A RISING

The Founding of the United State

A celebration from the collections o

PHILADELPHIA, PENNSYLVAN

PEOPLE

1765 to 1789

The American Philosophical Society

The Historical Society of Pennsylvania

The Library Company of Philadelphia

NINETEEN HUNDRED & SEVENTY SIX

A joint exhibition, from April 28
through November 1976, by
The American Philosophical Society
105 South Fifth Street
Philadelphia, Pennsylvania 19106

The Historical Society of Pennsylvania
1300 Locust Street
Philadelphia, Pennsylvania 19107

The Library Company of Philadelphia
1314 Locust Street
Philadelphia, Pennsylvania 19107

This exhibition
was made possible
by grants from
the three institutions
and from

The National Endowment for the
    Humanities
The Commonwealth of Pennsylvania
    Bicentennial Commission
The Philadelphia National Bank
The Dolfinger-McMahon Foundation
The City of Philadelphia
The Lindback Foundation
The CPC Corporation
The Independence Foundation

Cover: The Declaration of
Independence, in the
handwriting of Thomas
Jefferson. APS

End papers: A view of the battle
between the British and French off
Brest. Neptune consoles Britannia for
the loss of America, which is represented
by a man holding an American flag
and carrying on his shoulder the French
cock as a symbol of the Franco-American
Alliance. *London Magazine,* XLVII
(1778), facing p. 339. LCP

Contents

Preface

This catalogue accompanies the exhibit entitled A RISING PEOPLE, with which the American Philosophical Society, the Historical Society of Pennsylvania, and the Library Company of Philadelphia are celebrating the American Bicentennial. The catalogue, like the show itself, is addressed to American citizens who wish both to know more about the formation of the American nation in the years from 1765 to 1789 and to see the very books and documents in which the men of that generation recorded their thoughts, decisions, and acts. The catalogue therefore excludes bibliographical data; but it contains commentaries on the significance of individual entries.

Although closely related, the catalogue and the exhibit are not identical. For reasons of space and design, a few items illustrated in the catalogue could not be exhibited, while other items not included in the catalogue have been chosen for display in the exhibition. Thus, while catalogue and show will each have greater meaning if read and viewed one with the other, each may be enjoyed profitably alone. Indeed, we hope the catalogue will retain its interest and value long after the show has been dismantled. If it is read carefully, the texts of the documents with the accompanying narrative and descriptive notes, the catalogue will be found full of instructive and rewarding information about the early years of A RISING PEOPLE.

The materials in both catalogue and exhibit are arranged in roughly chronological order, modified by considerations of logical unity. Thus the sections on military history are separated from those on politics and diplomacy, even though they were historically closely interrelated.

The materials shown in A RISING PEOPLE have been drawn exclusively from the collections of the three sponsoring institutions.

The Sponsors

THE AMERICAN PHILOSOPHICAL SOCIETY, HELD AT PHILADELPHIA, FOR PROMOTING USEFUL KNOWLEDGE was first founded by Benjamin Franklin and his friends in 1743, re-established on its present foundation in 1769, and chartered by the Commonwealth of Pennsylvania in 1780. Its hall, erected in 1785-1789, is on a portion of the State House Yard (Independence Square) that was deeded to it by the Commonwealth in 1785. Patterned on the Royal Society of London

I

and the Society of Arts of Dublin, it is the oldest learned society in the United States, and often served the young republic as a sort of national library, national museum, and national academy of science. Franklin was its first president, and Thomas Jefferson its third. The Society's library, especially rich in the writings of men of science, also contains invaluable books and manuscripts illustrating the early history of the American Colonies and the United States. One of its important collections is of the papers of Franklin, from which many exhibits in A RISING PEOPLE have been taken.

THE HISTORICAL SOCIETY OF PENNSYLVANIA was founded in 1824, about fifty years after the events celebrated in this exhibition. Its purposes were the collection, preservation, and publication of material concerning Pennsylvania. Because of the central importance of the Commonwealth to the early history of the Nation, much of that larger story can be told from the Society's collections of manuscripts, maps, prints, and the like. In addition to these research materials, the Society also has a great collection of paintings of this period, some of which are in the exhibit but many more are available for continuing study. It has moved its location many times in the past century and a half; its present building has been recently enlarged and renovated. The Society's interests in things historical increase with the years.

THE LIBRARY COMPANY OF PHILADELPHIA, too, was founded by Benjamin Franklin and his friends and grew rapidly from its beginning in 1731 to be *the* library of the city by the time of the Revolution. As the largest book resource available, it played a major role during the period when the United States was brought into being. Its rooms were on the second floor of Carpenters' Hall when the First Continental Congress met there in 1774, and it offered the courtesy of its collections to the members of Congress, the Constitutional Convention, and the government of the new nation. Nine Signers of the Declaration were among its members, and such prominent patriots as John Dickinson and Charles Thomson served it as Directors. In 1850 it was the second largest library in the country. Today its holdings of the pamphlet literature of the Revolutionary and Federal periods constitute a collection of national importance, and the extensive papers of Dr. Benjamin Rush and John Dickinson are rich in historical material.

Acknowledgments

Most of the members of the staffs of the sponsoring institutions at one time or another in the past year, in small or large degree, have been involved in the preparation of this catalogue and exhibit. They have located and fetched books, prints, and manuscripts, cleaned and mounted them, carried them to the photographer, measured and re-measured individual pieces, checked bibliographical references, typed and retyped copy; and they have performed all these tasks efficiently and cheerfully, even against deadlines of time. For these and many other services, those who read and view A RISING PEOPLE should be grateful to:

Bertram V. Dodelin, Jr., Carl F. Miller, Carolyn B. Milligan, Murphy D. Smith, Willman Spawn, and Jean T. Williams at the American Philosophical Society Library;

Gary J. Christopher, Heather C. Egan, Lucy L. Hrivnak, David McKee and his housekeeping staff, Louis W. Meehan, Peter J. Parker, John H. Platt, Jr., Sarah B. Pomerantz, and Linda Stanley at the Historical Society of Pennsylvania; and

Anne Davis, Ellen S. Dorn, Lacy G. Edwards, A. Dorsey Fiske, Angela E. Fitzgerald, Karen K. Helm, Marie E. Korey, Phillip S. Lapsansky, Gordon M. Marshall, Kaspar Reder, and Bernard F. Reilly, Jr. at the Library Company of Philadelphia.

The preparation of this catalogue and exhibit is also indebted to:

Mrs. Sara L. Day, who made the preliminary selection of items for inclusion in the catalogue and then, that task completed, worked with the designers of the exhibition in identifying additional items for display.

Charles P. Mills & Son, which did some of the photography.

Meriden Gravure Company, especially John F. Peckham and Buell H. Hunt, whose contribution to the catalogue is far greater than is indicated by the plain statement that they printed it.

Sam Maitin, assisted by Beth Wickenden, who designed the catalogue.

Neil/Carter Design Associates, especially Tim Carter and Don Murray, who designed and mounted the exhibit.

The costs of preparing and printing this catalogue, of designing and mounting the exhibit, and of providing guides for visitors have been defrayed by the sponsoring institutions and by grants from The Dolfinger-McMahon Foundation and The Lindback Foundation to the American Philosophical Society; The National Endowment for the Humanities and The Philadelphia National Bank to the Historical Society of Pennsylvania; The Commonwealth of Pennsylvania Bicentennial Commission, The City of Philadelphia, The CPC Corporation, and The Independence Foundation to the Library Company of Philadelphia. On behalf of all who may read this catalogue and view the exhibit the sponsors express their warm thanks for indispensable financial support.

The content of the exhibition was chosen, and the text of the catalogue was written, by Whitfield J. Bell, Jr., Library of the American Philosophical Society, James E. Mooney, Historical Society of Pennsylvania, and Edwin Wolf 2nd, Library Company of Philadelphia.

A RISING PEOPLE

Introduction

As the nation approached its fiftieth anniversary, in peace and prosperity and with colonies of Spain and Portugal following the lead of English America by asserting their independence, John Adams recalled the story of a soldier of the Revolution standing on the highest summit of the Hudson highlands. Perhaps, we may imagine, this was at Stony Point after Anthony Wayne's notable victory there. But wherever it was, as Adams told it in his inimitable way, the soldier lifted his face to the stars and shouted in a drill-master's voice: "Attention, Universe! Kingdoms of the Earth, to the right about Wheel!! March!!!!" The story may or may not be apocryphal and the soldier may or may not have been as inspirited by his daily ration of rum as he was by patriotic fervor. But his command to the kingdoms of the world voiced a deep feeling which animated the American people in this first and greatest of modern revolutions.

They were profoundly conscious that they were a rising people, starting afresh in a new land and sharing its untold promise with the oppressed of other lands. Theirs was not a nationalism confined to the narrow object of political independence. It was one committed to eternal hostility against all forms of tyranny over the mind of man —against government not accountable to the people, against the age-old alliance of church and state, against ignorance, superstition, bigotry, and intolerance, against any power on earth which sought to violate the inherent and inviolable right of every man to life, liberty, and the pursuit of happiness.

But the greatness of the American Revolution was not that it was a declaration of war against old tyrannies. It was rather that, in transferring sovereignty from a crown to the citizen with all of the rights and awesome duties which this implied, it held out the promise of general improvement in the condition of man. Its cause, as Thomas Paine expressed it, was the cause of all mankind. This was a tremendous wager on the proposition that man's humane dispositions, guided by principles of reason and justice, would triumph over his capacity for evil. Throughout the centuries many wise and good men had held that the idea of self-government, especially over a vast extent of territory, was inherently impracticable and that some form of authoritarian restraint imposed from above was essential to the preservation of peace and good order. The peoples' submission to many absolute despotisms through many centuries in many lands seemed to lend support to such counsels.

But the invention of printing, the discovery of America, the beginning of scientific inquiry, and the diffusion of enlightenment in Europe seemed to make it inevitable that in time the old walls would crumble. The fateful issue was joined here in the British colonies in North America two centuries ago. But aspirations for human liberty and equal right and justice went back to the city states of Greece and to the republican citizenry of Rome and far beyond. The moral and philosophical propositions set forth in the Declaration of Independence which proclaimed as self-evident the truth that all men are created equal, that they are endowed with inherent rights including the right to life, liberty, and the pursuit of happiness, that all government rests on the consent of the governed, and that any government violating these rights might be altered or abolished by the people who could substitute such new forms as might effect their safety and happiness—all of these fundamental propositions had been fought for in many painful struggles over the centuries. Not one of them was new or distinctively American. But it was here two centuries ago that a new nation was brought forth which, for the first time in history, proclaimed at the outset that these principles would be the foundation on which its government would rest.

The American colonists were privileged to build upon these old foundations not because they were the victims of an "absolute Despotism" as the Declaration of Independence claimed, but because they were so free. For generations they had been prepared through long experience in governing themselves as virtually autonomous dominions. Unlike the colonists of other European powers, those settled by England were almost unfettered. They had brought with them the rights and privileges of Englishmen, guaranteed to them by their charters which they regarded as fundamental law. Through their own legislative assemblies they had long regulated their internal affairs. They had more than once challenged royal authority. They had already become a mixed people—English, Welsh, Swedes, Dutch, French, Swiss, Jews, Irish, Scots, Africans—and all, whether coming to America voluntarily or involuntarily, shared the promise of the new land and the goal of a commitment to human rights.

What was to happen in 1776 was foreshadowed a century earlier in Pennsylvania and in New Jersey, where William Penn sought "to lay a foundation for after ages" so that the oppressed from every land might "understand their liberty as men and christians, that they may not be brought in bondage, but by their own consent," and that they might have freedom of conscience along with other inestimable rights. It was Virginia, the oldest of the English colonies, not surprisingly, which had the first legislative assembly in North America, which first called for a resolution of independence, which produced the first constitution to be created by self-governing freemen, which adopted the first American Bill of Rights, and which enacted the first statute in the world calling for complete and absolute religious freedom. And it was those which followed in Puritan New England which created those indigenous nurseries of democracy in the form of free public schools and town meetings. For upwards of a century this diverse people sharing a common experience had begun to think of themselves as Americans, united by common aims and strengthened by their diversity of language, customs, religion, and cultural backgrounds. Long before that they had been groping toward some form of intercolonial confederation. By 1776, after a decade in which they had been discussing the fundamental principles of government in the press, in the pulpit, in the taverns, and in their homes from New Hampshire to Georgia and in the British islands, they were prepared to make the hazardous wager on man's capacity for self-government. In this new land, fortified by old principles of right and justice, they had become pragmatic, self-reliant, and politically astute.

But what made their revolution a truly transforming one was the deep and pervasive conviction, echoed in a quaint way by the soldier in the Hudson highlands, that Americans were leading the vanguard of a long procession of the kingdoms of the world toward a new and better world. It was this animating conviction which enabled the people to elevate and sustain in power leaders who, facing the problems of government with imagination as well as realism, were able to provide new solutions to old problems. They created the first machinery for settling war-provoking boundary questions by adjudication. They conceived the idea of constituent assemblies for framing fundamental laws. In their various states, they released claims to vast tracts of land in order to cement the union. For the governance of the resultant public domain they abandoned the idea of a colonial system as incompatible with republican principles and, in its place, brought forth the greatest single innovation in government of that remarkable generation—the concept of self-governing territories admissible to the union on terms of equality with the original states. It was this remarkably astute act of statesmanship which enabled the nation in time to extend itself across the continent and, in our own day, into the Arctic and the far reaches of the Pacific. The climax of this age of innovation in government came with the framing of the federal Constitution, adopted in 1788 after another elevated debate by the whole nation on the fundamental principles of government and the forms best calculated to preserve those to which the nation had committed itself a decade earlier.

It is thus not surprising that the soldier on the mountaintop and American citizens generally should have been inspired by what another soldier, unwittingly echoing Thomas Jefferson, called "this glorious cause." Throughout the land the people were convinced that a new era in human history had begun, that, as Tocqueville expressed it, it had been reserved to them to try to give reality to what philosophers had dreamed of for centuries. The founders even expressed this inspiring consciousness in the great seal of the republic —*Novus Ordo Seclorum.* Out in what was described as a remote part of the wilderness, soon after the federal government began operations, one citizen proclaimed that the establishment of "such an empire is one of the boldest experiments that has ever been made by man . . . which bids fair to be by far the most extensive of any upon the globe." It has in fact become the oldest and most extensive constitutional democracy in existence. It has survived tragic ordeals. It has been deeply divided on great issues, just as it was in the beginning. This always will be a divided people so long as it remains a democracy, since the right of dissent and the toleration of diversity of opinion of every sort are the very preconditions of a free society. But it has been and must ever be united on the great moral and philosophical propositions to which the nation committed itself in the Declaration of Independence. Without this, its national character and what Lincoln called the last best hope of earth will be forfeited.

These are the foundations on which all else rests and the task of keeping them from crumbling is never-ending. The founders of the nation well understood that the preservation of self-government is not a battle that can be won and its victory taken for granted. Thomas Jefferson, who through a long life served as advocate and exemplar of the principles he set forth in the Declaration of Independence, was only restating the conviction of Roman republicans when he said that the preservation of these principles depended upon the virtue of the people. And Benjamin Rush was one of many of the founders who recognized that the revolution begun in 1776 had not ended and must always be a continuing one. After two centuries, the revolution is still in progress. Old injustices are being righted while new ones are being placed on the consciences of the people. The foundations are, as yet, still solid.

To present in a single volume this series of transforming events which we call the American Revolution is impossible. The present assemblage of manuscripts, books, pamphlets, prints, portraits, maps, and objects does not and cannot attempt to trace the roots that reach from the Declaration of Independence back to the Bill of Rights of 1689, the Petition of Right of 1628, the great writ of Magna Carta of 1215 and far beyond. It does not and cannot show how the American people have responded to the great roll calls during the past two centuries in accordance with or in violation of their declared principles of government. It can only present, in this year of commemoration and reaffirmation, some of the things which tell of the epochal achievements of the leaders and the people of the nation in that remarkable period from 1765 to 1789. Even within these limitations it can only provide a few glimpses of the most notable landmarks along the road to independence and self-government. It is only a modest sampling of the historical record, drawn from many unrivalled collections that have been gathered and preserved over the generations.

It is a happy circumstance that this exhibit is the result of the collaboration of three institutions of learning, all created and sustained by individual citizens who have understood that a people who care nothing for the record of their past achievements are not likely to achieve much worth recording for the future. The Library Company of Philadelphia, proposed by Benjamin Franklin, was founded in 1731. The American Philosophical Society, also proposed by him, is the oldest learned society in America. The Historical Society of Pennsylvania has just celebrated its 150th anniversary and its *Pennsylvania Magazine of History and Biography,* the oldest historical journal in the nation, is currently in its centennial year. All have made and are making incalculable contributions to the intellectual and cultural life of the nation. The founders and patrons of these institutions well understood that, as James Madison expressed it, liberty and learning depend upon each other for their mutual support. These three institutions, with their immense collections of records of all forms portraying the history of the American people, stand as testimonials to the fact that many generations of American citizens have shared that belief. Theirs is only one of many evidences that Americans have recognized from the beginning that public duties devolved upon them along with the rights proclaimed for them two centuries ago. At that time John Jay, one of many who were somewhat reluctant to enter upon the experiment of self-government but who did much to make it succeed, expressed the thought that it would take "Time to make Sovereigns of Subjects." So it does.

But where else has this been done so quickly, so generally, and with such benefit to posterity? The kingdoms of the world have by no means followed the command of the soldier on the Hudson heights. Nor indeed have Americans themselves always done so. But this rising people is still in the vanguard, still marching, still able—as an admiring European of the 18th century expressed it and as Tocqueville echoed later—to make any constitution work.

Julian P. Boyd
February 17, 1976

Great Seal of the United States. Engraving by James Trenchard. *Columbian Magazine*, I (1786), facing p. 49. APS

"Tyranny of all kinds is to be abhorred."

—James Otis. *Rights of the British Colonies*, 1764

The Repeal, or the Funeral of Miss Ame Stamp. [London, 1766].

LCP

In order to defray "the Expences of defending, protecting, and securing" the American colonies, Parliament passed the Stamp Act. On March 22, 1765, the bill received the royal assent. By it stamp duties were placed on virtually everything written or printed: deeds, decrees, licenses, land warrants, indentures, pamphlets, newspapers, almanacs, and even playing cards. The stamped paper was to be shipped to an officer in each colony appointed to sell and distribute it. Franklin secured this official printing of the act. The sheet of stamped paper was saved when a shipment of paper to New York was burned by opponents of the law.

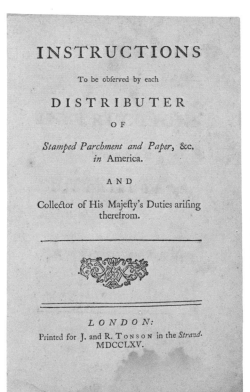

INSTRUCTIONS

To be observed by each

DISTRIBUTER

O F

Stamped Parchment and Paper, &c.
in America.

A N D

Collector of His Majesty's Duties arising
therefrom.

L O N D O N:
Printed for J. and R. TONSON in the *Strand.*
MDCCLXV.

*Instructions To be observed by each
Distributor of Stamped Parchment
and Paper, &c. in America. London:
J. and R. Tonson, 1765.* HSP

To be sure, it was necessary to issue a set of rules and regulations for each
of the stampmen. They provided for the orderly distribution of the taxed
sheets, but, unfortunately for the appointed officials, gave no guidance in
cases of downright opposition and violence. The pamphlet is inordinately
rare. The present one was preserved in the papers of John Hughes, Stamp
Agent at Philadelphia.

Ship *Royal Charlotte.* Invoice for
stamped paper consigned to
John Hughes, Esq., at Philadelphia,
London, July 16, 1765. HSP

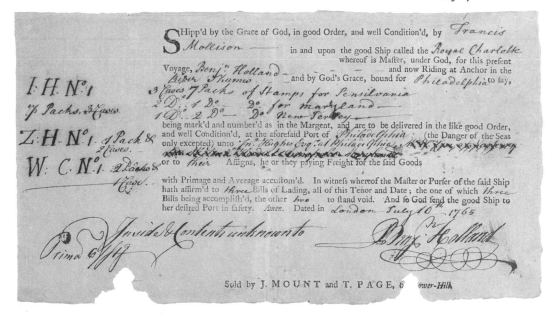

Three cases containing seven packs of stamped paper, referred to as
"Stamps," were to be distributed by Hughes for use in Pennsylvania.
The rest of the cargo was originally consigned directly to Zachariah Hood
in Maryland and William Coxe in New Jersey, but their names were
crossed out. Shrewdly, Captain Holland of the *Royal Charlotte* indicated
he had no knowledge of the contents of the cases.

Deborah Franklin. *Letter to Benjamin Franklin,* [Philadelphia], September 22, 1765. APS

Resistance to the Stamp Act. Engraved by Daniel-Nicholas Chodowiecki in *Historisch-genealogischer Calender, oder Jahrbuch der merkwürdigsten neuen Welt.* Leipzig, 1784. LCP

It was widely rumored that Franklin had not opposed, if indeed he had not favored, the Stamp Act. Not foreseeing the opposition, he had recommended the appointment of his friend Hughes as distributor for Pennsylvania. When rioting against the stampmen broke out elsewhere, radicals in Philadelphia tried to force Hughes's resignation, and, it was felt, might attack Franklin's house. Deborah told her husband how Franklin Court was turned into an armed fort. Friends and relatives came to her defense. "I ordered sum sorte of defens up Statirs such as I Cold manig my self," she wrote, and continued, "but if aney one Came to disturbe me I wold show a proper resentement. . . . I was told that thair was 8 hundred men readey to asiste aney one that shold be molested." No violence occurred.

[handwritten letter — John Hughes to John Swift, Alexander Barclay & Thomas Graeme, November 5, 1765]

John Hughes. *Letter to John Swift, Alexander Barclay & Thomas Graeme,* Philadelphia, November 5, 1765. APS

Upon the arrival of the ship carrying the stamp paper, Philadelphia was thrown into a turmoil. Hughes, the harassed stampman, explained at considerable length why he was unable to deliver stamp paper. "I am to inform you," he wrote, "that on Saturday the fifth of October last, The State House & Christ Church Bells *were rung, muffled* & two Negroe Drummers (one of whom belonged to Alderman Saml. Mifflin) beat thro' all parts of the City, *with muffled Drums*—Thereby alarming the Inhabitants;—In Consequence whereof a large Number of People was raised & assembled at the State House, where it was publickly declared, as I am informed, That if I did not immediately resign my Office, my House should be pulled down and my Substance destroyed." Needless to say, Hughes issued no stamp paper.

When the provisions of the Stamp Act became known, indignation was widespread through the colonies. On May 30, the Virginia House of Burgesses adopted a series of strong objections to it, which was quickly printed in newspapers to the north. On June 8, the Massachusetts House of Representatives sent a circular letter inviting the other colonies to meet at New York in October. It was, Caesar Rodney of Delaware stated, "an Assembly of the greatest Ability I ever Yet saw." The result of deliberation and debate was a declaration stating, among other articles, that it was "the undoubted Right of *Englishmen,* that no Taxes be imposed on them, but with their own Consent." Dickinson, a Philadelphia lawyer, composed the document which the Congress adopted.

John Dickinson. *Draft of the Resolves of the Stamp Act Congress.* [October, 1765]. Manuscript. LCP

The Pennsylvania Journal, October 31, 1765. LCP

Generally throughout the colonies newspapers temporarily ceased publication as the effective date of the Stamp Act, November 1, drew near. Mourning bands and skull-and-crossbones festooned the final angry pages. After the critical day, Franklin and Hall's *Pennsylvania Gazette* put out a single sheet with the defiant legend, "No Stamped Paper to be had," in place of the mast-head. Gradually publication returned to normal on unstamped paper as the law was universally disregarded.

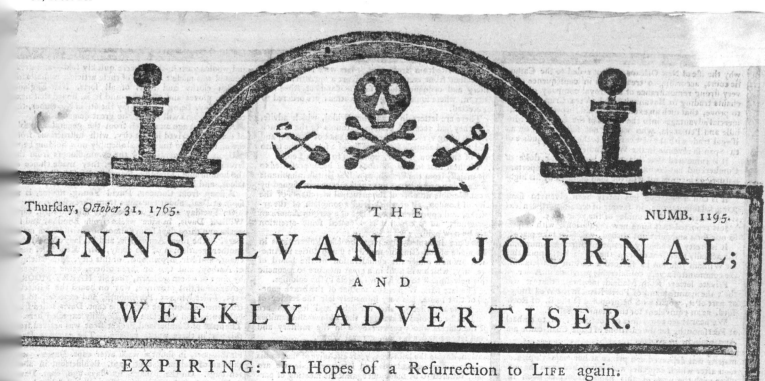

Thursday, October 31, 1765.　　THE　　NUMB. 1195.

PENNSYLVANIA JOURNAL;

AND

WEEKLY ADVERTISER.

EXPIRING: In Hopes of a Resurrection to LIFE again.

[Benjamin Church]. *Liberty and Property vindicated, and the St—pm-n burnt.* [Hartford]: "Published at the Desire of some of the Hearers," 1765. LCP

[Daniel Dulaney]. *Considerations on the Propriety of imposing Taxes in the British Colonies.* [Annapolis: Jonas Green], 1765, LCP

[Stephen Hopkins]. *The Rights of Colonies Examined.* Providence: William Goddard, 1765. LCP

[James Otis]. *A Vindication of the British Colonies, against the Aspersions of the Halifax Gentleman.* Boston: Edes and Gill, 1765. LCP

[John Dickinson]. *The Late Regulations respecting the British Colonies on the Continent of America considered.* Philadelphia: William Bradford, 1765. LCP

A New Collection of Verses applied to the First of November, A.D. 1765, &c. New Haven: B. Mecom, [1765]. LCP

Up and down the Atlantic coast pamphlets attacking the Stamp Act fluttered off the presses like leaves in a late autumn storm. Angered by the act itself and indignant that the British ministry and its supporters claimed the parliamentary right to tax the colonies, the aroused colonists rhetorically, logically and effectively defended their opposition to the impost. These pamphlets and others were responsible for the almost universal reaction of the American colonies.

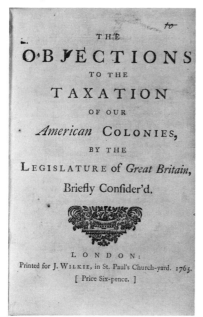

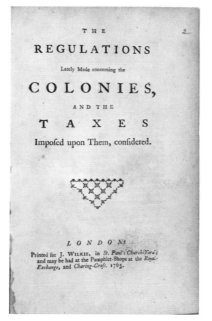

By the summer of 1765 the substance of the administration's justification of its action reached America in the form of pro-government pamphlets. Many of them were reprinted in the newspapers and added fuel to the fire of the colonies' resistance. Whately expressed the official position to such an extent that his pamphlet was once thought to have been written by Grenville. In London during the crisis Franklin in many instances annotated the printed arguments dealing with American affairs. In the margins of several of them he answered the points they made with a vigorous and angry pen, as evidenced by his copies of Tucker's piece and the anonymous *Good Humour.*

Good Humour: or, A Way with the Colonies. London: Printed for the Author, 1766. HSP

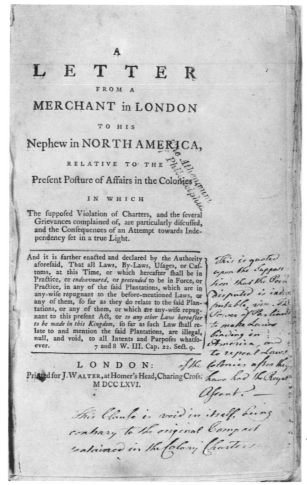

The Deplorable State of America. Engraved by John Singleton Copley. [Boston, November 1, 1765]. LCP

There was a strong pro-American feeling in London, particularly among the merchants. The day that the King approved the Stamp Act, a cartoon was published depicting its potential grievous result. The cartoon found its way to Boston, where the painter Copley greatly elaborated on the theme and introduced many local Boston references. It is so full of symbolism as almost to lose its point. No other example of Copley's version is known, but a Philadelphia engraver made a copy of it.

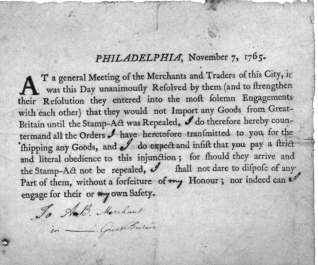

Philadelphia, November 7, 1765. At a general Meeting of the Merchants and Traders of this City . . . . [Philadelphia, 1765]. Broadside. A

Not satisfied with refusing the stamp paper, many Philadelphians joined together in a non-importation agreement to last until the Stamp Act was repealed.

A form to be sent to agents in England was printed up, countermanding all orders theretofore transmitted. Such a form Franklin got and added "To A. B. Merchant in Great Britain." In New York similar feelings were aroused. A committee of the Sons of Liberty wrote the radical newspaper publisher Bradford in Philadelphia urging him to form a local group "to correspond with those of this and the Neighbouring Provinces, who are willing to enter into a Firm Union, for the preservation of our inestimable & Undoubted rights."

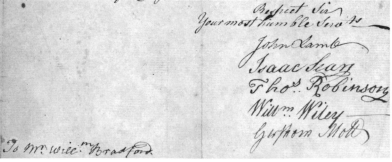

John Lamb, Isaac Sears, Thomas Robinson, William Wiley and Gershom Mott. *Letter to William Bradford,* New York, February 13, 1766. APS

8

Magna Britannia: her Colonies Reduc'd. [London: Benjamin Franklin, 1766]. LCP

Franklin, after his initial misjudgment of the temper of the colonies, became a strong and effective advocate of the repeal of the Stamp Act. He was not much of an artist, but he knew that a picture was worth a thousand words. His cartoon, showing a maimed Great Britain, was printed on cards which he handed to the members of Parliament at the time of the debate on repeal. This copy, preserved by Pierre Eugene Du Simitière, is the only one which has survived.

Few of Franklin's public appearances were more theatrical than his questioning before Parliament during the debate on the repeal of the Stamp Act. Carefully worded queries had been planted with sympathetic members, as his notes amply reveal. The hostile questions Franklin, with his sound knowledge of American affairs, was able to handle extemporaneously and in a masterly fashion. His role as an advocate of repeal was a great triumph for the sharp-witted Philadelphian.

Benjamin Franklin. *Notes of Questions asked by friendly Members of Parliament during the Debate on the Repeal of the Stamp Act,* [London], 1766]. Manuscript. HSP

The Examination of Doctor Benjamin Franklin, before an August Assembly, relating to the Repeal of the Stamp-Act, &c. [Philadelphia: Hall and Sellers, 1766]. LCP

The EXAMINATION of Doctor BENJAMIN FRANKLIN, *before an* AUGUST ASSEMBLY, *relating to the Repeal of the* STAMP-ACT, *&c.*

Q. WHAT is your name, and place of abode?
A. Franklin, of Philadelphia.
Q. Do the Americans pay any confiderable taxes among themfelves?
A. Certainly many, and very heavy taxes.
Q. What are the prefent taxes in Pennfylvania, laid by the laws of the Colony?
A. There are taxes on all eftates real and perfonal, a poll tax, a tax on all offices, profeffions, trades and bufineffes, according to their profits; an excife on all wine, rum, and other fpirits; and a duty of Ten Pounds per head on all Negroes imported, with fome other duties.
Q. For what purpofes are thofe taxes laid?
A. For the fupport of the civil and military eftablifhments of the country, and to difcharge the heavy debt contracted in the laft war.
Q. How long are thofe taxes to continue?
A. Thofe for difcharging the debt are to continue till 1772, and longer, if the debt fhould not be then all difcharged. The others muft always continue.
Q. Was it not expected that the debt would have been fooner difcharged?
A. It was, when the peace was made with France and Spain----But a frefh war breaking out with the Indians, a frefh load of debt was incurred, and the taxes, of courfe, continued longer by a new law.
Q. Are not all the people very able to pay thofe taxes?
A. No. The frontier counties, all along the continent, having been frequently ravaged by the enemy, and greatly impoverifhed, are able to pay very little tax. And therefore, in confideration of their diftreffes, our late tax laws do exprefly favour thofe counties, excufing the fufferers; and I fuppofe the fame is done in other governments.
Q. Are not you concerned in the management of the Poft-Office in America?
A. Yes. I am Deputy Poft-Mafter General of North-America.
Q. Don't you think the diftribution of ftamps, by poft, to all the inhabitants, very practicable, if there was no oppofition?
A. The pofts only go along the fea coafts; they do not, except in a few inftances, go back into the country; and if they did, fending for ftamps by poft would occafion an expence of poftage, amounting, in many cafes, to much more than that of the ftamps themfelves.
Q. Are you acquainted with Newfoundland?
A. I never was there.
Q. Do you know whether there are any poft roads on that ifland?
A. I have heard that there are no roads at all; but that the communication between one fettlement and another is by fea only.
Q. Can you difperfe the ftamps by poft in Canada?

A   A. There

Phillis Wheatley. *To the King's most excellent Majesty on his repealing the american Stamp act.* [Boston, 1766]. Manuscript. HSP

Among the many Americans who celebrated the repeal of the Stamp Act in prose and verse was Phillis Wheatley, the remarkable black poetess. Her poem was somewhat kinder to King George than most other effusions, giving him full credit for the beneficent act.

SUPPLEMENT to the PENNSYLVANIA JOURNAL, EXTRAORDINARY.

PHILADELPHIA, May 19, 1766.

This Morning arrived Capt. WISE, in a Brig from POOL in 8 Weeks, by whom we have the GLORIOUS NEWS of the

REPEAL OF THE STAMP-ACT,

As paſſed by the *King, Lords* and *Commons.* It received the ROYAL ASSENT the 18th of March, on which we moſt ſincerely congratulate our Readers.

An Act to repeal an Act made in the laſt Seſſion of Parliament; entitled, *An Act for granting and applying certain Stamp Duties, and other Duties, in the* Britiſh *Colonies and Plantations in* America, *towards further defraying the Expences of defending, protecting and ſecuring the ſame; and for amending ſuch Parts of the ſeveral Acts of Parliament, relating to the Trade and Revenues of the ſaid Colonies and Plantations, as direct the Manner of determining and recovering the Penalties and Forfeitures therein mentioned.*

Supplement to the Pennsylvania Journal. Extraordinary. Philadelphia, May 19, 1766. This Morning arrived Capt. Wise . . . by whom we have the Glorious News of the Repeal of the Stamp-Act. [Philadelphia: William and Thomas Bradford, 1766]. HSP

What the historian Carl Van Doren described as "happy tumult" broke out in England and America upon the news of the repeal of the Stamp Act. A London printseller found a ready market for a cartoon showing George Grenville and his supporters in a funeral procession—a print which Franklin sent home to his wife and which was hung up in a Philadelphia tavern and copied by a local engraver.

The Repeal, or the Funeral of Miss Ame Stamp. [London, 1766]. LCP

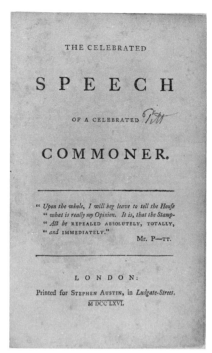

THE CELEBRATED

SPEECH

OF A CELEBRATED *Pitt*

COMMONER.

" *Upon the whole, I will beg leave to tell the House*
" *what is really my Opinion. It is, that the Stamp-*
" *Act be repealed* ABSOLUTELY, TOTALLY,
" *and* IMMEDIATELY."

Mr. P—TT.

LONDON:

Printed for STEPHEN AUSTIN, in *Ludgate-Street.*
M DCC LXVI.

[William Pitt]. *The
Celebrated Speech of a
celebrated Commoner.*
London: Stephen Austin,
1766. LCP

The Snare broken.

A

Thanksgiving-Discourse,

PREACHED

At the Desire of the West Church

IN

BOSTON, *N. E.* Friday *May* 23, 1766.

OCCASIONED BY THE

REPEAL

OF THE

Stamp-Act.

BY

JONATHAN MAYHEW, D. D.

Pastor of said Church.

——Brethren, ye have been called unto LIBERTY ; *only use not*
LIBERTY *for an occasion to the flesh, but by love serve one
another.* Ap. PAUL.

BOSTON:

Printed and Sold by R. & S. DRAPER, in New-
bury-Street ; EDES & GILL, in Queen-Street ;
and T. & J. Fleet, in Cornhill. 1766.

Jonathan Mayhew. *The
Snare broken. A
Thanksgiving-Discourse
. . . occasioned by the
Repeal of the Stamp-Act.*
Boston: R. & S. Draper;
Edes & Gill; and T. & J.
Fleet, 1766. LCP

A

New Song,

On the Repeal of the Stamp-Act, Tune,
A late worthy Old Lyon.

OF old times we read how the De'el tempted Eve
And told her fine stories, which she did believe ;
How in eating the apple, 'twould open her eyes,
And make her quite happy, as well as quite wise.
Taral, Laddey, &c.

She eagerly listen'd and gap'd at the fruit,
And swallow'd it down, but alas ! 'twould not suit :
The Devil was victor, be that as it will,
He tempted her just as he tempted Gr.nv.ll.
Taral Laddey, &c.

Quoth the Devil to Gr.nv.ll. I've drawn up a plan,
And think in my conscience that thou art the MAN ;
When e'er I intend any evil to do,
You may always be sure I will pitch upon you.
Taral Laddey, &c.

O'er-joy'd at the news like a courtier polite,
He thanked the Devil, and thought all was right ;
Expecting large share, of the profits in fact,
Arising by virtue of the *Noble Stamp-Act.*
Taral Laddey, &c.

This tickl'd his fancy, he tho't it would suit,
To commune with his *friends* such as H sk and dear B.te.
Who pleas'd with the *Scheme,* on wickedness bent,
All three to the Devil they lovingly went.
Taral Laddey, &c.

The Devil surpriz'd and almost struck mute
Yet rejoic'd at the sight of his *old* friend, J.hn B.te :
He kindly receiv'd them for better for worse,
And told them be sure put the Stamp-Act in force.
Taral Laddey, &c.

Recommended it strongly as a *Scheme* that would fit,
But told them like Devils to *out-brazen* P I T T,
And not fail to oppose *him* on ev'ry occasion, (nation.
Else his *tongue* like the serpents would beguile the whole
Taral Laddey &c.

Now alas ! it is truth tho' odd it doth seem,
From old Devils, young Devils certainly came ;
The old Devil *plann'd it,* but H.sk, Gr.nv.lle and B.te
Three Devils *incarnate* were to execute.
Taral Laddey &c.

But behold ! *one* arises, unrival'd in MERIT !
With *eloquence* fitted to his noble spirit :
With the sound of *cheek music,* this politick *Messiah,*
Knock'd Gr.nn.v.ll. quite stiff, as did *David, Goliah.*
Taral Laddey, &c.

Now rejoice ye *Americans,* they're left in the *lurch,*
Fairly flung by the Devil, no friend to the *church ;*
Conspicuous *PITT !* stands and displays truth his shield,
Come give him a bumper, *the Stamp-Act's repeal'd.*
Taral Laddey, &c.

Long life to great PITT see the bumpers do smile,
A statue erect for his *labour and toil* ;
Let his name be *immortal* and ne'er be forgot,
Whilst those of his *foes* do corrupt, stink and rot.
Taral Laddey, &c.

*A New Song, On the
Repeal of the Stamp-Act.*
[Philadelphia, 1766]. LCP

"The Americans are the sons, not the bastards of England,"
Pitt declaimed in Parliament as he opened the debate on
behalf of the repeal of the Stamp Act. He had been ill
and absent when the act was passed. By his stirring
defense of the colonists and their rights he made himself
an American hero. In the joy as expressed by Mayhew,
it was overlooked that by a Declaratory Act Parliament
restated its right to legislate for the colonies. He presented
this copy of his thanksgiving sermon to his colleague the
Reverend Dr. Samuel Eliot. The song was a goody-and-
baddy doggerel: down with Grenville and Bute, up
with Pitt.

William Pitt. Engraving
by J. E. Nilson of a
painting by William
Hoare. APS

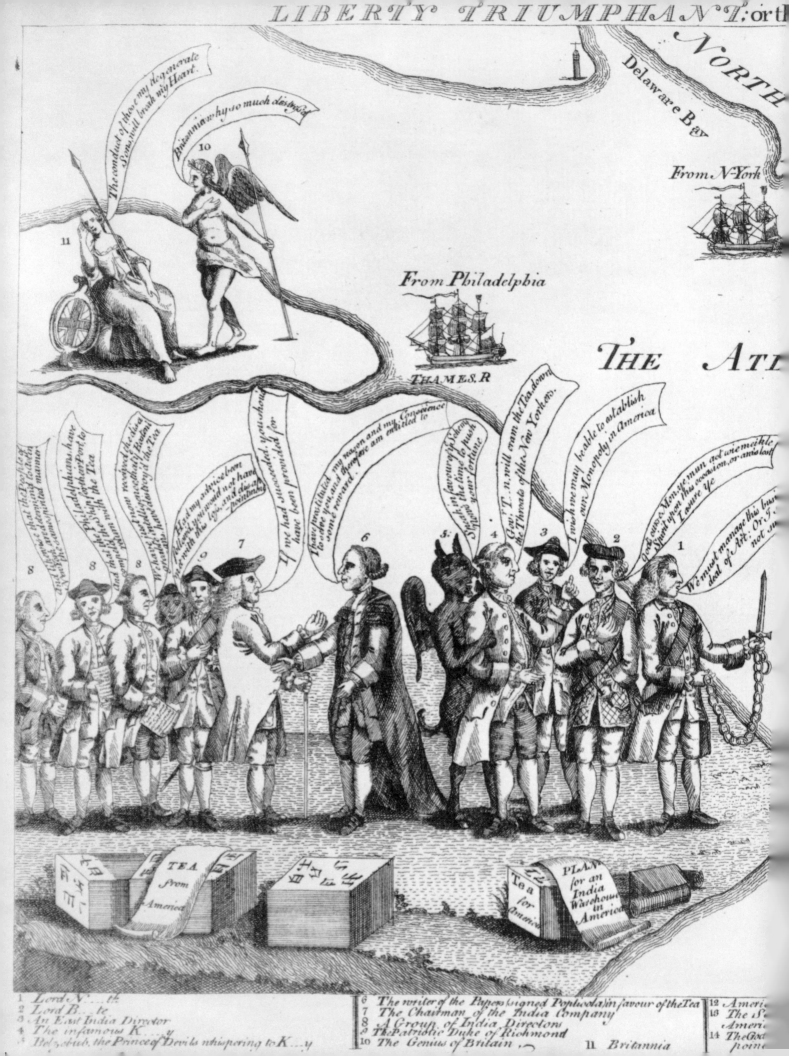

wnfall of OPPRESSION.

I will Trumpet their Noble Deeds, from Pole to Pole

Behold the Ardour of my Sons, and let not their brave Actions be buried in Oblivion

AMERICA

York

Long Island

TIC OCEAN

Provocations to Rebellion, 1766-1775

"Mutual provocation will go on to complete the separation."
—Benjamin Franklin. Letter to William Strahan, November 29, 1769

Aid me my Sons, and prevent my being Fetterd

We will secure your freedom, or die in the Attempt

Lead us on to Liberty or Death

Lead on Lead on

I am ready to die with grief and vexation at our Disappointment & it will blast my hope of preferment

Damn the Bostonians, they have been a great means of frustrating our design

We must now make a Virtue of necessity & join against landing the Tea

I approve of your Scheme as it will have appearances with the People who are easily deceived

Agreed

Agreed

... them, we ... to regain ...

Tea Act ...

Woman ... vented by the Natives of ... garb ... essing herself to Fame and ... Fame.

16 *A view of the Tea Ships in the Harbour of Boston.*
17 *Capt Lorings Vessel with Tea Shipwreck'd on Cape Cod.*
18 *A Group of Disappointed Americans who were for landing the Tea, in hopes of sharing in the Plunder of their Country.*

Liberty Triumphant, or the Downfall of Oppression. [Philadelphia?, 1774]. LCP

13

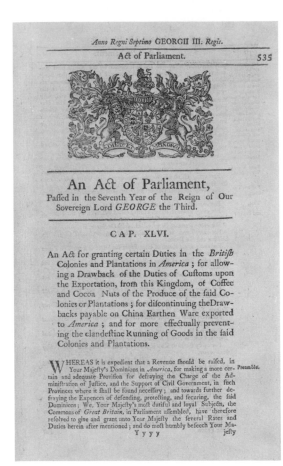

An Act of Parliament, Passed in the Seventh Year of the Reign of Our Sovereign Lord George the Third. . . . An Act for granting certain Duties in the British Colonies and Plantations in America. [Boston: Richard Draper, John Green, and Joseph Russell, 1767]. HSP

No sooner had the irritation of the Stamp Act been removed than the British government passed a series of new laws affecting the colonies. Named for Charles Townshend, the Chancellor of the Exchequer, the 1767 acts stirred up trouble once again. Of the four Townshend Acts the one most onerous was that levying import duties on lead, painters' colors, paper, glass and tea. Particularly galling was the fact that part of the income from these duties would go to pay for the salaries of royal officers in the colonies, thus freeing them from local control.

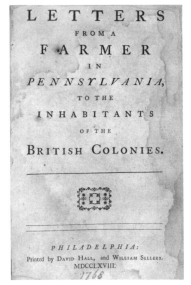

The *Letters* appeared first in William Goddard's *Pennsylvania Chronicle* from November 30, 1767, to February 8, 1768, and were quickly reprinted in newspapers up and down the seaboard and in pamphlet form. In the series, Dickinson conceded Parliament's right to regulate the trade of the Empire, but denied its right to tax the colonies in order to raise revenue. The work was the most influential of all the political pamphlets in the pre-Revolutionary era and, Dickinson's authorship made known, he became an American hero. So great was his reputation that a Town Meeting in Boston formally thanked him for his *Letters*. Smither's portrait was one of the tributes to his fame.

[John Dickinson]. *Letters from a Farmer in Pennsylvania, to the Inhabitants of the British Colonies.* Philadelphia: David Hall, and William Sellers, 1768. LCP

The Patriotic American Farmer. J-n D-k-ns-n Esqr. Barrister at Law. Engraving by James Smither. [Philadelphia]: R. Bell, [1768]. LCP

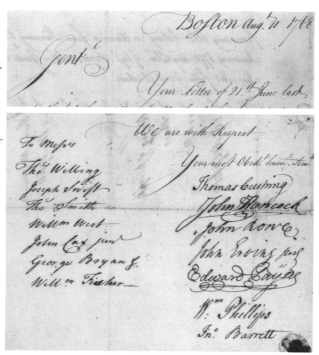

Thomas Cushing, John Hancock, John Rowe, John Erving, Jr., *et al.*, Committee of Boston Merchants. *Letter to Thomas Willing, Joseph Swift, et al., Merchants of Philadelphia*, Boston, August 11, 1768. APS

Philadelphia Non-Importation Agreement. Manuscript. Philadelphia, March 10, 1769. LCP

On August 11, 1768, a committee of Boston merchants sent a Philadelphia committee a copy of the non-importation agreement they had adopted. They begged the Philadelphians to "Chearfully & Unanimously Co-operate with us in this lawful, prudent & Salutary measure." The latter were hesitant. They tried to get the merchants of London to intervene to get the acts of Parliament repealed. When nothing came of that appeal, the Philadelphians bound themselves not to import from Great Britain goods shipped after April 1. When word came that Parliament was considering the removal of some of the duties, excitement spread through the colonies, some merchants wishing to end the boycott, others determined to continue it until all American grievances were redressed. The Boston merchants told Franklin late in 1769 that they were ready to accept British goods on condition that the duties on tea, glass, paper and colors be repealed.

Isaac Smith, Ebenezer Storer, William Greenleaf, Thomas Cushing, *et al.*, Merchants of Boston. *Letter to Benjamin Franklin*, Boston, December 29, 1769. APS

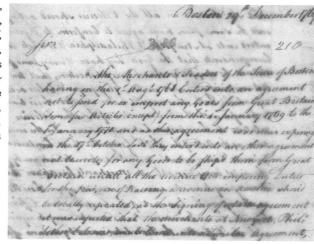

Charles Thomson, George Roberts, Jeremiah Warder, William Fisher, Abel James, Henry Drinker, *et al.*, Merchants of Philadelphia. *Letter to Benjamin Franklin*, Philadelphia, April 18, 1769. APS

A particular Account of the most barbarous and Horrid Massacre! Committed in King-Street, Boston, on Monday, March 5, 1770, by the Soldiery quartered in said Town. [Boston]: John Boyle, 1770. Broadside. LCP

S·G S·M J· C·A P·C

A particular Account of the moſt barbarous and

HORRID MASSACRE!

Committed in King-Street, *Boſton*, on Monday, *March* 5, 1770, by the Soldiery quartered in ſaid Town.

AMIDST the impending Wrecks and Ruins of Power that threaten a wide Deſtruction to American FREEDOM, the Revolutions of Time have produced a Day ever memorable for the moſt cruel and inhuman Maſſacre, perpetrated by the Hands of Men, who may be juſtly ſtiled more ſavage than the ſavage Beaſts.—An uncultivated *Indian* of the Woods, Stranger as he naturally is to every tender feeling of *Humanity*, would *ſcorn* to own himſelf concerned in an Action like this.—The Annals of no paſt Age, nor the moſt antient Records of Hiſtory, can furniſh us with ſo ſtriking an Inſtance of the *barbarity* of one *Britiſh* Subject towards another.—*Britannia* muſt hear it with Horror! and bluſh with Indignation to read what will ſtain the Character of a *Briton*, and reflect eternal diſgrace on the Pages of Engliſh Hiſtory. ——We have ſeen with the higheſt grief and concern, the ill-timed neceſſity of quartering the King's Troops in the Town of *Boſton*, who have often interrupted it's uſual Peace and good Order: We have remonſtrated in the higheſt Tokens of Reſentment againſt the Danger of ſubjecting a *free* and *peaceable* Government to the horrors of a Military Power, who have been *vainly* uſing every *baſe* and *diabolical* Method, they could poſſibly invent, to *intimidate* and *awe* the Inhabitants to a *tame* Submiſſion, that they might with more impunity, brandiſh their Weapons of Death: But the Spirit of LIBERTY will always prevail, whilſt Engliſh Blood flows in the veins of free-born *Americans*. ——In a firm, ſteady and united Principle of Affection to our injured Country, we have undauntedly reſolved againſt the unconſtitutional Meaſures of placing Troops among us in a Time of Peace, the fatal Effects of which, we have ſorrowfully ſeen in too many inſtances. We have obſerved with the greateſt Surprize and Concern, a Party of Soldiers without the leaſt Provocation, in the face of Day, diſcharge a loaded Muſket at the Inhabitants; Men, Women and Children repeatedly aſſaulted in the Streets, and oftentimes put in the moſt eminent hazard of their Lives; and even the Magiſtrates abuſed and treated with the higheſt indignity, while in the execution of their Office, and atrocious Offenders reſcued from the juſt and ſevereſt Puniſhments of the Law. It is natural to ſuppoſe, that when the Inhabitants of this Town ſaw thoſe Laws which were enacted for their own Safety and Security, thrown into ſuch Contempt, by the unwarrantable interpoſition of *Military Power*, the Laws of Nature might juſtly teach them to reſent for themſelves. We have ſeen theſe *valiant Heroes* ſally out in Parties to aſſault a ſingle Inhabitant, and have known them to be repelled by the courage, activity and bravery of inferior Numbers. We have alſo of late ſeen theſe *martial Oracles of Bravery*, fire upon unarmed People; at this Time, we beheld with the tendereſt feelings of Humanity and Compaſſion, *INNOCENCE*, in its defenceleſs ſtate, fall an unſeaſonable Victim to the cowardly Rage of thoſe *mercileſs Miſcreants*, whoſe Glory is their Shame.

MONDAY, *March* 5, 1770. In the Evening ſeveral ſoldiers were ſeen parading the Streets with drawn cutlaſſes and bayonets, abuſing and wounding numbers of the inhabitants: about nine o'clock five youths paſſing down cornhill, through the narrow alley leading to *Murray*'s barrack, obſerved three ſoldiers brandiſhing their broad ſwords, of an uncommon ſize againſt the walls, out of which they ſtruck fire plentifully. One of the youths admoniſhed the others to avoid the weapons, upon which one of the ſoldiers inſtantly turn'd about and ſtruck him on the arm, then pierced another thro' his cloaths inſide the arm cloſe to the arm-pit, and grazed the ſkin; the lads then ſtruck the ſoldiers, and a ſmart ſquabble enſued, which laſted for ſeveral minutes, during which time, one of the ſoldiers was knocked down twice by one of the lads and badly bruiſed; the ſoldiers then finding themſelves unable to ſtand the combat, retreated to their barrack, in order to augment their force; while they were recruiting, more lads gathered; in leſs than a minute from the time they left the place of action, ten or twelve (ſome ſay twenty) of them came out with drawn cutlaſſes, clubs and bayonets, and ſet upon the unarmed boys and young folks, who ſtood them a little while, but finding the inequality of their equipment, diſperſed.—On hearing the noiſe, one Samuel Atwood, came up to ſee what was the matter, and entering the alley from dock-ſquare, heard the latter part of the combat, and when the Boys had diſperſed he met the 10 or 12 ſoldiers aforeſaid ruſhing down the alley towards the ſquare, and aſked them if they intended to murder people? They anſwered Yes by G—d, root and branch! With that one of them ſtruck Mr. Atwood with a club, which was repeated by another, and being unarmed he turned to go off, and received a wound on the left ſhoulder which reached the bone and gave him much pain. Retreating a few ſteps, Mr. Atwood met two officers and ſaid, Gentlemen, what is the matter? They anſwered you'll ſee by and by. Immediately after, thoſe heroes appeared in the ſquare, aſking where were theſe boogers? where were theſe cowards? - - - - - But notwithſtanding their fierceneſs to the naked men, one of them advanced towards a youth who had a ſplit of a raw ſtave in his hand, and ſaid damn them here is one of them; but the young man ſeeing a perſon near him with a drawn ſword and good cane ready to ſupport him, held up his ſtave in defiance, and paſſed by him up the little alley by Mr. Silſby's to King-ſtreet, where they attacked ſingle and unarmed perſons 'till they raiſed much clamour, and then turned down Cornhill-ſtreet, inſulting all they met in like manner, and purſuing ſome to their very doors. Thirty or forty perſons, moſtly lads, being by this means gathered in King-ſtreet, Capt. Preſton, with a party of men with charged bayonets, came from the main guard to the commiſſioners houſe, the ſoldiers puſhing their bayonets, crying, Make way; They took place by the cuſtom-houſe, and continuing to puſh to drive the people off, pricked ſome in ſeveral places; on which they were clamorous, and, it is ſaid, threw ſnow-balls. On this, the Capt. commanded them to fire, and more ſnow-balls coming, again ſaid, Damn you, Fire, be the conſequence what it will! One ſoldier then fired, and a townſman with a cudgel ſtruck him over the hands with ſuch force that he dropt his firelock; and ruſhing forward aimed a blow at the Capts. head, which graz'd his hat and fell pretty heavy upon his arm; However the ſoldiers continued the fire, ſucceſſively, 'till 7 or 8, or as ſome ſay 11 guns were diſcharged.

By this fatal manœuvre, three men were laid dead on the ſpot, and two more ſtruggling for life; but what ſhewed a degree of cruelty unknown to Britiſh troops, at leaſt ſince the houſe of Hanover has directed their operations, was an attempt to fire upon or puſh with their bayonets, the perſons who undertook to remove the ſlain and wounded.

Return of the KILLED and WOUNDED in this Bloody Maſſacre.

SAMUEL GRAY, Ropemaker, killed on the Spot, the Ball entered his Head and broke the Skull.

CRISPUS ATTUCKS, a Mollatto Man, who was born in Framingham, but lately belonging to New-Providence, and was in Boſton in order to go to North Carolina, killed on the Spot, two Balls entering his Breaſt.

JAMES CALDWELL, Mate of Captain Morton's Veſſel, killed on the Spot, two Balls entering his Breaſt.

SAMUEL MAVERICK, a promiſing Youth of 17 Years of Age, Son of the Widow Maverick, and an Apprentice to Mr. Greenwood, Turner, mortally wounded, a Ball went thro' his Belly, and came out at his Back, he died next Morning.

CHRISTOPHER MONK, a Lad about 17 Years of Age, an Apprentice to Mr. Walker, Shipwright; dangerouſly wounded, a Ball entered his Side and came out at his Back.

JOHN CLARK, a Lad about 17 Years of Age, whoſe Parents live at Medford, and an Apprentice to Capt. Samuel Howard of this Town; dangerouſly wounded, a Ball entered juſt above his Groin and came out at his Hip, on the oppoſite Side.

EDWARD PAYNE, of this Town, Merchant, ſtanding at his Entry-Door, received a Ball in his Arm, and ſhattered ſome of the Bones.

JOHN GREEN, Taylor, wounded; he received a Ball juſt under his Hip, and lodged in the under Part of his Thigh, which was extracted.

ROBERT PATTERSON, a Seafaring Man, wounded; a Ball went thro' his right Arm.

PATRICK CARR, Leather Breeches Maker, mortally wounded, a Ball entered his Hip and went out at his Side; died 14th March.

DAVID PARKER, an Apprentice to Mr. Eddy, Wheelwright, wounded; a Ball entered his Thigh.

The People were immediately alarmed with the Report of this horrid Maſſacre, the Bells were ſet a ringing, and great Numbers ſoon aſſembled at the place where this tragical Scene had been acted; their Feelings may be better conceived than expreſſed; and while ſome were taking Care of the Dead and Wounded, the Reſt were in Conſultation what to do in thoſe dreadful Circumſtances. But ſo little intimidated were they, notwithſtanding their being within a few Yards of the Main-Guard, and ſeeing the 29th Regiment under Arms, and drawn up in King-ſtreet; they kept their Station and appear'd as an Officer of Rank expreſs'd it, ready to run upon the very Muzzels of their Muſkets. The Lieutenant Governor ſoon came into the Town-Houſe, and there met ſome of his Majeſty's Council and a Number of Civil Magiſtrates; a conſiderable Body of the People immediately entered into the Council-Chamber and expreſſed themſelves to his Honor with a Freedom and Warmth becoming the Occaſion. He uſed his utmoſt Endeavours to pacify them, requeſting that they would let the Matter ſubſide for the Night, and promiſing to do all in his Power that Juſtice ſhould be done, and the Law have its Courſe; Men of Influence and Weight with the People were not wanting on their part to procure their Compliance with his Honor's Requeſt,——by repreſenting the horrible Conſequences of a promiſcuous and raſh Engagement in the Night, and aſſuring them that ſuch Meaſures ſhould be entered upon in the Morning, as would be agreeable to their Dignity, and a more likely way of obtaining the beſt Satiſfaction for the Blood of their Fellow-Townſmen. The Inhabitants attended to theſe Suggeſtions, and the Regiment under Arms being ordered to their Barracks which was inſiſted upon by the People, they then ſeperated and returned to their Dwellings by One o'Clock. At 3 Capt. Preſton was committed, as were the Soldiers who fired, a few hours after him.

TUESDAY, *March* 6. At eleven o'clock the Inhabitants met at Faneuil-Hall, and choſe a Committee of 15 reſpectable Gentleman to wait upon the Lieut. Governor in Council, to requeſt of him to iſſue his orders for the immediate removal of the troops.

The Meſſage was in theſe words.

THAT it is the unanimous opinion of this meeting that the Inhabitants and ſoldiers can no longer live together in ſafety; that nothing can rationally be expected to reſtore the peace of the Town and prevent blood and carnage, but the immediate removal of the Troops; and that we therefore moſt fervently pray his Honor that his power and influence may be exerted for their inſtant removal.

His Honor's Reply.

GENTLEMEN, I am extremely ſorry for the unhappy differences between the Inhabitants and troops, and eſpecially for the action of the laſt evening, and I have exerted myſelf upon that occaſion that a due enquiry may be made, and that the law may have its courſe. I have in council conſulted with the commanding officers of the two regiments which are in town. They have their orders from the General at New-York. It is not in my power to countermand thoſe orders. The Council have deſired that the two regiments may be removed to the Caſtle. From the particular concern which the 29th regiment has had in your differences, Col. Dalrymple who is the commanding officer of the troops has ſignified to me that that regiment ſhall without delay be placed in the barracks at the Caſtle until he can ſend to the General and receive his further orders concerning both the regiments, and that the main guard ſhall be removed, and the 14th regiment ſo diſpoſed & laid under ſuch reſtraint that all occaſion of future diſturbances may be prevented.

The foregoing Reply having been read and fully conſidered—the queſtion was put, Whether the report be ſatisfactory? Paſſed in the Negative, (only one 1 diſſentient.) out of upwards of 4000 Voters.

It was then moved and voted that *John Hancock*, Eſq; Mr. *Samuel Adams*, Mr. *William Molineux*, *William Phillips*, Eſq; Dr. *Joſeph Warren*, *Joſhua Henſhaw*, Eſq; and *Samuel Pemberton*, Eſq; be a Committee to wait on his Honor the Lieut. Governor, and inform him, that it is the unanimous Opinion of this Meeting, that the Reply made to a Vote of the Inhabitants preſented his Honor in the Morning, is by no Means ſatisfactory; and that nothing leſs will ſatiſfy, than a total and immediate removal of all the Troops.

The Committee having waited upon the Lieut. Governor agreeable to the foregoing Vote; laid before the Inhabitants the following Vote of Council received from his Honor.

His Honor the Lieut. Governor laid before the Board a Vote of the Town of Boſton, paſſed this Afternoon, and then addreſſed the Board as follows,

Gentlemen of the Council,

"*I lay before you a Vote of the Town of Boſton which I have juſt now receiv'd from them, and I now aſk your Advice what you judge neceſſary to be done upon it.*"

The Council thereupon expreſſed themſelves to be *unanimouſly* of opinion, "that it was abſolutely neceſſary for his Majeſty's ſervice, the good order of the Town, and the Peace of the Province, that the Troops ſhould be immediately removed out of the Town of Boſton, and thereupon adviſed his Honor to communicate this Advice of the Council to Col. Dalrymple, and pray that he would order the Troops down to Caſtle-William." The Committe alſo informed the Town, that Col. Dalrymple after having ſeen the Vote of Council, ſaid to the Committee, "That he now gave his word of Honor that he would begin his Preparations in the Morning, and that there ſhould be no unneceſſary delay until the whole of the two Regiments were removed to the Caſtle."

Upon the above Report being read, the Inhabitants could not avoid expreſſing the high Satiſfaction it afforded them.

After Meaſures were taken for the Security of the Town in the Night by a ſtrong Military Watch the Meeting was Diſſolved.

Both Regiments were afterwards remov'd to Caſtle-Iſland *with all convenient ſpeed.*

THURSDAY, *March* 8. Agreeable to a general requeſt of the inhabitants, and by the conſent of parents and friends, were carried to the GRAVE in ſucceſſion, the bodies of *Samuel Gray*, *Samuel Maverick*, *James Caldwell*, and *Criſpus Attucks*, the unhappy Victims who fell in the bloody Maſſacre of the Monday Evening preceeding!——On this occaſion moſt of the Shops in town were ſhut, all the bells in town were ordered to toll a ſolemn peal, as were alſo thoſe in the neighbouring towns of Charleſtown, Roxbury, &c. The proceſſion began to move between the hours of 4 and 5 in the Afternoon; two of the unfortunate ſufferers, viz. Meſſ. *James Caldwell* and *Criſpus Attucks*, who were ſtrangers, were borne from Faneuil-Hall, attended by a numerous train of perſons of all ranks; and the other two, viz. *Samuel Gray*, from the Houſe of Mr. *Benjamin Gray*, (his brother) on the South ſide of the Exchange, and *Samuel Maverick*, from the houſe of his diſtreſſed mother, Mrs. *Mary Maverick* in Union-ſtreet, each followed by their reſpective relations and friends: The ſeveral hearſes forming a junction in King-ſtreet, the theatre of that inhuman TRAGEDY! proceeded from thence through the main ſtreet, lengthened by an immenſe concourſe of people ſo numerous as to be obliged to follow in ranks of ſix, and bro't up by a long train of carriages belonging to the principal gentry in town.—The bodies were depoſited in one vault in the middle burying ground.—The aggravated circumſtances of their death, the diſtreſs and ſorrow viſible in every countenance, together with the peculiar Solemnity with which the whole funeral was conducted, ſurpaſs deſcription.

SATURDAY, *March* 17. The Remains of *Patrick Carr*, who died of the Wounds he received in King-Street, on the bloody and execrable Night of the 5th Inſt. were attended by a numerous Train of Mourners to the *ſame* Grave, in which thoſe who fell by the *ſame* Hands of Violence were interr'd the laſt Week.

Amidſt the Change of Fortune and of Time,
Youth falls a Victim in it's early Prime:
Snatch'd from the Stage of Action and of Life,
By Hands embroil'd in guiltleſs Blood and Strife.
Whilſt throbbing Wounds their Agonies impart,
Or guſh with Anguiſh from a bleeding Heart;
In wreking Gore their wallowing Corpſe are toſs'd,
Till they by Death to ſenſe of Pain are loſt.
Tho' Powers neglect this horrid Scene to trace,
And mark with angry Eye the fatal Place:
Yet FREEDOM'S SONS in queſt of Truth purſue,
On guilty Wretches ſtill for Vengeance ſue.
And o'er the Spot, the ſculptur'd Marble raiſe,
Which unborn Youths may read in future Days.
Whilſt INNOCENCE amongſt the ſilent dead,
In mouldering Duſt reclines it's peaceful Head:
Come, ſpotleſs FREEDOM! bring thy filial Race,
The darling Offſpring of a fond Embrace!
Round the cold Grave where Innocence doth ſleep,
Let all thy Guards their conſtant Vigils keep:
O'er the heap'd Turf that hides each peaceful Head,
Vouchſafe, Fair Maid! thy ſheltering Wings to ſpread,
Shield the ſtill Aſhes from Oppreſſion's Eyes,
From penſion'd Tyrants, and from B——d's Lies!
Whilſt to the World, th' engraven Stone ſhall ſhow
The ſlaughter'd Victims in the Duſt below.

TYPIS JOHANNES BOYLES, MDCCLXX.

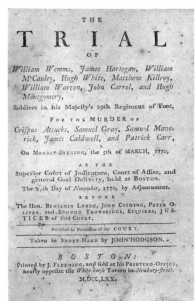

The Trial of William Wemms, James Hartegan, William M'Cauley, Hugh White, Matthew Killroy, William Warren, John Carrol, and Hugh Montgomery, Soldiers in his Majesty's 29th Regiment of Foot. Boston: J. Fleeming, 1770. LCP

A Short Narrative of The Horrid Massacre in Boston, perpetrated In the Evening of the Fifth Day of March, 1770. Boston: Printed by Order of the Town of Boston, And sold by Edes and Gill, and T. & J. Fleet, 1770. LCP

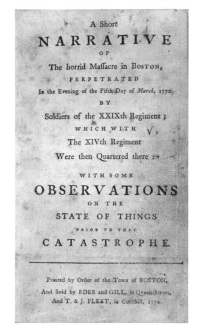

William Cooper, Town Clerk. Extract from minutes of the Town Meeting, Boston, March 22, 1770. APS

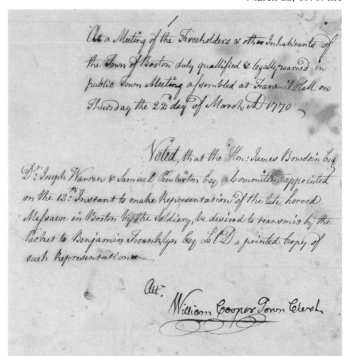

It was probably inevitable that the presence of troops amid a restless and resentful populace would occasion violence. A mob in Boston's King Street so harassed a group of British soldiers that they fired into the crowd and killed five men: Samuel Gray, ropemaker; Crispus Attucks, mulatto laborer; James Caldwell, seaman, Samuel Maverick, teenager; and Patrick Carr, breeches maker. The first "martyrs" of the American Revolution were widely hailed. Quickly the account of the massacre was sent to all the colonies, where it became inflammatory propaganda material. The town of Boston ordered James Bowdoin, Joseph Warren and Samuel Pemberton to write a *Narrative* of the event and voted to send a copy to Franklin, then acting as the agent for Massachusetts in London. When the soldiers were tried for murder, they were ably defended by John Adams and James Otis; all but two of the soldiers were acquitted, and they were punished but lightly. However, the memory of the Boston Massacre remained green.

A Pennsylvanian. *To the Inhabitants of
the City and County of Philadelphia.
Gentlemen, You are come here this
Day to determine whether you will be
Freemen or Slaves.* [Philadelphia,
1770]. Broadside. LCP

John Harris Cruger, Isaac Low, Henry
Remsen, Jr., and Thomas Walton,
merchants of New York. *Letter to the
Committee of Merchants in Philadelphia,*
New York, July 10, 1770. HSP

After a bitter struggle between radicals and moderates,
the New York merchants decided, in view of the repeal
of almost all the Townshend duties, to permit the
importation of everything except tea. Even then there
were defectors, as the satirical poem about an unpatriotic
wife indicated. A committee of the New York merchants
sent news of their decision to Philadelphia. It was received
with indignation. A call for renewed determination on
the part of Pennsylvanians in the face of the "Meanness
and Cowardice" of the Yorkers was circulated at a public
meeting held in the State-House yard on July 14, 1770.

New-York May 10th. 1770.

The FEMALE PATRIOT, No. I.

ADDRESSED TO THE

TEA-DRINKING LADIES OF NEW-YORK.

WHEN ADAM firft fell into SATAN's Snare,
    And forfeited his Blifs to pleafe the Fair;
GOD from his Garden drove the finful Man,
And thus the Source of human Woes began.
'Twas weak in ADAM, for to pleafe his Wife,
To lofe his accefs to the Tree of Life :
His dear bought Knowledge all his Sons deplore,
DEATH their Inheritance, and SIN their Store.
But why blame ADAM, fince his Brainlefs Race
Will lofe their ALL to obtain a beautious FACE;
And will their Honour, Pride, and Wealth lay down
Rather then fee a lovely Woman frown.
The Ladies are not quite fo complifant,
If they want TEA, they'll ftorm and rave and rant,
And call their Lordly Hufbands Afs and CLOWN,
The jeft of Fools and Sport of all the Town.
A pleafant Story lately I heard told
Of MADAM HORNBLOOM, a noted Scold,
Laft Day her Hufband faid, " My deareft Life,
My Kind, my Fair, my Angel of a Wife ;
Juft now, from LONDON, there's a Ship come in
Brings noble News will raife us Merchants Fame,
The Fruits of our non-importation Scheme.
The Parliament, dear Saint, may they be bleft
Have great part of our Grievances redreft :"
" Have they indeed," replies the frowning Dame,
" Say, is there not fome Tea and China come."
" Why, no! We can't import that Indian Weed,
That Duty's ftill a Rod above our Head."
" Curfe on your Heads, you nafty fumbling Crew,
Then round his Shoulders the hard Broom-Stick flew,
Go, dirty CLOD-POLE! get me fome Shufhong,
This Evening I've invited MADAM STRONG.
--- Silence --- you BLOCKHEAD --- hear, the Lady
        knocks !
Get to your Cock-Loft or expect fome Strokes."
    --- " Your Servant Madam, Tea is on the Board
I really tho't you once had broke your Word."
" I afk your Pardon, dear Mifs HORNBLOOM,
My fpraling Brats kept me fo long at Home;
My ftupid Hufband too has gone aftray
To wait upon the SONS of LIBERTY.'

The Female Patriot, No. I. *Addressed to
the Tea-Drinking Ladies of New-York.*
[New York, 1770]. Broadside. LCP

Samuel Adams. *Letter to Richard Henry Lee,* Boston, April 10, 1773. APS

Extract from the Journal of the House of Representatives of the Province of Massachusetts Bay, June 16, 1773. APS

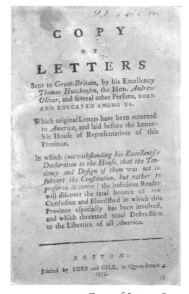

Copy of Letters Sent to Great-Britain, by his Excellency Thomas Hutchinson, the Hon. Andrew Oliver, and several other Persons, BORN AND EDUCATED AMONG US. Boston: Edes and Gill, 1773. LCP

The radical Sam Adams begins to form links with a like-minded Virginian. As early as 1773 he was talking of independence. "I have often thought it a Misfortune, or rather a Fault in the Friends of American Independence and Freedom," he wrote, "their not taking Care to open every Channel of Communication." Adams regretted the Compliance of New York in making annual Provision, for a military force, designed to carry Acts of Tyranny into Execution. . . . But the active Vigilance, the manly Generosity and the steady Perseverance of Virginia and South Carolina, gives us Reason to hope, that the Fire of true Patriotism will at length spread throughout the Continent."

Franklin, by means never disclosed, secured copies of letters written by the governor and lieutenant-governor of Massachusetts chiefly to Thomas Whately, then active in American affairs. In them the colonial officials expressed frankly their distrust of the provincials and suggested the use of force to effect compliance with the acts of Parliament. Franklin sent copies to Boston, it was said, in hopes that they would calm the rising storm by showing that the ministry received such information and advice from native Americans. The opposite proved to be the case. The letters added oil to the fires of resentment. The House of Representatives adopted a series of resolves citing the unfriendly sentiments expressed in the letters and asking for the recall of Hutchinson and Oliver. An official copy, with the heading written by Samuel Adams, was sent to Franklin.

Frontispiece in George Bickham. *Penmanship in its utmost Beauty and Extent.* London: H. Overton and I. Hoole, 1731. LCP

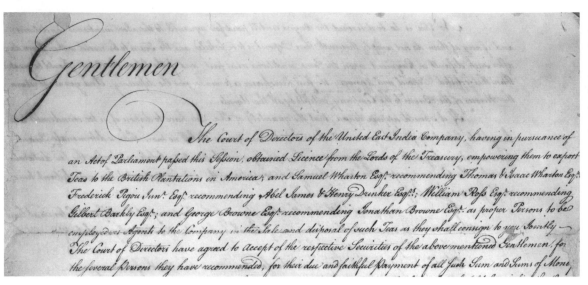

Account of Tea exported by the East India Company to his Majesty's Colonies in North America. [London, September, 1773]. LCP

The Boston Tea Party. Engraved by Daniel-Nicholas Chodowiecki in *Historisch-genealogischer Calender, oder Jahrbuch der merkwürdigsten neuen Welt.* Leipzig, 1784. LCP

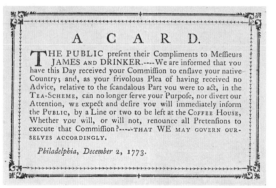

TO THE
Delaware Pilots.

WE took the Pleasure, some Days since, of kindly admonishing you *to do your Duty*; if perchance you should meet with the (Tea,) SHIP POLLY, CAPTAIN AYRES; a THREE DECKER which is hourly expected.

We have now to add, that Matters ripen fast here, and that *much is expected from those Lads who meet with the Tea Ship.*----There is some Talk of A HANDSOME REWARD FOR THE PILOT WHO GIVES THE FIRST GOOD ACCOUNT OF HER.----How that may be, we cannot *for certain* determine; But ALL agree, that TAR and FEATHERS will be his Portion, who pilots her into this Harbour. And we will answer for ourselves, that, whoever is committed to us, as an Offender against the Rights of *America*, will experience the utmost Exertion of our Abilities; as

THE COMMITTEE FOR TARRING AND FEATHERING.

P. S. We expect you will furnish yourselves with Copies of the foregoing and following Letter; which are printed for this Purpose, that the Pilot who meets with Captain *Ayres* may favor him with a Sight of them.

Committee of Taring and Feathering.

TO
Capt. AYRES,

Of the SHIP *POLLY*, on a Voyage from *London* to *Philadelphia.*

SIR,

WE are informed that you have, imprudently, taken Charge of a Quantity of Tea; which has been sent out by the *India* Company, *under the Auspices of the Ministry*, as a Trial of *American* Virtue and Resolution.

Now, as your Cargo, on your Arrival here, will most assuredly bring you into hot water; and as you are perhaps a Stranger *to these Parts*, we have concluded to advise you of the present Situation of Affairs in *Philadelphia*----that, taking Time by the Forelock, you may stop short in your dangerous Errand----secure your Ship against the Rafts of combustible Matter which may be set on Fire, and turned loose against her; and more than all this, that you may preserve your own Person, from the Pitch and Feathers that are prepared for you.

In the first Place, we must tell you, that the *Pennsylvanians* are, *to a Man*, passionately fond of Freedom; the Birthright of *Americans*; and at all Events are determined to enjoy it.

That they sincerely believe, no Power on the Face of the Earth has a Right to tax them without their Consent.

That in their Opinion, the Tea in your Custody is designed by the Ministry to enforce such a Tax, which they will undoubtedly oppose; and in so doing, give you every possible Obstruction.

We are nominated to a very disagreeable, but necessary Service.---- To our Care are committed all Offenders against the Rights of *America*; and hapless is he, whose evil Destiny has doomed him to suffer at our Hands.

You are sent out on a diabolical Service; and if you are so foolish and obstinate as to compleat your Voyage, by bringing your Ship to Anchor in this Port, you may run such a Gauntlet, as will induce you, in your last Moments, most heartily to curse those who have made you the Dupe of their Avarice and Ambition.

What think you Captain, of a Halter around your Neck----ten Gallons of liquid Tar decanted on your Pate----with the Feathers of a dozen wild Geese laid over that to enliven your Appearance?

Only think seriously of this----and fly to the Place from whence you came----fly without Hesitation----without the Formality of a Protest----and above all, Captain *Ayres* let us advise you to fly without the wild Geese Feathers.

Your Friends to serve

Philadelphia, Nov. 27, 1773   THE COMMITTEE *as before subscribed*

The detailed instructions of the East India Company, which had been given a monopoly of tea by Parliament, did not reach its American agents until the orders were virtually obsolete. The list of tea ships, cargoes and consignees indicated that one ship with 698 cases of tea was destined for Philadelphia. As early as October 15, 1773, a group of radicals, including Thomas Mifflin, William Bradford and Benjamin Rush, began to arouse the populace to prevent the landing of the tea. Many years later John Adams told Rush that it was Philadelphia's example which gave the Bostonians the courage to have their Tea Party. By November a Committee for Tarring and Feathering warned pilots and Captain Ayres of the tea ship *Polly* what would happen to them were the ship brought up the Delaware. James and Drinker and other consignees were told in no uncertain terms not to accept the shipment. A mass meeting on December 27, at which Ayres was present, so adamantly backed the refusal to permit him to land that he returned to England with the tea undelivered.

A CARD.

THE PUBLIC present their Compliments to Messieurs JAMES AND DRINKER.----We are informed that you have this Day received your Commission to enslave your native Country; and, as your frivolous Plea of having received no Advice, relative to the scandalous Part you were to act, in the TEA-SCHEME, can no longer serve your Purpose, nor divert our Attention, WE expect and desire you will immediately inform the PUBLIC, by a Line or two to be left at the COFFEE HOUSE, Whether YOU will, or will not, renounce all Pretensions to execute that Commission?----THAT WE MAY GOVERN OURSELVES ACCORDINGLY.

Philadelphia, December 2, 1773.

Monday Morning, December 27, 1773.

THE TEA-SHIP being arrived, every Inhabitant, who wishes to preserve the Liberty of America, is desired to meet at the STATE-HOUSE, This Morning, precisely at TEN o'Clock, to advise what is best to be done on this alarming Crisis.

Thomas & Elisha Hutchinson, Richard Clarke
& Sons and Benjamin Faneuil, Jr., Boston
merchants. *Letter (copy) to Thomas & Isaac
Wharton, Abel James & Henry Drinker,* et al.,
Philadelphia merchants, Castle William,
[Boston], December 4, 1773. HSP

Samuel Franklin. *Letter to
Benjamin Franklin,* Boston,
December 17, 1773. APS

Animated by the Philadelphia example, Sam Adams
and his Sons of Liberty determined to teach the British a
lesson as the tea ship neared Boston. The Boston
consignees informed their Philadelphia colleagues that
in face of "the outrage of the People against the plan of
the Honble. East India Company," they had agreed
to store the tea, but would not consent to send it back.
On the night of December 16, 1773, the famous Boston
Tea Party took place. As Samuel Franklin wrote to his
cousin in London on the following day: "after three
or four meetings of ye Committees of ye Near towns
with a good number of ye Inhabitants of Boston & our
Committe they Had yesterday a grand Meeting of
about 5000 persons at ye old South to putt into Execution
ye sending ye Ships back With ye Tea & I think ye
Body Waited with a great deal of patience both upon
ye Consignees & Mr Rotch & finding ye Governer
would not give the Vessell a pass about 6 oclock the
Meeting was Desolv'd & a parcell of men Calld Indians
appear'd & by Nine oclock I heard that all the Tea
was Destroyed by throwing it into ye Sea." The British
were mocked in a cartoon, instigated by pro-American
interests in England, which celebrated the debacle of
the tea.

*Liberty Triumphant, or the
Downfall of Oppression.*
[Philadelphia?, 1774]. LCP

Franklin before the Lords in Council. Print of painting by Christian Schuessele. APS

Benjamin Franklin.
Letter to Jane Mecom,
London, February 17,
1774. HSP

The administration of Lord North decided openly to attack and punish Franklin for having sent the Hutchinson and Oliver letters to Boston. He was hailed before a council of the House of Lords and there excoriated by the solicitor-general, Alexander Wedderburn. It was a humiliating experience for Franklin, but one which made him a martyr in the colonies. At the same time he was stripped of his office as postmaster-general in America. Telling his sister of the action, he wrote: "Intending to disgrace me, they have rather done me Honour. No Failure of Duty in my Office is alledg'd against me; such a Fault I should have been asham'd of. But I am too much attach'd to the Interests of America, and an Opposer of the Measures of the Administration.—The Displacing me therefore is a Testimony of my being uncorrupted."

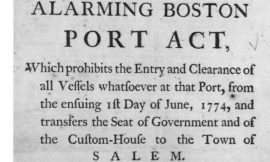

To punish Bostonians for having thrown the tea into the harbor the House of Commons passed the Boston Port Bill, which closed the port and cut off sea-borne trade. A group of Americans in London, including Franklin, Ralph Izard and William Middleton of South Carolina and Arthur and William Lee of Virginia, petitioned the House of Lords to reject the act. It was in vain. Samuel Adams wrote to Richard Henry Lee that things were in a bad state, but the inhabitants of Boston, "far from being in the least Degree intimidated, are resolved to undergo the greatest Hardships, rather than submit in any Instance to the Tyrannical Act." Adams spoke of other punitive measures and wondered if the Americans would look on them as an attack on one colony or on all. "Will they, as unconcern'd Spectators, look upon it to be design'd only to lop off the exuberant Branches of Democracy in the Constitution of this Province? Or, as part of a plan to reduce them all to Slavery? These are Questions, in my Opinion of Importance, which I trust will be thoroughly weighed in a general Congress. May God inspire that intended Body with Wisdom and Fortitude, and unite and prosper their Councils!" One of the most trenchant attacks upon the Boston Port Bill was the pamphlet of the thirty year-old Quincy. He presented this copy to James Bowdoin, one of the leading Boston radicals.

THE ALARMING BOSTON PORT ACT,

Which prohibits the Entry and Clearance of all Veſſels whatſoever at that Port, from the enſuing 1ſt Day of June, 1774, and transfers the Seat of Government and of the Cuſtom-Houſe to the Town of SALEM.

An ACT to diſcontinue, in ſuch manner, and for ſuch time as are therein mentioned, the landing and diſcharging, lading or ſhipping, of goods, wares, and merchandiſe, at the town, and within the Harbour of Boſton, in the province of Maſſachuſetts Bay, in North America.

WHEREAS dangerous commotions and inſurrections have been fomented and raiſed in the town of Boſton, in the province of Maſſachuſetts Bay, in New England, by divers ill-affected perſons, to the ſubverſion of his Majeſty's government, and to the utter deſtruction of the publick peace, and good order of the ſaid town; in which commotions and inſurrections certain valuable cargoes of teas, being the property of the Eaſt India Company, and on board certain veſſels lying within the bay or harbour of Boſton, were ſeized and deſtroyed: And whereas, in the preſent condition of the

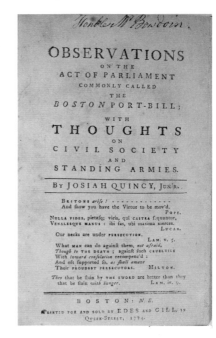

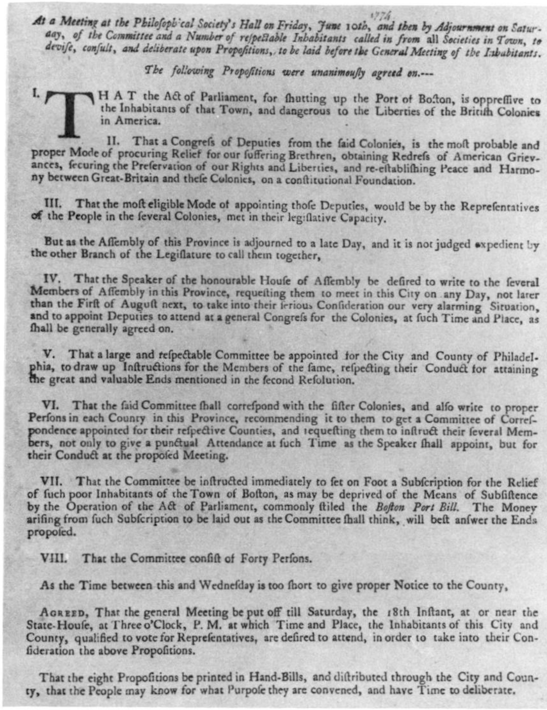

At a Meeting at the Philosophical Society's Hall on Friday, June 10th, and then by Adjournment on Saturday, of the Committee and a Number of respectable Inhabitants called in from all Societies in Town, to devise, consult, and deliberate upon Propositions, to be laid before the General Meeting of the Inhabitants.

1774

The following Propositions were unanimously agreed on.---

I. THAT the Act of Parliament, for shutting up the Port of Boston, is oppressive to the Inhabitants of that Town, and dangerous to the Liberties of the British Colonies in America.

II. That a Congress of Deputies from the said Colonies, is the most probable and proper Mode of procuring Relief for our suffering Brethren, obtaining Redress of American Grievances, securing the Preservation of our Rights and Liberties, and re-establishing Peace and Harmony between Great-Britain and these Colonies, on a constitutional Foundation.

III. That the most eligible Mode of appointing those Deputies, would be by the Representatives of the People in the several Colonies, met in their legislative Capacity.

But as the Assembly of this Province is adjourned to a late Day, and it is not judged expedient by the other Branch of the Legislature to call them together,

IV. That the Speaker of the honourable House of Assembly be desired to write to the several Members of Assembly in this Province, requesting them to meet in this City on any Day, not later than the First of August next, to take into their serious Consideration our very alarming Situation, and to appoint Deputies to attend at a general Congress for the Colonies, at such Time and Place, as shall be generally agreed on.

V. That a large and respectable Committee be appointed for the City and County of Philadelphia, to draw up Instructions for the Members of the same, respecting their Conduct for attaining the great and valuable Ends mentioned in the second Resolution.

VI. That the said Committee shall correspond with the sister Colonies, and also write to proper Persons in each County in this Province, recommending it to them to get a Committee of Correspondence appointed for their respective Counties, and requesting them to instruct their several Members, not only to give a punctual Attendance at such Time as the Speaker shall appoint, but for their Conduct at the proposed Meeting.

VII. That the Committee be instructed immediately to set on Foot a Subscription for the Relief of such poor Inhabitants of the Town of Boston, as may be deprived of the Means of Subsistence by the Operation of the Act of Parliament, commonly stiled the *Boston Port Bill.* The Money arising from such Subscription to be laid out as the Committee shall think, will best answer the Ends proposed.

VIII. That the Committee consist of Forty Persons.

As the Time between this and Wednesday is too short to give proper Notice to the County,

AGREED, That the general Meeting be put off till Saturday, the 18th Instant, at or near the State-House, at Three o'Clock, P. M. at which Time and Place, the Inhabitants of this City and County, qualified to vote for Representatives, are desired to attend, in order to take into their Consideration the above Propositions.

That the eight Propositions be printed in Hand-Bills, and distributed through the City and County, that the People may know for what Purpose they are convened, and have Time to deliberate.

At a Meeting at the Philosophical Society's Hall on Friday, June 10th, . . . of the Committee and a Number of respectable Inhabitants called in from all Societies in Town. [Philadelphia, 1774]. LCP

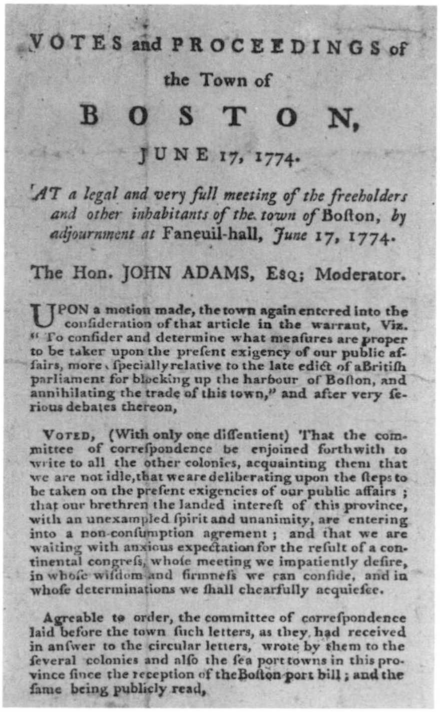

VOTES and PROCEEDINGS of the Town of BOSTON, JUNE 17, 1774.

AT a legal and very full meeting of the freeholders and other inhabitants of the town of Boston, *by adjournment at* Faneuil-hall, *June 17, 1774.*

The Hon. JOHN ADAMS, Esq; Moderator.

UPON a motion made, the town again entered into the consideration of that article in the warrant, Viz. "To consider and determine what measures are proper to be taken upon the present exigency of our public affairs, more especially relative to the late edict of a British parliament for blocking up the harbour of Boston, and annihilating the trade of this town," and after very serious debates thereon,

VOTED, (With only one dissentient) That the committee of correspondence be enjoined forthwith to write to all the other colonies, acquainting them that we are not idle, that we are deliberating upon the steps to be taken on the present exigencies of our public affairs; that our brethren the landed interest of this province, with an unexampled spirit and unanimity, are entering into a non-consumption agrement; and that we are waiting with anxious expectation for the result of a continental congress, whose meeting we impatiently desire, in whose wisdom and firmness we can confide, and in whose determinations we shall chearfully acquiesce.

Agreable to order, the committee of correspondence laid before the town such letters, as they had received in answer to the circular letters, wrote by them to the several colonies and also the sea port towns in this province since the reception of the Boston port bill; and the same being publicly read,

Votes and Proceedings of the Town of Boston, June 17, 1774. [Boston, 1774]. LCP

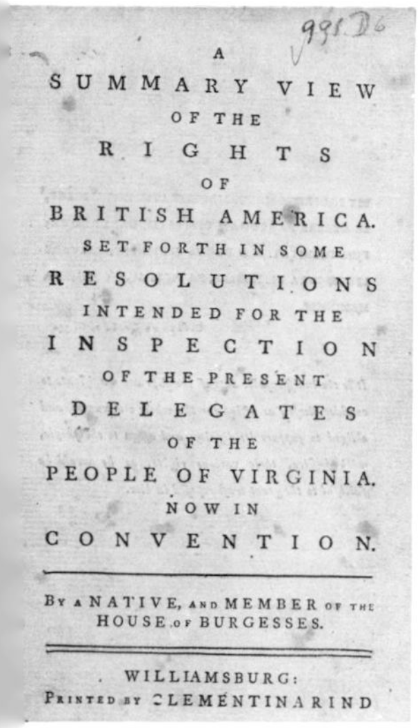

No sooner had news of the Boston Port Bill reached America than General Gage arrived to replace Governor Hutchinson and enforce the "Coercive Acts." Boston appealed to the other colonies for sympathy and support. The reaction was quick and favorable. In Philadelphia one meeting adopted a number of resolutions, among which was a call for "a Congress of Deputies from the said Colonies." Another set up a "Subscription for the relief of such poor Inhabitants of the Town of Boston" as were suffering from the effects of the bill. Boston, grateful, on June 17 enjoined a committee of correspondence to let the other colonies know that they had entered into a non-consumption agreement and were "awaiting with anxious expectation for the result of a continental congress, whose meeting we impatiently desire, in whose wisdom and firmness we can confide, and in whose determination we shall chearfully acquiesce."

[Thomas Jefferson]. *A Summary View of the Rights of British America.* Williamsburg: Clementina Rind, [1774]. LCP

995 D6

A SUMMARY VIEW OF THE RIGHTS OF BRITISH AMERICA. SET FORTH IN SOME RESOLUTIONS INTENDED FOR THE INSPECTION OF THE PRESENT DELEGATES OF THE PEOPLE OF VIRGINIA. NOW IN CONVENTION.

BY A NATIVE, AND MEMBER OF THE HOUSE OF BURGESSES.

WILLIAMSBURG: PRINTED BY CLEMENTINARIND

to be expected that those here, much less able at that time to oppose the designs of despotism, should be exempted from injury.

Accordingly that country, which had been acquired by the lives, the labours, and the fortunes, of individual adventurers, was by these princes, at several times, parted out and distributed among the favourites and * followers of their fortunes, and, by an assumed right of the crown alone, was erected into distinct and independent governments; a measure which it is believed his majesty's prudence and understanding would prevent him from imitating at this day, as no exercise of such a power, of dividing and dismembering a country, has ever occurred in his majesty's realm of England, though now of very antient standing; nor could it be justified or acquiesced under there, or in any other part of his majesty's empire.

That the exercise of a free trade with all parts of the world, possessed by the American colonists, as of natural right, and which no law of their own had taken away or abridged, was next the object of unjust encroachment. Some of the colonies having thought proper to continue the administration of their government in the name and under the authority of his majesty king Charles the first (whom, notwithstanding his late deposition by the commonwealth of England, they continued in the sovereignty of their state) the parliament for the commonwealth took the same in high offence, and assumed upon themselves the power of prohibiting their trade with all other parts of the world, except the island of Great Britain. This arbitrary act, however, they soon recalled, and by

Jefferson drew up a series of resolutions, which he intended as instructions for the Virginia delegates to the First Continental Congress. While he was absent, some friends had them printed up in their present pamphlet form. They are framed as an address to the King and set forth, as did the Declaration of Independence two years later, the injustices of which the colonies complained. The present copy is one of those with autograph corrections by Jefferson himself. It is his first printed work.

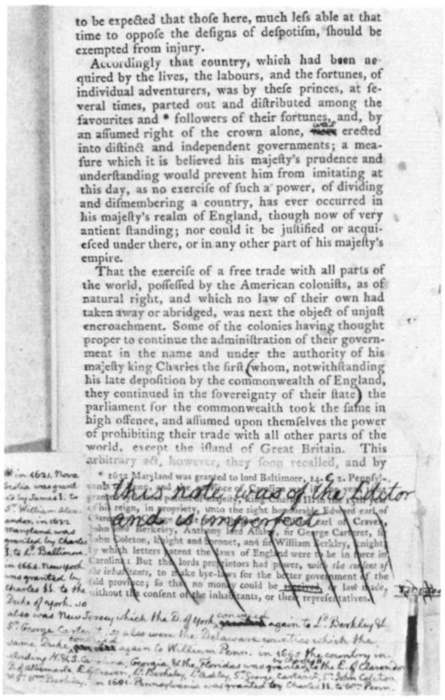

[Thomas Bradbury Chandler]. *A Friendly Address to all Reasonable Americans, on the Subject of our Political Confusions.* [New York: James Rivington], 1774. LCP

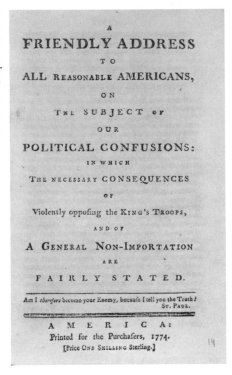

[John Gray]. *The Right of the British Legislature To Tax the American Colonies Vindicated.* London: T. Becket, 1774. LCP

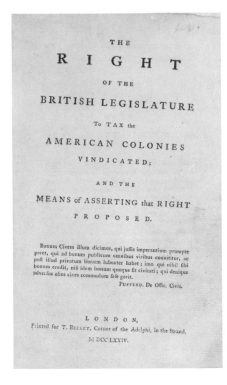

A Letter to a Member of Parliament on the Present Unhappy Dispute between Great-Britain and her Colonies. Wherein the Supremacy of the Former is Asserted and Proved. London: J. Walter, 1774. LCP

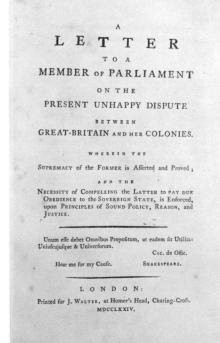

[Jabez Fisher]. *Americanus Examined, and his Principles compared with those of the Approved Advocates for America.* Philadelphia, 1774. LC

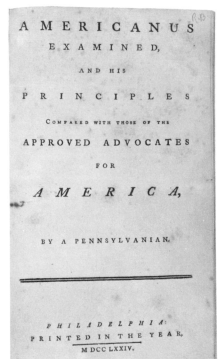

In England there were plenty of pro-government writers, and in America a vocal minority of Tories tried to persuade the people that compliance was better than resistance.

[John Cartwright]. *American Independence the Interest and Glory of Great Britain.* ondon: Printed for the Author, by H. S. Woodfall. Sold by J. Wilkie, 1774. LCP

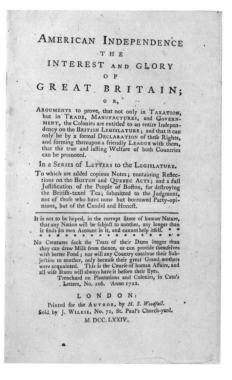

[Arthur Lee]. *An Appeal to the Justice and Interests of the People of Great Britain, in the Present Disputes with America.* London: J. Almon, 1774. HSP

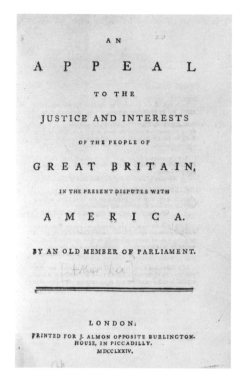

[Philip Livingston]. *The Other Side of the Question: or, A Defence of the Liberties of North-America. In Answer to a late Friendly Address to All Reasonable Americans.* New York: James Rivington, 1774. LCP

[Richard Wells]. *A Few Political Reflections submitted to the Consideration of the British Colonies.* Philadelphia: John Dunlap, 1774. LCP

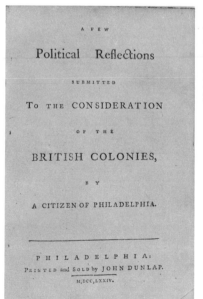

As the gulf between Great Britain and her American colonies widened the propaganda war intensified. On both sides of the Atlantic pamphlets were published supporting the Americans and deploring the punitive acts which Parliament had passed to maintain its right to govern the colonies as it saw fit.

Clash
of Arms,
1775-1777

"These are the times that
try men's souls."—Thomas
Paine. *The Crisis*, 1776

A Correct View of The Late
Battle at Charlestown June 17th
1775. *Pennsylvania Magazine*,
September 1775. LCP

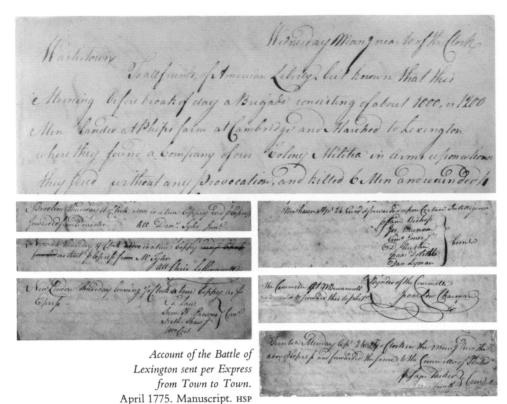

Account of the Battle of Lexington sent per Express from Town to Town. April 1775. Manuscript. HSP

The Battle of Lexington. Engraved by Daniel-Nicholas Chodowiecki in *Historisch-genealogischer Calender, oder Jahrbuch der merkwürdigsten neuen Welt.* Leipzig, 1784. LCP

PHILADELPHIA, *April* 24, 1775.

An Exprefs arrived at Five o'Clock this Evening, by which we have the following Advices.

Watertown, Wednefday Morning, near 10 *of the Clock.*

TO all Friends of American Liberty, be it known, that this morning before break of day, a brigade confifting of about 1000 or 1,200 men landed at Phipps's Farm, at Cambridge, and marched to Lexington, where they found a Company of our Colony Militia in arms, upon whom they fired without any provocation, and killed fix men, & wounded four others. By an exprefs from Bofton we find another brigade are now upon their march from Bofton, fuppofed to be about 1000. The bearer, Trail Biffel is charged to alarm the country quite to Connecticut; and all perfons are defired to furnifh him with frefh horfes, as they may be needed. I have fpoken with feveral, who have feen the dead and wounded. Pray let the Delegates from this colony to Connecticut fee this, they know Col. Forfter, one of the Delegates.

Massachusetts. [*News of the battle of Lexington*]. Philadelphia: W. and T. Bradford, [1775]. Broadside. HSP

Suffering because of the closing of the Port of Boston in retribution for the Boston Tea Party, and further aroused by the military activity of the British army occupying the town, the colonists of the area began to arm and to collect military stores, including a supply at Concord. A British force sent out on April 18-19, 1775, to seize the Concord munitions fired on minutemen encountered at Lexington on the way, and the Revolution was on. Reaching Concord, the invaders found the weapons, many in the hands of minutemen, and then retreated to Boston, bloodily harassed enroute by the embattled farmers, who then laid siege to the British in Boston. News of the battles was sent posthaste to the other colonies. The despatch was certified by the committees of correspondence of the towns through which it passed, until the express rider reached Philadelphia at five in the afternoon on April 24, 1775. The news was immediately set in type and printed for distribution.

VOL. IV. NUMB. 186.

DUNLAP's

Pennsylvania | **Packet**

OR,

GENERAL THE ADVERTISER.

MONDAY, MAY 15th, 1775.

AFFIDAVITS AND DEPOSITIONS, *Relative to the Commencement of the late Hos-TILITIES in the province of MASSACHUSETTS BAY: Together with an ADDRESS from the PROVINCIAL CONVENTION of said province, to the INHABITANTS of GREAT-BRITAIN, transmitted to the CONGRESS now sitting in this city, and published by their order.*

CHARLES THOMSON, Secretary.

WE SOLOMON BROWN, JONATHAN LORING, and ELIJAH SANDERSON, all of lawful age, and of Lexington, in the County of Middlesex, and Colony of the Massachusetts-Bay, in New-England, do testify and declare, that on the evening of the 18th of April, instant, being on the road between Concord and Lexington, and all of us mounted on horses, we were about ten of the clock suddenly surprized by nine persons, whom we took

gular troops (if they should approach) unless they should insult or molest us;—and upon their sudden approach I immediately ordered our Militia to disperse and not to fire.——Immediately said troops made their appearance and rushed furiously, fired upon and killed eight of our party, without receiving any provocation therefor from us.

JOHN PARKER.

Lexington, April 24th, 1775. I JOHN ROBINS being of lawful age, do testify and say, that on the 19th inst. the company under the command of Capt. John Parker, being drawn up (sometime before sun rise) on the green or common, and I being in the front rank, there suddenly appeared a number of the King's troops, about a thousand as I thought, at the distance of about 60 or 70 yards from us, huzzaing and on a quick pace towards us, with three officers in their front on horse back and on full gallop towards us, the foremost of which cried, throw down your arms ye villains, ye re-

Affidavits and Depositions relative to the Commencement of the late Hostilities. *Pennsylvania Packet,* May 15, 1775. LCP

Dear Elly New York 24th April 1775

We were alarmed yesterday with many melancholy accounts from Boston of a Skirmish having Happened between the Inhabitants & a party of Soldiers an Express was forwarded last Evening to the Southward and I suppose you will be all in an uproar about it this morning. I should be glad to inform you a true State of the matter but that is...

In this letter from a substantial merchant of New York to his friend, Pintard noted alarm at having heard "many melancholy accounts from Boston of a Skirmish having Happened between the inhabitants & a party of Soldiers." The news had affected New Yorkers in many ways, including the unloading of two sloops that had been full of provisions for the British troops in Boston, and the "whole city was in an uproar, altho it was Sunday." In Boston the siege settled.

...ewis Pintard. *Letter to Elias ...oudinot,* New York, April 24, ...775. HSP

Colonel Ethan Allen. *Letter to the New York Provincial Congress,* [May 1775]. HSP

Gentlemen in the Narrative Contained in the Inclosed was too materially Omitted the Valour and Intrepidity of Col. James Easton and forty Six Veteran Soldiers from the Massachusets Bay who assisted in Taking of Ticonderoga Col. Easton is Just returned from the Provincial Congress of the Massachusets Bay and to this Place and I Expect he will Soon have the Command of a Regiment & from that Province Yours &c.

Ethan Allen

While Boston was besieged, Fort Ticonderoga, commanding the route between Lakes Champlain and George and a strategic point on the waterway between Canada and the colonies to the south, was captured in a surprise attack led by Colonels Ethan Allen and Benedict Arnold on May 10, 1775. A major purpose of the assault was to seize the fort's artillery for use in that siege at Boston. Allen's letter was to give proper credit to Colonel James Easton for his part in the capture.

A Correct View of The Late Battle at Charlestown June 17th 1775. *Pennsylvania Magazine,* September 1775. LCP

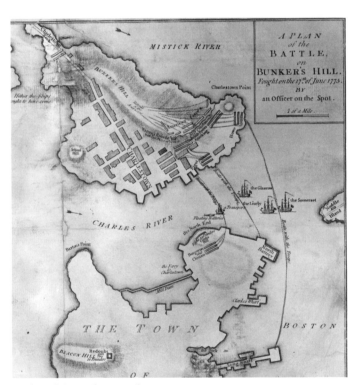

A Plan of the Battle on Bunkers Hill. London: R. Sayer & J. Bennett, 1775. HSP

The Battle of Bunker Hill. Engraved by Daniel-Nicholas Chodowiecki in *Historisch-genealogischer Calender, oder Jahrbuch der merkwürdigsten neuen Welt.* Leipzig, 1784. LCP

In an ill-conceived, undermanned, and undergunned attempt to force the British from Boston, American militia besieging the town fortified several hills on the Charlestown peninsula, notably Breed's Hill, opposite the north end of Boston. On June 17, 1775, British General William Howe attacked in force, driving the Americans off. But the British losses were so heavy and the American defense so staunch that the defeat came to be hailed as virtually a victory for the Patriot cause. One cause for American sorrow was the death of General Joseph Warren, an early patriot of Massachusetts, who had been brought down by a British bullet.

The Death of Warren. In [Hugh Henry Brackenridge]. *The Battle of Bunkers-Hill. A Dramatic Piece, of Five Acts, In Heroic Measure.* Philadelphia: Robert Bell, 1776. HSP

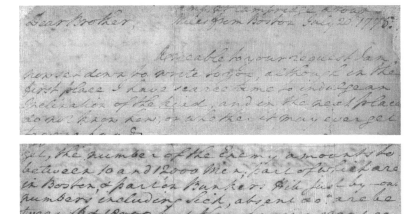

Appointed by Congress to command the Continental Army still sprawled about Boston, Washington left Philadelphia a day before news of Bunker Hill reached the Congress there. He arrived at Cambridge on July 2, 1775, and began to reorganize the recently defeated American forces. In this letter, a week after his arrival, Washington admitted, "Between you and me I think we are in an exceedingly dangerous situation." A few days later, in a long letter to his brother Samuel, he reported on the situation as he found it: "a numerous Army of Provincials under very little command, discipline, or order—I found our Enemy who had drove our People from Bunker Hill strongly Intrenching, and from Accts. had reason to expect before this, another attack from them; but, as we have been incessantly (Sunday not excepted) employed in the throwing up works of defence I rather begin to believe now, that they think it rather a dangerous experiment . . . the number of the Enemy amounts to between 10 and 12,000 men; part of which are in Boston, and part on Bunker Hill just by—our numbers including sick, absent &ca. are between 16 & 18,000." The growing strength of Washington's position forced the British to evacuate Boston in March 1776.

General George Washington.
Letter to Richard Henry Lee,
Camp at Cambridge, July 10,
1775. APS

General George Washington.
Letter to Samuel Washington,
Camp at Cambridge,
July 20, 1775. HSP

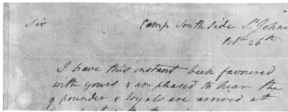

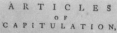

General Richard Montgomery. *Letter to Colonel Clement Biddle*, Camp South Side, St. John's, October 26, [1775]. HSP

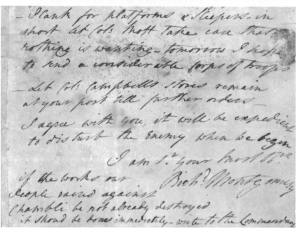

General Richard Montgomery and Inhabitants of Montreal. *Articles of Capitulation.* [Philadelphia]: John Dunlap, [1775]. Broadside. LCP

Anxious to "liberate" Canada from British rule and to make it the fourteenth colony, the Americans late in 1775 had launched a two-pronged attack. General Richard Montgomery advanced on Montreal, reducing the fort at St. John's on November 2 and capturing Montreal a few days later. He then moved his forces down the Saint Lawrence to Quebec, where Benedict Arnold's troops had already arrived. In a desperate assault on the town on the last day of the year, the Americans were defeated and Montgomery killed. The remnants of the army then returned to the theater of war in New York.

A View of St. John's, upon the River Sorell, in Canada, with the Redoubts, Works, etc. Taken in the Year 1776, during the late War in America. In [Thomas Anburey], *Travels through the Interior Parts of America* (London, 1789). LCP

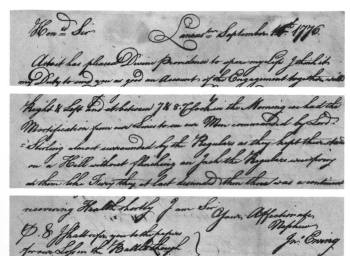

John Ewing. *Letter to Jasper Yeates, Lancaster,* September 14, 1776. With a map of the Battle of Long Island. HSP

The Taking of Pensacola. Engraving by François Godefroy. *Recueil d'Estampes représentant les différens Évènemens de la Guerre qui a procuré l'Indépendance aux États unis de l'Amérique.* Paris: Godefroy, [1783]. APS

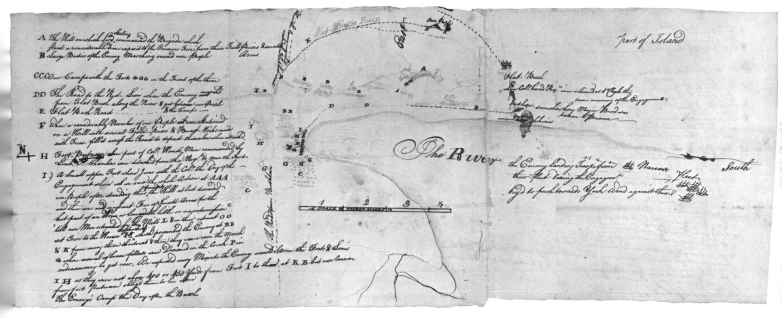

The evacuation by sea of the British Army from Boston forecast their reappearance elsewhere. Washington moved his army to protect New York City. In August 1776 General Howe's greatly reinforced army was conveyed in a vast fleet to New York Bay. Landing on Long Island, the British defeated the American army on August 27, but, not following up their advantage, allowed it to escape. Washington, however, was forced to withdraw even further to prevent entrapment, and New York fell to the enemy.

By RICHARD Viscount HOWE of the Kingdom of Ireland, and WILLIAM HOWE, Esq; General of His Majesty's Forces in America, the KING's Commissioners for restoring Peace to His MAJESTY's Colonies and Plantations in North-America, &c. &c. &c.

DECLARATION.

ALTHOUGH the Congress, whom the misguided Americans suffer to direct their Opposition to a Re-establishment of the constitutional Government of these Provinces, have disavowed every Purpose of Reconciliation, not consonant with their extravagant and inadmissable Claim of Independency, the KING's Commissioners think fit to declare, that they are equally desirous to confer with His MAJESTY's well-affected Subjects, upon the Means of restoring the public Tranquillity, and establishing a permanent Union with every Colony, as a Part of the BRITISH Empire.

Admiral Richard, Viscount Howe and General Sir William Howe. *Declaration [appealing to the rebels to return to their allegiance to the Crown].* [New York, 1776]. HSP

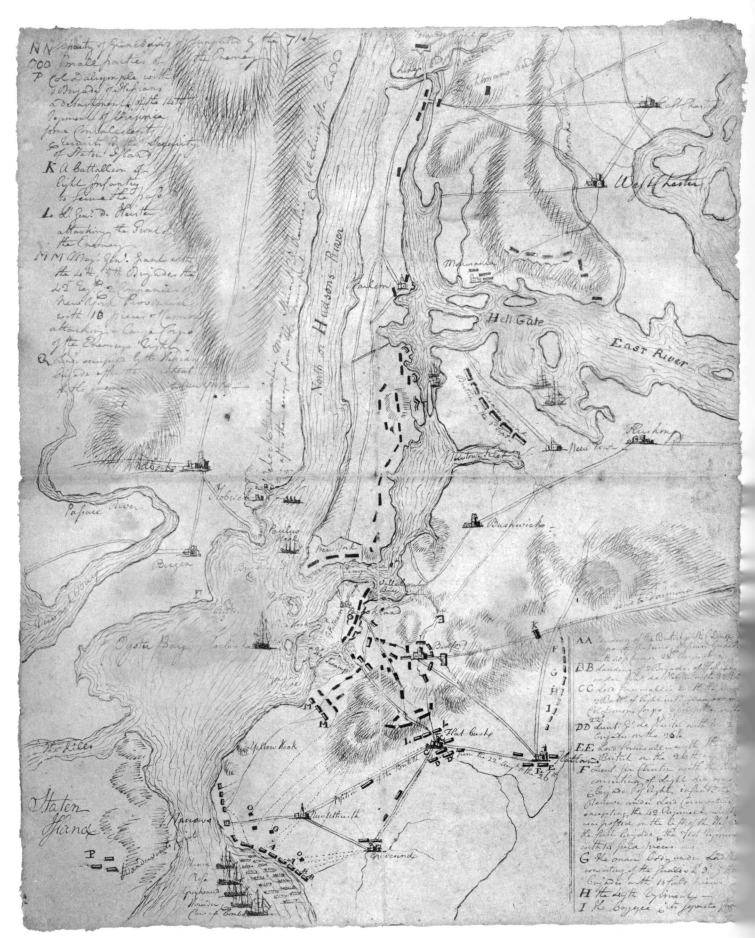

Charles Willson Peale.
*Map of the Battle of
Long Island.* [1776]. APS

Peale had enlisted in the Philadelphia Militia as a private but was soon elected to higher rank. He and Ewing were among those to whom the Howe brothers appealed to return to their allegiance to the King.

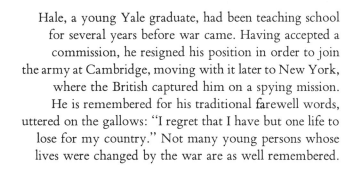

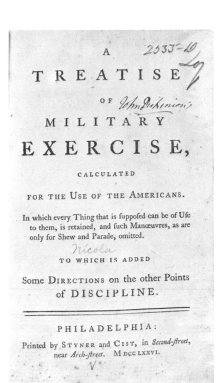

Hale, a young Yale graduate, had been teaching school for several years before war came. Having accepted a commission, he resigned his position in order to join the army at Cambridge, moving with it later to New York, where the British captured him on a spying mission. He is remembered for his traditional farewell words, uttered on the gallows: "I regret that I have but one life to lose for my country." Not many young persons whose lives were changed by the war are as well remembered.

During the Revolution, Lewis Nicola, an experienced soldier who had come to Philadelphia about 1766, wrote three military manuals, copies of which were purchased by many Americans just recently turned soldiers. This one bears the autograph of John Dickinson, who, with other Pennsylvanians, was soon to find the war nearer home.

IN COUNCIL OF SAFETY,

Philadelphia, November 14th 1776,
12 o'Clock, Thursday.

SIR,

WE have certain Intelligence that the Enemy has actual[ly] failed from New-York Five Hundred Ships for this Cit[y] and that great Numbers had got out of the Hook on 12 o'Clo[ck] Yesterday and were steering towards our Capes: As you value th[e] Safety of your Country, and all that is dear and valuable to Me[n] we most earnestly solicit your immediate Assistance, and that yo[u] will march all your Battalion to this City without the lea[st] Delay.

As nothing but the most hasty Marching of the Militia wi[ll] enable us to make a Stand, it is hoped that your Battalion w[ill] manifest their usual Spirit, and come forth on this trying Occasio[n] with the Alacrity that will do them Honour. If you can collect an[y] Shovels, Spades, Grubbing Hoes and Pitching Axes, beg you w[ill] bring them forward and the People shall be paid for them a fu[ll] Price.

By Order of Council,

THOMAS WHARTON, Jun. President

In Council of Safety. Philadelphia, November 14th, 1776. [Appeal to the commanding officers of battalions]. [Philadelphia, 1776]. Broadside. LCP

In Council of Safety. Philadelphia, December 8, 1776. To the Colonels . . . of the respective Battalions of this State. [Philadelphia, 1776]. Broadside. LCP

IN COUNCIL OF SAFETY,

PHILADELPHIA, *December* 8, 1776.

SIR,

THERE is certain intelligence of General Howe's army being yesterday on its march from Brunswick to Princetown, which puts it beyond a doubt that he intends for this city.—This glorious opportunity of signalizing himself in defence of our country, and securing the Rights of America forever, will be seized by every man who has a spark of patriotic fire in his bosom. We entreat you to march the Militia under your command with all possible expedition to this city, and bring with you as many waggons as you can possibly procure, which you are hereby authorized to impress, if they cannot be had otherwise—Delay not a moment, it may be fatal and subject you and all you hold most dear to the ruffian hands of the enemy, whose cruelties are without distinction and unequalled.

By Order of the Council,

DAVID RITTENHOUSE, Vice-President.

To the COLONELS *or* COMMANDING OFFICERS *of the respective* Battalions *of this* STATE.

TWO O'CLOCK, P.M.

THE Enemy are at Trenton, and all the City Militia are marched to meet them.

In Council of Safety.

~

Philadelphia, December 2, 1776.

RESOLVED,

THAT it is the Opinion of this Board, that all the Shops in this City be shut up, that the Schools be broke up, and the Inhabitants engaged solely in providing for the Defence of this City, at this Time of extreme Danger.

By Order of Council,

DAVID RITTENHOUSE, Vice-President.

[Philadelphia, Printed by Henry Miller, in Race-street.]

In Council of Safety. Philadelp[hia,] December 2, 1776. [Resolutio[n] directing shops to be shut an[d closed]. Philadelphia: Henry [Miller,] 1776. Broadside. LCP

Thomas Paine. Engraved by William Sharp, London, 1793, after a painting by George Romney. APS

General George Washington. *Letter to Colonel John Cadwalader*, McKonkey's Ferry, December 25, 1776. HSP

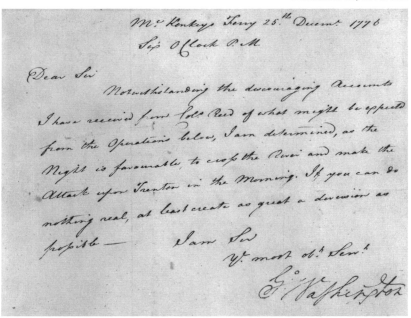

General George Washington. *Letter to Colonel John Cadwalader*, McKonkey's Ferry, December 25, 1776. HSP

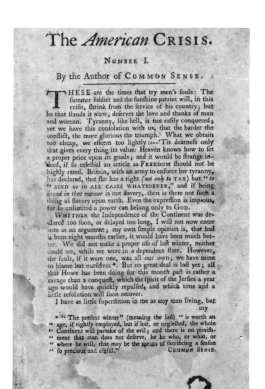

The *American* CRISIS.

NUMBER I.

By the Author of COMMON SENSE.

THESE are the times that try men's souls: The summer soldier and the sunshine patriot will, in this crisis, shrink from the service of his country; but he that stands it NOW, deserves the love and thanks of man and woman. Tyranny, like hell, is not easily conquered; yet we have this consolation with us, that the harder the conflict, the more glorious the triumph. What we obtain too cheap, we esteem too lightly:—'Tis dearness only that gives every thing its value: Heaven knows how to set a proper price upon its goods; and it would be strange indeed, if so celestial an article as FREEDOM should not be highly rated. Britain, with an army to enforce her tyranny, has declared, that she has a right (*not only to* TAX) but "*to* "BIND us in ALL CASES WHATSOEVER," and if being *bound in that manner* is not slavery, then is there not such a thing as slavery upon earth. Even the expression is impious, for so unlimited a power can belong only to GOD.

WHETHER the Independence of the Continent was declared too soon, or delayed too long, I will not now enter into as an argument; my own simple opinion is, that had it been eight months earlier, it would have been much better. We did not make a proper use of last winter, neither could we, while we were in a dependent state. However, the fault, if it were one, was all our own*. But no great deal is lost yet; all that Howe has been doing for this month past is rather a ravage than a conquest, which the spirit of the Jersies a year ago would have quickly repulsed, and which time and a little resolution will soon recover.

I have as little superstition in me as any man living, but my

> * "The present winter" (meaning the last) "is worth an age, if rightly employed, but if lost, or neglected, the whole Continent will partake of the evil; and there is no punishment that man does not deserve, be he who, or what, or where he will, that may be the means of sacrificing a season so precious and useful." COMMON SENSE.

Thomas Paine. *The American Crisis*. Number I. [Philadelphia, 1776]. APS

The autumn of 1776 found the Continental Army, discouraged and defeated, in full retreat across the Jerseys, closely pursued by the foe. The warnings to Americans published by the Council of Safety were no source of comfort. Washington sought safety on the Pennsylvania side of the Delaware, where his army was heartened by the eloquence of Thomas Paine's *Crisis:* "These are the times that try men's souls." The copy here is stained by human blood. Afraid that a large number of his troops would not remain when their enlistments ran out at the first of January, Washington recrossed the Delaware on Christmas night and defeated and captured a force of Hessians holding Trenton. Washington's report on the victory at Trenton cheered a people badly in need of news of victory.

General George Washington. *Letter to Colonel John Cadwalader*, Headquarters at Newtown, December 27, 1776. HSP

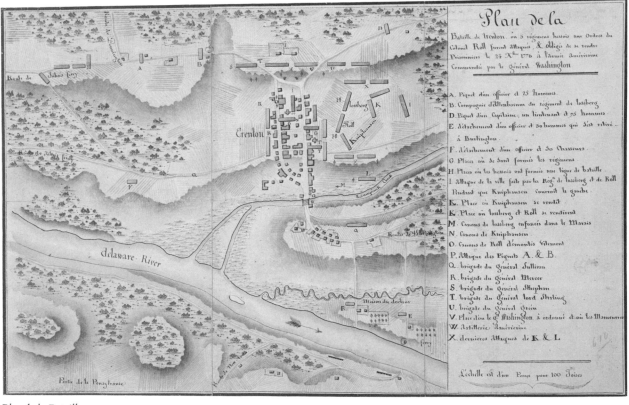

*Plan de la Bataille
de Trenton.*
Manuscript. HSP

Though another victory was soon in coming, there was
time to savor the happy defeat of the Hessians at Trenton.
The journal kept by Sergeant Young brings the drama
of the war down from high command to the ranks, and
his writing reflects the concerns of the troops with waiting
and prayer and writing home between marches in the
rain. The map drawn by a French military engineer
gives the positions of the American and Hessian troops
in the battle which routed the latter from their holiday
celebrations.

Extract of a Letter from New-Town, (Bucks County,) December 27. 1776

"WE have returned with much Honor from our *Trenton* Expedition, having brought off about Seven Hundred and Fifty *Heffians*, one Lieutenant Colonel, two Majors, four Captains, fifteen Subalterns, three Standards, fix Brafs Field Pieces, and near one thoufand Arms.

"We came on them by Surprife, at about half after Seven o'Clock.——Their Guard at the End of the Town, and their Parties in Town, gave a fmart Refift-ance for a while; and I they pufhed up the Creek, back of the Meeting-Houfe, where they formed, and I thought we fhould have had a fmart Engagement ; but they were by that Time near furrounded, and fo pufhed at all Points, that they furrendered with their Arms. &c.

"Our Officers and Men all behaved with moft remarkable Bravery, and by their Activity and Zeal, they foon put a moft honorable End to this important Affair.——Indeed, I never could conceive that *one Spirit* fhould fo *univerfally* animate, both OFFICERS and MEN, to rufh forward into Action.

"Colonel *Rohle*, and feveral Officers, wounded, were left on Parole at *Trenton*. They muft have loft thirty Men.——I hear of but two of our Men killed, and Captain *Wafhington*, and a few more wounded."

Extract of a Letter from New-Town, (Bucks County), December 27 [1776]. Broadside. LCP

Hessian prisoners taken at Trenton marched through Philadelphia. Engraved by Daniel-Nicholas Chodowiecki in *Historisch-genealogischer Calender, oder Jahrbuch der merkwürdigsten neuen Welt.* Leipzig, 1784. LCP

Benjamin Rush. *Letter to Richard Henry Lee,* Princetown, N. J., January 7, 1777. APS

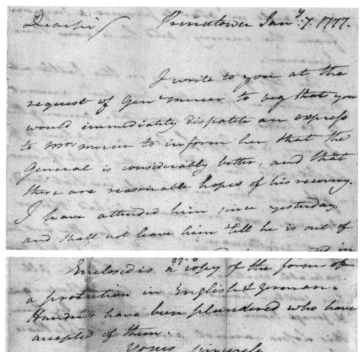

This new spirit of victory at Trenton kept the American cause at a high and happy pitch, and the victory at Princeton a few days later added to the joy. One of the sad moments of the battle was the wounding of General Hugh Mercer, shown in the middle distance in the painting done by his son. Carried from the field, the General was attended by Dr. Benjamin Rush, who wrote to Richard Henry Lee to tell Mrs. Mercer that his patient was improving. The news was premature, for Mercer died a few days later. The surprise attack on the British at Princeton was successful, much of New Jersey was cleared of enemy troops, and the threat of British incursions into Pennsylvania was removed.

Battle of Princeton, January 3, 1777. By William Mercer, ca. 1786-90. Oil on canvas. HSP

The Continental Congress, 1774-1776

A Declaration By The Representatives of the United Colonies . . . Setting forth the Causes and Necessity Of their taking up Arms. Portsmouth, [1775]. HSP

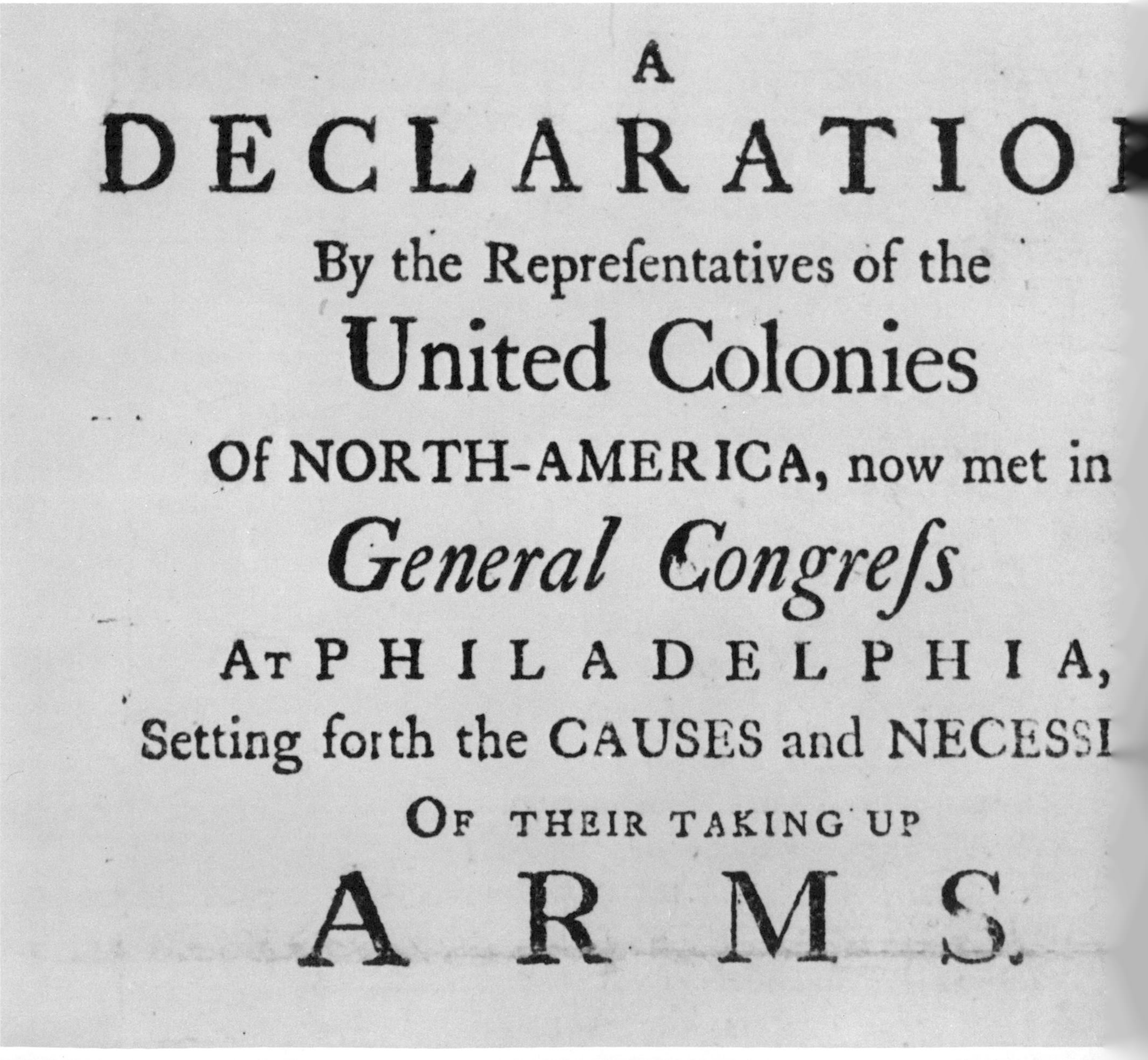

A

DECLARATIO

By the Repreſentatives of the

United Colonies

Of NORTH-AMERICA, now met in

General Congreſs

At PHILADELPHIA,

Setting forth the CAUSES and NECESSI

Of their taking up

ARMS.

"By *uniting* we stand,
by *dividing* we fall."
—John Dickinson.
A Song for American Freedom, 1768

View of that great and flourishing City of
OSTON, when in its purity, and out of the
nds of the Philistines.

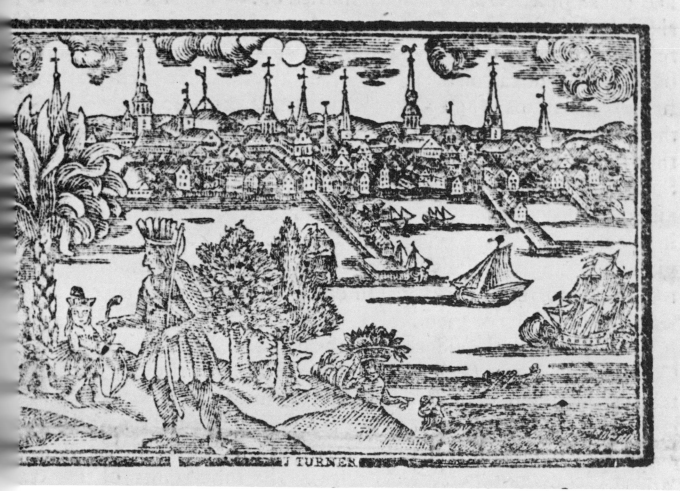

As the colonies up and down the seaboard approved a congress to be held in Philadelphia in September, they took steps to choose the delegates who would represent them. Deane, as clerk of the Committee of Correspondence in Connecticut, informed other members of the committee that it was decided to meet at New London on July 13 to select that colony's representatives. The clerk of the Pennsylvania Assembly formally set down the action of the House appointing Galloway, Rhoads, Mifflin,

Humphreys, Morton, Ross and Biddle as delegates to "meet such Committees or Delegates from the other Colonies as have been or may be appointed." This was presumably one of the official copies sent to the speaker of the House of Representatives of another colony in accordance with resolutions. A similar document signed by De Hart on behalf of Crane, Kinsey, Livingston and Smith, informed the Virginians that they had been appointed to represent New Jersey at the congress.

Silas Deane. *Letter to Messrs. Williams, Wales, Parsons & Trumbull,* Hartford, June 28, 1774. HSP

Charles Moore. *Extract from the Journal of the Assembly,* [Philadelphia], July 22, 1774. Manuscript. HSP

John De Hart. *Letter to the Committee of Correspondence of Virginia,* Elizabeth Town, N.J., July 25, 1774. HSP

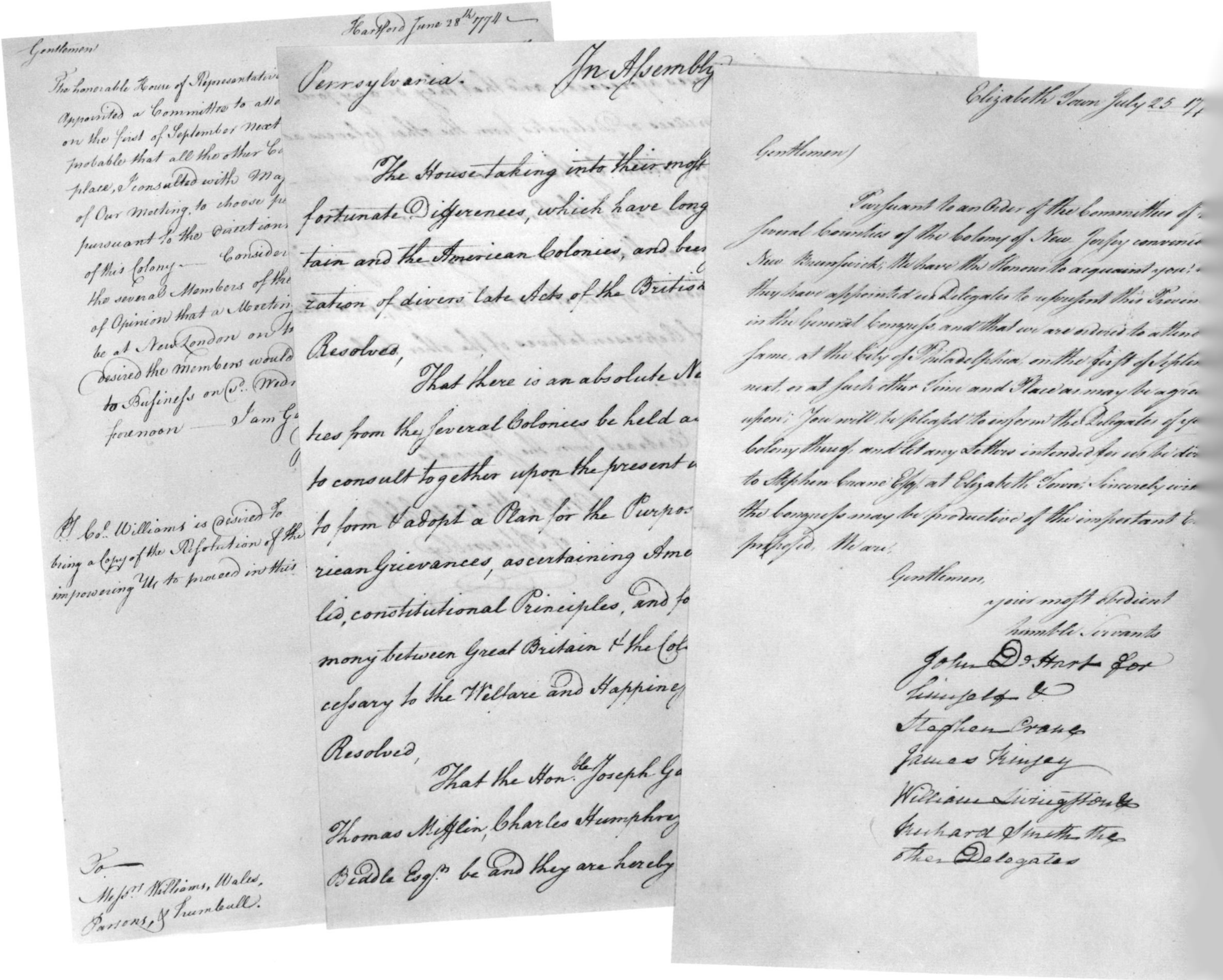

Instructions for the Deputies appointed to meet in General Congress on the Part of this Colony. [Williamsburg: Clementina Rind, 1774]. LCP

Inſtructions for the DEPUTIES appointed to meet in GENERAL CONGRESS on the Part of this Colony.

THE unhappy Diſputes between Great Britain and her American Colonies, which began about the third Year of the Reign of his preſent Majeſty, and ſince, continually increaſing, have proceeded to Lengths ſo dangerous and alarming as to excite juſt Apprehenſions in the Minds of his Majeſty's faithful Subjects of this Colony that they are in Danger of being deprived of their natural, ancient, conſtitutional, and chartered Rights, have compelled them to take the ſame into their moſt ſerious Conſideration; and, being deprived of their uſual and accuſtomed Mode of making known their Grievances, have appointed us their Repreſentatives to conſider what is proper to be done in this dangerous Criſis of American Affairs. It being our Opinion that the united Wiſdom of North America ſhould be collected in a General Congreſs of all the Colonies, we have appointed the Honourable PEYTON RANDOLPH, Eſquire, RICHARD HENRY LEE, GEORGE WASHINGTON, PATRICK HENRY, RICHARD BLAND, BENJAMIN HARRISON, and EDMUND PENDLETON, Eſquires, Deputies to repreſent this Colony in the ſaid Congreſs, to be held at Philadelphia on the firſt Monday in September next.

And that they may be the better informed of our Sentiments touching the Conduct we wiſh them to obſerve on this important Occaſion, we deſire that they will expreſs, in the firſt Place, our Faith and true Allegiance to his Majeſty King George the Third, our lawful and rightful

At the beginning of August a provincial convention met in Williamsburg to appoint Virginia's delegates to Congress and to frame instructions for them. Among the most important of these was the Virginians' desire to put off the adoption of a non-importation agreement until August 10, 1775, to avoid sudden economic dislocation. In his letter to Lee, Washington wonders if it would not be wise to come prepared with statistics of imports and exports. "If you should travel to Phila. by land, instead of water," he added in a postscript, "I should be glad of your Company—Mr. Henry & Coll. Pendleton are to be at my House on their way Tuesday the 30th. Instt."

George Washington. *Letter to Richard Henry Lee,* Fredericksburg, August 9, 1774. APS

George Washington. By Joseph Wright, 1784. Oil on canvas. HSP

Library Company of Philadelphia. *Minute Book*, August 31, 1774. LCP

Upon Motion, Ordered; That the Librarian furnish the Gentlemen who are to meet in Congress in this City, with the use of such Books as they may have occasion for during their sitting, taking a Receipt for them. The Secy is desired to deliver a Copy of this Minute to their Chairman.

As early as August 30 John Adams in his diary referred to Carpenters' Hall as the place "where Congress is to sit." The Directors of the Library Company must have known that, too, although officially the decision to meet in the Hall rather than the State House had not been reached. The library was on the second floor of Carpenters' Hall. Courteously, the delegates to the Congress were offered "the use of such Books as they may have occasion for during their sitting." It was believed that the radicals had decided on the neutral meeting place rather than the rooms of the Pennsylvania Assembly, of which Joseph Galloway was the Speaker, in order to be free of his conservative influence. When the sessions opened on September 5, Peyton Randolph was chosen president and Charles Thomson, "the Sam Adams of Philadelphia," secretary. The next day the Directors of the Library Company were officially thanked for "their obliging order."

Charles Thomson. Bust by William Rush. APS

PAINTED BY C.W. PEALE.   ENGRAVED BY GOODMAN & PIGGOTT.

Peyton Randolph. After a painting by Charles Willson Peale. HSP

Perhaps the Middle — All the Seven delegates from appointed
for Virginia are in here, & more Sensible fine fellows you'd
never wish to See, in Short it is the greatest Assembly (in pro
portion to the Number) that ever was Collected in America
And the Bostonians who (we know) have been Condemned by
many for their Violence, are Moderate men When Compared
to Virginia, South Carolina and Rode Island. in Short all the
the Colonies Seem to be hearty in the Cause. and have

Caesar Rodney. *Letter to Thomas Rodney*, Philadelphia, September 9, 1774. HSP

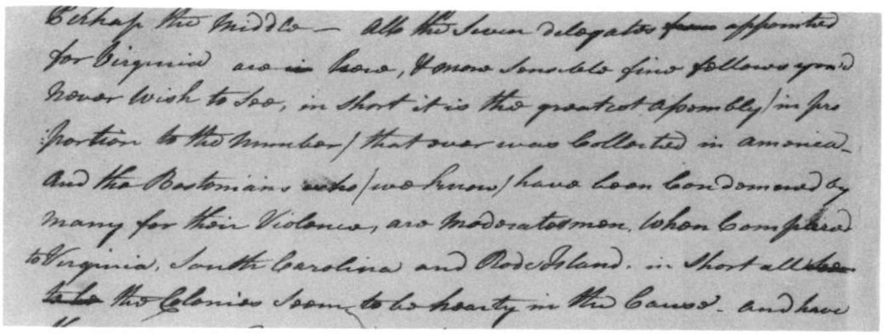

Most of the delegates to the First Continental Congress met in a spirit of high optimism. Rodney's chronicle of events for the benefit of his brother echoed the sentiments of all but the most conservative. "All the Seven delegates appointed for Virginia are here, & more sensible fine fellows you'd never wish to See, in Short it is the greatest Assembly (in proportion to the Number) that ever was Collected in America—And the Bostonians who (we know) have been Condemned by many for their Violence, are Moderate men, When Compared to Virginia, South Carolina and Rode Island, in Short all the Colonies Seem to be hearty in the Cause, and have the greatest Respect paid them by all the first people here."

Suddenly, a report was received that British warships had fired on the town of Boston. The report proved false, but on September 16 Paul Revere arrived in Philadelphia bearing a copy of the Suffolk Resolves. To all the indignities heaped on Boston, General Gage had just added another, which threatened the safety of the city. As Rodney reported it: "They Complain of the General's Seizing the Powder at Cambridge Which they say was private property; and also that he is now fortifying the only pass that leads from the town of Boston into the Country." Indignation in Philadelphia was widespread; Gage's actions strengthened the hands of the radicals.

Philadelphia Saturday Sepr. 17th. 1774

Sir

By Express Which arrived here Yesterday, from the Committee of the Town of Boston to the general Continental Congress, We are Informed the County of Suffolk of Which the Town of Boston is the Capital, had entered into Certain Resolutions, a Copy of Which was inclosed us. Generally to the purport of not Suffering the Commander in Chief, to Execute the Act of Parliament changing their Government by Persuading, protesting and Compelling officers under the new Regulation to Resign and by a Refusal in Jurymen to Serve &c., That they have ordered all those able to bear arms to keep in Readiness. to defend their inherent Rights, Even with Loss of Blood & Treasure; That they are determined not Injure the General or any of the Kings Troops, unless Compelled thereto by an Attack made by the Troops on them —
They Complain that of the General's Seizing the Powder at Cambridge Which they say was private property: and also that he is now fortifying the only pass that leads from the Town of Boston into the Country from whence the inhabitants of the Town are ... This pass is a Narrow Neck of Land about 120 Yards

I am Yrs.
Caesar Rodney

Caesar Rodney. *Letter to Thomas Rodney*, Philadelphia, September 17, 1774. HSP

Philadelphia. In Congress, Thursday, September 22, 1774. Resolved, That the Congress request the Merchants and Others, in the several Colonies, not to send to Great Britain any Orders for Goods. [Philadelphia]: W. and T. Bradford, [1774]. LCP

PHILADELPHIA.

In CONGRESS, Thurſday, September 22, 1774.

RESOLVED,

THAT the Congreſs requeſt the Merchants and Others, in the ſeveral Colonies, not to ſend to Great Britain any Orders for Goods, and to direct the execution of all Orders already ſent, to be delayed or ſuſpended, until the ſenſe of the Congreſs, on the means to be taken for the preſervation of the Liberties of *America*, is made public.

An Extract from the Minutes,
CHARLES THOMSON, *Sec.*

Printed by *W.* and *T. BRADFORD.*

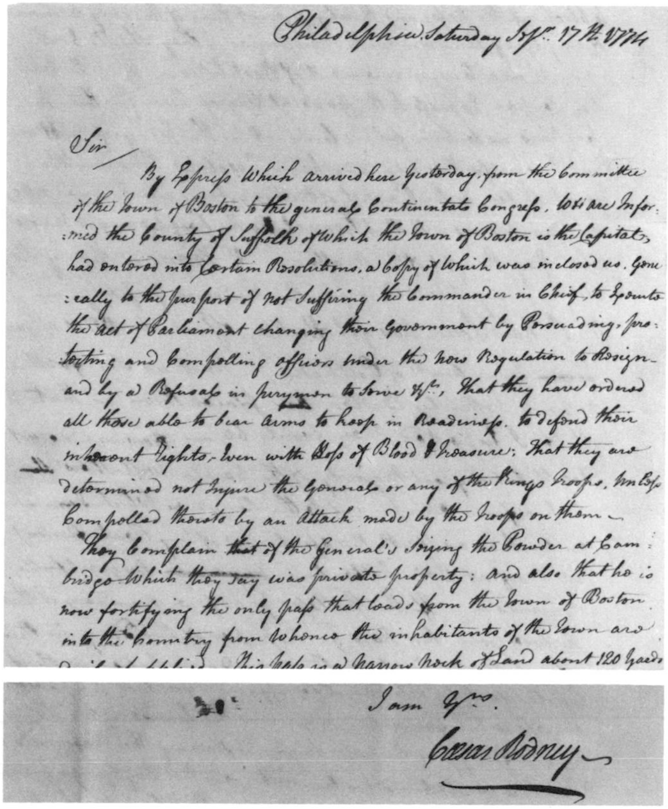

At the outset, the delegates had agreed that the proceedings of the Congress should be confidential until officially published. The brief resolution supporting the Suffolk Resolves had been given to the newspapers. The first order for a separate publication—Government Document No. 1—was the brief notice of September 22, which laid the ground for a full-fledged non-importation agreement.

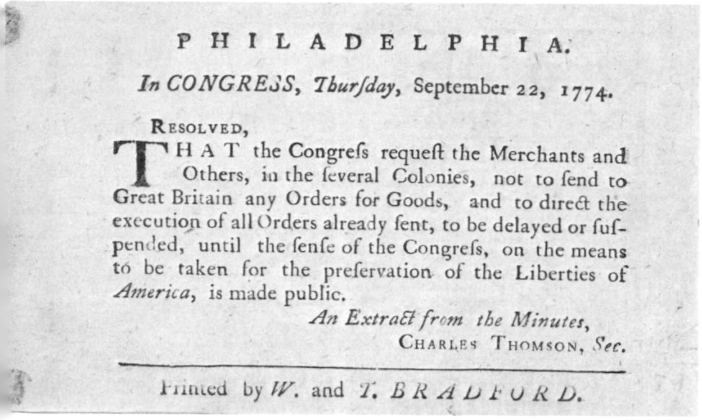

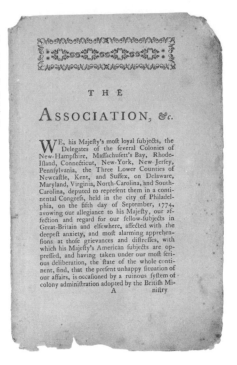

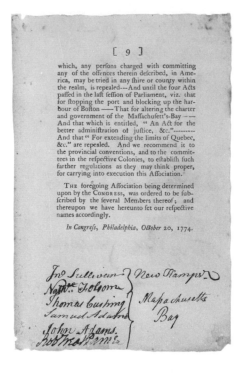

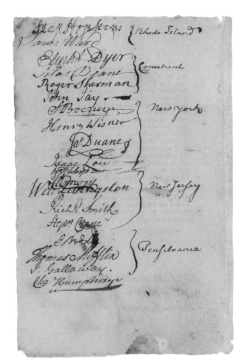

The most important action taken by the Congress was the adoption of the non-consumption, non-importation, non-exportation agreement known as the Association. The delegates agreed that after December 1, 1774, no goods, wares or merchandise would be imported from Britain or her colonies in the East and West Indies, nor would anything be exported to them, except—at the insistence of South Carolina—rice to Europe. Furthermore, "every species of extravagance and dissipation" would be discouraged, including horse-racing and elaborate funerals.

More important was the order to establish in every local jurisdiction a committee to enforce the agreement, the first practical step taken by the colonies to set up independent authorities. The actual printed Association was signed by all the members of Congress, Washington signing on behalf of Randolph, Bland and Harrison, who had left town. Galloway, and perhaps others, signed, unconvinced but afraid of reprisals. In this pamphlet are signatures of men who later signed the Declaration. This copy was sent to Maryland.

Patrick Henry. *Draft of the Address to the
King.* [October, 1774]. LCP

John Dickinson. *Draft of the Address to the
King.* [October 22–24, 1774]. LCP

To satisfy those who still hoped that reconciliation might yet be possible, Congress on October 1 appointed a committee to prepare an address to the King. Two drafts were composed, but the delegates liked neither. After John Dickinson was added to the Pennsylvania delegation, on October 21 he was put on the drafting committee and succeeded in producing a text satisfactory to the Congress. The gesture proved a futile one; no official acknowledgment of the address was made to the Americans.

John Dickinson. *Draft of a Letter to the Inhabitants of the Province of Quebec.* [October 25-26, 1774]. LCP

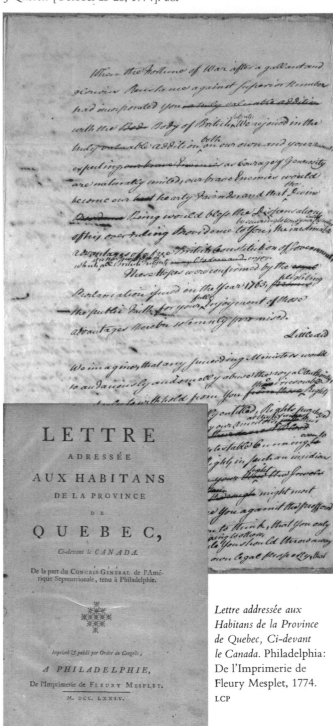

Extracts From the Votes and Proceedings Of the American Continental Congress, Held at Philadelphia on the 5th of September 1774. Philadelphia: William and Thomas Bradford, 1774. LCP

Journal of the Proceedings of the Congress, Held at Philadelphia, September 5, 1774. Philadelphia: William and Thomas Bradford, 1774. LCP

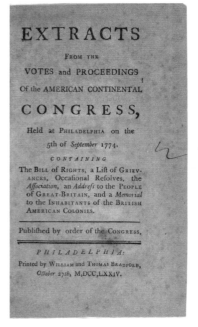

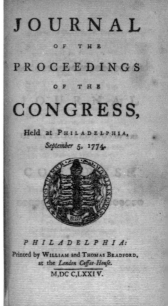

Lettre addressée aux Habitans de la Province de Quebec, Ci-devant le Canada. Philadelphia: De l'Imprimerie de Fleury Mesplet, 1774. LCP

One of the final acts of the First Continental Congress was the drafting of a message to the French-Canadians, asking them to join the British colonies to the south and send delegates to the Congress which would meet in May 1775. Once again it was Dickinson who drafted a document acceptable to the members of Congress. The English text was first printed both seperately and as a part of the *Extracts from the Votes.* The French translation, made by Pierre Eugène Du Simitière, was intended for wide distribution in Canada.

As the Congress drew near to adjournment a spate of documents was released for publication. On October 21 the address *To the People of Great-Britain* and that *To the Inhabitants of the Colonies* were sent to the printer. On October 22 the *Journal* was ordered to be prepared. Even before this work was completed, the *Extracts* came from the press. They consisted of the most important documents approved by the delegates, including the Declaration of Rights, the Association, and various addresses. Before the end of the year the *Extracts* were reprinted in a dozen colonial towns from Boston to Newbern, N. C. It took longer for Secretary Thomson to see the full *Journal* through the press, and the *Petition to the King* was not added until after the first of the new year in order that, observing diplomatic nicety, Congress might be sure the document was delivered before the text was published. On the title of the *Journal* is the first attempt at a seal for the United Colonies.

Samuel Ward. *Letter to John Dickinson (with enclosures)*, Westerly, R. I., December 14, 1774. LCP

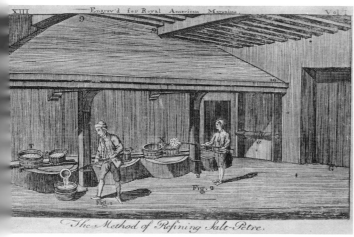

Thomas Cushing. *Letter to Benjamin Franklin*, [Boston, December 30, 1774]. APS

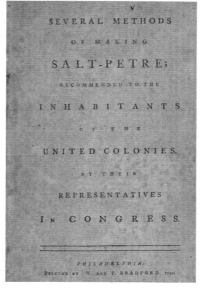

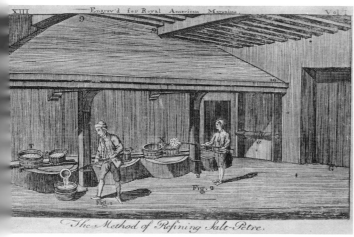

The Method of Refining Salt-Petre. *Royal American Magazine*, August 1774, facing p. 285. LCP

SEVERAL METHODS OF MAKING SALT-PETRE; RECOMMENDED TO THE INHABITANTS OF THE UNITED COLONIES, BY THEIR REPRESENTATIVES IN CONGRESS.

PHILADELPHIA: PRINTED BY W. AND T. BRADFORD. 1775.

Several Methods of making Salt-Petre; recommended to the Inhabitants of the United Colonies by their Representatives in Congress. Philadelphia: W. and T. Bradford, 1775. LCP

The British government thought that one of the more effective ways of preventing open rebellion in America was to confiscate all available gunpowder, arms and other military supplies and to prevent their free importation into the colonies. Ward of Rhode Island sent Dickinson copies of the recently received orders of the ministry on the subject and informed him that their Provincial Congress had removed all such material into its care and hoped other colonies would do likewise. He went on, "if We must either become Slaves, or fly to Arms, I shall not and I hope No American will hesitate one Moment which to chuse." The same information was sent to Cushing in Boston, who passed it on to Franklin, noting: "The Colonies apprehend this Political Manoevre of the Ministry forebodes the most vigorous exertions of Martial Force. They are therefore adopting the most Effectual Methods to defend themselves." After hostilities broke out, Congress gave serious attention to the production of saltpetre, and circulated a pamphlet on its manufacture which owed much to the research of Dr. Benjamin Rush and Thomas Paine, who had published articles on the subject in the *Pennsylvania Magazine,* which were reprinted elsewhere.

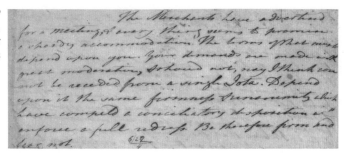

Arthur Lee. *Letter to Richard Henry Lee,* London, December 22, 1774. APS

Royal Coat of Arms. Masthead of the *Pennsylvania Chronicle.* Philadelphia: William Goddard, 1767. APS

John Almon. *Letter to John Dickinson,* London, February 4, 1775. LCP

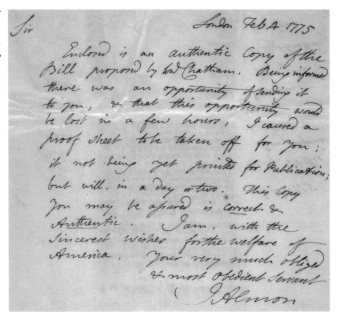

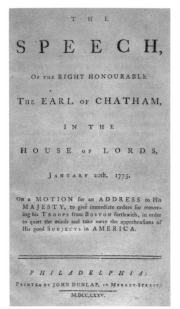

William Pitt, Earl of Chatham. *The Speech, Of the Right Honourable The Earl of Chatham, in the House of Lords, January 20, 1775.* Philadelphia: John Dunlap, 1775. LCP

[William Lee]. *Letter to John Dickinson,* London, February 6, 1775. LCP

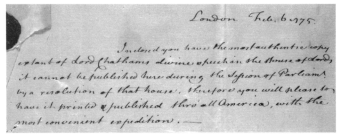

When news of the actions of Congress reached England, there was a surge of hope that the government might relax its policies. Lee tells his brother that the petition to the King was favorably received. "The Merchants have advertised for a Meeting. . . . Depend upon it the same firmness & unanimity which have compeld a conciliatory disposition will enforce a full redress." William Pitt, Earl of Chatham, was the prime mover in trying to effect a reconciliation. A copy of a confidential letter from him was quoted by Lee: "I have not words to express my satisfaction, that the Congress has conducted this most arduous & delicate business, with such manly wisdom & calm Resolution." On January 20, 1775, Chatham moved that the King be asked to order the troops out of Boston as the first step in allaying the crisis. In a vigorous speech he argued the colonists' case and urged moderation. Almon sent Dickinson a copy of the bill Chatham proposed, a proof sheet "taken off for you; it not being yet printed for Publication." Two days later William Lee sent the Philadelphia patriot "the most authentic copy extant of Lord Chathams divine speech in the House of Lords." He continued: "it cannot be published here during the Session of Parliamt. by a resolution of that house, therefore you will please to have it printed & published thro' all America, with the most convenient expedition." This Dickinson did, and the Dunlap printing resulted. The text is recognized as far better than that eventually printed in London.

To the Honourable the Commons of Great Britain,
in Parliament assembled.

The humble PETITION of the Merchants, Traders, and
others, of the City of London, concerned in the Commerce of North America,

SHEWETH,

THAT your Petitioners are all essentially interested in the
Trade to North America, either as Exporters and Importers,
or as Venders of British and Foreign Goods for Exportation
to that Country.

William Lee. *Letter
hn Dickinson,
don, February 6,
. LCP*

ur and William
*Letter to John
inson, London,
ary 13, 1775.*

William Lee. *Letter to John
Dickinson, [London],
February 21, 1775.* LCP

Arthur Lee. *Letter
to John Dickinson,
[London], February
23, [1775].* LCP

To the Honourable
the Commons of
Great Britain, in
Parliament
assembled. The
humble Petition of
the Merchants,
Traders, and others,
of the City of
London, concerned
in the Commerce
of North-America.
[London, 1775]. LCP

William Lee. *Letter
to John Dickinson,
London, February,
1775.* LCP

William Lee. *Letter
to John Dickinson,
London, March 28,
1775.* LCP

As the British administration's determination to put
down American resistance by force became clear, the
Lee brothers in a series of newsletters, unsigned for
safety's sake, kept Dickinson informed of the events
as they occurred. Since the harbor of Boston was
closed and mail to Virginia uncertain, the Philadelphian
was chosen as the conduit to pass on information to
Samuel Adams to the north and Richard Henry Lee
to the south. "Genl. Gage's Army is to be immediately
augmented to 10,000 effective men . . . 9000 Ton of
Transports are already taken up in this port to carry
the troops . . .," William Lee wrote at the beginning
of February. To his brother's letter written a week
later, William added: "Take care of Traitors in Phila.
viz. Dr. Smith, as well as the De Lanceys, Lott, Watts,
McEvers, Jay &c in N. York." Although Arthur Lee
favored some gesture of conciliation, he felt it would be
in vain; "if we must draw the Sword let us do it,
with as much apparent reluctance & justice on our
side as possible." The petition of the merchants
of London was also sent over to America.

By the end of the month affairs had reached a climax:
"I think an express shd. go instantly to Boston or the
Massachusetts Bay, & to Genl. [Charles] Lee
wherever he is: as War agt. America is formally
declared here." From a distance William Lee
presumed to suggest what should be done: "Genl. Lee
shd. command in this business if he will undertake
it & Col. George Washington of Virga. shd. be
second in command."

FREE THOUGHTS,
ON
The PROCEEDINGS of
THE
CONTINENTAL CONGRESS,
Held at PHILADELPHIA Sept. 5, 1774:
WHEREIN
Their Errors are exhibited,
THEIR
REASONINGS CONFUTED,
AND
The fatal Tendency of their Non-Importation, Non-Ex-
portation, and Non-Consumption Measures, are
laid open to the plainest Understandings;
AND
The ONLY MEANS pointed out
For Preserving and Securing
Our present HAPPY CONSTITUTION:
IN
A LETTER
TO
The FARMERS,
AND OTHER INHABITANTS of
NORTH AMERICA
In General,
And to those of the Province of New-York
In Particular.

By a FARMER.
Hear me, for I WILL speak!

PRINTED IN THE YEAR M.DCC.LXXIV.

[Samuel Seabury]. *Free Thoughts,
on The Proceedings of the
Continental Congress, Held at
Philadelphia Sept. 5, 1774:
wherein Their Errors are
exhibited.* [New York: James
Rivington], 1774. LCP

A
FULL VINDICATION
OF THE
Measures of the Congress,
FROM
The CALUMNIES of their ENEMIES;
In ANSWER to
A LETTER,
Under the Signature of
A. W. FARMER.
WHEREIN
His Sophistry is exposed, his Cavils confuted, his
Artifices detected, and his Wit ridiculed;
IN
A GENERAL ADDRESS
To the Inhabitants of America,
AND
A Particular Address
To the FARMERS of the Province of New-York.

Veritas magna est & prævalebit.
Truth is powerful, and will prevail.

NEW-YORK:
Printed by JAMES RIVINGTON. 1774.

[Alexander Hamilton]. *A Full
Vindication of the Measures of
the Congress, from The
Calumnies of their Enemies.*
New York: James Rivington,
1774. LCP

*Jacob Rush,
secretary. The
Committee,
taking into
Consideration the
Tenth Article
of the Association
of the General
Congress . . . ,
December 6,
1774.* [Philadelphia,
1774]. HSP

COMMITTEE CHAMBER, *December 6, 1774.*

THE COMMITTEE, taking into Consideration the *Tenth* Article of the Association of the General Congress, do unanimously resolve, that the said Arti-
requires the opening of all Packages of Goods imported after the *first* Day of
cember, and before the *first* of *February;* but at the same Time, the COMMITTEE
tending that the Sale of such Goods shall be conducted with as little Inconve-
ence as is consistent with the said Association.--

RESOLVED, That though all Bales and Packages delivered to the COMMIT
for Sale, must be opened, yet that the Goods shall be sold in Lots or Parce
and that such Sales shall be made by the City Vendue Master under the Direc
of the COMMITTEE.

RESOLVED, That in disposing of Goods in Lots or Parcels, no Lot shal
made of less Value upon the sterling Invoice than £ 3, nor of any greater
£ 15; except in the former Case, where an entire Package is of less Value
£ 3; and in the latter, where the Value of any single Piece shall exceed £ 15

RESOLVED, That Salt and Coal, imported from Great-Britain or Irel
may be sold at Public Vendue by the Cargo, or smaller Quantity, at the Ele
of the Owner or Consignee, under the Direction of the Committee; and th
Freight of Nine-pence per Bushel shall be allowed on all Kinds of Salt impo
as aforesaid; and a Freight of Twelve-pence per Bushel on all Coal importe
aforesaid.

RESOLVED, That it is expected, all Importers of Goods, after the *Fi
December,* do apply to the Committee of the District where the Vessel so impo
has arrived, and make their Election of sending back, storing or selling all
Goods; for which Purpose, the said Committee will attend at the Coffee-
every Day, from Ten till One o'Clock.

THE Committee also recommend to all Importers of Goods a Perusal of
Attention to the *Eleventh* Article of the General Congress, viz. " That a Com
tee be chosen in every County, City, and Town, by those, who are qualifie
vote for Representatives in the Legislature, whose Business it shall be, attent
to observe the Conduct of all Persons touching this Association: And when it
be made to appear to the Satisfaction of a Majority of any such Committee,
any Person within the Limits of their Appointment has violated this Associa
that such Majority do forthwith cause the Truth of the Case to be published i
Gazette, to the End that all such Foes to the Rights of British America m
publicly known, and universally contemned as the Enemies of American L
ty: And thenceforth we respectively will break off all Dealings with him or

By Order of the COMMITTEE,

JACOB RUSH, *pro temp.* Secreta

No sooner were the proceedings of Congress made
known than a pamphlet war began, *pro* and *con.*
One of the first to attack the major action taken,
the non-importation, non-exportation,
non-consumption Association, was the New York
Anglican clergyman, Samuel Seabury. This copy of
the earliest of his polemics against Congress was
bought by the Philadelphia Quaker schoolmaster,
Robert Proud, soon after it came out. Seabury
was almost immediately answered by the 17-year-old
King's College student, Alexander Hamilton, who
ably defended the proceedings of the delegates.

With extraordinary zeal committees were set up
throughout the colonies to oversee and force
compliance with the non-importation,
non-exportation, non-consumption section of the
Association of the First Continental Congress. These
were in fact the first bodies independent of Great
Britain given powers and responsibilities. In
Philadelphia the Committee of Inspection and
Observation established the rules covering imports,
and sub-committees in each district carried them
out. The records show that cargos entering the
port were sold or stored. Under the control of the
city's radicals, the embargo was effective.

*Manuscript Record
of the Control over
Imports by the
Sub-Committee
of Inspection and
Observation for
District No. 3.*
[Philadelphia],
December 20,
1774. APS

FOR STORING.

To Thomas Mifflin, James Mease, Thomas Barkley, Lamber
Cadwalader, Jacob Rush, Sharp Delany, Blathwait Jones
Thomas Pryor, Joseph Dean, Benjamin Harbinson, th
COMMITTEE *for the*
FOURTH DISTRICT.

GENTLEMEN,

HAVING imported the undermentioned Articles in th
Ship *Brig Jamaica Prequet* commanded by Cap
tain *Rich Newbury* lately arrived from *Jamaica*
I do hereby authorize and request you, or any of you, t
receive the said Goods into your Possession, and to store ther
in such Places as you think proper, at *my* Expence an
Risque, until the Non-Importation Agreement shall cease, o
I shall by a Request in Writing desire the same to be Sold.

Philad December
Daniel Roberdeau

WH & WH
12 Punch
1 Butt } Coffee
8 Tierces
1 Barr

Amounting of Invoice
to £293.12.11 *Jam.* Currency

Daniel Roberdeau, *Printed Rules
and Forms filled out to put Goods
in storage under care of the Sub-
Committee of Inspection and
Observation for District No. 4.*
Philadelphia, December 13, 1774.
HSP

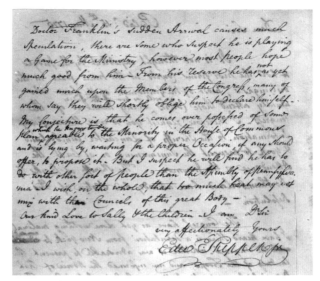

Edward Shippen, Jr. *Letter to Jasper Yeates,* Philadelphia, May 15, 1775. HSP

Dr. Franklin, convinced that he could accomplish nothing further in London on behalf of the colonies, came home. He had been away so long that the new radicals were not quite sure where he stood. After telling Yeates that Congress had advised the New Yorkers not to fight to prevent the landing of troops, Shippen went on: "Doctor Franklin's sudden Arrival causes much Speculation. There are some who suspect he is playing a Game for the Ministry, however most people hope much good from him—From his reserve he has not as yet gained much upon the Members of the Congress, many of whom say they will shortly oblige him to declare himself."

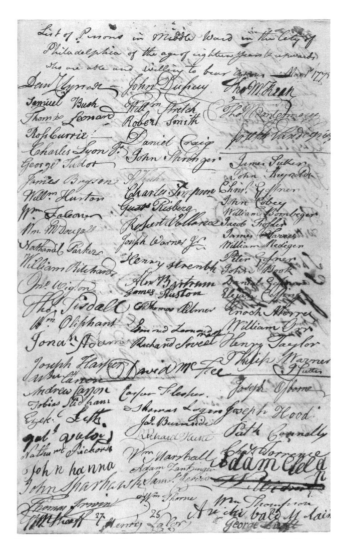

"List of Persons in Middle Ward in the City of Philadelphia of the age of eighteen years & upwards who are able and willing to bear Arms," May 1, 1775. Manuscript. HSP

With the outbreak of fighting in Massachusetts, there was a flurry of activity throughout the colonies to prepare militarily. In Philadelphia companies of militiamen, known as Associators, joined the militia. The name of Thomas McKean, a delegate to the Continental Congress from Delaware, heads the list of those in the Middle Ward ready, willing and able to join up.

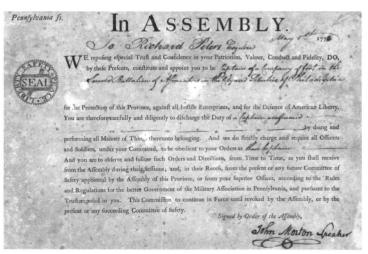

John Morton, Speaker. *Commission to Richard Peters as "Captain of a Company of foot in the Second Battalion of Associators,"* [Philadelphia], May 1, 1775. HSP

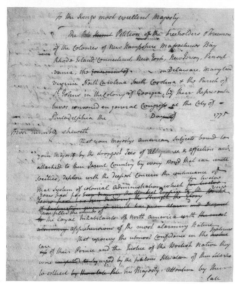

On May 26, 1775, among the items on an agenda which Congress set for itself was a second address to the King. On June 3 its composition was referred to a committee consisting of Dickinson, Johnson, John Rutledge, Jay and Franklin. The whole matter became extremely controversial and evoked the strongest opposition from John Adams and other radicals. Adams called it a "Measure of Imbecility," and in a letter to Joseph Warren, which was intercepted and made public, referred to Dickinson as "a certain great Fortune and piddling Genius." Jay wrote the first draft, which was not satisfactory to the committee, who then entrusted the writing to Dickinson. His version was accepted, much as he had drafted it, on July 5. Jefferson and his colleagues from Virginia informed the Convention that the business of Congress was preventing them from returning. "A petition to the king is already sent away, earnestly entreating the royal interposition to prevent the further progress of civil contention by redressing American grievances; but we are prevented from transmitting a copy of it, because a public communication, before it has been presented, may be improper." In spite of the delicacy of Congress, the petition was never presented to the King. Dickinson's hope for conciliation once again foundered.

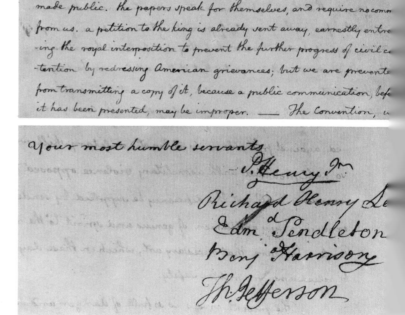

Only two days after Thomas Jefferson arrived in Philadelphia to take the place of the ailing Peyton Randolph in Congress, a committee was appointed to "draw up a declaration, to be published by General Washington, upon his arrival at the camp before Boston." The first draft proved unsatisfactory, and on June 26 Jefferson and Dickinson were added to the committee. The former wrote a version, which the latter extended and changed in a few places. Although it was commonly believed that Dickinson softened the harshness of Jefferson's statements, Julian P. Boyd has shown that in some instances his language was bolder than the Virginian's, and that the whole can be considered of joint authorship. Adopted on July 6, 1775, it was the most important document issued by the first session of the Second Continental Congress.

A Declaration By The Representatives of the United Colonies . . . Setting forth the Causes and Necessity Of their taking up Arms. Portsmouth, [1775]. HSP

A DECLARATION

By the Representatives of the

United Colonies

Of NORTH-AMERICA, now met in

General Congress

AT PHILADELPHIA,

Setting forth the CAUSES and NECESSITY

OF THEIR TAKING UP

ARMS.

A View of that great and flourishing City of BOSTON, when in its purity, and out of the Hands of the Philistines.

IF it was possible for Men, who exercise their Reason, to believe, that the Divine Author of our Existence intended a Part of the human Race to hold an absolute Property in, and an unbounded Power over others, marked out by his infinite Goodness & Wisdom, as the Objects of a legal Domination, never rightfully resistible, however severe and oppressive, the Inhabitants of these Colonies might at least require from the Parliament of Great Britain, some Evidence, that this dreadful Authority over them has been granted to that Body. But a Reverence for our Great CREATOR, Principles of Humanity, and the Dictates of common Sense, must convince all those who reflect upon the Subject, that Government was instituted to promote the Welfare of Mankind, and ought to be administered for the Attainment of that End. The Legislature of Great-Britain, however stimulated by an inordinate Passion for a Power not only unjustifiable, but which they know to be peculiarly reprobated by the very Constitution of that Kingdom, and desperate of Success in any Mode of Contest, where Regard should be had to Truth, Law, or Right, have at length, deserting those, attempted to effect their cruel and impolitic Purpose of enslaving these Colonies by Violence, and have thereby rendered it necessary for us to close with their last Appeal from Reason to Arms.—Yet however blinded by that Assembly may be, by their intemperate Rage for unlimited Domination so to slight Justice and the Opinion of Mankind, we esteem ourselves bound by Obligations of Respect to the rest of the World, to make known the Justice of our Cause.

Our Forefathers, Inhabitants of the Island of Great-Britain, left their native Land to seek on these Shores a Residence for civil and religious Freedom. At the Expence of their Blood, at the Hazard of their Fortunes, without the least Charge to the Country from which they removed, by unceasing Labor and an unconquerable Spirit, they effected Settlements in the distant & inhospitable Wilds of America, then filled with numerous and warlike Nations of Barbarians.—Societies or Governments, vested with perfect Legislatures, were formed under Charters from the Crown, and an harmonious Intercourse was established between the Colonies and the Kingdom from which they derived their Origin.—The mutual Benefits of this Union became in a short Time so extraordinary, as to excite Astonishment: It is universally confessed, that the amazing Increase of the Wealth, Strength and Navigation of the Realm, arose from this Source; and the Minister who so wisely and successfully directed the Measures of Great-Britain in the late War, publicly declared, that these Colonies enabled her to triumph over her Enemies.—Towards the Conclusion of that War, it pleased our Sovereign to make a Change in his Counsels.—From that fatal Moment, the Affairs of the British Empire began to fall into Confusion, and gradually sliding from the Summit of glorious Prosperity to which they had been advanced by the Virtues and Abilities of one Man, are at length distrated by the Convulsions that now shake it to its deepest Foundations.—The new Ministry finding the brave Foes of Britain, though frequently defeated, yet still contending, took up the unfortunate Idea of granting them a hasty Peace, and of then subduing her faithful Friends.

These devoted Colonies were judged to be in such a State, as to present Victories without Bloodshed, and all the easy Emoluments of statuteable Plunder.— The uninterrupted Tenor of their peaceable and respectful Behaviour from the Beginning of Colonization, their dutiful, zealous and useful Services during the War, though so recently and amply acknowledged in the most honorable Manner by his Majesty, by the late King, and by Parliament, could not save them from the meditated Innovations.— Parliament was influenced to adopt the pernicious Project, & assuming a new Power over them, have in the Course of eleven Years, given such decisive Specimens of the Spirit and Consequences attending this Power, as to leave no Doubt concerning the Effects of Acquiescence under it. They have undertaken to give and grant our Money without our Consent, tho'

we have ever exercised an exclusive Right to dispose of our own Property; Statutes have been passed for extending the Jurisdiction of Courts of Admiralty and Vice Admiralty beyond their ancient Limits: For depriving us of the accustomed and inestimable Privilege of Trial by Jury in Cases affecting both Life and Property; for suspending the Legislature of one of the Colonies; for interdicting all Commerce of another; and for altering fundamentally the Form of Government established by Charter, and secured by Acts of its own Legislature solemnly confirmed by the Crown; for exempting the "Murderers" of Colonists from legal Trial, and in Effect, from Punishment; for erecting in a neighbouring Province acquired by the joint Arms of Great Britain and America, a Despotism dangerous to our very Existence; and for quartering Soldiers upon the Colonists in Time of profound Peace. It has also been resolved in Parliament, that Colonists charged with committing certain Offences, shall be transported to England to be tried.

But why should we enumerate our Injuries in Detail? By one Statute it is declared, that Parliament can " of Right make Laws to bind us IN ALL CASES WHATSOEVER." What is to defend us against so enormous, so unlimited a Power? Not a single Man of those who assume it, is chosen by us; or is subject to our Controul or Influence: but on the contrary, they are all of them exempt from Operation of such Laws, and an American Revenue, if not directed from the ostensible Purposes for which it is raised, would actually lighten their own Burdens in Proportion, as they increase ours. We saw the Misery to which such Despotism would reduce us. We for ten Years incessantly and ineffectually besieged the Throne as Supplicants; we reasoned, we remonstrated with Parliament in the most mild and decent Language. But Administration, sensible that we should regard those oppressive Measures as Freemen ought to do, sent over Fleets and Armies to enforce them. The Indignation of the Americans was roused it is true; but it was the Indignation of a virtuous, loyal, and affectionate People. A Congress of Delegates from the united Colonies was assembled at Philadelphia, on the fifth Day of last September. We resolved again to offer an humble and dutiful Petition to the King, and also addressed our Fellow Subjects of Great Britain. We have pursued every temperate, every respectful Measure, we have even proceeded to break off our commercial Intercourse with our Fellow Subjects, as the last peaceable Admonition, that our Attachment to no Nation upon Earth should supplant our Attachment to Liberty.— This, we flattered ourselves, was the ultimate Step of the Controversy: But subsequent Events have shewn, how vain was this Hope of finding Moderation in our Enemies.

Several threatening Expressions against the Colonies were inserted in his Majesty's Speech; our Petition, though we were told it was a decent one, that his Majesty had been pleased to receive it graciously, and to promise laying it before his Parliament, was hudled into both Houses amongst a Bundle of American Papers, and there neglected. The Lords and Commons in their Address, in the Month of February last, said, "that a Rebellion at that Time actually existed within the Province of Massachusetts Bay; and that those concerned in it, had been countenanced and encouraged by unlawful Combinations and Engagements, entered into by his Majesty's Subjects in several of the other Colonies; and therefore they besought his Majesty, " that he would take the most effectual Measures to inforce due Obedience to the Laws and Authority of the supreme Legislature."— Soon after the commercial Intercourse of whole Colonies, with foreign Countries and with each other, was cut off by an Act of Parliament; by another, several of them were intirely prohibited from the Fisheries in the Seas near their Coasts, on which they always depended for their Sustenance; and large Re-inforcements of Ships and Troops were immediately sent over to General Gage.

Fruitless were all the Entreaties, Arguments and Eloquence of an

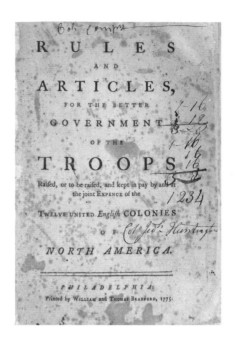

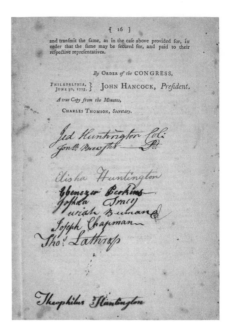

Less than a fortnight after Washington was entrusted with the command of the army, Congress adopted on June 30, 1775, a detailed set of rules for the discipline of the troops. In every sense these were the first American army regulations. Copies were widely distributed to the troops already in the field. This copy went to Col. Jedediah Huntington of the Connecticut militia; members of his regiment signed it at the end, undoubtedly to signify that they had read the rules.

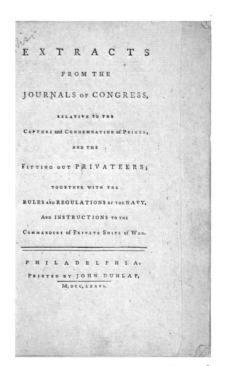

Until the United Colonies were able to build up a fleet of men-of-war, aggressive action on the sea was in the hands of privateers. Congress officially recognized their importance by establishing rules for them and for the tiny navy. This copy was Charles Thomson's, with some notes in the text and a continuation of pertinent extracts from July 24, 1776, to May 9, 1778, the last ordering American vessels to refrain from harassing neutral ships.

Directions to the Deputy Post-Masters, for keeping their Accounts. [Philadelphia, 1775]. HSP

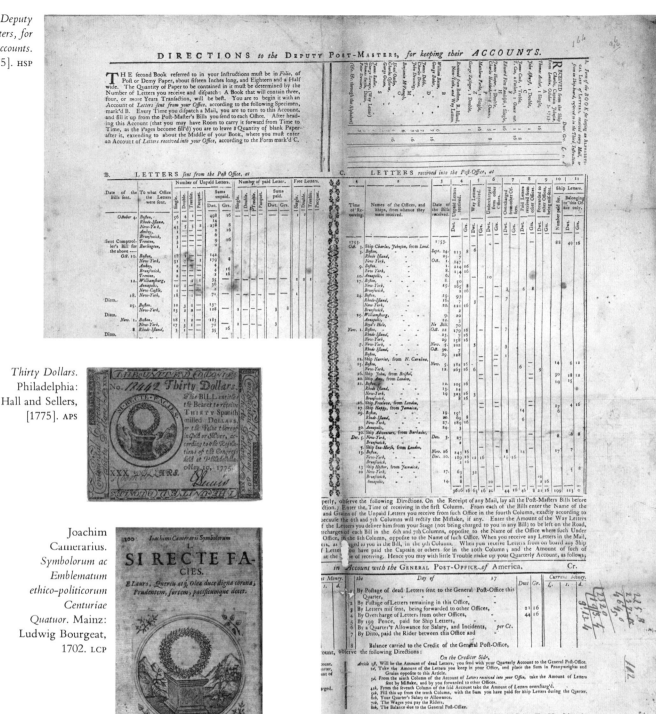

Thirty Dollars. Philadelphia: Hall and Sellers, [1775]. APS

Joachim Camerarius. *Symbolorum ac Emblematum ethico-politicorum Centuriae Quatuor.* Mainz: Ludwig Bourgeat, 1702. LCP

On July 22, 1775, Congress ordered the emission of two million dollars in paper money "for the defence of America," the first federally issued money. The following day a committee, including Franklin, was appointed to get proper plates engraved and oversee the production of the bills. The Continental currency thus printed in various denominations was decorated with emblems selected from Camerarius' work, a copy of which Franklin owned and which is now in the Library Company.

A regular method of assuring intercolonial communication was essential to the transmission of information and intelligence. On July 26, 1775, Congress authorized the formation of a post office headed by a postmaster general. Benjamin Franklin, who had served in that office under the Crown, was chosen to fill it under the Congress of the United Colonies. His printed signature is at the foot of the huge broadside of instructions, which marks the beginning of a separate American post office.

[Thomas Paine]. *Common
Sense; addressed to the
Inhabitants of America.*
Philadelphia: R. Bell, 1776. LCP

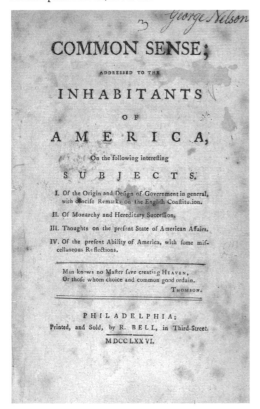

*Extract from the Minutes of
Congress,* May 15, 1776.
Philadelphia: John Dunlap,
[1776]. Broadside. LCP

The time was ripe and the contents of the pamphlet
were compelling. When Paine's *Common Sense*
appeared anonymously in January 1776, it was an
immediate bestseller, with edition after edition
coming off the presses of the colonies. In strong,
no-nonsense phrases Paine called for immediate
independence. If any single piece of propaganda
may be said to have brought forth the Declaration
of Independence, it was Paine's.

Even before Congress itself took action to sever the colonies
from the mother country finally and irrevocably, it
recommended that the several Assemblies and Conventions of
the colonies take action to set up popular governments.
In effect, this was the call to the colonies to adopt new
constitutions and become states.

John Dickinson. *Draft of an Address to the Inhabitants of the Colonies,* [Philadelphia, January, 1776]. HSP

James Wilson. *Draft of an Address to the Inhabitants of the Colonies* (with emendations by John Dickinson and William Hooper), [Philadelphia, February, 1776]. HSP

On January 24, 1776, Congress appointed Dickinson, Wilson, Hooper, Duane and Alexander a committee to draw up an address to the American colonists. Dickinson made the first attempt to draft it; then Wilson took over the composition, incorporated some of Dickinson's wording and presented it to Congress on February 13, when it was tabled. It was, in some degree, a precursor of the Declaration of Independence, for, as Wilson told Madison, "it was meant to lead the public mind into the idea of Independence, of which the necessity was plainly foreseen by Congress." Richard Smith called it "very long, badly written and full against Independence," but the text hardly bears out those unkind words. The final words are hardly equivocal: "That the Colonies may continue connected, as they have been, with Britain, is our second Wish: Our first is — THAT AMERICA MAY BE FREE."

On his way to Canada with other commissioners to try to persuade the Canadians to join the other American colonies, Franklin, held up by ice on the lakes, had time to appraise the progress of Congress. In answer to Quincy's query when was Congress going to take the steps to make it an independent body, he replied: "I can only answer at present, that nothing seems wanting but that 'general Consent'; — The Novelty of the Thing deters some, the Doubt of Success others, the vain Hope of Reconciliation many. But our Enemies take continually every proper Measure to remove these Obstacles."

Benjamin Franklin. *Letter to Josiah Quincy,* Saratoga, N.Y., April 15, 1776. HSP

Less than a week before Richard Henry Lee introduced his motion for independence, a select committee of Congress began making arrangements to procure arms in the French West Indies. "You are earnestly to endeavor to procure from him [the French general at Martinique]," the Committee directed Bingham, "Ten Thousand good Musquets, well fitted with Bayonets." Payment would be "the Produce of this Country." In addition, Bingham was to find out if the large French fleet assembling in the islands was for or against America, and generally to keep his ears open and send what intelligence he got through Silas Deane.

Benjamin Franklin, Benjamin Harrison, John Dickinson and Robert Morris, Committee of Secret Correspondence. *Letter to William Bingham,* Philadelphia, June 3, 1776. HSP

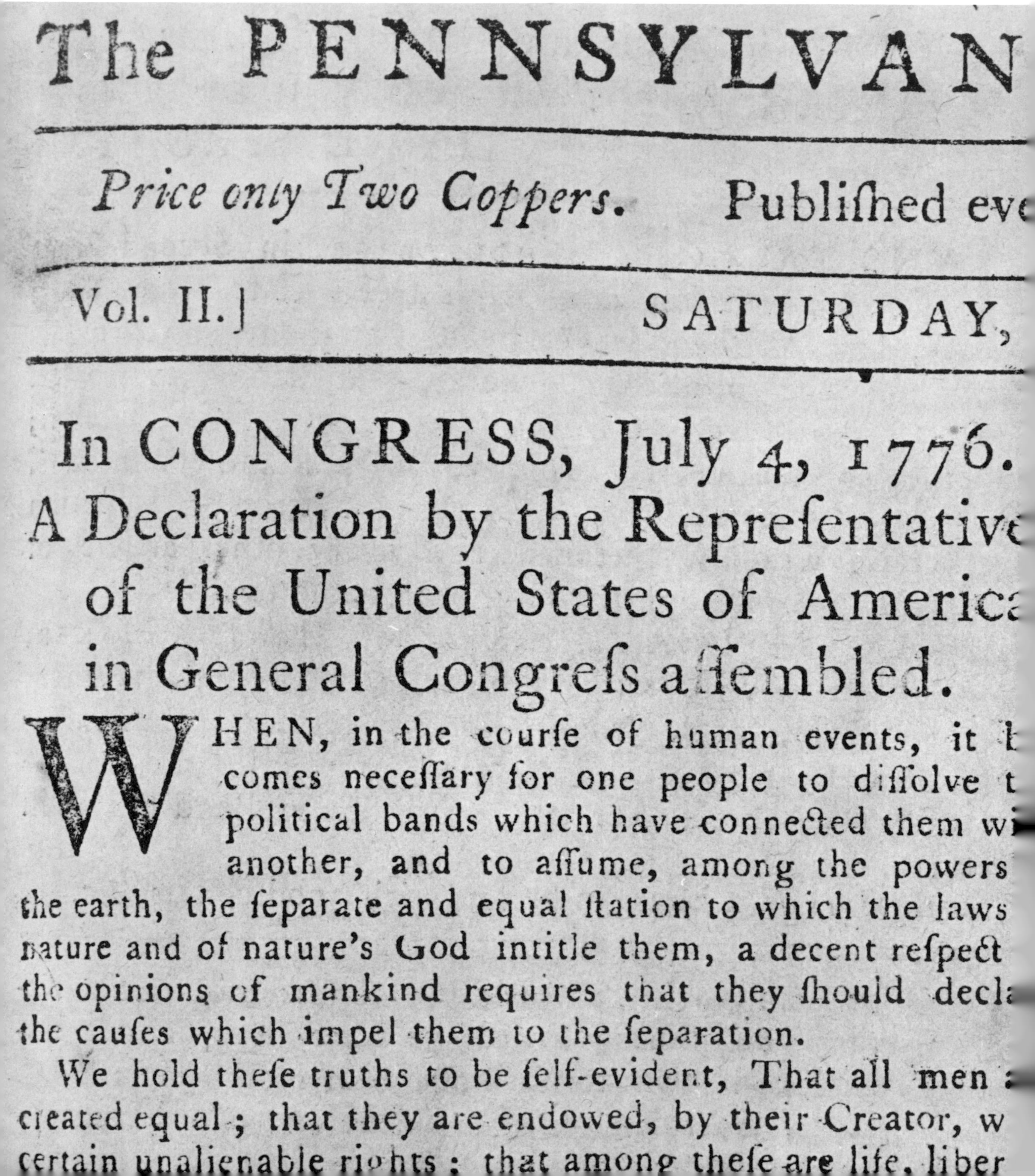

The PENNSYLVAN

Price only Two Coppers. Publiſhed eve

Vol. II.]   SATURDAY,

In CONGRESS, July 4, 1776.

A Declaration by the Repreſentative of the United States of America in General Congreſs aſſembled.

WHEN, in the courſe of human events, it b comes neceſſary for one people to diſſolve t political bands which have connected them wi another, and to aſſume, among the powers the earth, the ſeparate and equal ſtation to which the laws nature and of nature's God intitle them, a decent reſpect the opinions of mankind requires that they ſhould decla the cauſes which impel them to the ſeparation.

We hold theſe truths to be ſelf-evident, That all men created equal; that they are endowed, by their Creator, w certain unalienable rights; that among theſe are life, liber

Pennsylvania Evening Post,
July 6, 1776. HSP

A EVENING POST.

uesday, Thursday, and *Saturday* Evenings.

LY 6, 1776. [Num. 228.

He has diſſolved Repreſentative Houſes repeatedly, for op-
ſing with manly firmneſs his invaſions on the rights of the
ple.

He has refuſed for a long time, after ſuch diſſolutions, to
ſe others to be elected; whereby the legiſlative powers,
apable of annihilation, have returned to the people at
ge for their exerciſe; the ſtate remaining in the mean time
oſed to all the dangers of invaſion from without, and con-
ſions within.

He has endeavoured to prevent the population of theſe
s; for that purpoſe obſtructing the laws for naturaliza-
of foreigners; refuſing to paſs others to encourage their
rations hither, and raiſing the conditions of new appro-
tions of lands.

He has obſtructed the adminiſtration of juſtice, by refuſing
aſſent to laws for eſtabliſhing judiciary powers.

He has made Judges dependant on his will alone, for the
re of their offices, and the amount and ayment of their

Resolved, That these United Colonies are, and of right ought to be, Free and Independant States; that they are absolved from all allegiance to the British crown, and that all political connection between them, and the state of Great-Britain, is and ought to be totally dissolved.

Journal of the Congress.
Philadelphia: R. Aitken,
1776. LCP

204   JOURNALS OF CONGRESS.

FRIDAY, *June* 7, 1776.

Certain resolutions respecting Independency being moved and seconded,

Resolved, That the consideration of them be referred till to-morrow morning; and that the members be enjoined to attend punctually

ally at ten o'clock, in order to take the same into their consideration.

SATURDAY, *June* 8, 1776.

Resolved, That the resolutions respecting Independency be referred to a committee of the whole Congress:

The Congress then resolved itself into a committee of the whole, and after some time the president resumed the chair, and Mr. Harrison reported that the committee have taken into consideration the matter to them referred, but not having come to any resolution thereon, directed him to move for leave to sit again on Monday.

Resolved, That this Congress will on Monday next, at 10 o'clock, resolve itself into a committee of the whole, to take into their farther consideration the resolutions referred to them.

238   JOURNALS OF CONGRESS.

Resolved, That this Congress will to morrow resolve itself in committee of the whole to take into consideration the declarat respecting independance.

Adjourned to nine o'clock to morrow.

TUESDAY, *July* 2d. 1776.

The Congress resumed the consideration of the resolution reported from the committee of the whole, which was agreed to, as follows:

Resolved, That these United Colonies are, and of right ought to be, Free and Independant States; that they are absolved from all allegiance to the British crown, and that all political connection between them, and the state of Great-Britain, is and ought to be totally dissolved.

Agreeable to the order of the day, the Congress resolved itself into a committee of the whole; and after some time, the president resumed the chair, and Mr. Harrison reported, that the committee have had under consideration the declaration to them referred, but not having had time to go through the same, desired him to move for leave to sit again:

Resolved, That this Congress will to-morrow again resolve itself into a committee of the whole, to take into their farther consideration the declaration respecting Independence.

In the Continental Congress on June 7, 1776, Richard Henry Lee of Virginia moved, "That these United Colonies are, and of right ought to be, free and independent States, that they are absolved from all allegiance to the British Crown, and that all political connection between them and the State of Great Britain is, and ought to be, totally dissolved." Discussion of the resolution was postponed until July 1. Meanwhile, on June 11, Congress appointed a committee to prepare a statement of reasons for the action, should it be taken. The committee was composed of John Adams, Benjamin Franklin, Roger Sherman, Robert R. Livingston, and Thomas Jefferson. Jefferson's colleagues asked him to draft the declaration. The committee presented its draft on June 28. On July 1 debate began, and on July 2 Lee's motion was adopted. By this vote the American colonies declared themselves states, and formally separated from Great Britain. "The Second Day of July 1776," John Adams wrote his wife on July 3, "will be the most memorable Epocha, in the History of America.—I am apt to believe that it will be celebrated, by succeeding Generations, as the great anniversary Festival. It ought to be commemorated, as the Day of Deliverance by solemn Acts of Devotion to God Almighty. It ought to be solemnized with Pomp and Parade, with Shews, Games, Sports, Guns, Bells, Bonfires and Illuminations from one End of this Continent to the other from this Time forward forever more."

There was no rush to independence; the movement was slow, and acceptance of the idea reluctant. The Pennsylvania Assembly, for example, instructed its delegates to the Continental Congress in November 1775 "utterly [to] reject any proposition (should such be made) that may cause or lead to a separation from the mother Country." Even this reference to independence alarmed moderate men, including some in arms against the British. General Charles Lee, second in command to Washington, writing from the army at Cambridge, Mass., here warns John Dickinson, a leader of moderation in Pennsylvania, that the Assembly's instructions were "ill timed and to the last degree impolitick." By providing Britain with evidence that some Americans aimed at independence, they would only strengthen British resolve to reject American appeals. "I cannot help wishing your People of Pennsylvania better represented— I mean more adequately."

Not every colony was prepared to vote for independence on June 7, when Richard Henry Lee introduced his resolution. In the ensuing weeks before July 2 advocates for independence encouraged and pressured the laggards, as is shown in this letter of a Massachusetts delegate to a constituent, which gently suggests that the interest of France in freer trade with America is the same as the colonies'.

Richard Henry Lee.
Engraving of a drawing by J. B. Longacre from a portrait miniature. HSP

Thomas Jefferson. *Letter to Benjamin Franklin,* [Philadelphia], "Friday morn." [June 21, 1776]. APS

Th:J. to Doct.r Franklyn.

The inclosed paper has been read & with some small altera-
-tions approved of by the committee. will Doct.r Franklyn be
so good as to peruse it & suggest such alterations as his
more enlarged view of the subject will dictate? the paper
having been returned to me to change a particular sentiment
or two, I propose laying it again before the committee to-
-morrow morning, if Doct.r Franklyn can think of it before
that time.

Friday morn.

By June 21 Jefferson had completed a draft of the Declaration, and, having shown it to Adams, Livingston, and Sherman, he asked Franklin to read it "and suggest such alterations as his more enlarged view of the subject will dictate."

Jacob Graff's House. Southwest corner, Market and Seventh Streets, Philadelphia. Photograph *ca.* 1880. LCP

Thomas Jefferson, while a member of Congress in 1776, occupied two furnished rooms—a bedroom and a parlor—on the second floor of the new house of the bricklayer Jacob Graff. Questioned in 1825 about the circumstances of his writing the Declaration of Independence, Jefferson replied firmly that he customarily did all his writing in the parlor, "and in it I wrote this paper particularly." The house was demolished in 1883.

Thomas Jefferson. By Jean Antoine Hondon. Plaster bust, 1787. APS

This bust, made in Paris by "the first statuary in the world," was once owned by astronomer David Rittenhouse. It may have been given to him by Jefferson.

opposite

On July 8 Thomas Jefferson sent Richard Henry Lee (who returned to Virginia since making his motion on June 7) manuscript copy of the Declaration of Independence essentially was first presented to Congress, and also a broadside printing o Declaration as revised and adopted. "You will judge whether the better or worse for the Critics," Jefferson remarked, sugge he thought the critics had not improved it. Lee and his br Arthur immediately compared the printed and manuscript vers noting Congress's changes and excisions in the ma and by underli

A Declaration by the Representatives of the UNITED STATES OF
AMERICA in General Congress assembled.

When in the course of human events it becomes necessary for one people to dis-
-solve the political bands which have connected them with another, and to assume
among the powers of the earth the separate and equal station to which the laws of
nature and of nature's god entitle them, a decent respect to the opinions of mankind
requires that they should declare the causes which impel them to the separation.

We hold these truths to be self-evident; that all men are created equal; that
they are endowed by their Creator with inherent and inalienable rights; that among these
are life, liberty, and the pursuit of happiness; that to secure these rights, governments
are instituted among men, deriving their just powers from the consent of the governed;
that whenever any form of government becomes destructive of these ends, it is the
right of the people to alter or to abolish it, and to institute new government, laying
it's foundation on such principles, and organising it's powers in such form as to
them shall seem most likely to effect their safety and happiness. prudence indeed
will dictate that governments long established should not be changed for light & trans-
-ient causes. and accordingly all experience hath shewn, that mankind are more dis-
-posed to suffer, while evils are sufferable than to right themselves by abolishing the forms to which
they are accustomed. but when a long train of abuses and usurpations, begun at a distin
-guished period & pursuing invariably the same object, evinces a design to reduce them under
absolute despotism, it is their right, it is their duty, to throw off such government, & to pro-
-vide new guards for their future security. such has been the patient sufferance of these
colonies; & such is now the necessity which constrains them to expunge their former systems
of government. the history of the present king of Great Britain, is a history of unremitting
injuries and usurpations, among which appears no solitary fact to contradict the
uniform tenor of the rest; but all have in direct object the establishment of an absolute
tyranny over these states. to prove this let facts be submitted to a candid world, for
the truth of which we pledge a faith yet unsullied by falsehood.

he has refused his assent to laws the most wholesome and necessary for the public good.
he has forbidden his governors to pass laws of immediate & pressing importance, unless su
-pended in their operation till his assent should be obtained; and when so suspend
-ed, he has neglected utterly to attend to them.
he has refused to pass other laws for the accomodation of large districts of people, unless
those people would relinquish the right of representation in the legislature; a right
inestimable to them, & formidable to tyrants only.

certain un-
alienable rights

v is the

left out

alter

repeated

left out

having

left out

utterly ne-
-lected

Thomas Jefferson. *A Declaration by the Representatives of the United States of America in*
General Congress assembled. With corrections by Richard Henry Lee and Arthur Lee. APS

67

John Penn. *Letter to
Samuel Johnson,* Philadelphia,
June 28, 1776. HSP

Knowing that Congress has scheduled a debate on Lee's resolution for July 1, John Penn, a North Carolina delegate, predicts, "The first day of July will be made remarkable; then the question relative to Independence will be agitated and there is no doubt but a total separation from Britain will take place. This Province is for it; indeed so are all except Maryland & her people are coming over fast."

Josiah Bartlett. *Letter to
General Nathaniel Folsom,*
Philadelphia, July 1, 1776. HSP

After the first day's debate on Lee's resolution, a New Hampshire delegate assures his correspondent he has "no Doubt but that by the next post I shall be able to send you a formal Declaration of Independency setting forth the reasons &c." But he warns that "in the Grand american Cause, we are now Come to the time, that requires harmony, together with all the wisdom, prudence, Courage, & resolution we are masters of . . . ."

State House in Philadelphia, 1778.
By Charles Willson Peale.
Engraving by Illman Brothers. APS

[handwritten manuscript]

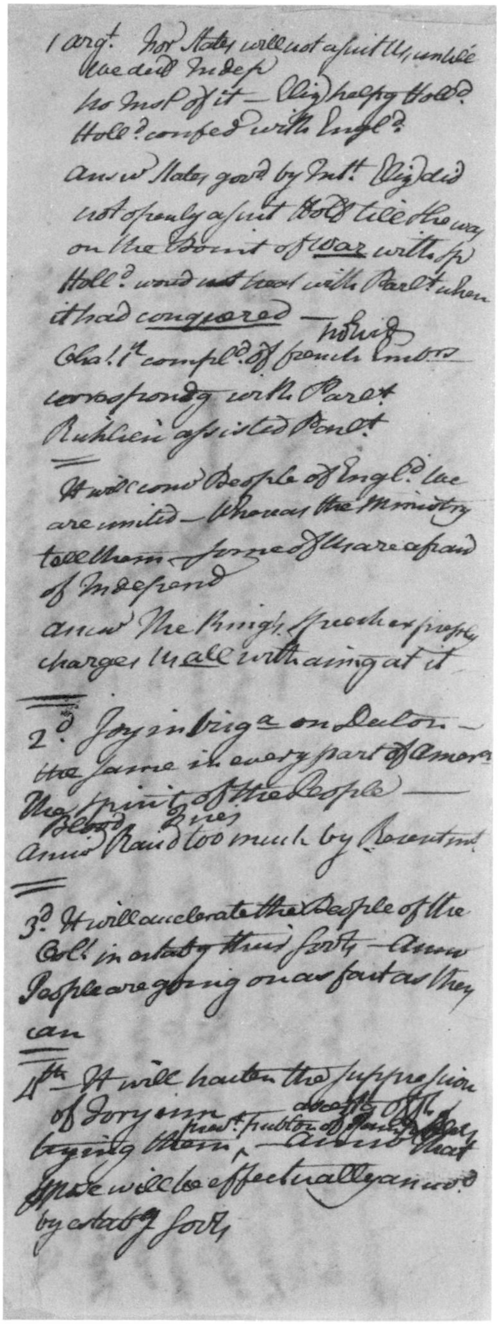

The members of Congress were by no means unanimous for independence on July 1, 1776. The ablest and best known spokesman for caution was John Dickinson, the Philadelphia lawyer whose pamphlets and state papers had strongly and eloquently asserted, explained, and defended Americans' claims against Britain for ten years past. In a carefully reasoned, clearly expressed address to Congress he opposed the motion for independence as premature. Dickinson's decision was especially poignant, for he knew he was in the minority. "My Conduct, this Day," he told his colleagues sadly, "I expect will give the finishing Blow to my once great, and now too diminished Popularity." He would rather vote away his own reputation, he continued, "than the Blood and Happiness of my Countrymen. . . . I should rather they should hate Me, than that I should hurt them." A week later, independence declared and the Declaration adopted, John Adams wrote of Dickinson that he had "fallen, like Grass before the Scythe."

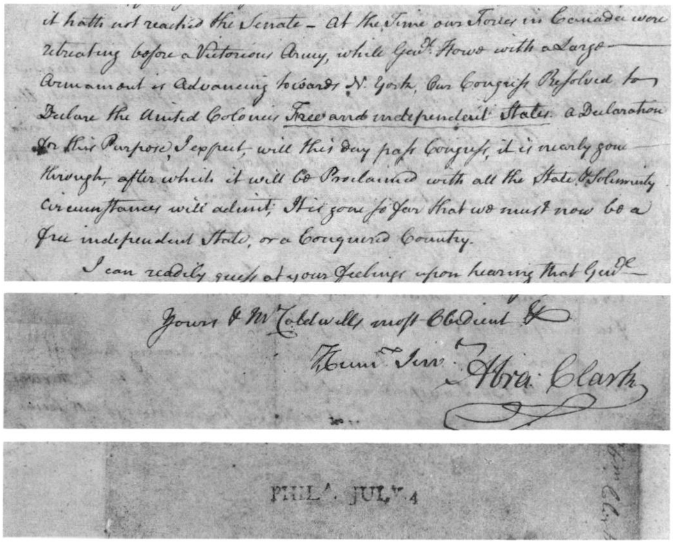

[handwritten letter]

Writing on the morning of July 4, while Jefferson's draft of the Declaration was under consideration, a New Jersey delegate informs a Jersey militia officer that the die is almost cast.

> Our Congress Resolved to Declare the United Colonies Free and independent States. A Declaration for the Purpose, I expect, will this day pass Congress. It is nearly gone through, after which it will be Proclaimed with all the State & Solemnity Circumstances will admit. It is gone so far that we must now be a free independent State, or a Conquered Country.

Of great philatelic interest is the postal cancellation "Phila. July 4."

In Congress, July 4, 1776,
A Declaration By the
Representatives of the United
States of America, In general
Congress assembled.
[Philadelphia: John Dunlap,
1776]. Proof. HSP

IN CONG

A DECI

BY THE REPR

UNITED STA

IN GENERAL

WHEN in the Courſe of human Events,
with another," and to aſſume among the
Nature's God entitle them," a decent Reſ
to the Separation.

WE hold theſe Truths to be ſelf-evi
unalienable Rights," that among theſe a
inſtituted among Men, " deriving their juſt Powers from the Co
Ends, " it is the Right of the People to alter or to aboliſh it,
its Powers in ſuch Form, as to them ſhall ſeem moſt likely to
tabliſhed ſhould not be changed for light and tranſient Cauſes
Evils are ſufferable, than to right themſelves by aboliſhing the F
ing invariably the ſame Objeƈt, evinces a Deſign to reduce them
and to provide new Guards for their future Security." Such has
them to alter their former Syſtems of Government." The Hi
having in direƈt Objeƈt the Eſtabliſhment of an abſolute Tyranny
HE has refuſed his Aſſent to Laws, the moſt wholeſome and
HE has forbidden his Governors to paſs Laws of immediate a
and when ſo ſuſpended, he has utterly negleƈted to attend to the
HE has refuſed to paſs other Laws for the Accommodation of
the Legiſlature, a Right ineſtimable to them, and formidable to
HE has called together Legiſlative Bodies at Places unuſual, u
fatiguing them into Compliance with his Meaſures.
HE has diſſolved Repreſentative Houſes repeatedly, for oppo
HE has refuſed for a long Time, after ſuch Diſſolutions, to ca
turned to the People at large for their exerciſe; the State remaini
HE has endeavoured to prevent the Population of theſe States;
to encourage their Migrations hither, and raiſing the Conditions

The Declaration of Independence was debated by Congress on July
and 3, and approved on July 4. A copy was sent at once to the print
John Dunlap, in whose shop on Market Street it was set up on the r
of July 4-5. This fragment, believed to be uncorrected printer's proo

ESS, JULY 4, 1776.

RATION

NTATIVES OF THE

ES OF AMERICA,

NGRESS ASSEMBLED.

ceſſary for one People " to diſſolve the Political Bands which have connected them
e Earth, the ſeparate and equal Station " to which the Laws of Nature and of
inions of Mankind requires " that they ſhould declare the cauſes which impel them

all Men are created equal," " that they are endowed by their Creator with certain
ty, and the Purſuit of Happineſs——That to ſecure theſe Rights, Governments are
overned," that whenever any Form of Government becomes deſtructive of theſe
e a new Government, laying its Foundation on ſuch Principles, and organizing
fety and Happineſs." Prudence, indeed, will dictate that Governments long eſ-
gly all Experience hath ſhewn, that Mankind are more diſpoſed to ſuffer, while
they are accuſtomed. But when a long Train of Abuſes and Uſurpations, purſu-
e Deſpotiſm, it is their Right, it is their Duty, to throw off ſuch Government,
nt Sufferance of theſe Colonies ;" and ſuch is now the Neceſſity which conſtrains
eſent King of Great-Britain is a Hiſtory of repeated Injuries and Uſurpations, all
s. To prove this, let Facts be ſubmitted to a candid World.
e public Good.
portance, unleſs ſuſpended in their Operation till his Aſſent ſhould be obtained ;

of People, unleſs thoſe People would relinquiſh the Right of Repreſentation in

and diſtant from the Depoſitory of their public Records, for the ſole Purpoſe of

y Firmneſs his Invaſions on the Rights of the People.
e elected ; whereby the Legiſlative Powers, incapable of Annihilation, have re-
ime expoſed to all the Dangers of Invaſion from without, and Convulſions within.
e obſtructing the Laws for Naturalization of Foreigners ; refuſing to paſs othes
riations of Lands.

e earlieſt appearance of the document in type. It was corrected not
than the morning of July 5, and copies pulled that day.
ompare this proof with the broadside as finally published, noting the
ges (such as dropping of quotation marks) made before final printing.

71

In Congress, July 4, 1776.
A Declaration by the Representatives
of the United States of America,
in general Congress assembled.
Philadelphia: John Dunlap,
[1776]. Broadside. APS

The printer delivered copies of the Declaration of Independence to Congress on the morning of July 5. This is one of those copies. Congress directed that they be sent at once to the several state assemblies, conventions and committees or councils of safety, and to the commanding officers of Continental troops; and that the Declaration be proclaimed in each of the states and at the head of the Army.

In conformity with this direction, the Declaration was publicly proclaimed in Philadelphia in the State House Yard at noon on July 8 in the presence of a great concourse of citizens. "The company declared their approbation by 3 repeated huzzas," wrote one of those present. "The Kings arms was taken down in court room [of the] state house [at the] same time." That night there were "bonfires, ringing bells with other great Demonstrations of Joy."

IN CONGRESS, JULY 4, 1776.

A DECLARATION

BY THE REPRESENTATIVES OF THE

UNITED STATES OF AMERICA,

IN GENERAL CONGRESS ASSEMBLED.

WHEN in the Courfe of human Events, it becomes neceffary for one People to diffolve the Political Bands which have connected them with another, and to affume among the Powers of the Earth, the feparate and equal Station to which the Laws of Nature and of Nature's God entitle them, a decent Refpect to the Opinions of Mankind requires that they fhould declare the caufes which impel them to the Separation.

WE hold thefe Truths to be felf-evident, that all Men are created equal, that they are endowed by their Creator with certain unalienable Rights, that among thefe are Life, Liberty, and the Purfuit of Happinefs—That to fecure thefe Rights, Governments are inftituted among Men, deriving their juft Powers from the Confent of the Governed, that whenever any Form of Government becomes deftructive of thefe Ends, it is the Right of the People to alter or to abolifh it, and to inftitute new Government, laying its Foundation on fuch Principles, and organizing its Powers in fuch Form, as to them fhall feem moft likely to effect their Safety and Happinefs. Prudence, indeed, will dictate that Governments long eftablifhed fhould not be changed for light and tranfient Caufes; and accordingly all Experience hath fhewn, that Mankind are more difpofed to fuffer, while Evils are fufferable, than to right themfelves by abolifhing the Forms to which they are accuftomed. But when a long Train of Abufes and Ufurpations, purfuing invariably the fame Object, evinces a Defign to reduce them under abfolute Defpotifm, it is their Right, it is their Duty, to throw off fuch Government, and to provide new Guards for their future Security. Such has been the patient Sufferance of thefe Colonies; and fuch is now the Neceffity which conftrains them to alter their former Syftems of Government. The Hiftory of the prefent King of Great Britain is a Hiftory of repeated Injuries and Ufurpations, all

ranging them into Compliance with his Meafures.

HE has diffolved Reprefentative Houfes repeatedly, for oppofing with manly Firmnefs his Invafions on the Rights of the People.

HE has refufed for a long Time, after fuch Diffolutions, to caufe others to be elected; whereby the Legiflative Powers, incapable of Annihilation, have returned to the People at large for their exercife; the State remaining in the mean time expofed to all the Dangers of Invafion from without, and Convulfions within.

HE has endeavoured to prevent the Population of thefe States; for that Purpofe obftructing the Laws for Naturalization of Foreigners; refufing to pafs others to encourage their Migrations hither, and raifing the Conditions of new Appropriations of Lands.

HE has obftructed the Adminiftration of Juftice, by refufing his Affent to Laws for eftablifhing Judiciary Powers.

HE has made Judges dependent on his Will alone, for the Tenure of their Offices, and the Amount and Payment of their Salaries.

HE has erected a Multitude of new Offices, and fent hither Swarms of Officers to harrafs our People, and eat out their Subftance.

HE has kept among us, in Times of Peace, Standing Armies, without the confent of our Legiflatures.

HE has affected to render the Military independent of and fuperior to the Civil Power.

HE has combined with others to fubject us to a Jurifdiction foreign to our Conftitution, and unacknowledged by our Laws; giving his Affent to their Acts of pretended Legiflation:

FOR quartering large Bodies of Armed Troops among us:

FOR protecting them, by a mock Trial, from Punifhment for any Murders which they fhould commit on the Inhabitants of thefe States:

FOR cutting off our Trade with all Parts of the World:

FOR impofing Taxes on us without our Confent:

FOR depriving us, in many Cafes, of the Benefits of Trial by Jury:

FOR tranfporting us beyond Seas to be tried for pretended Offences:

FOR abolifhing the free Syftem of Englifh Laws in a neighbouring Province, eftablifhing therein an arbitrary Government, and enlarging its Boundaries, fo as to render it at once an Example and fit Inftrument for introducing the fame abfolute Rule into thefe Colonies:

FOR taking away our Charters, abolifhing our moft valuable Laws, and altering fundamentally the Forms of our Governments:

FOR fufpending our own Legiflatures, and declaring themfelves invefted with Power to legiflate for us in all Cafes whatfoever.

HE has abdicated Government here, by declaring us out of his Protection and waging War againft us.

HE has plundered our Seas, ravaged our Coafts, burnt our Towns, and deftroyed the Lives of our People.

HE is, at this Time, tranfporting large Armies of foreign Mercenaries to compleat the Works of Death, Defolation, and Tyranny, already begun with circumftances of Cruelty and Perfidy, fcarcely paralleled in the moft barbarous Ages, and totally unworthy the Head of a civilized Nation.

HE has conftrained our fellow Citizens taken Captive on the high Seas to bear Arms againft their Country, to become the Executioners of their Friends and Brethren, or to fall themfelves by their Hands.

HE has excited domeftic Infurrections amongft us, and has endeavoured to bring on the Inhabitants of our Frontiers, the mercilefs Indian Savages, whofe known Rule of Warfare, is an undiftinguifhed Deftruction, of all Ages, Sexes and Conditions.

IN every ftage of thefe Oppreffions we have Petitioned for Redrefs in the moft humble Terms: Our repeated Petitions have been anfwered only by repeated Injury. A Prince, whofe Character is thus marked by every act which may define a Tyrant, is unfit to be the Ruler of a free People.

NOR have we been wanting in Attentions to our Britifh Brethren. We have warned them from Time to Time of Attempts by their Legiflature to extend an unwarrantable Jurifdiction over us. We have reminded them of the Circumftances of our Emigration and Settlement here. We have appealed to their native Juftice and Magnanimity, and we have conjured them by the Ties of our common Kindred to difavow thefe Ufurpations, which, would inevitably interrupt our Connections and Correfpondence. They too have been deaf to the Voice of Juftice and of Confanguinity. We muft, therefore, acquiefce in the Neceffity, which denounces our Separation, and hold them, as we hold the reft of Mankind, Enemies in War, in Peace, Friends.

WE, therefore, the Reprefentatives of the UNITED STATES OF AMERICA, in GENERAL CONGRESS, Affembled, appealing to the Supreme Judge of the World for the Rectitude of our Intentions, do, in the Name, and by Authority of the good People of thefe Colonies, folemnly Publifh and Declare, That thefe United Colonies are, and of Right ought to be, FREE AND INDEPENDENT STATES; that they are abfolved from all Allegiance to the Britifh Crown, and that all political Connection between them and the State of Great-Britain, is and ought to be totally diffolved; and that as FREE AND INDEPENDENT STATES, they have full Power to levy War, conclude Peace, contract Alliances, eftablifh Commerce, and to do all other Acts and Things which INDEPENDENT STATES may of right do. And for the fupport of this Declaration, with a firm Reliance on the Protection of divine Providence, we mutually pledge to each other our Lives, our Fortunes, and our facred Honor.

Signed by ORDER and in BEHALF of the CONGRESS,

JOHN HANCOCK, PRESIDENT.

ATTEST.
CHARLES THOMSON, SECRETARY.

PHILADELPHIA: PRINTED BY JOHN DUNLAP.

John Hancock. *Letter to the Committee of Safety of Pennsylvania*, Philadelphia, July 5, 1776. HSP

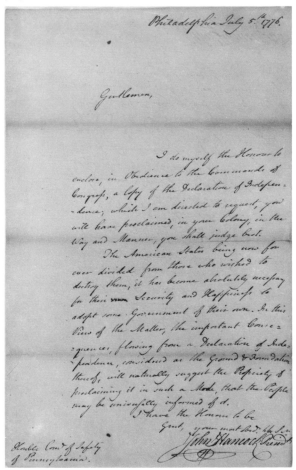

John Adams. *Letter to Mary Palmer*, Philadelphia, July 5, 1776. HSP

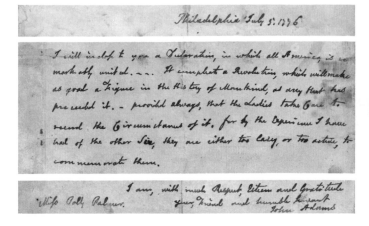

Enclosing a copy of the Declaration to a relative, John Adams speaks of its significance in a mixture of seriousness and gallantry. "It compleats a Revolution, which will make as good a Figure in the History of Mankind, as any that has preceeded it—provided always, that the Ladies take Care to record the Circumstances of it, for by the Experience I have had of the other Sex, they are either too lazy, or too active, to commemorate them."

George Ross. *Letter to Peter Grubb*, Lancaster, Pa., July 6, 1776. HSP

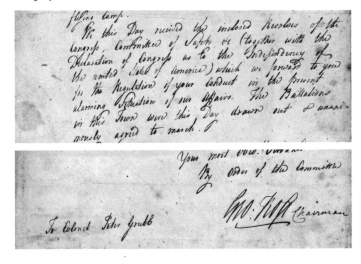

The President of Congress forwarded a copy of the Declaration to the Pennsylvania Committee of Safety in these formal phrases:

> The American States being now for ever divided from those who wished to destroy them, it has become absolutely necessary for their Security and Happiness to adopt some Government of their own. In this view of the Matter, the important Consequences, flowing from a Declaration of Independence, considered as the Ground & Foundation thereof, will naturally suggest the Propriety of proclaiming it in such a Mode, that the People may be universally informed of it.

From Lancaster the chairman of the Committee of Safety, who became a Signer, forwards "the Declaration of Congress as to the Independency of the united States of America" to a member of the Committee of Safety of Berks County so they may govern their conduct "in the present alarming Situation of our Affairs."

The PENNSYLVANIA EVENING POST.

Price only Two Coppers.   Publiſhed every *Tuesday, Thursday,* and *Saturday* Evenings.

Vol. II.]   SATURDAY, JULY 6, 1776.   [Num. 228.

In CONGRESS, July 4, 1776.   He has diſſolved Repreſentative Houſes repeatedly, for op-
A Declaration by the Representatives   poſing with manly firmneſs his invaſions on the rights of the people.

sylvania Evening Post, July 6, 1776. HSP

1776. Dienſtags, den 9 July.   Henrich Millers   813 Stück

Pennſylvaniſcher Staatsbote.

Dieſe Zeitung kommt alle Wochen zweymal heraus, näml. Dienſtags und Freytags, für Sechs Schillinge des Jahrs.
N.B. All ADVERTISEMENTS to be inſerted in this Paper, or printed ſingle by HENRY MILLER, Publiſher hereof, are by him tranſlated gratis.

Im Congreß, den 4ten July, 1776.

nsylvanischer Staatsbote, July 9, 1776. HSP

MONDAY, July 15, 1776.   THE   [No. 1292]

NEW-YORK GAZETTE: AND THE WEEKLY MERCURY.

Containing the freſheſt Advices.   Foreign and Domeſtick.

PRINTED BY HUGH GAINE, Printer, Bookseller, and Stationer, at the BIBLE and CROWN, in HANOVER-SQUARE.

New-York Gazette, July 15, 1776. LCP

[161]

The London Chronicle   Nº 3073.

Vol. XL.

From THURSDAY, AUGUST 15, to SATURDAY, AUGUST 17, 1776.

ndon Chronicle, August 17, 1776. LCP

THE LONDON CHRONICLE for 1776.   August 15—17.

164   ADVICES *from* AMERICA.

In CONGRESS, *July* 4, 1776.
A Declaration *by the* REPRESENTATIVES *of the* UNITED STATES *of* AMERICA, *in* GENERAL CONGRESS *assembled.*

WHEN in the courſe of human events it becomes neceſſary for one people to diſſolve the political bands which have connected them with another, and to aſſume among the powers of the earth the ſeparate and equal ſtation to which the laws of nature and of nature's God entitle them, a decent reſpect to the opinions of mankind requires that they ſhould declare the cauſes which impel them to the ſeparation.
We hold theſe truths to be ſelf-evident; that all men are created equal; that they are

juſtice, by refuſing his aſſent to laws for eſtabliſhing judiciary powers.
He has made judges dependent on his will alone, for the tenure of their offices, and the amount and payment of their ſalaries.
He has erected a multitude of new offices, and ſent hither ſwarms of officers to harraſs our people and eat out their ſubſiſtence.
He has kept among us, in times of peace, ſtanding armies, without the conſent of our legiſlatures.
He has affected to render the military independent of, and ſuperior to, the civil power.
He has combined with others to ſubject us to a juriſdiction foreign to our conſtitution, and unacknowledged by our laws; giving his aſſent to their pretended acts of legiſlation:
For quartering large bodies of armed troops among us:

and hold them, as we hold the reſt of mankind, enemies in war, in peace friends.
We, therefore, the repreſentatives of the United States of America, in general congreſs aſſembled, appealing to the Supreme Judge of the World for the rectitude of our intentions, do, in the name and by the authority of the good people of theſe colonies, ſolemnly publiſh and declare, that theſe United Colonies are, and of right ought to be, free and independent ſtates, and that they are abſolved from all allegiance to the Britiſh crown, and that all political connections between them and the ſtate of Great Britain is and ought to be totally diſſolved; and that as free and independent ſtates, they have full power to levy war, conclude peace, contract alliances, eſtabliſh commerce, and to do all other acts and things which independent ſtates may of right do. And for the ſupport of

Two days after it was adopted by Congress and the day after it was first printed as a broadside, the Declaration was published in Philadelphia's *Pennsylvania Evening Post.* Three days later, translated into German, it appeared in the *Pennsylvanischer Staatsbote.* From Philadelphia copies of the broadside and the newspaper were carried to other cities and towns, where local printers published the Declaration as quickly as printing schedules allowed.

Thus it appeared in Baltimore on July 9, New York on July 10, New Haven on July 12, Providence on July 13, Exeter, N. H., on July 16, Boston and Newport, R. I., on July 18, Williamsburg, Va., on July 20—in all, in not fewer than 30 newspapers before the end of the month. On August 17 the *London Chronicle* published the Declaration, and thus began its dissemination through Great Britain and Europe.

Benjamin Rush. *Letter to Patrick Henry,* Philadelphia. July 16, 1776.

The "inestimable blessings" of freedom and independence would "be cheaply bought at the loss of all the towns and of every . . . third man in America." In such heated phrases Dr. Rush, physician, member of Congress, and Signer, assesses the significance of the Declaration of Independence in a letter to one of the first and most eloquent advocates of American rights.

Major Alexander Graydon. *Letter to John Lardner,* Mount Washington, [New York], July 18, 1776. HSP

Not every American, however, not even those in the army, thought the Declaration of Independence wise or timely, or that its consequences would be unmixed blessings. From Fort Washington on the northern end of Manhattan Island Major Graydon discussed such reservations frankly in a private letter.

The Declaration of Independancy is variously relish[ed] here, some approving, others condemning it. For [my] own part, I have not the least Objection did I kno[w] my Rulers and the Form of Government. Innovati[ons] are always dangerous particularly here, where the Populace have so great an Ascendancy & popular Governments I cou'd never approve of. However I acquiesce in the Measure as it became daily more necessary, altho' I am of Opinion that delaying it awhile longer cou'd have had no bad Tendency. . . But perhaps you will tell me that 'of two Evils we must chuse the least,' either submit to Britain or declare Independancy.—Granted! but there is no Reason that we should not have put it off as long [as] possible.—However the Matter is now settled, and Salvation depends upon supporting the Measure.

Charles Thomson. *Letter to John Dickinson,* Philadelphia, August 16, 1776 HSP

Consistent to the end in opposing independence, John Dickinson refused to sign the Declaration, and lost his seat in Congress. Charles Thomson, long a principal leader of the revolutionary movement in Pennsylvania and now secretary of Congress, here expresses regret that Dickinson's vote and subsequent withdrawal from political life had opened the way for inexperienced and unqualified persons to organize the new government of Pennsylvania.

"Our Declaration of Independancy has given Vigor to the Spirits of the People." It also required the new nation to organize and reorganize its institutions. Articles of confederation were under consideration, Adams writes; and plans were being drafted to establish relations with foreign governments and even to enter into alliances.

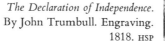

Samuel Adams. *Letter to Richard Henry Lee, Philadelphia, July 15, 1776.* APS

Congress Voting Independence. By Robert Edge Pine and/or Edward Savage. Oil on canvas. *ca.* 1788. HSP

The Declaration of Independence. By John Trumbull. Engraving. 1818. HSP

No single event in American history is so deeply impressed on the national memory as the Declaration of Independence, and no scene is more readily recognizable by Americans than that of Congress voting independence. Though the best known representation is by John Trumbull, Pine's is thought to be more accurately detailed. For example, it shows the Assembly Room (now called the Declaration Chamber) as it undoubtedly was in 1776. Some of the portraits of individuals are good likenesses.

This painting, like Trumbull's, shows Thomas Jefferson formally presenting the draft of the Declaration of Independence to John Hancock, president of Congress. The 70-year-old Benjamin Franklin is seated in a chair in the foreground.

In Congress, July 4, 1776. The Unanimous Declaration of the Thirteen United States of America. Facsimile. Washington: Benjamin Owen Tyler, 1818. APS

circumstances of our emigration and settlement here. We have appealed to their native

these usurpations, which would inevitably interrupt our connexions and correspondence

the necessity, which denounces our Separation, and hold them, as we hold the rest of ma

UNITED STATES of AMERICA, in General

of the world for the rectitude of our intentions. Do, in the Name, and by Authority

are, and of Right ought to be **FREE AND INDEPENDEN**

that all political connexion between them and the state of Great-Britain, is and ought to

full Power to levy War, conclude Peace, contract Alliances, establish Commerce

may of Right do. (**AND**) for the support of this **Declaration**, with a

pledge to each other our **LIVES,** our **FORTUNES,** and our sacred **HO**

John H

Wm Hooper

Joseph Hewes

John Penn

Button Gwinnett

Lyman Hall

Geo Walton.

Edward Rutledge

Tho? Heyward Junr

Samuel Chase

Wm Paca

Tho Stone

Charles Carroll of C

Department of State Thomas Lynch Junr
September 1, 1817.

Arthur Middleton

The foregoing copy of the declaration of
Independence, has been collated with the original
instrument and found correct. I have, myself,
examined the signatures to each. Those executed
by Mr. Tyler are curiously exact imitations; so
much so that it would be difficult if not
impossible for the closest scrutiny, to distinguish
them, were it not for the hand of time, from the
originals.

Richard Rush
Acting Secretary of State

George W

Richard H

Th Jeff

Benj Harr

Tho? Nelson jr

Francis Lightfo

Carter Braxt

Copied from the original Declaration of Independence in the Department of State, and Published by BENJAMIN OWEN TYLER Professor of Penmanship, City of

78

The Signers

"Gentlemen . . . most conspicuous for their talents and virtues"—Benjamin Rush. "Characters of the Revolutionary Patriots," 1776

magnanimity, and we have conjured them by the ties of our common kindred to ... avow ... have been deaf to the voice of justice and of consanguinity. We must, therefore, acquiesce in ... enemies in **WAR**, in **Peace Friends.** ———— We, therefore, the representatives of the ... ... Assembled, appealing to the **SUPREME JUDGE** ... people of these Colonies, solemnly publish and Declare, That these ... ... that they are Absolved from all Allegiance to the British Crown, and ... dissolved, and that as **Free and Independent States** they have ... ... to do all other Acts and Things which Independent States ... ... on the Protection of **DIVINE PROVIDENCE, WE** mutually —

Rob Morris
Benjamin Rush
Benj. Franklin
John Morton
Geo Clymer
Ja. Smith
Geo Taylor
James Wilson
Geo. Ross
Casar Rodney
Geo Read
Tho M. Kean

Wm Floyd
Phil. Livingston
Fran. Lewis
Lewis Morris

Rich Stockton
Jno Witherspoon
Fras Hopkinson
John Hart
Abra Clark

Josiah Bartlett
Wm Whipple
Sam. Adams
John Adams
Rob Treat Paine
Elbridge Gerry
Step. Hopkins
William Ellery
Roger Sherman
Sam. Huntington
Wm Williams
Oliver Wolcott
Matthew Thornton

...signed and executed the ornamental writing, and has been particular to copy the Facsimiles exact, and has also observed the same punctuation, and copied every Capital as in the original. Engraved by PETER MAVERICK

John Adams

John Adams (1735-1826). Massachusetts

One of the most powerful minds and influences in the formation of America, Adams was a member of the First and Second Continental Congresses, proposed Washington as commander-in-chief of the Army, was on the committee which drafted the Declaration, served with Franklin and Arthur Lee as one of the commissioners to France, was minister to Holland, a member of the American commission to negotiate the treaty of peace, 1783, and the first American minister to Great Britain. Subsequently he was Vice-President and President of the United States. For more than 60 years his warmest thoughts and highest hopes were for his country. He was, in the words of Benjamin Rush, "a real American in principle and conduct."

*Letter to Samuel Huntington, Amsterdam, December 31, 1780. HSP

Saml Adams

Samuel Adams (1722-1803). Massachusetts

For a generation before the outbreak of war in 1775 Adams spoke, wrote, planned, schemed, and agitated against British authority and for American independence. His arenas were the Massachusetts Assembly and the Boston Town Meeting. "Adams I believe has

the most thorough Understanding of Liberty, and her Resources, in the Temper and Character of the People, tho not in the Law and Constitution, as well as the most habitual, radical Love of it, of any of them," wrote his cousin John Adams, "—as well as the most correct, genteel and artful Pen." Again in John Adams' words: Samuel was "born and tempered a wedge of steel to split the knot of *lignum vitae*, which tied North America to Great Britain."

Letter to Peyton Randolph, Boston, January 1, 1775. HSP

Josiah Bartlett

Josiah Bartlett (1729-1795). New Hampshire

A physician who served in the New Hampshire Assembly, was a justice of the peace, and commanded militia, Bartlett was elected to the First Continental Congress, but did not attend. In the Second he showed himself, in Benjamin Rush's words, "warmly attached to the liberties of his country." After leaving Congress he was chief justice of the New Hampshire Superior Court, president of New Hampshire, and the state's first governor.

Letter to General Nathaniel Folsom, Philadelphia, November 23, 1775. HSP

Carter Braxton

Carter Braxton (1736-1797). Virginia

A planter who had spent several years in England, Braxton served several terms in the Virginia House of Burgesses before 1776. He was agreeable and sensible in public life, in private life an accomplished gentleman; but his political views, Benjamin Rush thought, were not sufficiently "detached . . . from his British prejudices." After leaving Congress he served many years in the Virginia legislature, where he supported Jefferson's bill for establishing religious freedom.

Letter to Jonathan Hudson, Williamsburg, November 29, 1777. HSP

Charles Carroll of Carrollton (1737-1832). Maryland

A Maryland Roman Catholic aristocrat, educated in France by English Jesuits and at the Inns of Court, London, he was perhaps the wealthiest man in the colonies in 1775. In the spring of 1776 he made a journey to Montreal with Benjamin Franklin, Samuel Chase, and his brother Father John Carroll, in what proved to be an unsuccessful effort to bring Canada to the side of the American colonies. Called "an inflexible patriot," he spoke seldom in Congress, but always sensibly and informedly. He was the last survivor of the 56 Signers.

Letter to_____, August 22, 1777. HSP

Samuel Chase (1741-1811). Maryland

Physically large, inclined to bully, liked by some, detested by many, Chase served 20 years in the Maryland Assembly and held a variety of other positions in government—sometimes simultaneously. John Adams characterized him as "violent and boisterous," and Benjamin Rush said "he possessed more learning than knowledge, and more of both than judgment." Though he opposed the Federal Constitution, after its adoption he was a strong Federalist, and was appointed by President Washington an associate justice of the Supreme Court. His conduct on the bench resulted in his impeachment; he was acquitted, but thereafter Supreme Court justices have generally observed high standards of good behavior and decorum.

(With Charles Carroll of Carrollton). Letter to General David Wooster, Montreal, May 25, 1776. HSP

Abraham Clark (1726-1794). New Jersey

A surveyor and farmer, who had been sheriff of Essex County, clerk of the Provincial Assembly, and secretary of the New Jersey Committee of Safety, Clark was plain-spoken, sometimes dour and cynical, quick to see the "weaknesses and defects of public men and measures." He strongly opposed privileges for lawyers and military men. In Congress he was "attentive to business and excelled in drawing up reports and resolutions." After the establishment of the Federal Government he served two terms in the House of Representatives.

Letter to Colonel Elias Dayton, Philadelphia, August 6, 1776. HSP

George Clymer (1739-1813).
Pennsylvania

A successful merchant in Philadelphia, Clymer was an early patriot, serving as captain of a volunteer military company and member of the Committee of Safety when the Revolution began. His colleague Benjamin Rush applied to him Lord Peterborough's encomium on William Law: "The mould in which this man's mind was cast was seldom used." As a member of the Federal Convention Clymer signed the Constitution, and in the Federal Government served a term in the House of Representatives.

Letter to Colonel Peter Grubb, Philadelphia, July 2, 1776. HSP

William Ellery (1727-1820).
Rhode Island

Ellery had a successful career of public service—deputy governor, naval officer, clerk of courts—before commencing the study of law at the age of 40. In Congress, where he served seven years, he was an effective committeeman—he held 14 appointments in 1777-78 alone.

He seldom spoke but often amused himself during debates by writing witty epigrams about his colleagues and Congress' business. After leaving Congress he served as chief justice of Rhode Island. President Washington appointed him collector of customs for Newport in 1790, and he held the post until his death. A learned man, on the morning he died he was reading Cicero.

Letter to General William Whipple, South Kingstown, Rhode Island, October 30, 1777. HSP

William Floyd (1734-1821). New York

A large landowner and major general of militia, he served in Congress almost continuously from 1774 to 1783. He seldom spoke, "but always voted with the zealous friends to liberty and independence." In the new Federal Government he served a term in Congress.

Letter to Governor George Clinton, Kingston, New York, October 10, 1777. HSP

Benjamin Franklin (1706-1790).
Pennsylvania

Printer, publisher, and journalist; provincial politician, intercolonial statesman, and diplomat; scientist, reformer, and philantropist, Franklin had had the most varied experiences and enjoyed the most extended reputation of all Americans on the eve of the Revolution. By example and precept he had improved the life of the community, and taught others how to do the same. He discovered the laws of electricity. As early as 1754 he drafted a plan of union for the British colonies in America, and since 1757 he had been the principal spokesman for America in Britain. At 70, the oldest man in Congress, he signed the Declaration and was appointed minister to France, where his diplomatic achievement was brilliant and indispensable. An admiring contemporary wrote of him that he snatched lightning from heaven and the scepter from tyrants. A modern biographer, with no less wonder, concluded that Franklin seemed more than any single man: rather "a harmonious human multitude."

Letter to Colonel Thomas McKean, Philadelphia, August 24, 1776. HSP

Elbridge Gerry (1744-1814). Massachusetts

Best known today for his part in the political redistricting of his state which is called "gerrymandering," Gerry in 1776 was "a respectable young merchant," in whom John Adams "found a faithfull Friend, and an ardent perservering Lover of his Country, who never hesitated to promote with all his Abilities and Industry the boldest measures reconcilable with prudence." He attended the Federal Convention but refused to sign the Constitution. He later served in Congress and as governor of his state, and in 1812 was elected Vice President of the United States.

Letter to John Wendell, Philadelphia, June 11, 1776. HSP

Button Gwinnett (1732-1777). Georgia

English-born, Gwinnett was a merchant in Savannah who was a justice of the peace and a member of the Georgia Assembly before the Revolution began. An admirer of the radical Pennsylvania State Constitution of 1776 (it provided for a unicameral legislature), he was influential in having Georgia adopt a similar basic law in 1777. He was acting President of the State but failed of election for the full term; and shortly afterwards died of wounds received in a duel. He is perhaps best known to the modern public because his autograph commands the highest price of all the Signers.

(With George Walton and Lyman Hall). Statement concerning Joseph Rice, Philadelphia, July 22, 1776. HSP

Lyman Hall

Lyman Hall (1724-1790). Georgia

First a minister, then a physician, finally a rice planter, Hall was a Connecticut man who settled in Georgia, where he was an early advocate of independence. John Adams described him and his fellow Georgia Signers as "intelligent and spirited Men, who made a powerful Addition to our Phalanx." During the war his house in Savannah and his plantation were destroyed. As governor of Georgia in 1783 he proposed that the legislature set aside a grant of land to support a state university—the foundation of Franklin College and the University of Georgia.

Letter to Jonathan Dickinson Sergeant, Philadelphia, July 17, 1775. HSP

John Hancock

John Hancock (1737-1793). Massachusetts

One of the principal leaders of the revolutionary movement in Massachusetts, Hancock was a rich merchant, who served several terms in the provincial Assembly and was president of the Provincial Congress in 1774, when he was sent to Congress. As president of that body, 1775-77, he was effective and popular, though

inclined to vanity. Believing in his own military capacities, he was disappointed when his colleague John Adams nominated Washington as commander-in-chief. He served nine terms as governor of Massachusetts. Dying in office, he was given a state funeral that must have satisfied even his taste for pomp.

Letter to George Washington, Philadelphia, August 22, 1776. HSP

Benj. Harrison

Benjamin Harrison (1726-1791). Virginia

A Virginia aristocrat, he was a member of the House of Burgesses continually from 1749 until the Revolution, serving often as its Speaker. He was one of the committee of Burgesses who issued a call for a Continental Congress in 1774, and was so firm in the cause that he said he "would have come on foot rather than not come" to Philadelphia. He was chairman of Congress' Committee of the Whole which discussed Richard Henry Lee's motion for independence in June 1776. After leaving Congress, Harrison served again in the Virginia House of Delegates.

Letter to the Pennsylvania Committee of Safety, [Philadelphia], May 12, 1776. HSP

John Hart

John Hart (1711?-1779). New Jersey

Described by Benjamin Rush as "a plain, honest, well-meaning Jersey farmer, with but little education, but with good sense and virtue eno' to discover and pursue the true interests of his country," Hart was a man of local influence—a member of the Provincial Assembly for 10 years, a judge, and a member of the New Jersey Provincial Congress in 1775, and of the Committee of Safety. After leaving Congress, he was Speaker of the first Assembly under the new State constitution of 1776 and chairman of the Council of Safety.

Letter to Francis Hopkinson, Princeton, September 12, 1776. HSP

Joseph Hewes (1730-1779).
North Carolina

A merchant, born of Quaker parents, of moderate views, reluctant to come to final separation from Britain, Hewes was convinced by John Adams of the popular strength of the independence movement in North Carolina: as Adams remembered, he "started suddenly upright, and lifting both his hands to Heaven, as if he had been in a trance, cried out, 'It is done! and I will abide by it,'" In Congress he was chairman of the Marine Committee, which got John Paul Jones (whom he knew) his first ship and "laid the first Foundations, the Corner stone of an American navy."

Letter to [Richard Caswell], Edenton, North Carolina, April 4, 1777. HSP

Thomas Heyward, Jr. (1746-1809).
South Carolina

Educated in the law at the Middle Temple, on his return from London Heyward was elected to the South Carolina Assembly, and was a member of the Council of Safety, which took over the functions of government in the province, 1775. Of amiable manners, with an appreciation of poetry and some talent for it, "on him," wrote John Adams, "We could always depend for sound Measures, though he seldom spoke in public." He was imprisoned after the fall of Charleston to the British, 1780, served some years as a judge, and was the founder and first president of the Agricultural Society of South Carolina.

Letter to Dr. John Morgan, Philadelphia, September 4, 1776. HSP

William Hooper (1742-1790).
North Carolina

A native of Boston, graduate of Harvard College, and a student of law under James Otis, Hooper settled in North Carolina in 1767, bringing to that colony some of New England's independence fervor. He served in the North Carolina Assembly and was a leader in the revolutionary movement, though strongly opposed to the more democratic aspirations of the frontiersmen. Benjamin Rush remembered him in Congress as "a sensible, sprightly young lawyer, and a rapid, but correct speaker," He lost heavily at the hands of the British during the war, and never regained his former political prominence and influence.

Letter to Joseph Hewes, Philadelphia, December 1, 1776. HSP

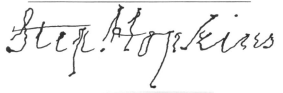

Stephen Hopkins (1707-1785). Rhode Island

Hopkins had a distinguished career of public service before coming to Congress —member of the General Assembly of Rhode Island and its speaker, chief justice of the Superior Court, governor, delegate to the Albany Congress which drafted a Plan of Union for the colonies, 1754. In Congress "his Experience and Judgment were very Usefull," John Adams wrote; but his principal service to his colleagues was of another kind: "When the Business of the Evening was over, he kept Us in Conversation till Eleven and sometimes twelve O Clock. His Custom was to drink nothing all day nor till Eight O Clock, in the Evening, and then his Beveredge was Jamaica Spirit and Water. It gave him Wit, Humour, Anecdotes, Science and Learning. . . . Hopkins never drank to excess, but all he drank was immediately not only converted into Wit, Sense, Knowledge and good humour, but inspired Us all with similar qualities."

Letter to Ruth G. Hopkins, Philadelphia, November 15, 1775. HSP

Francis Hopkinson (1737-1791). New Jersey

Though a lawyer by profession, Hopkinson is best known as one of the first American musicians, poets, and essayists. "He is one of your pretty little, curious ingenious Men," wrote John Adams on meeting him. "His Head is not bigger, than a large Apple." In Congress he served effectively as chairman of the Continental Navy Board and as Treasurer of Loans, and he designed the American flag. He organized and directed 20,000 marchers in "the Grand Federal Procession" in Philadelphia on July 4, 1788, which signalized the ratification of the Federal Constitution. President Washington appointed him a federal judge in 1789.

(With John Nixon and John Wharton). Letter to Council of Safety of Pennsylvania, [Philadelphia], April 10, 1777. HSP

Samuel Huntington (1731-1796). Connecticut

Huntington served in Congress for eight years, several of them as president; and showed himself to be, in Benjamin Rush's phrase, "a sensible, candid and worthy man, and wholly free from State prejudices." He was a lawyer, who had served some years in the Connecticut Assembly and as a judge of the Superior Court of the Province.

After leaving Congress in 1784, he became chief justice of the court, and in 1786 he was chosen governor.

Letter to Rev. James Cogswell, Philadelphia, March 30, 1776. HSP

Thomas Jefferson (1743-1826). Virginia

Of the many and various accomplishments of a long life, he chose three by which he wished most to be remembered—that he was "Author of the Declaration of American Independence, of the Statute of Virginia for religious freedom, & Father of the University of Virginia."
His genius, declared his friend Benjamin Rush, was "of the first order. It was universal in its objects."

(With Patrick Henry, Jr., Richard Henry Lee, Edmund Pendleton, and Benjamin Harrison). Letter to the President of the Virginia Convention [Peyton Randolph], Philadelphia, July 11, 1775. HSP

Francis Lightfoot Lee (1734-1797). Virginia

A member of the Virginia House of Burgesses for almost 20 years before coming to Congress, Lee was considered a more ardent patriot than his older brother Richard Henry Lee, who was better known; Benjamin Rush thought

his mind was "more acute and correct" than his brother's. In Congress he was an excellent committee-man and had considerable influence. "I never knew him wrong eventually upon any question," was Rush's judgment.

Letter to Thomas Jefferson, Philadelphia, September 17, 1776. HSP

Richard Henry Lee (1732-1794). Virginia

The author of the famous resolution of June 7, 1776, "That these United Colonies are, and of right ought to be, free and independent States," was a Virginia aristocrat who opposed the Stamp Act, worked harmoniously with Patrick Henry, and was warmly supported by the New Englanders in Congress for his strong stand for independence. He was, Jefferson said, "eloquent, bold and ever watchful at his post." Shortly after offering his resolution he returned to Virginia to participate in the Virginia constitutional convention, and so could not vote for his own motion. He opposed the Federal Constitution but under the new government served as United States senator. Fearful of the consequences of giving Congress power over both "purse and sword," he warned: "The first maxim of a man who loves liberty should be never to grant to Rulers an atom of power that is not most clearly & indispensably necessary for the safety and well-being of Society."

Letter to James Searle, "Chantilly," Virginia, August 7, 1779. HSP

Francis Lewis (1713-1803). New York

A native of Wales, a successful merchant who had retired before the Revolution began, Lewis took a moderate stand in politics. In Congress he was valuable in committee work, and, in Benjamin Rush's judgment, was "a very honest man." During the war his house was destroyed by the British, his wife died of the effects of imprisonment by the enemy, and he poured most of his wealth into the American cause. The last 20 years of his life he lived retired in the homes of his sons.

Letter to Governor Thomas Johnston, Baltimore, January 27, 1777. HSP

Philip Livingston (1716-1778). New York

Member of one of the rich manorial families of New York, Livingston was an aristocrat, "blunt but honest," with a fund of knowledge and experience in commercial matters, which he put at the service of Congress. He was also a philanthropist—one of the first to advocate the founding of King's (now Columbia) College, benefactor of Yale College, a founder of the New York Society Library, the New York Hospital and the New York Chamber of Commerce, and president of the St. Andrews Society of New York. He died in York, Pa., where Congress had moved when the British occupied Philadelphia.

Letter to Robert Livingston, Hurley, New York, March 25, 1778. HSP

Thomas Lynch, Jr. (1749-1779). South Carolina

Educated at Eton, Cambridge, and the Middle Temple, London, Lynch soon quit the practice of law to manage his plantation. He was a delegate to the South Carolina Provincial Congress in 1775, and a member of the General Assembly of that state. Benjamin Rush thought him a man of only moderate ability and inclined to be fearful in hard circumstances. He was lost at sea at 30, and his autograph is the scarcest of all the Signers' signatures.

Signature (with letter of explanation from General James Hamilton, the Signer's nephew, to Robert Gilmor, a collector of autographs, Charleston, April 6, 1836). HSP

Thomas McKean (1734-1817). Delaware

Born in Pennsylvania, McKean spent the early years of his public life in the

service of Delaware, then for some years held offices in both Delaware and Pennsylvania simultaneously, and ended his political career as a three-term governor of Pennsylvania. Though cold, vain, and often tactless, McKean was able, energetic, honest, and independent. He voted for independence but, having returned to Delaware to help draft a constitution for the state, he did not actually affix his signature to the Declaration until some time in 1777.

Letter to Colonel John Nixon, [Philadelphia], February 3, 1776. HSP

Arthur Middleton (1742-1787). South Carolina

Though he was a rich aristocrat, who had read law at the Middle Temple, London, and was an excellent classical scholar, Middleton was a leader of the South Carolina patriots from 1774 onward. John Adams thought "he had little Information and less Argument;" he was sometimes rude and sarcastic in debate, and refused to serve on Congress' Committee on Accounts, saying that "he hated accounts, did not even keep his own, and knew nothing about them." After leaving Congress he was elected governor of South Carolina, but refused to serve; but he held a variety of other state offices.

Letter to Thomas Burke, Charleston, October 18, 1779. HSP

Lewis Morris (1726-1798). New York

Lord of the Manor of Morrisania on the Hudson River in Westchester County, he took a lead in the call for a provincial congress in 1775. He left Congress in June 1776 to command the Westchester County militia, but returned in September, when he signed the Declaration. Three sons served in the Continental Army at one time. He suffered heavy losses to his property from the enemy's depredations, but he never complained or wavered. "Every attachment of his heart," wrote Benjamin Rush, "yielded to his love of his country."

Letter to Governor George Clinton, Camp at White Plains, New York, September 6, 1778. HSP

Robert Morris (1734-1806). Pennsylvania

One of the richest merchants in Philadelphia, Morris opposed the Stamp Act, but was slow in committing himself to the patriot cause. He questioned the timing of the Declaration, but signed the document and later publicly acknowledged he had been mistaken. "I think he has a masterly

Understanding, an open Temper and an honest Heart," John Adams wrote. In the darkest days of the Revolution Congress made him Superintendent of Finance—virtually financial dictator; his policies restored the nation's credit. "The United States may command every thing I have," Morris declared, "except my integrity. . . ." He was a member of the Constitutional Convention, and under the Federal Government served a term as United States senator.

(With Josiah Bartlett, Philip Livingston, Joseph Hewes, Thomas McKean, and Richard Henry Lee). Letter to William Bingham, Philadelphia, September 24, 1776. HSP

John Morton

NO AUTHENTIC
PORTRAIT
KNOWN

John Morton (1724-1777). Pennsylvania

A surveyor by profession, Morton had considerable experience in public affairs as member of the Pennsylvania Assembly and its speaker, delegate to the Stamp Act Congress, justice of the peace, sheriff, judge of the Chester County Court of Common Pleas, and associate justice of the Provincial Supreme Court. He cast the deciding vote in the Pennsylvania delegation in support of Richard Henry Lee's resolution for independence. He died soon after signing the Declaration, but Benjamin Rush remembered him as "a plain farmer . . . [who] was well acquainted with the principles of government and public business."

Letter to General Anthony Wayne, Philadelphia, August 16, 1776. HSP

Thos Nelson jr.

Thomas Nelson, Jr. (1738-1789). Virginia

Educated at Trinity College, Cambridge, he was first elected to the Virginia House of Burgesses while still on his journey home. He was an early advocate of independence. In Congress he spoke well and, despite his weight, was alert and lively. He succeeded Thomas Jefferson as governor of Virginia in 1781; and in the siege of Yorktown (in which his house was heavily damaged) he joined Washington at the head of 3000 militia.

Letter to John Page, Philadelphia, July 16, 1776. HSP

Wm Paca

William Paca (1740-1799). Maryland

A lawyer trained at the Inns of Court, London, Paca was a member of the Maryland Provincial Assembly, of the state's Council of Safety, and of Maryland's first State Senate. During the Revolution he spent thousands of pounds of his own fortune to support the patriot cause. In Congress he impressed John Adams as "a deliberater," and Benjamin Rush thought his influence and reputation were less than his abilities deserved because he loved his ease too much. After leaving

Congress he served his state as chief judge of the Superior Court and governor. President Washington appointed him a federal judge in 1789.

(With Thomas Johnson, Jr. and Samuel Chase). Letter to Committee of Safety of Pennsylvania, Philadelphia, March 19, 1776. HSP

Robert Treat Paine (1731-1814). Massachusetts

In the trial of the British soldiers involved in the Boston Massacre Paine was one of the prosecutors, while John Adams was one of the defense counsel. Though Paine had an amiable temper and was droll and witty in speech and conversation, he "opposed nearly every measure that was proposed by other people," Benjamin Rush wrote, "and hence he got the name of 'The Objection Maker' in Congress." He was, however, eminently useful in committees, which he attended regularly and punctually. After leaving Congress he served as attorney general of Massachusetts, helped draft the State's Constitution in 1779-80, and sat for 14 years on the State Supreme Court.

Letter to General Philip Schuyler, Philadelphia, January 3, 1776. HSP

John Penn (1741-1788). North Carolina

A native of Virginia, where he read law with Edmund Pendleton (a member of the first Continental Congress), Penn settled in North Carolina, practiced his profession and became a local leader in the patriotic cause. "My first wish," he said, "is that America may be free; the second is that she may be restored to Great Britain in peace and harmony upon Just terms."

Letter to Richard Caswell, Philadelphia, June 25, 1777. HSP

George Read (1733-1798). Delaware

A lawyer who was attorney general of Delaware before the Revolution, Read protested the Stamp Act and in the conflict between the colonies and Britain was a moderate, like John Dickinson; and, like Dickinson, he voted against independence on July 2, 1776. However, he signed the Declaration later. "He was firm, without violence, in all his purposes," wrote Benjamin Rush of him in Congress, "and was much respected by all his acquaintances." In the Federal Convention he was a tireless—and some thought tiresome—advocate of the smaller states. In the Federal Government he was one of Delaware's first two senators, resigning in 1793 to become chief justice of that state.

Letter to George Washington, Newark, Delaware, November 25, 1777. HSP

Caesar Rodney (1728-1784). Delaware

Like others of his class and place Rodney held a succession of public offices before the Revolution—sheriff of Kent County, justice of the peace, member of the Assembly and its speaker, judge of the Superior Court, captain of militia. He is famous for his breakneck ride from Dover to Philadelphia to cast his vote for independence. John Adams thought him "the oddest looking Man in the World. . . . Yet there is Sense and Fire, Spirit, Wit and Humour in his Countenance." After leaving Congress Rodney served as major general of the Delaware militia and as president of the State.

Letter to Thomas Rodney, Philadelphia, May 29, 1776. HSP

George Ross (1730-1779). Pennsylvania

A successful lawyer, a member of the Pennsylvania Assembly for several years before the Revolution, Ross was witty and good humored, and enjoyed the comforts of life. In Congress, Benjamin Rush recalled, his speeches commanded attention; but he disliked committee work and other business and so had little influence in that body. After leaving Congress he became judge of admiralty, but died soon afterwards. On his deathbed—in mid-July—he announced with satisfaction that he was going on a long journey to a cool place —"there were most excellent wines there"—and that he should fare very well.

Letter to James Wilson, Elizabeth Town, New Jersey, November 28, 1776. HSP

Benjamin Rush (1745-1813). Pennsylvania

Though his political achievement was almost limited to his signing the Declaration, Rush was perhaps the most famous physician in the United States when he died, and he had a parallel career of equal distinction as a moralist and reformer. He worked to abolish the slave trade and slavery, to improve the lot of prisoners and abolish capital punishment, to provide schools for women, blacks, and poor children. He was a tireless advocate of temperance, peace, and of an American education to train Americans for citizenship and public service. In the Pennsylvania Hospital he treated the insane with compassion and understanding. "I know of no Character living or dead," declared his friend John Adams, "who has done more real good for America."

Letter to James Searle, York Town, Pennsylvania, January 29, 1778. HSP

Edward Rutledge

Edward Rutledge (1749-1800).
South Carolina

Trained in the law in England, a
member of the planter aristocracy of
South Carolina, he was a delegate to
the First Continental Congress, where
his appearance and manner excited John
Adams' contempt:"Young Ned Rutledge
is a perfect Bob o'Lincoln—a Swallow—
a Sparrow—a Peacock—excessively
vain, excessively weak, and excessively
variable and unsteady—jejeune, inane,
and puerile." The judgment was too
harsh. Rutledge played an important
role in the decision of his delegation
to vote for independence. At 27 he was
the youngest Signer.

Letter to Dr. John Morgan, [Philadelphia],
July 1, 1776. HSP

Roger Sherman

Roger Sherman (1721-1793).
Connecticut

By trade a shoemaker, Sherman became
well informed through reading; he
acquired land, was elected to local and
provincial offices, became a lawyer,
then a merchant. He was one of the
committee of five who drafted the
Declaration, but seems to have had no
influence on content or form. As his
portrait by Earle shows, he was, in

John Adams' words, "an old Puritan,
as honest as an Angell and as firm in
the Cause of American Independence as
Mount Atlass." In the Constitutional
Convention, of which he was a member,
his rustic appearance and Yankee speech
and accent seemed "grotesque and
laughable;—and yet," wrote a colleague,
"no Man has a better Heart or a clearer
Head. If he cannot embellish, he can
furnish thoughts that are wise and
useful." He served in both the House
of Representatives and the Senate
under the Federal Government.

Letter to Governor Jonathan Trumbull, Philadelphia,
April 17, 1777. HSP

Jas. Smith

James Smith (1719-1806). Pennsylvania

Born in Northern Ireland, brought to
Pennsylvania as a lad, Smith was a
surveyor on the frontier, then became
a lawyer (successful) and ironmaster
(unsuccessful). He was a leader of
back-country sentiment for independence
and the colonel of the militia of York
County. His speeches in Congress were
witty, humorous, and often entertaining.
After leaving Congress, he served in
the State Assembly and was a judge of
the High Court of Errors and Appeals;
but mostly he devoted himself to his
legal practice.

Letter to the Lancaster County Committee of Safety,
York Town, Pennsylvania, January 1, 1776. HSP

Richard Stockton (1730–1781).
New Jersey

A lawyer with a large practice, Stockton served on the Governor's Council in New Jersey and as a member of the provincial Supreme Court. A graduate and trustee of the College of New Jersey, he was instrumental in bringing his fellow delegate John Witherspoon to America to head the institution. "His habits as a lawyer and a judge," wrote his son-in-law, "produced in him a respect for the British constitution, but this did not lessen his attachment to the independence of the United States." That attachment was tested soon after he signed the Declaration, for he was captured by the British, was badly treated during imprisonment, and never fully recovered his health thereafter. His home "Morven" in Princeton is now the official residence of the governors of New Jersey.

Letter to Mrs. Elizabeth Ferguson, "Morven,"
Princeton, February 26, 1777. HSP

Thomas Stone (1743–1787). Maryland

An able lawyer of moderate political views, Stone is little known because he rarely spoke in Congress, held no outstanding office, left few papers, and died relatively young. "A friend to universal liberty," he sometimes deluded himself "on plain subjects," Benjamin Rush remembered, citing as an example Stone's assertion that "he had never known a single instance of a negro being contented in slavery." After leaving Congress, Stone served several years in the Maryland State Senate.

Letter to Matthew Tilghman, Philadelphia,
October 11, 1776. HSP

George Taylor (1716–1781).
Pennsylvania

A native of Northern Ireland, an ironmaster in Pennsylvania, Taylor was a member of the Provincial Assembly, a justice of the peace and judge of county courts, and a colonel of militia. In provincial politics before 1775 he had consistently opposed British policies; in Congress, except for voting for independence, he seems not to have distinguished himself in any way.

Letter to Timothy Matlack, Durham, Pennsylvania,
May 24, 1777. HSP

Matthew Thornton (1714–1803).
New Hampshire

Born in Northern Ireland, by profession a physician, Thornton was a military surgeon on the expedition to Louisbourg, 1745, colonel of militia, a justice of the peace, and president of the New Hampshire Provincial Congress in 1775. Elected to Congress in September 1776, he signed the Declaration in November. "As droll and funny as Tristram Shandy," Thornton had a fund of anecdotes with which he clinched his arguments and entertained his fellow delegates. After leaving Congress he was an associate judge of the Superior Court of New Hampshire. His gravestone characterizes him as "An Honest Man."

Letter to Meshech Weare, Philadelphia, April 2, 1777. HSP

George Walton (1741-1804). Georgia

Born in Virginia, apprenticed to a carpenter, largely self-taught, he was admitted to legal practice in Georgia in 1774. He took an early part in the Revolutionary movement and was secretary of the Provincial Congress and president of the Council of Safety. During the war he fought at the siege of Savannah, 1779, where he was wounded and made prisoner. He was subsequently chief justice of Georgia, governor of the State, and a United States senator.

Letter to General Lachlan McIntosh, Savannah, Georgia, April 26, 1778. HSP

William Whipple (1730-1785). New Hampshire

Formerly a sea captain who had engaged in the slave trade, Whipple gave up the sea for a merchant's life ashore. He held violent sentiments toward Loyalists: "I think it high time they were all Hung or Banished." He commanded troops at the battle of Saratoga, 1777. After the war he was an associate judge of the Superior Court of his state.

Letter to———, Portsmouth, New Hampshire, September 15, 1776. HSP

William Williams (1731-1811). Connecticut

Williams held a number of local and provincial offices in Connecticut before the Revolution, to which he gave himself, his pen, and his wealth. Though he voted for independence, he disapproved Philadelphia's celebration of July 4 in 1777 as a waste. "A great Expenditure of Liquor, Powder &c. took up the Day, and of Candles thro the City good part of the night," he reported grumpily. "I suppose and I conclude much Tory unilluminated Glass will want replacing &c." After leaving Congress he held county judicial posts in Connecticut almost until his death.

Letter to Colonel Jedediah Elderkind, Lebanon, Connecticut, June 6, 1777. HSP

James Wilson

James Wilson (1742-1798).
Pennsylvania

Born in Scotland, trained by John Dickinson, Wilson was a student of constitutional law. "Government seems to have been his peculiar Study," wrote a contemporary, "all the political institutions of the World he knows in detail, and can trace the causes and effects of every revolution from the earliest stages of the Greecian commonwealth down to the present time." He denied that Parliament had any authority over the colonies: "All the different members of the British empire are *distinct states, independent of each other, but connected together under the same sovereign.*" Of him in Congress Benjamin Rush wrote that "his mind, while he spoke, was one blaze of light." With James Madison he was the principal author of the Federal Constitution. President Washington appointed him one of the first associate justices of the Supreme Court.

Letter to Jasper Yeates, Philadelphia, July 10, 1776. HSP

John Witherspoon (1723-1794).
New Jersey

Born and educated in Scotland, where he was a Presbyterian clergyman for 23 years, Witherspoon became president of the College of New Jersey at Princeton in 1768. He believed that education should fit a man for public services. John Adams said of him in 1774 that he was "as high a Son of Liberty as any Man in America." Though Witherspoon served some years in Congress, the fact that he was a clergyman limited his influence. After the war he divided his energies between continued public services and the revival of the College, much hurt by the war. Noting the use and abuse of the English language in the United States, he coined the word "Americanism" to describe them.

Letter to David Witherspoon, Philadelphia, November 15, 1776. HSP

Oliver Wolcott (1726-1797).
Connecticut

A lawyer who had been a county sheriff, county judge, and member of the Connecticut Assembly, Wolcott alternated service in Congress with service in the field. Absent from Congress on August 2, 1776, he signed the Declaration on his return in October. Thomas Rodney's judgment was balanced: "a man of Integrity, is very candid in Debate and open to Conviction and does not want abilities; but does not appear to be possessed of much political knowledge." He was elected governor of Connecticut in 1796.

Letter to Deputy Governor Matthew Griswold, New York, July 1, 1776. HSP

George Wythe

George Wythe (1726-1806). Virginia

One of the ablest lawyers in Congress, Wythe had served in the Virginia House of Burgesses and been its clerk before coming to Congress. He was Thomas Jefferson's law teacher. He designed the state seal of Virginia with its republican motto: "Sic semper tyrannis." After leaving Congress he was appointed chancellor of the Commonwealth. One who served with him in the Federal Convention wrote of Wythe: "He is remarkable for his exemplary life, and universally esteemed for his good principles. No Man it is said understands the history of Government better than Mr. Wythe . . . yet from his too favorable opinion of Men, he is no great politician." He died from poisoning by one of his servants.

Letter to George Washington, Williamsburg, October 25, 1781. HSP

This is the only known copy of the Declaration printed on vellum. It was made after the first printing on July 4-5 and before July 19, and from a different setting of type.

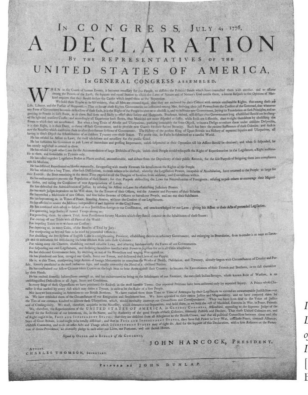

In Congress, July 4, 1776. A Declaration By the Representatives of the United States of America, In General Congress assembled. [Philadelphia]: John Dunlap, [1776]. Broadside on vellum. APS

Victory
and Defeat,
1777

"There now appeared no doubt of the ability and resolution of the States to maintain their independency"—Arthur Lee. *Journal*, December 6, 1777

General George Washington at Princeton. By Charles Peale Polk. Oil on canvas. HSP

Robert Morris for the Committee of Correspondence. *Letter to the American Commissioners in Paris,* Philadelphia, March 28, 1777. APS

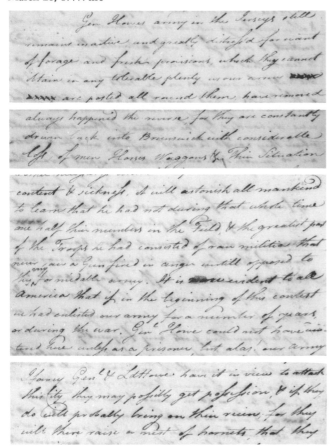

George Washington. *Letter to General Lord Stirling,* Camp near the Clove, July 24, 1777. HSP

Writing to the American Commissioners in France in the spring of 1777, Robert Morris reported that after defeat at Princeton, "Gen. Howes army in the Jerseys still remains inactive and greatly distress'd for want of forage and fresh provisions, which they cannot obtain in any tolerable plenty as our army are posted all round them." The British troops on forays were "constantly driven back into Brunswick with considerable loss" amounting to three or four thousand killed or taken. The British were plagued with desertion, yet Washington never had enough strength to carry destruction to them, for "it will astonish all mankind to learn that he had not during that whole time one half their numbers in the Field," many of them *raw militia that never saw a Gun fired in anger*" and were really quite undependable over the long haul compared to enlisted regular troops. Morris was confident that "the Garrison at Ticonderoga will be strong enough to dispute the passage" of the British, and predicted that if the Howes attacked and took Philadelphia, it "will probably bring on their ruin, for they will there raise a nest of hornets, that they do not expect and are taught to believe very differently."

Still concerned with present military realities in northern Jersey, Washington wrote Lord Stirling at Peekskill in late July that he had made plans to cover Philadelphia while still worrying the British. He discussed the possibility of a campaign against New York City; but, more realistically, noted the British fleet movements in the harbor, where "170 Sail of Topsail Vessels and about 50 or 60 smaller ones—this with the Report of the Pilots being Southern ones," led to the idea that Philadelphia was their target. With the British in "absolute Command of the Water," Washington realized that the American army at that point could only be observers and await the enemy's moves.

In COUNCIL.

PHILADELPHIA, April 9, 1777.

To the PEOPLE of *Pennsylvania.*

BY the Intelligence which the Council have this Day received from General *Putnam,* the Enemy are in Motion toward *South-Amboy,* and it is probable they will, once more, attempt to pass through *New-Jersey,* and endeavour to gain Possession of the City of *Philadelphia.*

The Council think it a Duty which they owe to the Public, to give them the earliest Intelligence of the Movements of the Enemy, that every possible Effort may be made effectually to oppose them, and prevent the many great Inconveniencies and disagreeable Consequences which must arise from the Loss of the City—Consequences which will affect not only the People of *Philadelphia* and the State of *Pennsylvania,* but also the whole Continent of *America.* This City has once been saved by the vigorous, manly Efforts of a few brave Associators, who generously stepped forward in the Defence of their Country—and it has been repeatedly and justly observed, and ought to be acknowledged as a signal Evidence of the Favour of Divine Providence, that the Lives of the Militia in every Battle, during this just War, has been remarkably spared—Confiding, therefore, in the Continuance of his Blessing who is indeed the GOD of Armies, let every Man among us hold himself ready to march into the Field whenever he shall be called upon so to do.—If the Enemy really intend to make an Attack on this State, no Time should be lost, every Moment should be employed in putting ourselves in perfect Readiness to repel them.

The Inconveniences which naturally and unavoidably arise from the Militia taking the Field, induceth the Council to wait as long as may be consistent with the Safety of the State, before they call them to Arms—In Justice, therefore, to yourselves and Posterity, we entreat you TO BE READY—for whenever the Time shall come wherein you must either tamely submit yourselves to the immediate Insults of haughty Tyrants, whose Lust and Avarice will make a Prey of *every Thing* which human Beings, while they retain their Senses, esteem worth possessing—or bravely determine to oppose your Enemies in the Field—the Notice will be short—the Call must and will be sudden—and it is too probable may happen in a few Days.

The Militia of this State, it is feared, cannot be arranged under the Law in Time for the present Emergency—yet we have not the least Doubt but that the same Spirit of Liberty which blazed forth in the Winter Campaign, will animate every virtuous Breast to act once more on the same generous Principles which, in the Depth of Winter, led you forward to a Harvest of Glory on the Hills of *Princetown*—The Cause is the same—and the Prize we contend for, far from losing its Lustre, is become more valuable to us by the Price which we have already paid for it.

Those who shall go into the Field on the present Occasion will be considered as having taken their Tour of Duty, and will not be called upon again until the whole Militia of the State shall have served in Turn, agreeable to the Spirit of the Militia Law.

CONGRESS propose to form a Camp near the City of *Philadelphia,* to which the Militia of *Pennsylvania* will, when called upon, repair.—Arms, Tents and the necessary Camp Equipage are provided, and the utmost Attention will be given to the Measures necessary to make a Spring Campaign as agreeable to you as possible.

It is on your own Virtue and Firmness, next to the Care and Protection of Heaven, that you must depend for your Liberty and Safety;—and a spirited Conduct in this Time of Danger will fix your Character both at home and abroad.

THOMAS WHARTON, jun. PRESIDENT.

Thomas Wharton, Jr. *In Council. Philadelphia, April 9, 1777. To the People of Pennsylvania.* Philadelphia: Styner and Cist, [1777]. Broadside. HSP

Morris' fear that the British would attack Philadelphia, the capital of the country and its most important city, was echoed in this warning in early April 1777 that that was a real possibility. The Pennsylvania Council under its president Thomas Wharton, Jr. called on "every Man among us [to] hold himself ready to march into the Field," warning them "TO BE READY—for whenever the Time shall come wherein you must either tamely submit yourselves to the immediate Insults of haughty Tyrants, whose Lust and Avarice will make a Prey of *every Thing* which human Beings . . . esteem worth possessing." Confident that the "Spirit of Liberty which blazed forth in the Winter Campaign" just ended and reaped a "Harvest of Glory on the Hills of Princetown," was not extinct, the state called on the militia to be ready when needed to repulse the invaders in "a Spring campaign as agreeable to you as possible."

Map of the Coastline from Long Island to Cape Henry. Manuscript. HSP

The spring passed without the attack Wharton expected, for the British under General Howe withdrew to safe quarters in New York City, leaving in the Jersey fields some of their Loyalist allies. But the British commander, lacking firm direction from London, planned to end the rebel uprising by seizing Philadelphia after all. He had two choices: to go by sea around Cape May and up the Delaware, which was heavily fortified; or to take the route, more than five times long, up Chespeake Bay and thence overland to the capital. Howe chose the latter route, so that his troops were confined to transports at sea for many extra days in the heat of a Chesapeake Bay summer. They disembarked at the head of the bay in mid-August.

My Dear Polly   Naamans Creek 26th Augst 1777

The Army are all on their march
and now pasing by this place in Order to
meet Genl Howe who has landed about thirty
Miles from here — just after I had wrote
the Inclosd — I Recd Orders to put myself
at the Head of my Division, and push with
all posible Dispatch for Wilmington, where
we shall Encamp this Evening — and the
Day after tomorrow in all probability we
shall try the Mettle of the British Troops
who seem Determined to push for Phila —

Give my best and Kindest Compliments
to our Mothers & Sisters and kiss our little
Girl and Boy for me Adieu my Dear Polly
and believe me with true Affection

Yours yours
Anty Wayne

Anthony Wayne. *Letter to his wife,* Naaman's Creek near Brandywine, August 26, 1777. HSP

General Wayne told his wife Polly in late August, that the American army on its way to meet Howe would "push with all possible Dispatch for Wilmington" to make a camp before "we shall try the mettle of the British Troops who seem determined to push" for Philadelphia. Knowing he would soon be in battle, he asked Polly to "kiss our Little Girl and Boy for me."

Aquila Giles. *Letter to Jonathan Potts,* Philadelphia, August 28, 1777. HSP

Washington's army of 10,000 men marched through Philadelphia on August 24 and put themselves between Philadelphia and the British, who had landed "at the mouth of Elk River in Maryland," where their fleet lay at anchor. General John Sullivan was expected to join Washington with 2,000 men. Giles, like many other citizens, expected an American victory.

George Washington.
Letter to John Cadwalader,
Wilmington, August 28,
1777. HSP

Wilmington Augt 28th 1777.

Dr Sir.

General Howe has advanced part of his Force about Two miles this side the Head of Elk, and from the information of Deserters and Prisoners, there is reason to believe, he is either marching or soon will be towards Philadelphia. If that is his Object, and of which there can be but little doubt, I think many important advantages would be derived from the Militia's hanging on his Rear or Right Flank, after he leaves Elk, while he is opposed by this Army in Front or in such other way as shall seem most adviseable from circumstances. But there I am wholly at a loss to whom to address myself respecting the Militia on the Eastern Shore, not knowing their Officers or where they are assembling. The [illegible] to point out Genl Smallwood

[illegible] Subject. For the requisition I have made, I shall offer no excuse. It is the result of necessity and founded in the most implicit confidence that you are, and will be ready upon all occasions to afford every aid in your power to advance the true interest and happiness of your Country. Influenced by these considerations I have made it, and have only to add that I am

with great regard & esteem
Dr Sir
Yr most Obedt Servt
Go Washington

P.S.
Several deserters have come in to day and our parties made between thirty & forty prisoners—

Meanwhile Washington was planning his moves. To General Cadwalader on August 28, he noted Howe's advance toward Philadelphia. Washington had clear ideas on his objectives, but was unsure how much he should rely on the militia of the Eastern Shore of Maryland; and he asked for Cadwalader's help. He appreciated that Cadwalader's "situation in this instance will be delicate and not a little embarrassing. I feel myself in that predicament." And a predicament it was.

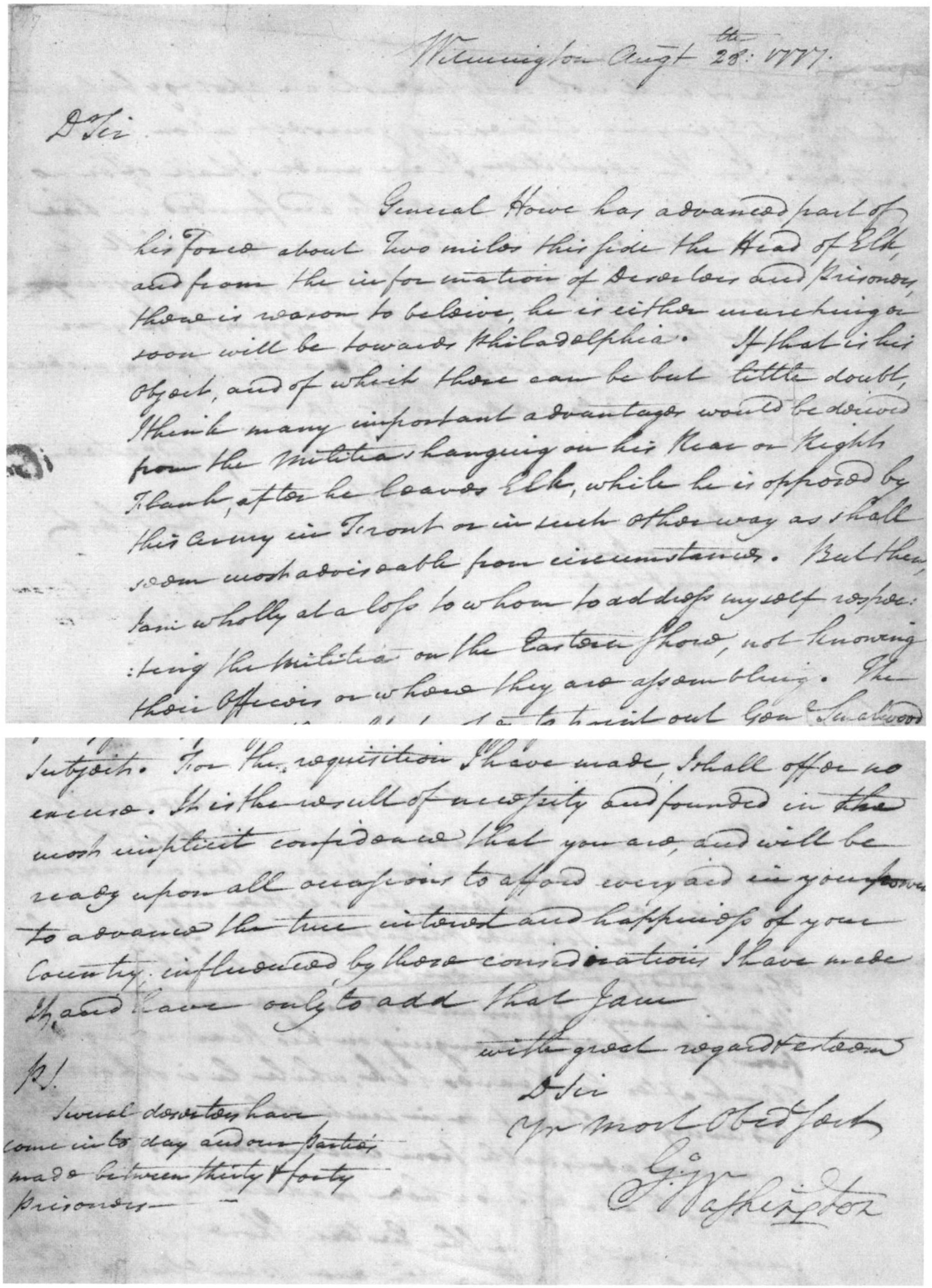

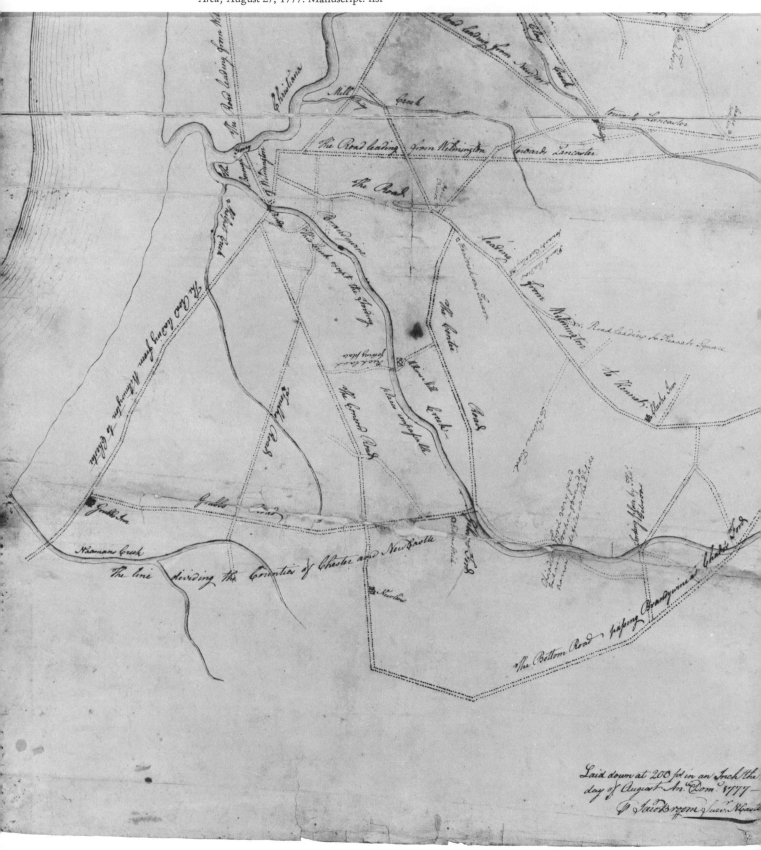

When the two armies met on the Brandywine the British had the advantage of numbers and attack, while Washington lacked accurate information about the terrain and the enemy's movements. "A contrariety of intelligence, in a critical and important point," he reported of the battle, "contributed greatly, if it did not entirely bring on the misfortunes of the day." This map was the Commander-in-Chief's, and bears many additions in his hand.

CHESTER, September 11, 1777. *Twelve o'Clock at Night.*

SIR,

I AM forry to inform you that in this day's engagement we have been obliged to leave the enemy maf-
ters of the field. Unfortunately the intelligence received of the enemy's advancing up the Brandywine,
and croffing at a Ford about fix miles above us, was uncertain and contradictory, notwithftanding all my
pains to get the beft. This prevented my making a difpofition adequate to the force, with which the enemy attacked us on our right ; in confequence of which the troops firft engaged were obliged to retire before they could be reinforced.—In the midft of the attack on the right, that body of the enemy which
remained on the other fide of Chad's Ford, croffed it, and attacked the divifion there under the command
of General Wayne and the light troops under General Maxwell ; who after a fevere conflict alfo retired.
The Militia under the command of General Armftrong, being pofted at a Ford about two miles below
Chad's, had no opportunity of engaging. But though we fought under many difadvantages, and were
from the caufes above mentioned, obliged to retire ; yet our lofs of men is not, I am perfuaded, very confiderable ; I believe much lefs than the enemy's. We have alfo loft feven or eight pieces of cannon, according to the beft information I can at prefent obtain.—The baggage having been previoufly moved off
is all fecure ; faving the men's blankets, which being at their backs, many of them doubtlefs were loft.

I have directed all the troops to affemble behind Chefter, where they are now arranging for this night.—
Notwithftanding the misfortune of the day, I am happy to find the troops in good fpirits ; and I hope
another time we fhall compenfate for the loffes now fuftained.

The Marquis La Fayette was wounded in the leg, and General Woodford in the hand. Divers other
officers were wounded, and fome flain, but the numbers of either cannot now be afcertained.

I have the honor to be, Sir, your obedient humble fervant,
G. WASHINGTON.

P. S. It has not been in my power to fend you earlier intelligence ; the prefent being the firft lei-
fure moment I have had fince the action.

Published by Order of Congrefs,

CHARLES THOMSON, Secretary.

PHILADELPHIA, Printed by JOHN DUNLAP.

The battle was slow in being joined; but the British soon attacked in earnest, first Sullivan on the right flank, then the main force under Washington late in the day. At midnight he despatched his report to Congress: "we have been obliged to leave the enemy masters of the field." The young French volunteer Lafayette was wounded, and some 1200-1300 others were dead, wounded, or prisoners. Boudinot judged the action "the most bloody Battle known on this Continent and perhaps the best fought on both sides." He thought the British losses were three times the American; in fact, they were less than half.

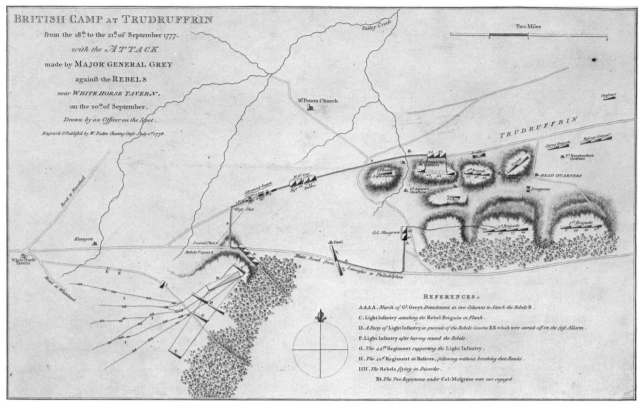

BRITISH CAMP AT TRUDRUFFRIN

from the 18th to the 21st of September 1777.

with the ATTACK

made by MAJOR GENERAL GREY

against the REBELS

near WHITE HORSE TAVERN.

on the 20th of September.

Drawn by an Officer on the Spot.

Engrav'd & Publish'd by W. Faden Charing Cross July 1st 1778.

British Camp at Truduffrin. London: William Faden, 1778. HSP

Conrad Harnett. *Letter to William Wilkinson,* Lancaster, September 25, 1777. HSP

The Americans' next engagement in battle was at Paoli on September 21, where General Grey made a surprise attack on Wayne's troops. Armed only with bayonets, without firing a shot and losing only eight men killed and wounded, the British killed or wounded 300 Americans and captured nearly 100 more. Wayne was charged with neglecting proper disposition of his troops "untill it was too late." Only the news from the North, where an American victory was expected over Burgoyne's army moving south from Canada, redressed the defeats at Brandywine and Paoli and the occupation of Philadelphia.

John Armstrong. *Letter to Thomas Wharton, Jr.*, Camp near the Trappe, October 5, [1777]. HSP

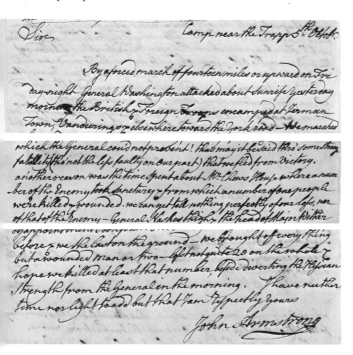

Anthony Wayne. *Letter to his wife*, Camp near Pauling Mill, October 6, 1777. HSP

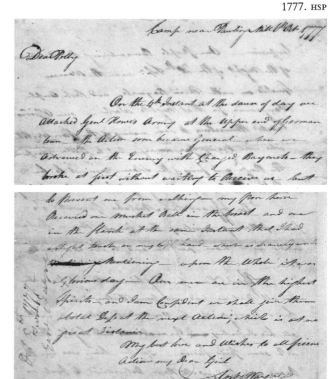

George Weedon. "The Disposition of the American Army for Battle . . . at German Town," October 4, 1777. *Orderly Book.* Manuscript. APS

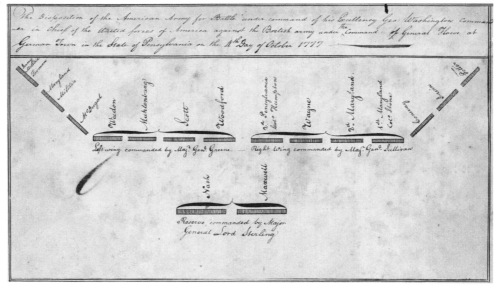

Washington prepared explicit, detailed orders for the battle of Germantown. He made a surprise attack at dawn on October 4 after a forced march; but he reckoned without an early autumn fog and the strong point the British improvised in the solidly-built, stone country house "Cliveden," home of the prominent Loyalist lawyer Benjamin Chew. Recalling his bitter defeat at Paoli two weeks before, General Wayne took satisfaction from the havoc done by his troops' bayonet charge. Though Germantown was another victory for the British, Wayne was "Confident we shall give them a total Defeat the next Action."

Nicholas Herkimer. *Letter to Peter Gansevoort,* Canajoharie District, July 12, 1777. HSP

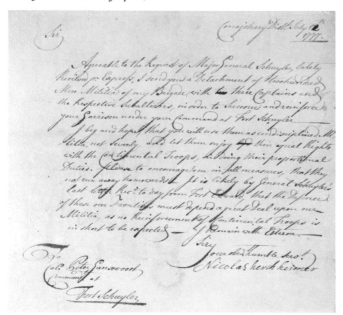

While Philadelphia was one center of warfare in the summer and fall of 1777, another campaign was going forward on Lake Champlain and along the upper Hudson River, where General Sir John Burgoyne was advancing southward with the aim of separating New England from the rest of the American states. A mixed force of Brunswick, British, Provincial and Indian troops under Colonel Baum, despatched to Bennington to seize stores Burgoyne badly needed, was defeated by Vermont troops—the famous "Green Mountain Boys." General Herkimer, a Mohawk Valley Dutchman, was mortally wounded and his forces defeated at Oriskany, on their way to reinforce Fort Stanwix, which had been invested by a British army en route from Oswego to join Burgoyne. But in two battles at Freeman's Farm and Bemis Heights—the battle of Saratoga—the British were defeated; and on October 17 "General Burgoyne and the whole remains of his Army surrendered to General Gates and the Army under his Command! The Enemy were allowed to march out of their lines or Encampment with the honors of war." This "glorious intelligence" travelled fast to Congress, now sitting in Lancaster, Pa.

The Surrender of Burgoyne's Army at Saratoga. Engraved by Daniel-Nicholas Chodowiecki in *Historisch-genealogischer Calender, oder Jahrbuch der merkwürdigsten neuen Welt.* Leipzig, 1784. LCP

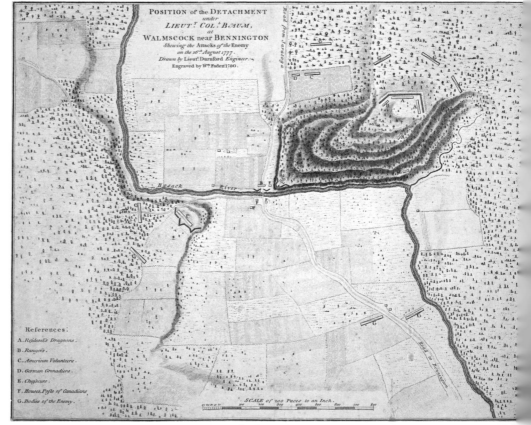

Lieutenant Durnford. *Position of the Detachment under Lieutt. Coll. Baum . . . near Bennington.* London: William Faden, 1780. HSP

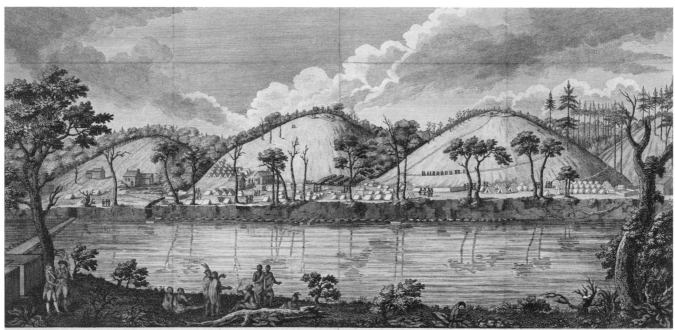

View of the West Bank of the Hudson's River 3. Miles above Still Water, upon which the Army under the command of Lt. General Burgoyne, took post on the 20th Sep. 1777.
(Shewing General Frazer's Funeral.)
Published as the Act directs, Jan 31. 1789, by William Lane, Leadenhall Street, London.

View of the West Bank of the Hudson's River . . . above Still Water.
In: Thomas Anburey. *Travels through the Interior Parts of North America.*
Two volumes. London: William Lane, 1789.

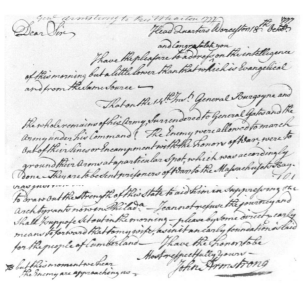

General John Armstrong. *Letter to
Thomas Wharton, Jr.,* Head Quarters,
Worcester, October 18, 1777. HSP

Glorious
Authentic Intelligence.
OCTOBER 21st, 1777.

Camp at Saratoga, October 12, 1777.
SIR,

I HAVE the satisfaction to acquaint your Excellency with the great success of the arms of the United States in this department.——On the 7th instant the enemy attacked our advanced piquets upon the left, which drew on an action, about the same hour of the day, and near the same spot of ground, where that of the 19th of September was fought, from 3 o'clock in the afternoon, until almost night, the conflict was very warm and bloody, when the enemy by a precipitate retreat determined the fate of the day,—— leaving in our hands eight pieces of Brass cannon, the tents and baggage of their flying army, a large quantity of fix'd ammunition, a considerable number of wounded and prisoners, amongst whom are

entrenched camp, which they occupied upon their advancing down the country.——The enemy have burnt all the houses before them as they retreated ;——The extensive buildings and mills, &c. belonging to Major General Schuyler, are also laid in ashes. This shameful behaviour occasioned my sending a drum, with the inclosed letter, to General Burgoyne.——I am happy to acquaint your Excellency that desertion has taken deep root in the royal army, particularly amongst the Germans, who come to us in shoals.——I am so much pressed on every side with business, that it is impossible for me to be more particular now; but I hope in a few days to have leisure, to acquaint your Excellency with every circumstance at present omitted.

I am, with great respect your
Excellency's most obedient

*Glorious Authentic Intelligence,
October 21st 1777.* Lancaster:
Francis Bailey, [1777]. Broadside. HSP

John Armstrong. *Letter to Thomas Wharton, Jr.,* Camp at Whitemarsh, November 29, 1777. HSP

Meanwhile, outside Philadelphia, Washington kept probing the British defenses, for he did not give up the idea of attacking the enemy in that city until the arrival of British and Loyalist reinforcements rendered his hope foolhardy. The approach of winter, too, put an end to the feasibility of an attack. Washington first considered Whitemarsh for winter quarters, then chose Valley Forge; but Colonel Armstrong favored a position across the Schuylkill River on its north bank.

George Washington. *Letter to Anthony Wayne,* [Headquarters], December 3, 1777. HSP

Still hoping to find support for his scheme to drive the British from Philadelphia, Washington sought support from General Wayne for the idea. But it was in vain. Washington then turned to the important task of quartering his army for the winter.

By His Excellency George Washington,
Esquire, General and Commander in Chief.
Lancaster: John Dunlap, [1777].
Broadside. HSP

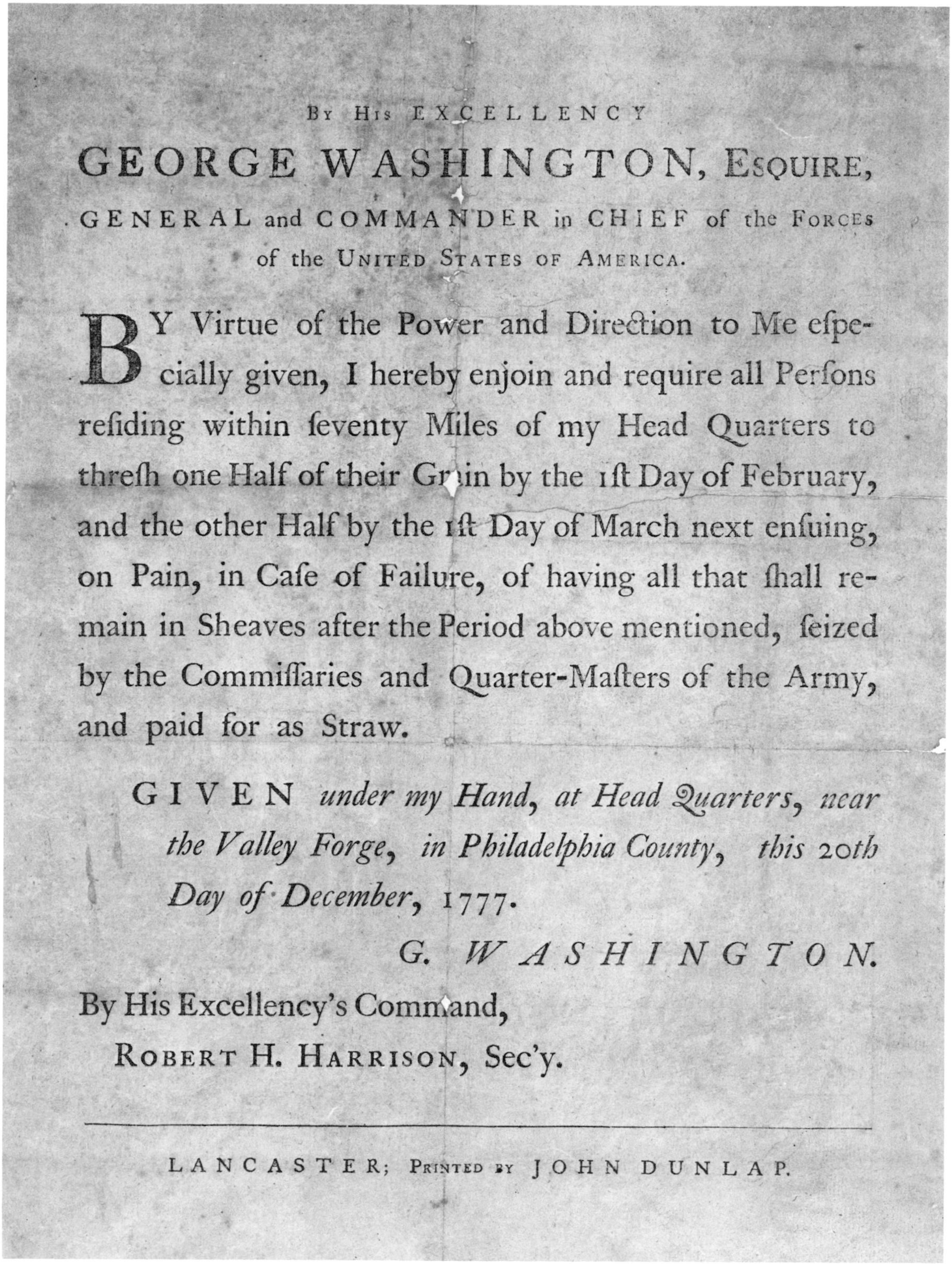

By His EXCELLENCY

GEORGE WASHINGTON, ESQUIRE,

GENERAL and COMMANDER in CHIEF of the FORCES

of the UNITED STATES of AMERICA.

BY Virtue of the Power and Direction to Me especially given, I hereby enjoin and require all Persons residing within seventy Miles of my Head Quarters to thresh one Half of their Grain by the 1st Day of February, and the other Half by the 1st Day of March next ensuing, on Pain, in Case of Failure, of having all that shall remain in Sheaves after the Period above mentioned, seized by the Commissaries and Quarter-Masters of the Army, and paid for as Straw.

GIVEN *under my Hand, at Head Quarters, near the Valley Forge, in Philadelphia County, this* 20th *Day of December,* 1777.

G. *WASHINGTON.*

By His Excellency's Command,

ROBERT H. HARRISON, Sec'y.

LANCASTER; PRINTED BY JOHN DUNLAP.

Desperate to provide food for his troops, General Washington ordered the farmers of the area to thresh their grain on penalty of having it seized and paid for as straw. Despite such measures as these, enforced or only threatened, the supply of the army worsened as the winter wore on.

York Town Decr. 20. 1777.

My Lord,

We have been much alarmed by a report that the Army was going into Winter quarters in and about Wilmington, thereby leaving New Jersey and a great part of Pennsa. intirely open to the Enemy – This Supposed measure produced several Resolutions of Congress, which, with a Remonstrance on that Subject from the Legislature of Pennsa. are forwarded to the Commander in Chief requesting his particular Attention to the Security of New Jersey &c. We had before Congress the Opinions of the General officers respecting proper places for Cantoning the Army, and with great pleasure find you in favour of the Valley near Schuylkill, which in the judgment of all or most I have met with is the only place for defending the Country and preventing Supplies to the Enemy, as the Army at Wilmington would leave great part of Pennsa. and Jersey greatly exposed to the Enemys Ravages, the Shiping up Delaware would be lost, and all the extensive Salt works in Jersey destroyed, and not unlikely a general defection take place in this State, and many parts of Jersey, and Supplies for the Army from the Eastern States greatly Obstructed. It is now said the Army are sitting down in the Valley which I heartily wish may be true.

A Ship from France lately arrived at Portsmouth in New Hampshire with 48 brass field pieces four pounders with Carriages Compleat – 19 Nine Inch Mortars with Shells, Cannon Shot, small Arms, Powder, & Sulphur. We have a prospect of soon having in our power a full Supply of Cloathing for the Army.

We have no late News from France, I have given the Substance of the latest. I am My Lord,

Your Obedt. Humr. Servt.

Abra. Clark

Lord Stirling

Abraham Clark. *Letter to General Lord Stirling*, York, December 20, 1777. HSP

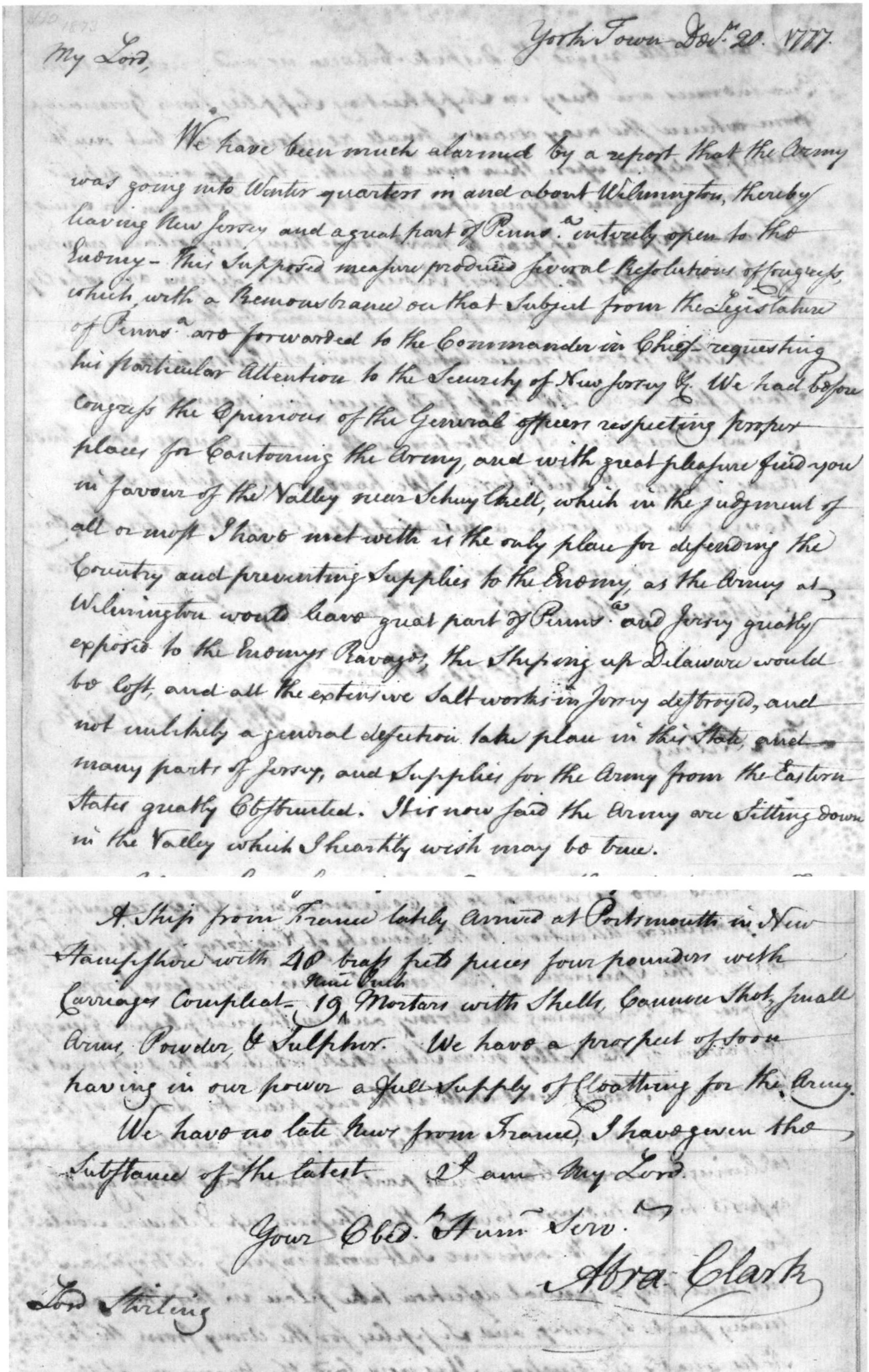

A member of Congress from New Jersey, Clark expressed to one of the Jersey generals his satisfaction with the choice of Valley Forge for the army's winter quarters. He had been afraid that Washington would spend the winter near Wilmington in Delaware, which would have left "great part of Pennsa. and Jersey greatly exposed to the Enemys Ravages, the Shiping up Delaware would be lost, and all the extensive Salt works in Jersey destroyed."

The muster rolls, which indicate whether a soldier was enlisted for eight months, three years, or the duration of the war, was also a grim record of sickness and death, with here and there the report of a discharge for a lucky man.

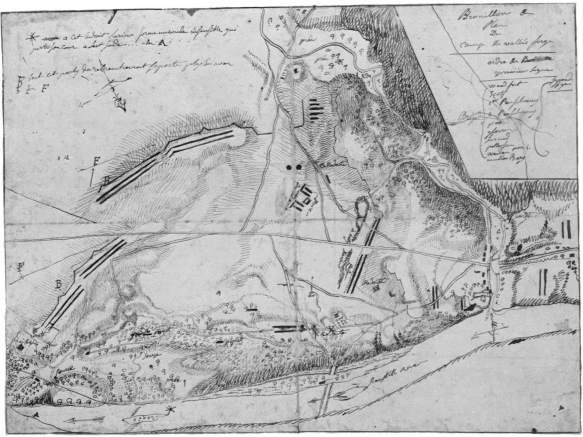

General Louis de Bèque du Portail. *"Plan Du Camp de vallié forge,"* 1778. Manuscript. HSP

The bleak prospects and suffering in the winter cantonment at Valley Forge were somewhat relieved as foreign volunteers joined the Americans to fight for liberty or advance their own careers. This map, made by an able French military engineer, is graphic testimony of the aid and support France and the French offered long before the two nations became formal allies.

William Shellingford. *Petition to General Anthony Wayne,* [Valley Forge, 1778].
HSP

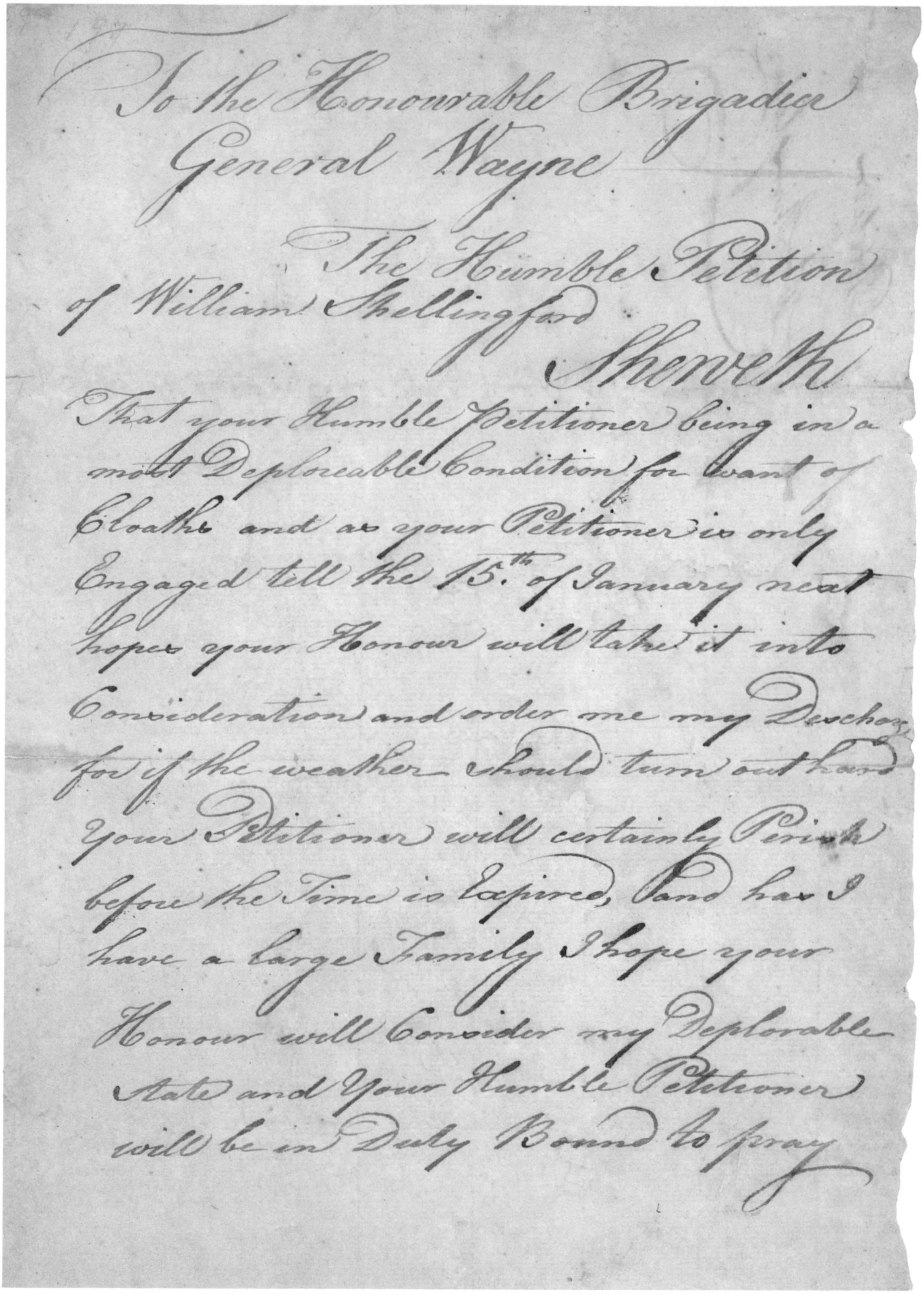

To the Honourable Brigadier
General Wayne
The Humble Petition
of William Shellingford
Sheweth
That your Humble Petitioner being in a
most Deploreable Condition for want of
Cloaths and as your Petitioner is only
Engaged till the 15th of January next
hopes your Honour will take it into
Consideration and order me my Discharge
for if the weather should turn out hard
your Petitioner will certainly Perish
before the Time is Expired, and has I
have a large Family I hope your
Honour will Consider my Deplorable
state and Your Humble Petitioner
will be in Duty Bound to pray

Such sharing of discomforts with others did little to lessen them; to many soldiers it seemed the only way to improve their lot was to get out. This humble petitioner, "being in a most Deploreable Condition for want of Cloathes," was concerned that he get an early discharge, "for if the weather should turn out hard your Petitioner will certainly Perish." The problem of expiring enlistments and expiring troops continued to plague the army throughout the winter of 1777-78.

Camp Jan.y 22d 1778 —

My Dear Sir, I am very Sorry to be Obliged to Inform you of the miserable State of our Army, I believe the Private men the best in the world Else they would Mutiny & Desert in Bodys, I think they have more virtue than half the Country, they have here built Towns amidst Snow & Frost naked, & now they have Comfortable Huts they have not A Blanket to five men, nor have they Even Straw through the Vilianous neglect of Quartermasters, I am very sorry to find also most of the Staff departments abused either through the Ignorance or Avarice or neglect of those Entrusted to Execute our Horses both Waggon & Officers Starving in Such a Country is Amasing, & this is not all, but I find Some of our best Officers kept under the Hatches, or Resigning, & Some Others of the Upper ones Arrogating to themselves all the power & Depriving their Brethren of their dignities; Col.os of Regts is nothing, they have not so much Authority as a British Ens.n so that their Command is ridiculous, & they are Either Clepid fools or Knaves & they seem to want Either Spirit or Knowledge to Resent it. I am truly grieved at our Situation, & I know it grieves our Worthy leader who is one of the first of men; Our

Our Regt. is gone to nothing & we see no likelihood of them being filled, too many trying to make fortunes while a few are striving against the Torrent of Oppression, those who have virtue & Courage are Stigmatised

that now thirteen Regiments has but one General Officer to look up to & them Dispersed in different Brigades & divisions, absolutely disgusted with the service, Its true General Wayne deserves the highest Encomiums for his bravery, Care and friendship to the Officers & Soldiers of the State but it is too much for one Gentleman to Attend to. I fear your Patience is tired therefore Conclude With the most Sincere declarations of Gratitude, & best wishes for the welfare of the best of men, whose friendship I have Experienced in So large and Extensive A maner that I want words to Express, And Am Dear Sir your Most Obed.t and very

Humble Serv.t

Rich.d Butler

my Compliments wait on Mrs Wilson
And your Sweet little family —

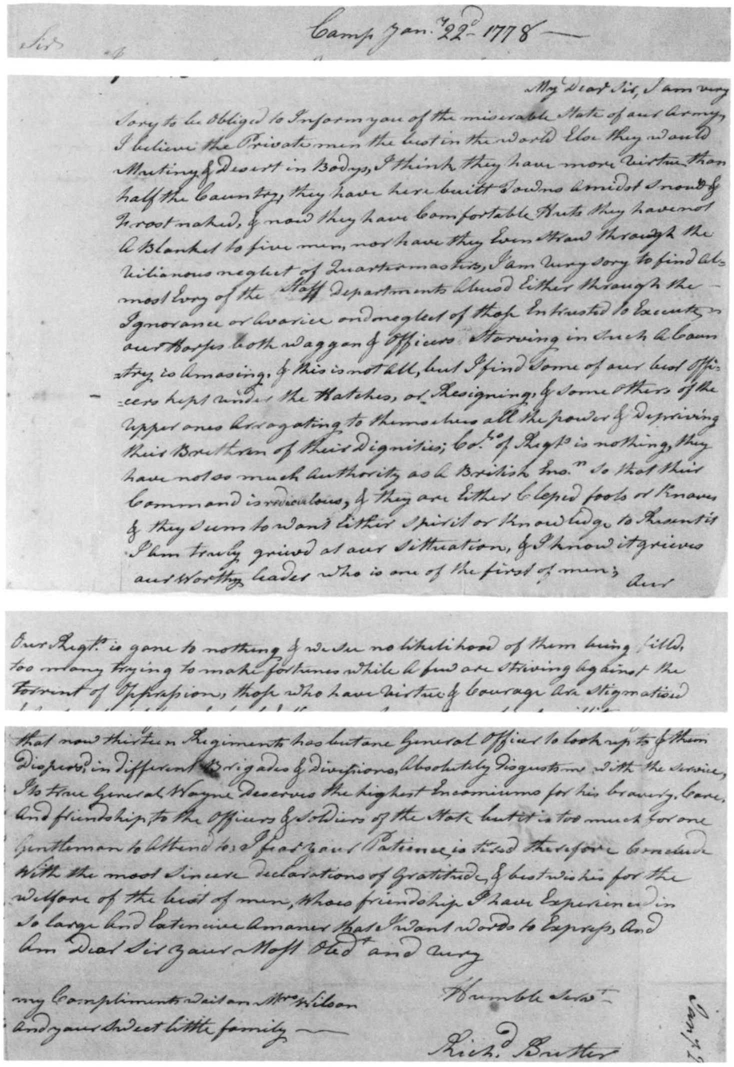

Richard Butler. *Letter to James Wilson,* Camp [at Valley Forge], January 22, 1778. HSP

Colonel Butler had been active in the Patriot campaigns and this letter describes some of those exciting moments, but, more tellingly, it describes "the miserable State of our Army. I believe the Private men the best in the world Else they would Munity & Desert in Bodys, I think they have more Virtue than half the Country, they have here built Towns amidst snows & Frost naked, & now they have Comfortable Huts they have not A Blanket to five men, nor have they Even Straw." Butler blamed the "Vilianous neglect" of the quartermasters and some others, enraged that men should be starving in the richest farmland in America.

(The whole of this letter is to be printed notwithstanding the cross lines)

Moore Hall, Camp Valley Forge Feb.y 16th 1778

My Worthy Friend

opinion upon the information of Col.o Blaine. Several Brigades complained they had been destitute of flour 2,3,& 4 days. We reexamined Col. Blaine who assured us that if such want took place it must be owing to neglect in the issuing Commissaries or Quart. Masters, as flour

In plain terms 'tis probable this army will disperse, if the Comm.y department is so damnably managed — Good God how absurd to attempt an expedition into Canada, when you cannot feed this reduced army. All the meat you have in magazines or can purchase in any part, and transport here, will not be more than sufficient to satisfy the daily wants of this army for months to come. This consideration induces me to set my face against that expedition, which I foresee will be extending from time to time, till it becomes a great object. I lament it was not confined to its original limits. 'Tis yet too late to reduce it — The passes on the North River must be seen or without question this & the neighbouring States of Jersey, Delaware and Maryland, must be evacuated by our army. They cannot be fed with meat, but from beyond that River — But more on this Subject when I have the pleasure of seeing you. Y.rs F. Dana.

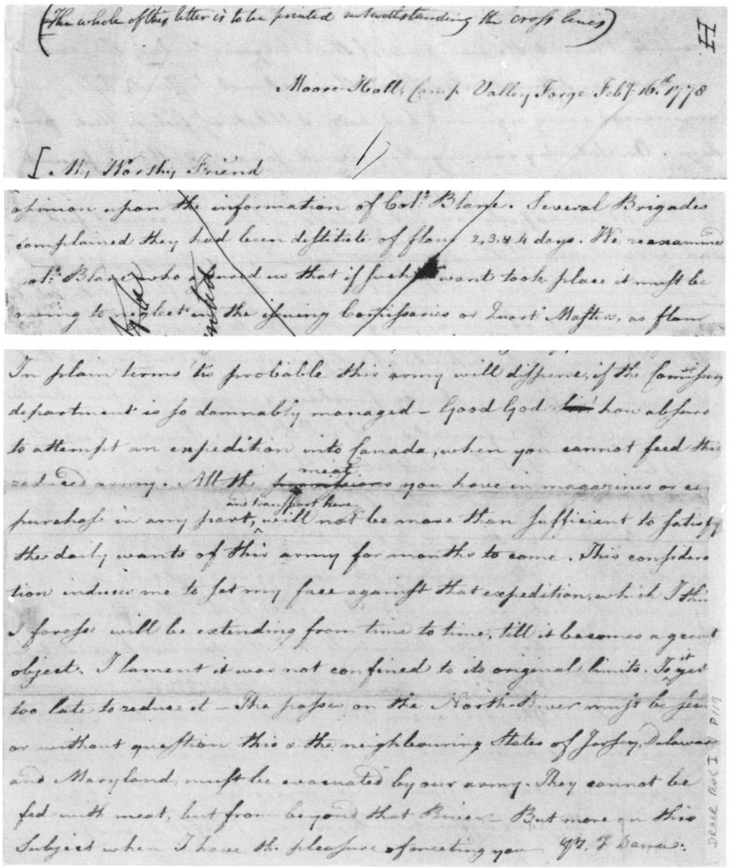

Francis Dana. *Letter to a friend,* Valley Forge, February 16, 1778. HSP

Dana expressed the sentiments of many in his passionate outcry against the miseries of the troops. Soldiers were "in a very suffering condition for want of necessary clothing," went days without "fish or flesh," and sometimes without flour for bread. He blamed the supply department, "so damnably managed—Good God how absurd to attempt an expedition into Canada, when you cannot feed" the troops in camp, he exclaimed.

Tench Tilghman. *Letter to John Cadwalader,* Head Quarters, Valley Forge, January 18, 1778. HSP

[Facsimile of handwritten letter:]

Head Quarter Valley Forge 18ᵗʰ January
—78

Dear General

hindered from doing the least damage to the inhabitants. A state of inactivity puts a stop to all news in the military line. In the underhand political there is a deal of jugling. But I trust the Storm will break upon the Heads

This damned faction founded solely upon the Ambition of one Man, for G—s is but a puppet, is so fraught with every mischief, that every honest Man ought upon the first discovery to give the Alarm, as he would upon the discovery of a fire which if suffered to get head, would destroy that Confidence which the whole Continent reposed him, supported the drooping Cause, and by a kind of Magic raised that very Army which humbled the proud Burgoyne. I have said enough to set you on fire, but be moderate — Adieu my good Friend and believe me

Tilghman also wrote of the wretched conditions in the camp in those times that tried men's souls, and he also traced in heated language the beginnings of the affair called the Conway Cabal, a "damned faction founded solely upon the Ambition of one Man." He observed to General Cadwalader that "a state of inactivity puts a stop to all news in the military line. In the underhand political there is a deal of jugling."

Officer of an Independent Company. Engraved by Daniel-Nicholas Chodowiecki in *Historisch-genealogischer Calender, oder Jahrbuch der merkwürdigsten neuen Welt.* Leipzig, 1784. LCP

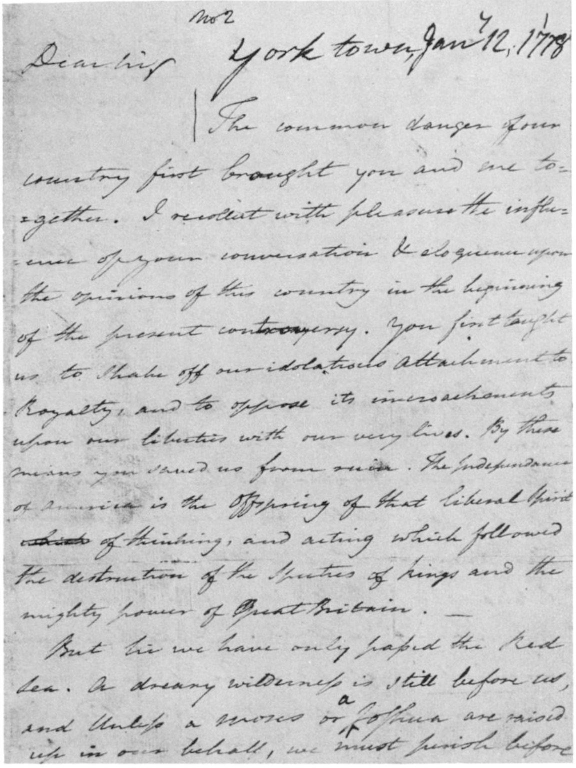

No 2

Dear Sir   Yorktown Jany 12, 1778

The common danger of our country first brought you and me together. I recollect with pleasure the influence of your conversation & eloquence upon the opinions of this country in the beginning of the present controversy. You first taught us to shake off our idolatrous attachment to Royalty, and to oppose its encroachments upon our liberties with our very lives. By these means you saved us from ruin. The Independance of America is the Offspring of that liberal Spirit ~~which~~ of thinking, and acting which followed the destruction of the Sceptres of kings and the mighty power of Great Britain. —

But Sir we have only passed the Red Sea. A dreary wilderness is still before us, and unless a Moses or a Joshua are raised up in our behalf, we must perish before

[Benjamin Rush]. *Letter to Patrick Henry,* Yorktown, Pa., January 12, 1778. HSP

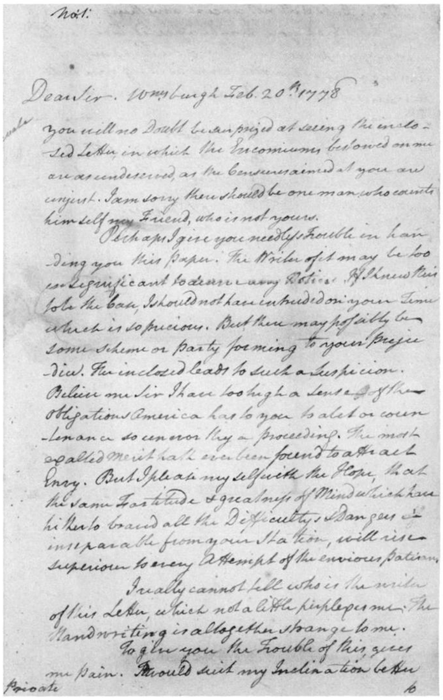

No 1.

Dear Sir.   Wmsburgh Feb. 20th 1778

You will no Doubt be surprized at seeing the inclosed Letter, in which the Encomiums bestowed on me are as undeserved, as the Censures aimed at you are unjust. I am sorry there should be one man who counts himself my Friend, who is not yours.

Perhaps I give you needless Trouble in handing you this paper. The Writer of it may be too insignificant to deserve any Notice. If I knew this to be the case, I should not have intruded on your Time which is so precious. But there may possibly be some Scheme or party forming to your prejudice. The inclosed leads to such a Suspicion. Believe me Sir I have too high a sense of the obligations America has to you to abet or countenance so unworthy a proceeding. The most exalted Merit hath ever been found to attract Envy. But I please my self with the Hope, that the same Fortitude & greatness of Mind which have hitherto braved all the Difficultys & Dangers inseparable from your Station, will rise superiour to every Attempt of the envious partisan.

I really cannot tell who is the writer of this Letter, which not a little perplexes me. The Handwriting is altogether strange to me.

To give you the Trouble of this gives me pain. It would suit my Inclination better

Private   to

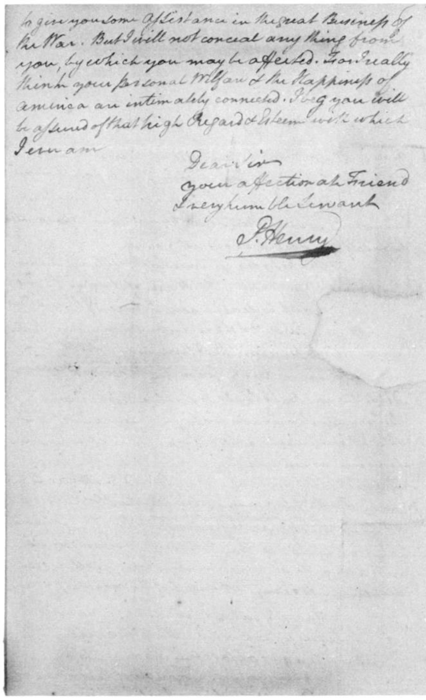

to give you some Assistance in the great Business of the War. But I will not conceal any thing from you, by which you may be affected. For I really think your personal Welfare & the Happiness of America are intimately connected. I beg you will be assured of that high Regard & Esteem with which I ever am

Dear Sir
your affectionate Friend
& very humble Servant

P. Henry

Patrick Henry. *Letters to George Washington,* Williamsburg, February 20 and March 5, 1778. HSP

The origins of the Conway Cabal were obscure, and they combined various elements, including jealousy of Washington, dissatisfaction with his leadership, and an understandable inclination to contrast the successes of General Horatio Gates at Saratoga with Washington's defeats at Brandywine and Germantown. Dr. Benjamin Rush expressed these sentiments in an unsigned letter to Governor Patrick Henry of Virginia. "The Northern Army has shewn us what Americans are capable of doing with a GENERAL at their head. The Spirit of the Southern Army [Washington's] is no way inferior to the Spirit of the Northern. A Gates— a Lee, or a Conway would, in a few Weeks render them an irresistable body of Men." Henry forwarded the letter to Washington, who recognized the author's handwriting. The conspirators (if they deserve that term) included members of Congress and the Board of War; but their own conduct betrayed them, no permanent mischief was done, and General Conway eventually apologized to Washington "for having done, written, or said anything disagreeable."

Henry Laurens, President of Congress. *Letter to Baron von Steuben,* York Town, January 14, 1778. HSP

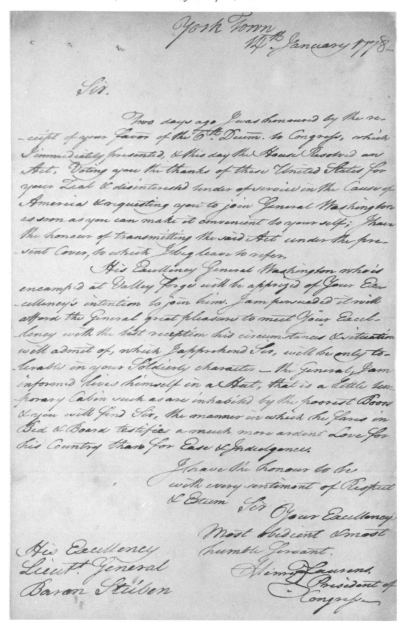

Henry Laurens. Drawn from life by Pierre E. DuSimitière and engraved by B. F. Prevost, 1781. APS

Horatio Gates. *Letter to Baron von Steuben,* York, March 23, 1778. HSP

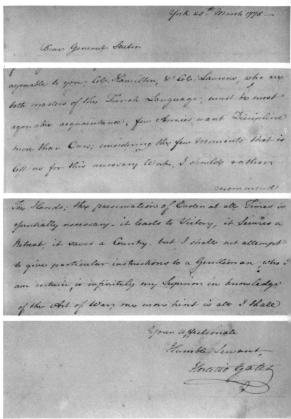

The American troops needed discipline, and that was brought to them by Steuben, the German professional soldier who had offered his services to America through Franklin at Paris. From Congress, where he presented himself, Steuben was sent to Washington at Valley Forge, with a warning from the President of Congress about the conditions at the camp and how he might be received by the commander-in-chief, who "lives himself in a Hut, that is a little temporary Cabin such as are inhabited by the poorest Boors & you will find Sir, the manner in which he fares in Bed & Board testifies a much more ardent Love for his Country than for Ease & Indulgence." Less than three months later Laurens wrote that Steuben had "hit the taste of the officers, gives universal satisfaction and I am assured has made an amazing improvement in discipline."

General Gates welcomed the German officer with the comment that "few Armies want Discipline more than Ours," and then gave Steuben some advice on what he should do: "The presence of Order at all Times is essentially necessary—it leads to Victory, it Secures a Retreat, it saves a Country;" but he quickly apologized for seeming to instruct an officer "infinitely my Superior in knowledge of the Art of War."

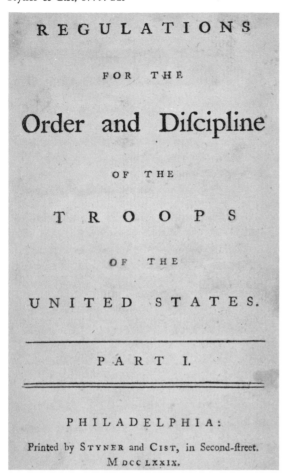

REGULATIONS

FOR THE

Order and Discipline

OF THE

TROOPS

OF THE

UNITED STATES.

PART I.

PHILADELPHIA:

Printed by STYNER and CIST, in Second-ſtreet.
M DCC LXXIX.

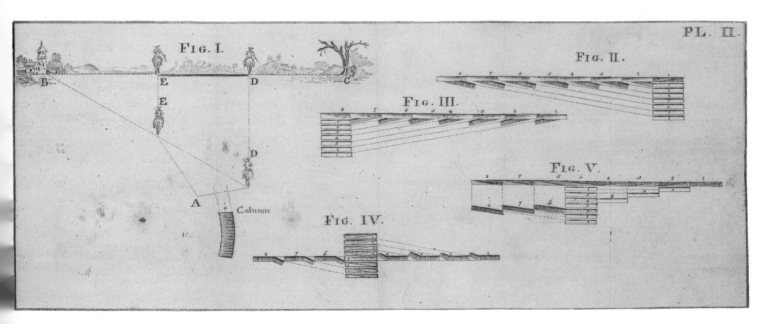

The military order and discipline that General von Steuben brought to the troops at Valley Forge and afterwards have become an indelible tradition of the war and of national history. Inevitably, the essentials of Steuben's system were codified and published, first in the edition shown here, later in many reprints and revised editions.

The figures in the plate show how to form the line by the points of view and how to form and display columns. Other military manuals were also in demand, including John Muller's on artillery—ironically the work of an English artillerist and military engineer.

General George Weedon.
Orderly Book, Valley
Forge, May 5, 1778.
Manuscript. APS

George Washington. *Letter to Richard Henry Lee*, Valley Forge, February 15, 1778. APS

Plagued by cold and hunger and conspiracy and disorder, Washington saw his personal trials increase when the British circulated an alleged letter from him to Mrs. Washington—"not one word of which did I ever write." Reacting with angry passion, Washington declared that the "Enemy are governed by no principles that ought to actuate honest Men—no wonder then that forgery should be amongst their crimes." And he concluded the denunciation with a lament for the continuing deficiencies of his own services of supply.

Rammer for 24 and 16 Pounders

Spunge and Rammer for Long Siege 12 Prs

From Valley Forge a French officer whom Franklin had recommended to the Continental Congress, sent Franklin a report of the grand celebration in the camp on receipt of the happy news of the French Alliance. The British at Philadelphia, he remarked with a smile, would not dance to the sound of this martial music. The long hard winter of Valley Forge was ending in an unusually welcome spring.

The arrival of spring brought relief from some of the sufferings of the long winter, and it also brought news of the French Alliance. In General Weedon's orderly book the report of the court martial of a deserter— "Sentenc'd to be hung by his neck till he be dead"—is followed by orders for May 6, when the announcement of the treaty to the army was celebrated with a triumphant salute of thirteen cannon, a running fire of musketry, and huzzas for the King of France and the American States.

Cannon. Sketch by
Charles Willson Peale.
1779. APS

This cannon, sketched by Peale for a recently commissioned portrait of Washington, may have been one of those captured by the Americans from the Hessians at the battle of Trenton.

"Philadelphia has taken Howe."

—Benjamin Franklin, 1777

John Bull Triumphant. By James Gillray. London: W. Humphrey, 1780. HSP

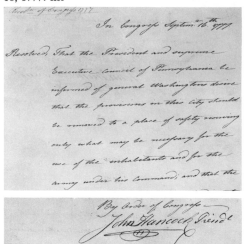

Defeated at Brandywine, General Washington realized that he could not prevent the British Army from occupying Philadelphia. At his request, Congress called on Pennsylvania to remove all surplus provisions out of the city, and to collect as many blankets as possible for the army, "as the general represents many of the Soldiers to be without Blankets, and that their health will be much exposed by remaining so."

In response to Congress' recommendation of June 11, the French volunteer General du Coudray inspected the Delaware defenses. In this memoir du Coudray concludes that the British could be barred from the river approach to Philadelphia only by strengthening the fort at Billingsport on the Jersey side. He urges that civilian laborers be used instead of soldiers as they cost less, worked harder, and did not waste so much equipment.

For all his ability, du Coudray was an embarrassment to the Americans. Though he neither spoke nor understood English very well, he expected to be put in command of the American artillery. Congress appointed him instead inspector general of ordnance on August 11, 1777. A month later he was drowned in the Schuylkill River when he rode his horse onto one end of a ferryboat and off the other. John Adams judged his premature death a "Dispensation that will save Us much Altercation."

The defeat of Washington's army at Brandywine and of Wayne's force at Paoli opened Philadelphia to the British. Congress arranged to move to Lancaster, ardent patriots fled, enemy patrols were reported near the city, and marauding bands sacked unoccupied houses. Those who remained awaited the British entry with mixed feelings. Quaker Elizabeth Drinker, whose husband Henry had been seized and imprisoned by the State authorities, records the event: "Well, here are the English in earnest. about 2 or 3000 came in, through second street, without opposition or interruption, no plundering on the one side or the oth"

Thomas Fisher.
*Letter to his
father*,
Winchester, Va.,
October 6,
1777. HSP

Richard Henry
Lee. *Letter to
Governor Patrick
Henry*,
Philadelphia,
September 8,
1777. HSP

Governments in wartime are not often careful to protect dissenters. To defend the state from those they deemed enemies of the people, the Pennsylvania Supreme Executive Council ordered some fifty Loyalists and suspected Loyalists apprehended. Some gave their oath not to leave their houses, but, predictably, 26— mostly Quaker pacifists—refused. On September 2 and 3 most of these were jailed, and on September 4 they were ordered sent out of Philadelphia into western Virginia. In this Remonstrance three of those seized protested the lawlessness of the arrest and demanded a hearing. The Council refused the petition; other petitions and protests to the Council and Continental Congress were also unavailing; and, defying a writ of habeas corpus, the authorities carried the prisoners away from their homes into exile.

Though "the Virginia exiles" had been unlawfully seized and carried out of Pennsylvania, they were not ill-treated. On the road to Virginia they were usually entertained by sympathetic citizens. At Winchester they were not confined, were adequately housed and fed, and were allowed to send and receive letters and have visitors. Two prisoners died during the winter, but from natural causes. In April 1778, without having been tried on any charge, the "exiles" were allowed to return home to Philadelphia—which was still in British hands.

Convinced that Philadelphia's Quaker pacifists were determined on a "mischievous interposition in favor of the enemy at this critical moment," one member of the Continental Congress warns the governor of Virginia, where the pacifists were to be confined, that they would "endeavor by means of the 'Friends' in Virginia to make disturbance and raise discontents there." Lee urges Henry to have the exiles "well secured . . . for they are mischievous people."

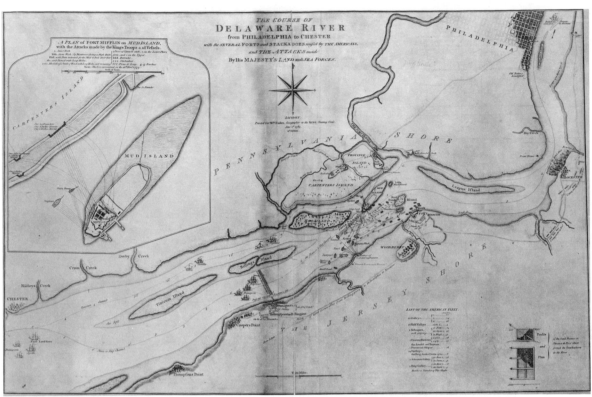

William Faden.
*The Course of
the Delaware
River.* London,
1785. HSP

This map, made by a British geographer and published
in London, locates the principal points at which the
Americans resisted—only to be overcome—the
British naval control of the approach to Philadelphia.

Continental Congress.
Resolutions, October 8 and
December 29, 1777. HSP

Though they occupied Philadelphia and had access to
the city by water, the British Army's control of the
surrounding countryside was limited by Washington's
position at Valley Forge and the hostility or

indifference of many civilians north and west of the
city. Drawing the noose tighter, Congress
authorizes courts martial to try anyone charged with
carrying information or supplies into Philadelphia.

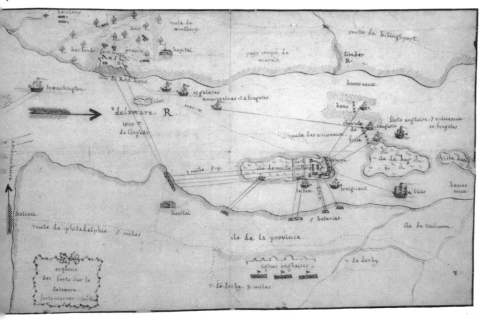

*Blowing up of the Frigate
Augusta, [October 22,
1777]. Artist
unknown.* HSP

simple sketch of the Delaware River defenses
ws the relative location of Forts Mifflin and Mercer,
chevaux-de-frise, and the positions of the   .
sh naval vessels and land batteries which shelled
American positions.

he large arrow in the Delaware points downstream
ch); the top of the map is east.

Several British frigates ran aground on October 22
during the attack on Fort Mercer at Red Bank in the
campaign to reduce the American defenses of
Philadelphia on the Delaware. The Americans opened
fire from the fort and from their row-galleys and
floating batteries; and the *Augusta* caught fire and blew
up. Until recent years her frame could be seen in
the river at low tide.

Colonel William Bradford.
*Letter to Governor Thomas
Wharton, Jr.,* "Sloop Speedwell
off Red Bank," November 16,
1777. HSP

British combined naval and military power soon cleared the Delaware
River. Admiral Howe moved against Billingsport, where a small,
unfinished redoubt guarded the first chevaux-de-frise in the river; the
garrison evacuated the place on October 2. The British attack on Fort
Mercer on October 22, however, was repulsed with heavy losses of men
and several vessels, including the *Augusta*.

On November 10 British men-of-war, frigates, and galleys opened their
bombardment of Fort Mifflin. Though intended to protect the second
line of chevaux-de-frise, Fort Mifflin was poorly designed—one observer
called it "a Burlesque upon the art of Fortification." The shelling continued
six days, "tore the Fort all to peices and knocked down all the Ambrusers
[embrasures], killed many of our People and wounded more." Unable
to withstand the attack longer, the Americans set fire to the buildings and
withdrew. "Thus Fort Mifflin is fallen," Bradford informed the Governor.

Fort Mercer's turn was next. On November 20, in the face of naval and
ground attack—the latter by 2000 troops under Lord Cornwallis—
the Americans abandoned the fort; and British control of Philadelphia
was finally secure.

127

By His EXCELLENCY
SIR WILLIAM HOWE,
General and Commander in Chief, &c. &c. &c

PROCLAMATIO[N]

WHEREAS Complaints ha[ve]
many of the Inhabitants, i[n]
phia, have been injured in their P[ro]
Persons, and that the Depredation[s]
encouraged by Citizens purchasing
others, what is thus unwarrantab[ly]
Neighbours, to the Prejudice of [?]
Discipline among the Troops, and [?]
the Inhabitants, to whom the full[est]
tended.

I DO therefore hereby declar[e]
emplary Punishment shall be infl[icted]
whatsoever, who shall be found guil[ty]
perty of others unwarrantably, of [?]
Sale, or of purchasing what may be [?]
in particular, or by any other Perso[n]
in the City, or of suspicious Charac[ter]

And I do hereby further requi[re]
the City and its Neighbourhood, [?]
within their Power for detecting an[d]
fenders, in order that they may be [?]
ate Justice.

Given under my Hand at Hea[d]
delphia, this 7th Day of Nov[ember]

By his Excellency's Command,
ROBERT MACKENZIE, Secretary.

Sir William Howe.
Proclamation,
November 7, 1777.
[Philadelphia,
1777]. LCP

ALL Persons having in their Possession any
Kind of Stores and Provisions, belonging to
the Rebel Army, are hereby required to report the
same to the Quarter-Master or Commissary-General,
and every one neglecting to do it, will be treated
with the utmost Rigour.

Any Person, who will give Information wher[e] [?]
[?] n to

By His EXCELLENCY
SIR WILLIAM HOWE
General and Commander in Chief, &c. &c

PROCLAMAT[ION]

WHEREAS It is expedient for the [?]
tants, the Suppression of Vice and [?]
servation of the Peace, the Support of the [Poor,]
of the nightly Watch and Lamps, and the Regul[ation]
kets and Ferries, with other Matters in which the [?]
and good Order of the City of Philadelphia an[d]
concerned, that a Police be established; I do ther[efore]
appoint JOSEPH GALLOWAY, Esq; SUP[ERINTENDENT]
GENERAL, assisted by three Magistrates of the [?]
after appointed, with Powers and Authority t[o]
and Regulations from Time to Time, as may mos[t]
the salutary Ends above proposed, and to nomin[ate]
a Number of inferior Officers under them as m[ay]
to carry the said Orders and Regulations into [?]
Authority shall extend in and over the Coun[ties]
Rivers Delaware and Schuylkill, and within t[he]
from River to River: And I do hereby enjoi[n]
whatever, to pay due Obedience to the SU[PERINTENDENT]
GENERAL, Chief Magistrates, and all oth[er]
under them, in the Execution of their Duty, [?]
commanding Guards, to aid and assist them [?]
necessary.

Given under my Hand at Head[?]
this 4th Day of December, [1777?]

By his Excellency's Command,
ROBERT MACKENZIE, Secretary.

✶✶✶✶✶✶✶✶✶✶✶✶✶✶✶✶✶✶✶✶✶

PHILADELPHIA, PRINTED BY JAMES HUMPHREYS, JUNR.
in Market-street, between Front and Second-streets.

Sir William Howe.
Proclamation,
December 4, 1777.
Philadelphia: James
Humphreys, Jr.,
1777. LCP

All Persons having in their
Possession any Kind of Stores
and Provisions . . ., September
29, 1777. [Philadelphia,
1777]. LCP

Philadelphia, December 8, 1777.

REGULATIONS,

Under which the Inhabitants may purchase the enume-
rated Articles, mentioned in the Proclamation of His
Excellency Sir WILLIAM HOWE, K. B. General and Commander in Chief, &c. &c. &c.

1st. NO RUM, or SPIRITS of inferior Quality,
are to be sold (except by the Importer) at one
Time, or to one Person, in any greater Quantity, than
one Hogshead, or in any less than ten Gallons, and not
without a Permit first obtained for the Quantity intended to be purchased, from the Inspector of the prohibited
Articles.

2d. MOLASSES is not to be sold (except by the
Importer) in any Quantity exceeding one Hogshead, at
one Time, nor without a Permit as aforesaid.

3d. SALT may not be sold (except by the Importer)
in any Quantity, exceeding one Bushel at one Time, for
the Use of one Family, nor without Permit as aforesaid.

4th. MEDICINES not to be sold, without a special
Permit by Order of the Superintendent General.

By Order of His Excellency Sir WILLIAM HOWE,

JOSEPH GALLOWAY, Superintendent General.

Joseph Galloway
Regulations,
December 8, 1777.
[Philadelphia,
1777]. LCP

By ORDER OF HIS EXCELLENCY
Sir William Howe, K. B.
General and Commander in Chief, &c. &c. &c.

PROCLAMATION.

[?]bitants of the
[?]t is the Order
[?]atever, living
[?]ll appear in
[?]too, at Half
[?]ing, and the
[?]us: And all
[?]me aforesaid,
[?]bles, and con-
[?]y Account of
[?]d require the
[?]aid City and
[?]e said Order,

[?] this 9th Day
[?] His Majesty's

[?]OWAY,
[?]ent-General.

Joseph Gallo[way]
Proclamation,
January 9, 17[78]
[Philadelphia,
1778]. LCP

PHILADELPHIA, October 31, 177[7]

FIVE OR SIX HUNDRED

BLANKET[S]

ARE WANTED FOR THE TROOPS

THE Inhabitants are requested to fur[nish]
that Number to the BARRACK-MAST[ER]
who will pay for them, or replace them i[n a]
few Days.

Five or Six Hundred
Blankets are wanted
for the Troops.
Philadelphia,
October 31, 1777.
Handbill. LCP

Having taken Philadelphia, the British Army found it had to control
and govern a civilian population which regarded it with mixed
feelings. Within a few days an inventory was ordered of all rebel
army property in the city. The citizens were forbidden to buy from
the soldiers (who probably had looted what they offered). The
importation and sale of spirituous liquors were regulated. Public
houses were licensed. To be Superintendent General in charge of
civilian affairs the Commander-in-Chief appointed Joseph Galloway,
who had practiced law in Philadelphia, served in the Pennsylvania
Assembly, and been an early advocate for the rights of America.
The appointment marked Galloway as one of the principal
"enemies of America."

Neither the American nor the British ar[my]
ever seemed to have enough blankets fo[r]
troops and for the sick and wounded in
hospitals. Shortly after they occupied
Philadelphia, British military authorities
on the citizens to supply their needs.

Lewis Nicola. *Plan of the English Lines near Philadelphia*, 1777. HSP

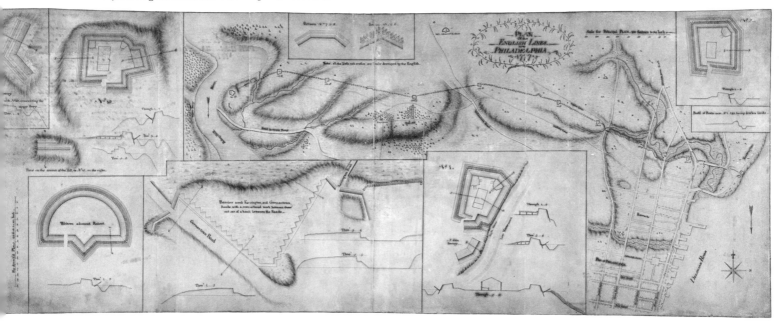

Nicola, formerly a British officer in Ireland, who joined the Continental Army and rose to the rank of colonel, explained the making of this map in 1778:

The Redoubts of the English lines are ten, besides two advanced ones. No 1 which I took a plan of in the month of July was then complete, but the heat of the weather and many avocations prevented our prosecuting the survey till October, by which time the wooden work of the other redoubts as well as the abaties were carried away. . . .

Regiments of American volunteers fought in the British Army. These Tory soldiers, though detested by their rebel countrymen and overlooked by historians, are evidence that the American Revolution was also a civil war. Major Colden was the son of Franklin's philosophical correspondent, the royal lieutenant governor of New York; Colonel Allen was a son of the aged respected former chief justice of Pennsylvania; while the English Major Simcoe was a distinguished cavalry leader, fighting through the war to Yorktown.

Return of the Strength of his Majesty's Provincial Forces in Philadelphia, December 24, 1777. HSP

First Battalion of Pennsylvania Loyalists . . . All Intrepid Able-Bodied Heroes, December 30, 1777. [Philadelphia, 1777]. LCP

TEUCRO DUCE NIL DESPERAND

First Battalion of PENNSYLVANIA LOYALISTS, commanded by His Excellency Sir WILLIAM HOWE, K.B.

ALL INTREPID ABLE-BODIED

HEROES,

WHO are willing to serve His MAJESTY KING GEORGE the Third, in Defence of their Country, Laws and Constitution, against the arbitrary Usurpations of a tyrannical Congress, have now not only an Opportunity of manifesting their Spirit, by assisting in reducing to Obedience their too-long deluded Countrymen, but also of acquiring the polite Accomplishments of a Soldier, by serving only two Years, or during the present Rebellion in America.
Such spirited Fellows, who are willing to engage,

December 30, 1777.

ALL GENTLEMEN

VOLUNTEERS,

Who have a Desire to serve on Board the STANLEY ARMED BRIG, belonging to His MAJESTY'S SHIP the

ROEBUCK,

Now lying down at the lower Ship Yards,

WILL meet with the warmest Encouragement from the Officer appointed to command her, who gives constant Attendance, and expects early Applications, as it is intended to fit her out immediately on an advantageous Cruize.

GOD Save the KING.

QUEEN'S

RANGERS.

All young and able-bodied

MEN,

[Seafaring Men excepted]

WHO are desirous of serving their KING and COUNTRY, during the present Rebellion, will repair to the Commanding Officer's Quarters of the Queen's Rangers at Kensington, where they will receive their full Bounty, Cloathing, Arms and Accoutrements.

PHILADELPHIA: Printed by JAMES HUMPHREYS, JUN. in Market-street, between Front and Second-streets.

All Gentleman Volunteers, December 30, 1777. Philadelphia: James Humphreys, Jr., [1777]. LCP

Queen's Rangers. All young and able-bodied Men. Philadelphia: James Humphreys, Jr., [1778]. LCP

Eine durch Seine Excellenz, Sir William Howe, Ritt vom Bad, General und Oberbefehlshaber, ꝛc. ꝛc. ꝛc. herausgegebene

Proclamation.

Wintemal es zur schleunigern und würklichern Unterdrückung der in Nord-America herrschenden unnatürlichen Rebellion für gut angesehen worden, eine Anzahl Provinzial Truppen anzuwerben um Seiner Majest getreuen und wohlgesinnten Unterthanen, Einwohner der Colonien, eine Gelegenheit an die Hand zu geben, sich von dem Elend zu retten welches Verwirrung und Tyranney begleitet, und zur Wiederherstellung des Seegen von Frieden und Ordnung, sammt gerechtem und gesetzmäßigem Gouvernment, mitzuwirken.—Als eine Belohnung für die Behändigkeit und Eif Seiner Majestät getreuen Unterthanen welche sich dem Chor der nun aufgebracht wird einverleiben mögen, thue ich hiemit, zufolge der mir von Seiner Majestät gegebenen Gewalt, allen Personen, die in einigen der gesagten Provinzial Corpsen angeworben worden, oder sich noch anwerben lassen werden, zwey Jahr oder während dem gegenwärtigen Krieg in Nord-America zu dienen, und getreulich nach solchen ihren Verpflichtungen im Dienst einiger der besagten Corpsen beharren werden, versprechen und versichern, daß nachdem sie abgedankt oder entlassen sind, sie in den Colonien worinnen d Corps aufgebracht worden oder werden wird, oder in solcher Colonie die S ne Majestät genehmigen mag, nach ihren respectiven Rängen folgende Quantitäten leere Ländereyen bekommen sollen

Jeder nicht-commissionirte Officier = = 200 Acker
Jeder gemeiner Soldat = = 50 Acker

Dasselbige soll solchen nicht-commissionirten Officiers und Soldaten durch Guvernör der respectiven Colonen verstattet werden, die sich persönlich da anmelden mögen, zwar ohne Belohnung oder Entgeld, doch müssen che Ländereyen, nach Verfliessung Zehn Jahren, denselben Quit Renten und andere Ländereyen in der Provinz in welcher sie verliehen werden, und g chen Bauungs und Verbesserungs Bedingungen unterworfen seyn.
Gegeben unter meiner Hand, im Haupt-Quartier zu Germantown, diesen Achten Tag October, 1777.

W. HOWE

Auf Seiner Excellenz Befehl,
Robert Mackenzie, Secretär.

Philadelphia, gedruckt bey Christoph Saur, jun. und Peter Saur.

General Sir William Howe. Proclamation, October 8, 1777. Philadelphia: Christopher Saur, Jr., [1777]. LCP

The recruiting-sergeant was seldom idle. The British here offer a variety of appeals to Americans to join their forces—an enlistment bounty, the satisfaction of restoring British authority, treatment due a gentleman, and, at the end, 50 acres of land, "where every gallant Hero may retire, and enjoy his Bottle and Lass." The Proclamation of October 8, issued a few days after the battle of Germantown, was directed to the German-speaking citizens of the state.

Sir William Howe. Engraved portrait. HSP

One day in January 1778 the Americans released a number of floating combustibles, charged with powder, into the Delaware River, where it was expected they would be carried downstream and explode upon coming in contact with the British shipping at Philadelphia. The British discovered these "infernals" and, manning the wharfs and ships, discharged cannon and small arms at everything they saw floating in the river at ebb tide. On these facts Hopkinson, lawyer, littérateur, Signer of the Declaration of Independence, composed the jingling verses which, immediately and widely reprinted, gave the Americans something to laugh at in the generally grim winter of 1777-78.

[Francis Hopkinson].
British Valour
Displayed: Or, The
Battle of the Kegs.
Pennsylvania Packet,
March 4, 1778. LCP

For the PENNSYLVANIA PACKET.

BRITISH VALOUR DISPLAYED:
Or, The BATTLE of the KEGS.

GALLANTS attend, and hear a friend
   Trill forth harmonious ditty;
Strange things I'll tell, which late befel
   In Philadelphia city.

'Twas early day, as Poets say,
   Just when the fun was rifing,
A foldier ftood on a log of wood
   And faw a fight furprifing.

As in a maze he ftood to gaze,
   The truth can't be deny'd, Sir;
He fpy'd a fcore of kegs, or more,
   Come floating down the tide, Sir.

A failor too, in jerkin blue,
   This ftrange appearance viewing,
Firft damn'd his eyes in great furprize,
   Then faid—" fome mifchief 's brewing :

" Thefe kegs now hold the rebels bold
   " Pack'd up like pickl'd herring,
" And they're come down t' attack the town
   " In this new way of ferrying."

The foldier flew, the failor too,
   And fear'd almoft to death, Sir,
Wore out their fhoes to fpread the news,
   And ran 'til out of breath, Sir.

Now up and down throughout the town
   Moft frantic fcenes were acted;
And fome ran here and others there,
   Like men almoft diftracted.

Some fire cry'd, which fome deny'd,
   But faid the earth had quaked;
And girls and boys, with hideous noife,
   Ran thro' the ftreets half naked.

Sir William he, fnug as a flea,
   Lay all this time a fnoring,
Nor dreamt of harm, as he lay warm
   In bed with Mrs. *Loring.*

Now in a fright he ftarts upright,
   Awak'd by fuch a clatter;
Firft rubs his eyes, then boldly cries,
   " For God's fake, what's the matter?"

At his bed fide he then efpy'd
   Sir Erfkine at command, Sir,
Upon one foot he had one boot
   And t'other in his hand, Sir.

" Arife, arife," *Sir Erfkine* cries,
   " The rebels—more's the pity!
" Without a boat, are all afloat
   " And rang'd before the city.

" The motley crew, in veffels new,
   " With Satan for their guide, Sir,
" Pack'd up in bags, and wooden kegs,
   " Come driving down the tide, Sir.

" Therefore prepare for bloody war,
   " Thefe kegs muft all be routed,
" Or furely we defpis'd fhall be,
   " And Britifh valour doubted."

The royal band now ready ftand,
   All rang'd in dread array, Sir,
On every flip, in every fhip,
   For to begin the fray, Sir.

The cannons roar from fhore to fhore,
   The fmall arms make a rattle;
Since wars began I'm fure no man
   E'er faw fo ftrange a battle.

The *rebel* dales—the *rebel* vales,
   With *rebel* trees furrounded;
The diftant woods, the hills and floods,
   With *rebel* echoes founded.

The fifh below fwam to and fro,
   Attack'd from ev'ry quarter;
Why fure, thought they, the De'il's to pay
   'Mong folks above the water.

The kegs, 'tis faid, tho' ftrongly made
   Of *rebel* ftaves and hoops, Sir,
Could not oppofe their pow'rful foes,
   The conqu'ring Britifh troops, Sir.

From morn to night thefe men of might
   Difplay'd amazing courage;
And when the fun was fairly down,
   Retir'd to fup their porridge.

One hundred men, with each a pen
   Or more, upon my word, Sir,
It is moft true, would be too few
   Their valour to record, Sir.

Such feats did they perform that day
   Againft thefe wicked kegs, Sir,
That years to come, *if they get home*,
   They'll make their boafts and brags, Sir.

LANCASTER: Printed by JOHN DUNLAP, in Queen-ftreet.

THE ROYAL PENNSYLVANIA GAZETTE.

[NUMBER X.]

PHILADELPHIA, FRIDAY,   APRIL 3, 1778.

PUBLISHED by JAMES ROBERTSON, in FRONT-STREET, between CHESNUT and WALNUT-STREETS.

At the SUBSCRIBER'S SCHOOL, | TO BE SOLD, WHOLESALE and RETAIL, by | JUST IMPORTED from LIVERPOOL, In the Schooner GALETEA,

The Royal Pennsylvania Gazette,
April 3, 1778. HSP

*On Monday . . . at the Theatre
in Southwark . . . The Constant
Couple.* Philadelphia: James
Humphreys, Jr., [1778]. LCP

Twenty Four American Country Dances.
London: Longman & Broderip, 1785. LCP

ON MONDAY,

The SECOND Day of MARCH, 1778

At the Theatre in Southwark,

For the Benefit of a PUBLIC CHARITY,

Will be represented a Comedy

CALLED THE

Constant Couple.

TO WHICH WILL BE ADDED, THE

Mock Doctor.

The CHARACTERS by the OFFICERS of the ARMY
and NAVY.

TICKETS to be had at the Printer's; at the Coffee-house in Market-
street; and at the Pennsylvania Farmer, near the New-Market, and
no where else.
BOXES and PIT, ONE DOLLAR.—GALLERY, HALF a DOLLAR.
Doors to open at Five o'Clock, and begin precisely at Seven.
No Money will, on any Account, be taken at the Door.
Gentlemen are earnestly requested not to attempt to bribe the
Door-keepers.
N. B. Places for the Boxes to be taken at the Office of the
Theatre in Front-street, between the Hours of Nine and Two o'clock:
After which Time, the Box-keeper will not attend. Ladies or Gen-
tlemen, who would have Places kept for them, are desired to send
their Servants to the Theatre at Four o'clock, otherwise their Places
will be given up.

PHILADELPHIA, Printed by JAMES HUMPHREYS, JUNR.

By midwinter life for many civilians in Philadelphia
returned to normal. The shops were filled again with
imported goods, artisans and mechanics plied their trades,
children went to school, as the newspaper advertisements
show.

In addition, the Army gave a variety of entertainments,
concerts, and shows. Thirteen theatrical performances
were presented by British officers during the winter.

Captain John André was a leading spirit in organizing
the plays, managed the theater, and painted the scenery.
Despite his charming manner, however, he is said not
to have been a good actor.

And if the British brought "The Constant Couple"
to Philadelphia, they took home to England some of the
simple country dances their captives in Philadelphia
and other cities taught them.

[John André]. *Ticket for th[e]
Meschianza* [Philadelphia,
May 18, 1778]. LCP

[John André]. *Sketch of
a Meschianza Costume.*
[Philadelphia, 1778]. LCP

*In the shield is a view of the sea, with a setting sun [Howe?],
and on the wreath the words, "Luceo discendens, aucto
splendore resurgam." At the top is General Howe's crest and
motto, "Vive, vale." But Howe never rose again to
comparable command.*

*The dress is that of the Ladies of the Knights of the
Blended Rose at Meschianza. Miss Margaret Shippen
(who later married Benedict Arnold) was to have been
one of these Ladies, but at the last moment her father
forbade it, and her place was taken by another.*

To pay tribute to their commanding officer, Sir William
Howe, upon his recall, the officers of the Army organized
an extravaganza that opened with a colorful regatta on
the Delaware, included a tournament between Knights of
the Blended Rose and those of the Burning Mountain,
and ended at the house of Joseph Wharton below the
city, where a ball, fireworks, and supper continued until
4 o'clock in the morning.

The principal architect of this "most splendid
entertainment" was Captain John André, who took
understandable pride in the achievement. He was
indefatigable, planning the entire theme, designing the
costumes of the Knights' Ladies, painting scenery, and
organizing the tables, which required 430 covers,
1200 dishes, and 300 wax tapers.

No doubt it pleased Sir William.

Though Captain André and his fellow officers might pride themselves on their salute to General Howe, and a few Philadelphia maidens took an exquisite delight from their invitation to the affair, the Meschianza was sharply criticized. A Philadelphia Quaker rebuked its authors for extravagance:

A shameful scene of dissipation,
The Death of sense and Reputation,
A Deep degeneracy of Nature,
A Frolic, for the Lash of Satire.

Table of Regiments in the British Army.
In: Adam Friedrich Geisler. *Geschichte
und Zustand der Königlich
Grosbrittannischen Kriegsmacht zu
Wasser und zu Lande.* Dessau and
Leipzig, 1784. HSP

[Jasper Mauduit]. *Strictures on the Philadelphia Mischianza or Triumph upon Leaving America Unconquered.* Philadelphia, 1780. LCP

Strictures, &c.

IF Sir W——M H——E had thought fit quietly to resign his command, and been content to enjoy in privacy the fortune he had acquired, till the nation had in some measure digested the disgraces and losses we had suffered under his command in America; or till the dangers and calamities, which, in consequence of them, threaten us here at home, were passed over; he might not then, perhaps, have been disturbed in his retirement.

But at a time when the British empire in America is sunk, and when thousands and thousands of good subjects in both countries are ruined by its fall; at a time when, with the loss of our colonies, the empire here in Britain itself, is shaken and endangered; at such a time of public calamity, when every good Englishman was trembling for the commonwealth; at such a time of distress, for a General to take to himself ovations and triumphs, greater than the duke of Marlborough, or any English commander ever thought of; to suffer himself to be crowned with laurels, and to have triumphal arches erected to his honour---is such an insult offered to our understandings, as cannot but raise in the mind of every man of sense, the highest degree of astonishment and indignation.

I do not at present bring any charge, or enquire now where we ought to fix the blame; but this we are sure of, that during the whole of G---l H---e's command, our attempts to subdue the rebellion have been every where unsuccessful; the British arms have been

---

STRICTURES

ON THE

PHILADELPHIA

MISCHIANZA OR TRIUMPH

UPON LEAVING

America Unconquered.

WITH

EXTRACTS, containing the Principal Part of a LETTER published in the AMERICAN CRISIS.

IN ORDER TO SHEW,

How far the King's Enemies think his GENERALS deserving the PUBLIC HONOURS.

N. B. A flattering Account of this Mischianza was published in the Philadelphia Gazette, and copied into the Morning Post of the 13th of July last; and a larger one by a still more flattering Panegyrist, may be found in the Gentleman's Magazine for August last.

LONDON PRINTED:

PHILADELPHIA,

Re-Printed by F. BAILEY, IN MARKET-STREET.
M,DCC,LXXX.

And a prominent American Loyalist, a refugee in London, voiced indignation that, "at a time when the British Empire in America is sunk, . . . the empire here in Britain itself, is shaken and endangered, . . . [and] every good Englishman is trembling for the commonwealth," Howe should accept ovations and triumphs greater than Marlborough ever thought of, and allow triumphal arches to be erected in his honor and himself to be crowned with laurels. First printed in London, Mauduit's *Strictures* were reprinted in Philadelphia, no doubt to the gratification of American patriots at this evidence of dissension among their enemies.

Even Loyalists had to recognize by early spring that the British must soon evacuate Philadelphia. James Allen was critical of Sir William Howe's "supineness" and "neglect" of true Loyalists. He expected better things from Howe's successor in America, Sir Henry Clinton.

Only a few hours after the British Army withdrew the American Army is ordered to march into Philadelphia. And the next day General Benedict Arnold, as military governor of the city, imposed martial law.

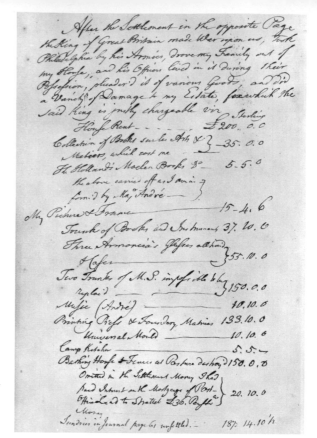

Benjamin Franklin. *Ledger*, 1764–1775. APS

Benjamin Franklin was only one of many citizens whose property was damaged, destroyed, or carried off by British soldiers during the occupation of Philadelphia. In this accounting he records the loss of books, scientific instruments, glasses for the armonica, irreplaceable manuscripts, sheet music, and "My Picture & Frame." The latter two were taken by Captain John André, who was billeted in the house. André gave the painting of Franklin to his commanding officer General Grey, and one of Grey's descendants in 1906 presented it to the United States. It now hangs in the White House.

General Benedict Arnold. *A Proclamation*, June 19, 1778. [Philadelphia, 1778]. LCP

By the Hon. Major General, ARNOLD, Commander in Chief of the forces of the United States of America, in the city of Philadelphia, &c.

A PROCLAMATION.

IN order to protect the perfons and property of the inhabitants of this city from infult and injury, to fecure the public and private ftores, which the enemy may have left in the city, and to prevent the diforder and confufion naturally arifing from want of government, his Excellency General WASHINGTON, in compliance with the following refolution of Congrefs, has thought proper to eftablifh military law in this city and fuburbs, until the civil authority of the state can refume the government thereof.

In CONGRESS, June 4, 1778.

Refolved, That fhould the city of Philadelphia be evacuated by the enemy, it will be expedient and proper for the Commander in Chief to take effectual care that no infult, plunder, or injury of any kind, may be offered to the inhabitants of the faid city: That, in order to prevent public or private injury from the operations of ill difpofed perfons, the General be directed to take early and proper care to prevent the removal, transfer, or fale of any goods, wares, or merchandize, in poffeffion of the inhabitants of the faid city, until the property of the fame fhall be afcertained by a Joint Committee, confifting of perfons appointed by Congrefs, and of perfons appointed by the Supreme Executive Council of the State of Pennfylvania, to wit, fo far as to determine whether any or what Part thereof may belong to the king of Great Britain, or to any of his fubjects.

Extract from the minutes. CHARLES THOMSON, Sec.

Given at head quarters, in the city of Philadelphia, June 19, 1778.

By his Honor's command, DAVID S. FRANKS, Sec. B. ARNOLD, Major Gen.

PENNSYLVANIA, ss.

A PROCLAMATION.

By the SUPREME EXECUTIVE COUNCIL of the Common-Wealth of PENNSYLVANIA.

WHEREAS the following named persons, late and heretofore inhabitants of this State—That is to say—Enoch Story, late merchant; Samuel Garrigues, the elder, late clerk of the market and trader; James Stevenson, late baker; Abraham Carlile, house-carpenter; Peter Deshong, miller; Alexander Bartram, trader; Christian Hook, attorney at law; Peter Miller, scrivener; Lodowick Kerker, butcher; Philip Marchinton, trader; Edward Hanlon, cooper and vintner; Alfred Cliffton, gentleman; and Arthur Thomas, breeches-maker; all now or late of the city of Philadelphia: And Thomas Leverley, late of the township of Roxborough, miller; John Roberts, late of the township of Lower-Merion, Miller; Robert Iredale, the younger, and Thomas Iredale, both late of the township of Horsham, labourers; Joshua Knight, late of the township of Abingdon, blacksmith; John Knight, tanner; Isaac Knight, husbandman; Albinson Walton, late of the township of Biberry, husbandman; John Smith, late guager of the port of Philadelphia; and Henry Hugh Ferguson, commissary of prisoners for General Howe, all late of the county of Philadelphia: And Samuel Biles, Esquire, late sheriff of the county of Bucks; Walter Willet, late of the township of Southampton, husbandman; Richard Hovenden, late of the

By order of COUNCIL,

THOMAS WHARTON, Junior, President.

GOD SAVE THE COMMON-WEALTH.

Attested by order of the Council,
T. MATLACK, Secretary.

LANCASTER, Printed by JOHN DUNLAP.

Supreme Executive Council. *Proclamation, May 8, 1778.* Lancaster: John Dunlap, 1778. LCP

TO BE SOLD

By PUBLIC AUCTION,
1778.

On Tuesday the eighth of September, at the late dwelling house of Samuel Shoemaker, in Arch-street,

ALL the Houshold Furniture, now seized and confiscated to the State, such as feather beds, bedsteads, tables, chairs, settees, looking glasses, china tea cups, saucers and plates, Queen's ware dishes and plates, andirons, tongs and shovels, oven stoves and common ditto, dressing tables, high and low drawers, desk and book case; a collection of books on various subjects, prints framed and glazed. Also all kinds of kitchen furniture, such as pots, kettles, stew pans, tubs, buckets, &c. Likewise a small fire engine, a pair of horses, a coach and harness. Any persons having claims on goods left at the said house, are desired to call on the Agents and make their claims good before the above day of sale.

PHILADELPHIA: PRINTED BY JOHN DUNLAP, in Market-street.

To Be Sold by Public Auction, September 8, 1778. Philadelphia: John Dunlap, 1778. LCP

Plunket Fleeson. *Register of Oaths,* Philadelphia, 1778. HSP

Pennsylvania citizens who had adhered to the British, joined their Army, or given them aid and comfort, were declared traitors and their property confiscated. Eventually two of the men proscribed by the Executive Council were hanged in Philadelphia. The respected Samuel Shoemaker not only lost his property but, refusing to take the oath of allegiance, was put in jail—to the acute embarrassment of both his fellow-Quakers and the authorities.

After the withdrawal of the British, the citizens of Philadelphia were required to renounce George III and swear allegiance to the Commonwealth of Pennsylvania as "a free and Independent State." In this register are the names of the Lutheran minister John C. Kunze (815), the Indian trader George Croghan (819), and the pharmacist and physician Robert Bass (821).

The French Alliance, 1778

"On the great stage of Europe"
—Silas Deane. Letter to
Mrs. Deane, March 3, 1776

*Franklin urging the Claims of the
American Colonies before Louis XVI.*
By George P. A. Healy. Oil on canvas. APS

Continental Congress. *Commission to Benjamin Franklin, Silas Deane, and Arthur Lee,* [Philadelphia], September 30, 1776. APS

This is Congress' commission to Franklin and his colleagues to negotiate a treaty of commerce with France. It was the first step in the diplomatic progress to a treaty of alliance and French military and naval aid in the war for American independence.

Continental Congress. *Extracts from the Journal,* September 26 and 28, 1776. APS

Congress appoints Benjamin Franklin, Silas Deane, and Thomas Jefferson commissioners to France, and authorizes them to "live in such stile and manner at the court of France as they may find suitable and necessary to support the dignity of their public character." This particular document is docketed in Franklin's hand, "Instructions. Allowance to Commrs. Sept. 26. 1776." Because of family obligations, Jefferson declined his appointment, much to Franklin's regret.

Benjamin Franklin. Portrait by Charles Nicolas Cochin. Engraved by Augu[st] de Saint Aubin, 17[..] APS

Made within a few weeks of Franklin's arrival in France and reproduced in countless small prints, on ceramics, watch faces and souvenirs of every sort, this is the Franklin most Frenchmen carried in their mind's eye.

A nineteenth-century artist's conception of Franklin's appeal to France for aid to the American states. In fact Franklin was first introduced to Louis XVI on March 20, 1778, in the King's dressing room, where he appeared in plain Quaker-like dress. A year later, on March 23, 1779, he presented his credentials as minister at a formal audience.

Commissioned by King Louis-Philippe for Versailles, the painting was completed only after his abdication in 1848. It received a medal at the Paris Universal Exposition of 1855 and was subsequently brought to Chicago, where it was destroyed in the fire of 1871. The painting is best known through engravings. This is the artist's original study.

Congress' instructions to Franklin and Deane, the American Commissioners to France, took the form of shopping lists. In October 1776 Congress wanted eight battleships of the line "of 74 and 64 guns well manned and fitted in every respect for service"; in February 1777 they wanted 80,000 blankets, 40,000 uniforms, 100,000 pairs of yarn stockings, 1,000,000 gun flints, and 200 tons of lead for bullets.

Benjamin Franklin and Robert Morris. *Letter to William Bingham,* Philadelphia, October 21, 1776. APS

Philadelphia October 21st 1776

Sir

We send you herewith a copy of what we wrote you the 19th Sept. per the Sloop Independance Capt Young and hope some of the articles that were to be forwarded to your Island or St. Eustatia by Monsr Hortalez have arrived. In that case you will apply for, receive and Ship them by these opportunities of our Continental Cruizers which are sent for that purpose, and also to bring back such Woolen Goods as can be procured agreable to the Orders of the Secret Committee.

Your obed Servts
B Franklin
Robt Morris

Wm Bingham Esqr

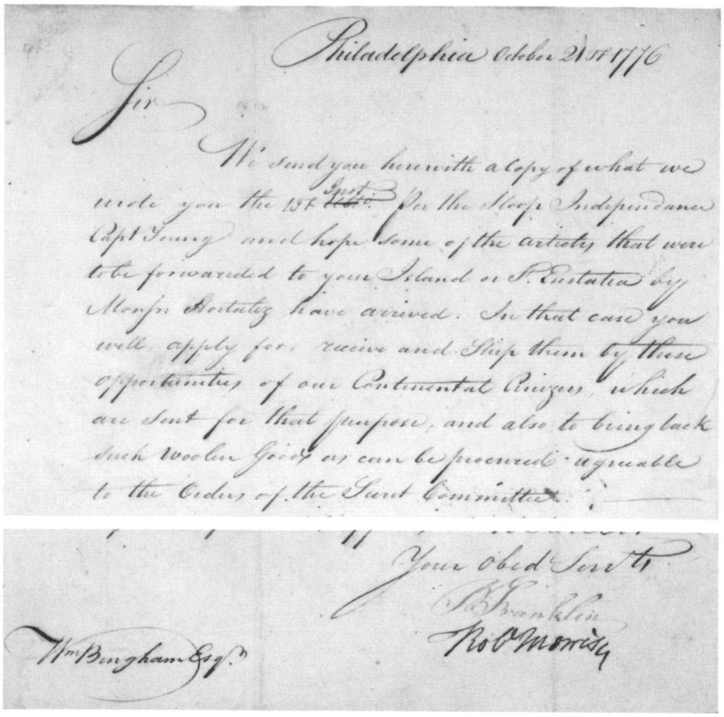

Immediately after the American colonies declared their independence, and months before the treaty of alliance and commerce was signed, France began to aid the Americans secretly. Trade was conducted by a dummy trading company Rodrigue Hortales & Cie. through the neutral port of St. Eustatius in the Dutch West Indies. In this letter the Committee of Congress informs its agent on Martinique, William Bingham, how to take possession of the French goods and forward them to Philadelphia.

Benjamin Harrison and Richard Henry Lee. *Letter to the American Commissioners in Paris,* Baltimore, Md., January 9, 1777. APS

Gentlemen Baltimore 9th January 1777

To Franklin, Adams & Deane

Captain Hammond having been detained longer than we expected, furnishes us with an opportunity of giving you the information we have since received from the Army, thro a Committee of Congress left at Philadelphia; for we have yet had no regular accounts from General Washington. On the 2d instant, General Washington having received information that the enemy were on their march to attack him at Trenton, ordered two brigades of militia to advance and annoy them on the road leading from Princeton to Trenton, who falling in with the enemy about 3 miles from the latter place, engaged them, but being overpowerd by numbers, made a retreating fight until they joined the main body who were drawn up on the heights west of a bridge that divides the village of Trenton nearly in two parts. The enemy attempting to force the bridge were repulsed with loss by a body of men with artillery placed there to receive them. In the mean time some batteries being opened on the heights soon drove the enemy from that part of the Town possessed by them. Thus the affair ended for that evening. But General Washington having received intel-

P.S.
In the engagement near Princeton we lost, 15 privates one Colonel, and Brigadier Gen. Mercer a very good Officer & a worthy Gentleman

Benj Harrison
Richard Henry Lee

In secret Committee

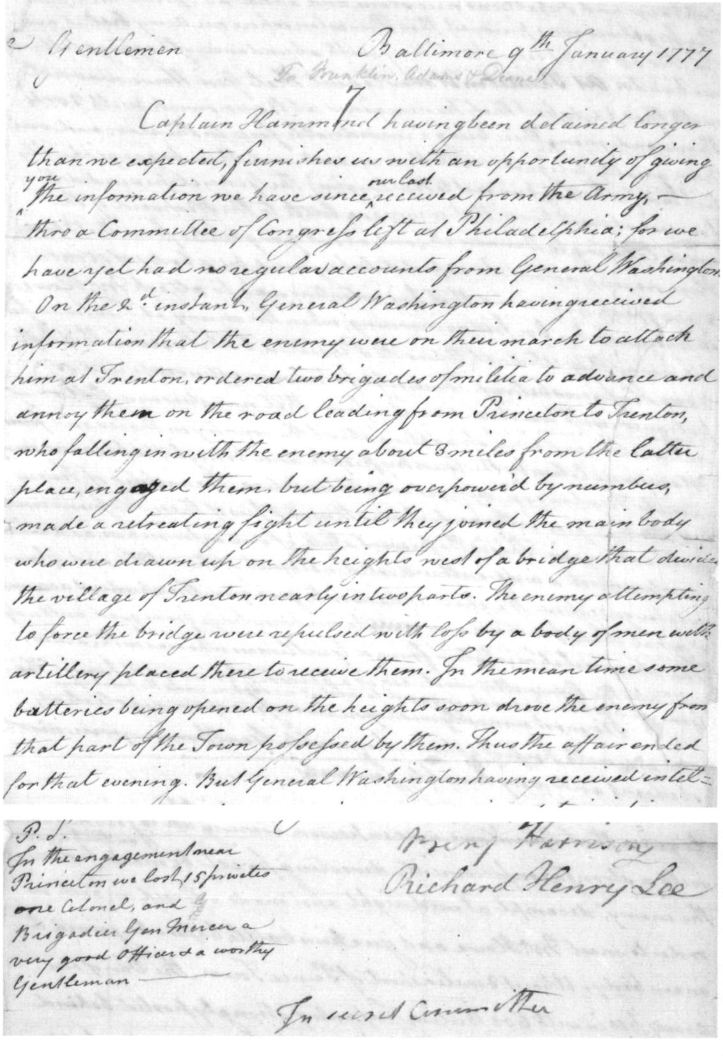

Congress kept its representatives abroad as well informed of military events in America as possible. Details of the battle at Princeton on January 2 took more than a week to reach Baltimore; but the Secret Committee took the opportunity of a vessel bound for France to send as much as they knew. Washington, they explained to Franklin and his colleagues, had been too busy to write; besides, they supposed, he awaited the final issue of the engagements with the British in New Jersey.

Roderigue Hortales & Cie. *Letter to the Secret Committee of Correspondence*, Paris, September 10, 1777. HSP

Three great objects strike my sight.

America in arms to support the liberty she affects, and the independency she has openly declared.

Britain perceiving too late her mistakes, respecting the Intrepidity and the forces of the Americans, and carrying on against them a ruinous war, for the sole purpose of obtaining, if possible, a less disadvantageous peace.

Finally France hesitating between those great events, and in your opinion, too long deferring to determine, whether or not she ought to engage in the quarrel.

This is the point on which the question turns.—America says succour us, and we will never make peace. France says prove to me that you will never make peace and I will succour you.

conduct the two nations to the most firm & durable alliance!—This is the sincere & constant wish of him who has the honor of being with the most respectful devotion, Gentlemen,

Your very humble & very obedient Servant

Paris ye 10th of Sept 1777 Roderigue Hortales & Co.

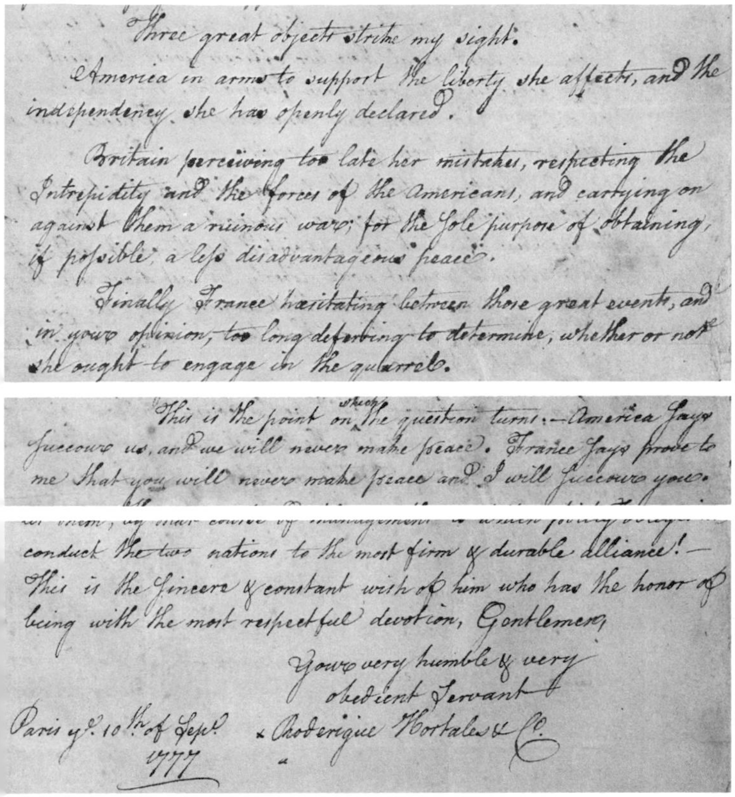

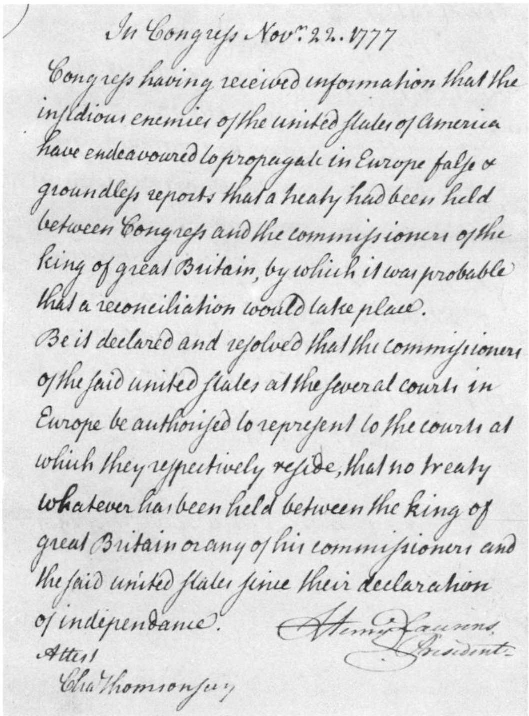

Months before King Louis XVI declared himself an ally of the American states, France secretly supplied the Americans with arms and other supplies. Roderigue Hortales & Company, managed by the playwright Caron de Beaumarchais, was the cover. In this remarkable letter Beaumarchais explains with the greatest clarity the differing interests of France and America. "This is the point on which the question turns:—America says, succour us, and we will never make peace. France says, prove to me that you will never make peace and I will succour you."

Continental Congress. *Declaration and resolution*, November 22, 1777. APS

In Congress Nov. 22. 1777

Congress having received information that the insidious enemies of the united states of America have endeavoured to propagate in Europe false & groundless reports that a treaty had been held between Congress and the commissioners of the king of great Britain, by which it was probable that a reconciliation would take place.

Be it declared and resolved that the commissioners of the said united states at the several courts in Europe be authorised to represent to the courts at which they respectively reside, that no treaty whatever has been held between the king of great Britain or any of his commissioners and the said united states since their declaration of independance.

Henry Laurens President

Attest

Cha Thomson secy

One reason why Britain's enemies in Europe hesitated to declare openly for America was their fear that the new republic might make peace and return to its former allegiance. British agents industriously spread such reports in European capitals, until Congress had to take formal notice of them. By this resolution Congress instructed their commissioners abroad to assert that the United States and Great Britain since the Declaration of Independence had entered into "no treaty whatever."

York Town Oct. 18th 1777

Honourable Gentlemen

54

We have the pleasure of inclosing to you the copy of a letter from General Gates containing the circumstances of a Victory gained over General Burgoyne on the 7th. This event must defeat the main view of General Clinton in proceeding up Hudson River. He has, it is true, got possession of Fort Montgomery, but with much loss, as we hear.

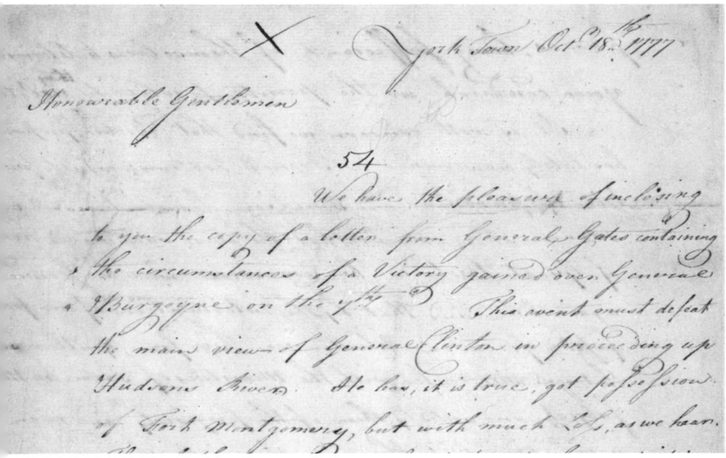

Committee of Foreign Affairs. *Letter to Benjamin Franklin, Silas Deane, and Arthur Lee, Commissioners in Paris*, York Town, Pa., October 18, 1777. APS

Congress sends news of General Gates' victory over Burgoyne at Saratoga—an event that frustrated the plans of the British General Clinton to proceed up the Hudson River from New York and so split New England from the Middle States. Gates' victory was followed by Burgoyne's surrender of his army on October 17, and *that* event proved to be an effective argument why France should publicly ally itself to the United States.

Mme. Anne-Louise d'Hardancourt Brillon de Jouy. *Marche des Insurgents*, [Paris, 1778]. APS

News of the Americans' victory over Burgoyne's army occasioned great rejoicing among the friends of America and of Franklin in Paris. One of them, Franklin's confidante and correspondent Mme. Brillon, composed a spirited march in salute to the conquering "insurgents."

Treaties of Amity and Commerce, and of Alliance . . . between His Most Christian Majesty and the Thirteen United States of America. Philadelphia: John Dunlap, 1778. APS

Traité d'Amitié et de Commerce, conclu entre le Roi et les États-Unis . . . le 6 Février 1778. Paris: L'Imprimerie Royale, 1778. HSP

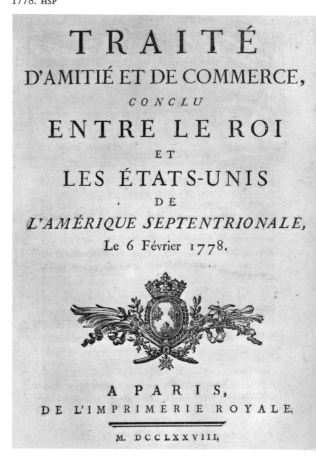

Encouraged by the Americans' victory at Saratoga and fearful that Britain and America might effect a reconciliation, France decided early in January 1778 to make a treaty of alliance. Signed on February 6, the treaties bound France to help the United States achieve independence, and the United States to make common cause with France should that country be attacked by Great Britain. Neither ally would make peace without the consent of the other, or lay down its arms until American independence was assured by treaty. Each country was to receive most-favored-nation treatment, and the ports of each were to be open to the trade of the other.

The treaties reached Congress in York, Pennsylvania, on May 2; and they were ratified on May 4.

Continental Congress. *Resolution of thanks*, May 4, 1778. APS

General Thomas Conway. *Letter to Colonel Marinus Willett*, Albany, May 18, 1778. HSP

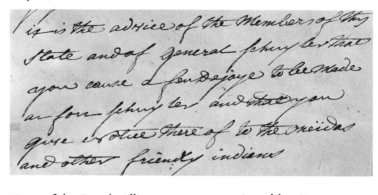

News of the French Alliance was communicated by Congress to General Washington. By his orders the treaty was read to the troops at Valley Forge on May 6, to the accompaniment of thirteen-gun salutes and huzzas for the King of France, the friendly European powers, and the American States. Similar events occurred elsewhere, as this order shows. At Fort Schuyler in the distant Mohawk Valley the news was greeted with a feu de joie, and "the Oneidas and other friendly Indians" were informed of this happy turn in their American allies' fortunes.

Congress expresses its grateful acknowledgment to the King of France "for his truly magnanimous Conduct . . . in the said generous & disinterested Treaties." This extract was received by John Adams and is docketed by him.

A Picturesque View of the State of the Nation for February 1778. [London, 1778]. LCP

In this satirical English comment on the Americans' Treaty of Alliance and Commerce with France, America saws off the horns of the "poor tame cow," which is British commerce, while a Dutchman milks the beast, and a Frenchman and a Spaniard take the milk. "A Free Englishman" is in despair that he cannot rouse the British Lion. In the background the Howe brothers slumber in Philadelphia "out of sight of fleet and army."

First printed in the *Westminster Magazine* of February 1778, the cartoon was republished in America, and appeared also in Dutch and French versions, with changes appropriate to national sensibilities.

GRATIS.

Benjamin Franklin. *Printed Seal.* From blank form of passport, Passy, 178-. APS

La Grande Bretagne mutilé.
Rotterdam, [1778]. APS

Inspired by Franklin's Stamp Act cartoon of 1766 (see p. 9), this represents Great Britain in 1778—her shipping idle in the harbor, her merchants kept from trading, New England lost, Philadelphia reclaimed by the rebels, Halifax beset by American privateers.

Samuel Adams. *Letter to Richard Henry Lee,* Boston, April 20, 1778. APS

Contrasting French "Magnanimity" with British "Meanness and Poverty of Spirit," Samuel Adams, signer of the Declaration of Independence and still a member of Congress, rejoices in the French Alliance, and warns against reconciliation with Britain. "The one is generously holding out the Arm of Protection to a People most cruelly oppressed; while the other is practicing the Arts of Treachery and Deceit to subjugate and enslave them."

which he would without doubt gladly furnish on credit. — the Genoese are among the richest people in Europe. being principally commercial they make great sums of money, which their sumptuary laws put it out of their power to expend. the consequence is that for a long time they have put their money into the banks of Europe for 3 and 3½ per cent. they have immense sums in the London bank, the state of which has for some time alarmed them: & nothing has prevented their drawing it out but the impossibility of disposing of it elsewhere. were they indeed to go pretty generally on the plan of selling out, it is probable they must sell to considerable loss, yet the high interest we pay would make amends for that, more especially when they contemplate the certain loss of their principal at no very distant period if suffered to remain there. there seems therefore reason to hope we might do something clever with them, which would be doubly beneficial by supplying our wants, and perhaps rendering our Enemies bankrupt by sudden & large calls on them. I throw out these things for your contemplation. if

...mas Jefferson. *Letter to John*
...ock, Albemarle County,
...nia, October 19, 1778. HSP

...w to obtain credit to purchase necessary supplies for the army was ...gging problem for the Continental Congress. Jefferson, now a ...ber of the Virginia House of Delegates, here suggests the Grand ...ny of Tuscany as a likely source of funds and his neighbor ...ppo Mazzei as a discreet person to make preliminary overtures. ...e the Grand Duke's funds were deposited in London banks, ...pport of the Americans "would be doubly beneficial by ...lying our wants, and perhaps rendering our Enemies bankrupt ...dden & large calls on them."

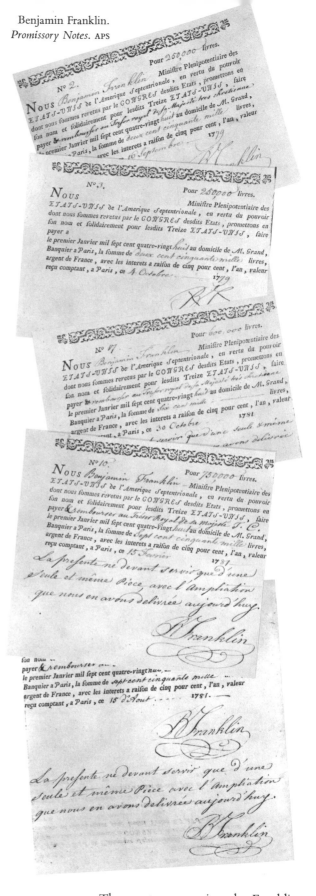

Benjamin Franklin.
Promissory Notes. APS

These notes were given by Franklin to the French government for loans made by France to the United States. A livre was worth about 25 cents. The forms were printed on Franklin's private press.

Arthur Lee. *Letter to George Washington,* Philadelphia, November 11, 1780. **HSP**

Sir   Philadelphia Nov. 11th 1780.

The manifest necessity of an immediate supply of money for the public service, & the difficulty, I am sure there will be in obtaining it from the Court of Versailles, induce me to suggest to your Excellency that, in my judgment, nothing will promote the attainment of it more than your opinion made known to that Court, of its being indispensible to the continuance of the War.

The very high respect they entertain for your cha...

His Excellency Genl. Washington

...roof of the incomparable reputation of General Washington, as well ...evidence of the erratic conduct of a former commissioner to ...ance, is this letter proposing that Washington use his influence to ...ge the French government to make another loan, which Lee ...ought "indispensible to the continuance of the War."

147

John Jay. *Letter to Benjamin Franklin*, Philadelphia, June 9, 1779. HSP

In Congress Philadelphia June 9 1779

Sir,

I inclose you an Act of Congress of the 8th of this Instant June directing that Bills should be drawn upon you to the Amount of three hundred and sixty thousand Livres Tournois for the Purpose of importing military Stores. I have accordingly drawn four Setts payable to the Honorable Henry Laurens, Francis Lewis, James Searle and John Fell the Commercial Committee of Congress or the Order of either of them, towit, one Sett for one hundred and fifty thousand, one for one hundred thousand, one for seventy thousand, and one for forty thousand Livres Tournois. Our Disappointment in not receiving the Supplies which we expected from France has rendered this Measure indispensibly necessary and we flatter ourselves that you will be able to make such Representations to the Court of France on this Subject as to induce them chearfully to put it in your Power to honor these Drafts.

John Jay
President

The Hon'ble Benjamin Franklin Esquire Minister Plenipotentiary for the United States of America at the Court of France.

Congress authorizes its Minister in Paris to spend 360,000 livres (approximately $90,000) for military supplies "indispensibly necessary" to carry on the war.

Major General Horatio Gates. Drawn from life by Pierre E. DuSimitière and engraved by B. L. Prevost, 1781. APS.

Major General Benedict Arnold. Drawn from life by Pierre E. DuSimitière and engraved by B. L. Prevost, 1781. APS.

The French Army at Newport. Engraved by Daniel-Nicholas Chodowiecki in *Historisch-genealogischer Calender, oder Jahrbuch der merkwürdigsten neuen Welt.* Leipzig, 1784. LCP

Benjamin Franklin.
Monogram "BF."
Brass stencil. APS

less important than troops were
ns, equipment and other supplies
for both America's army and
rican civilians. Despite Franklin's
best efforts and the good will of
many French officials, it was not
usually easy to assemble such
shipments for "les Américains."
hen a ship did go off, it might be
red at sea by British men-of-war
r privateers— a fate which befell
he *Marquis de la Fayette,* a French
ssel bound for Boston laden with
0 bags of salt petre, thousands of
uskets and uniforms, wine, cloth
other manufactured goods, and
(sweet conquest for the British!)
"a Bust of Dr. Franklin."

To advance at the Rate of 1 *per Cent.*
through this S A L E.

First Day's Sale,

Tuesday, January 29, 1782.

A Bust of Dr. FRANKLIN.
Lot 1   1 Bust

C L O A T H I N G.

Public 8995 Coats, Regimental, of Blue Cloth, with White
Serge Linings and Metal Buttons, in 91 Lots, at
per Coat.

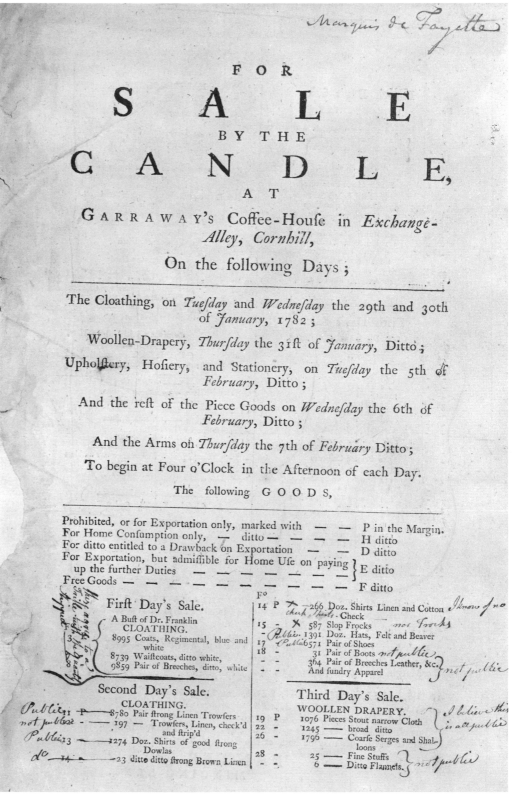

Marquis de Fayette

FOR
SALE
BY THE
CANDLE,
AT
GARRAWAY's Coffee-House in *Exchange-
Alley, Cornhill,*

On the following Days;

The Cloathing, on *Tuesday* and *Wednesday* the 29th and 30th
of *January,* 1782;

Woollen-Drapery, *Thursday* the 31st of *January,* Ditto;

Upholstery, Hosiery, and Stationery, on *Tuesday* the 5th of
February, Ditto;

And the rest of the Piece Goods on *Wednesday* the 6th of
February, Ditto;

And the Arms on *Thursday* the 7th of *February* Ditto;

To begin at Four o'Clock in the Afternoon of each Day.

The following G O O D S,

Prohibited, or for Exportation only, marked with — — P in the Margin.
For Home Consumption only, — ditto — — — — — H ditto
For ditto entitled to a Drawback on Exportation — — D ditto
For Exportation, but admissible for Home Use on paying } E ditto
up the further Duties — — — — — — — —
Free Goods — — — — — — — — — — — F ditto

F°

First Day's Sale.
A Bust of Dr. Franklin
CLOATHING.
8995 Coats, Regimental, blue and
white
8739 Waistcoats, ditto white,
9859 Pair of Breeches, ditto, white

14 P — 266 Doz. Shirts Linen and Cotton *I know of no*
check Shirts - Check
15 X — 587 Slop Frocks *not Frocks*
Public 1391 Doz. Hats, Felt and Beaver
17 *Public* 6571 Pair of Shoes
18 — 31 Pair of Boots *not public*
— 364 Pair of Breeches Leather, &c. } *not public*
And sundry Apparel

Second Day's Sale.
CLOATHING.
Public 31 P — 8780 Pair strong Linen Trowsers
not public — 197 — Trowsers, Linen, check'd
and strip'd
Public 13 — 1274 Doz. Shirts of good strong
Dowlas
dc 14 — 23 ditto ditto strong Brown Linen

Third Day's Sale.
WOOLLEN DRAPERY.
19 P 1076 Pieces Stout narrow Cloth
22 - 1245 — broad ditto
26 - 1796 — Coarse Serges and Shal-
loons
28 - 25 — Fine Stuffs
- 6 — Ditto Flannels } *not public*

Panter & Co.
For Sale by the Candle . . . .
[London, 1782]. APS

Continental Congress.
Resolve, October 21,
1778. APS

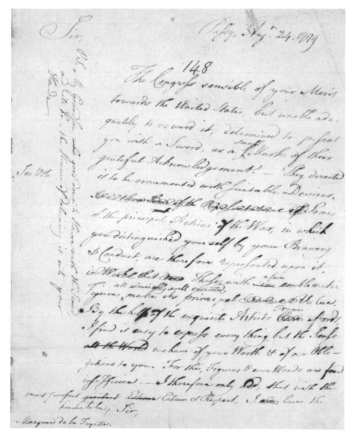

*Major General the Marquis de la
Fayette.* Portrait by Jean Urbain
Guerin; engraved by Frantz
Gabriel Fiesinger. [1789]. APS.

Benjamin Franklin.
*Letter to the Marquis
de la Fayette,* Passy,
August 24, 1779.
Draft. APS

The presence of the young French nobleman la Fayette
in the American Army was striking proof of French
sympathy with the Americans' cause. On October 21, 1778,
Congress voted its thanks for la Fayette's "disinterested
zeal" and outstanding services, and directed the American
minister at Versailles "to cause an elegant sword, with
proper devices, to be made and presented" to him. Made
by "the best Artists in Paris" at a cost of 200 guineas,
the sword was highly ornate, with la Fayette's arms
and motto on one side, and on the other a rising moon
illuminating a land partly forested and partly cultivated,
with the motto *Crescam ut prosim* ("Let me wax to
benefit mankind.")

The sword, with Franklin's handsomely phrased letter
of presentation, was delivered to la Fayette at Le Havre,
where he was planning an invasion (soon aborted) of
England. It was cited in Franco-American propaganda
of the period. This "noble present from Congress,"
la Fayette reported, had an "immense effect" upon the
French army at Le Havre, and Franklin admitted that
"some of the Circumstances" of the gift were "agreable
to this nation."

P. P. Burdett. *Letter to Benjamin Franklin*, Karlsruhe, June 1777. APS

One of Franklin's opportunities—and burdens—as the American agent in Paris was to select professional European soldiers to send General Washington, whose army badly needed experienced officers. Some of the volunteers had no qualifications, others were woefully uninformed about America and Americans; but a few made unique and memorable contributions to the American cause. One of these was the German von Steuben, whom one of Franklin's English friends here introduces as "a Gentleman of Family, Merit and great experience."

INFORMATION

TO THOSE

WHO WOULD REMOVE

TO AMERICA.

M ANY Perfons in Europe having directly or by Letters, exprefs'd to the Writer of this, who is well acquainted with North-America, their Defire of tranfporting and eftablishing themfelves in that Country; but who appear to him to have formed thro' Ignorance, miftaken Ideas & Expectations of what is to be obtained there; he thinks it may be ufeful, and prevent inconvenient, expenfive & fruit-lefs Removals and Voyages of improper Perfons, if he gives fome clearer & truer Notions of that Part of the World than appear to have hitherto pre-vailed.

He finds it is imagined by Numbers that the In-habitants of North-America are rich, capable of rewarding, and difpos'd to reward all forts of Ingenuity; that they are at the fame time ignorant of all the Sciences; & confequently that ftrangers poffeffing Talents in the Belles-Letters, fineArts, &c. muft be highly efteemed, and fo well paid as to become eafily rich themfelves; that there are alfo abundance of profitable Offices to be difpofed of,

A

Benjamin Franklin. *Information to those who would remove to America.* [Passy, 1784]. APS

Major General Frederick William Augustus von Steuben. Drawn from life by Pierre E. DuSimitière and engraved by B. L. Prevost, 1781. APS

As the most famous and knowledgeable American in Europe, Franklin was "pestered continually," he complained, by persons wishing to go to America. Most of these would-be emigrants had no accurate idea of America; they would not recognize the country needed farmers and mechanics, not painters, poets, and peruke-makers. To provide his correspondents with practical advice, as well as to save himself the trouble of writing scores of similar personal replies, Franklin composed this little essay and printed it on his private press. It was quickly reprinted in Paris, London, Hamburg, Dublin, Cremona, and elsewhere.

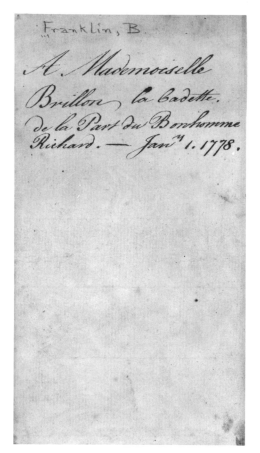

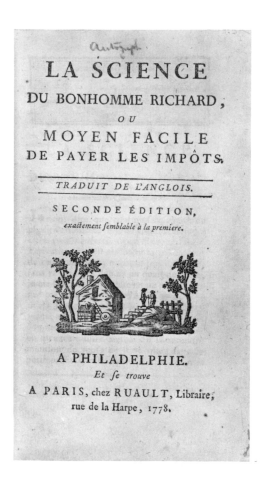

Benjamin Franklin. *La
Science du Bonhomme Richard.*
Paris: Ruault, 1778. APS

*Franklin's Audience with
Louis XVI.* Engraved by
Daniel-Nicholas
Chodowiecki in
*Historisch-genealogischer
Calender, oder Jahrbuch
der merkwürdigsten neuen
Welt.* Leipzig, 1784. LCP

Jean S. Bailly. *Exposé des
Expériences qui ont été faites
pour l' Examen du
Magnétisme Animal.* Paris:
L'Imprimerie Royale, 1784. APS

Franklin succeeded as a diplomat partly because of his scientific achievement, his personal charm, and the legend which grew around him and which he himself fostered. *The Way to Wealth* was translated into French; he was chosen master of the Masonic Lodge of the Nine Sisters, was an active member of the Académie des Sciences, and the most popular guest in the most famous salons. "His reputation," wrote John Adams some years afterwards, "was more universal than that of Leibnitz or Newton, Frederick or Voltaire, and his character more beloved and esteemed than any or all of them. . . . His name was familiar to government and people, to kings, courtiers, nobility, clergy and philosophers, as well as plebeians, to such a degree that there was scarcely a peasant or a citizen, a *valet de chambre*, coachman or footman, a lady's chambermaid or a scullian in a kitchen who was not familiar with it, and who did not consider him as a friend to human kind. . . . He was considered as a citizen of the world, a friend to all men and an enemy to none."

The copy of *La Science du Bonhomme Richard* shown here was presented by Franklin to the daughter of his good friends M. and Mme. Brillon. Note that the business of the Lodge meeting to which Franklin was invited was the initiation of Dr. Edward Bancroft (an American who was a secret agent for the British), sponsored on the occasion by Captain John Paul Jones.

Mme. Anne Catherine d'Autricourt Helvétius. *Invitation to Benjamin Franklin,* Auteuil, October 21, 1778. APS

Benjamin Franklin. Portrait Medallion by Jean Baptiste Nini, 1777. Terra Cotta. APS

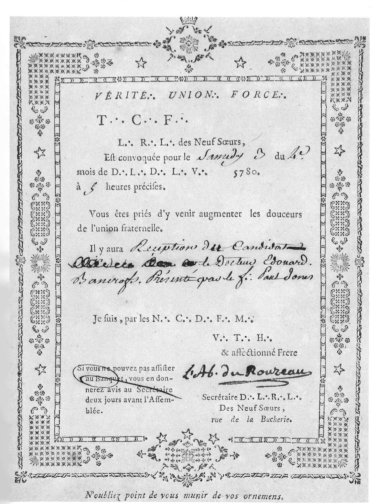

Though not done from life, this portrait medallion, made in the spring of 1777, was thought by Franklin's family to be an excellent likeness. This particular medallion was presented in 1778 or 1779 to the artist Charles Willson Peale by the French minister to the United States.

Loge des Neuf Soeurs. *Meeting Notice to Benjamin Franklin,* Paris, April 3, 1780. APS

Defeat
and Victory,
1778-1781

"The World Turned Upside
Down"—English tune,
played at Yorktown, 1781

Surrender of Cornwallis' Army.
Engraving by François
Godefroy. *Recueil d'Estampes
représentant les différens Événemens
de la Guerre qui a procuré
l'Indépendance aux États unis de
l'Amérique.* Paris: Godefroy,
[1783]. APS

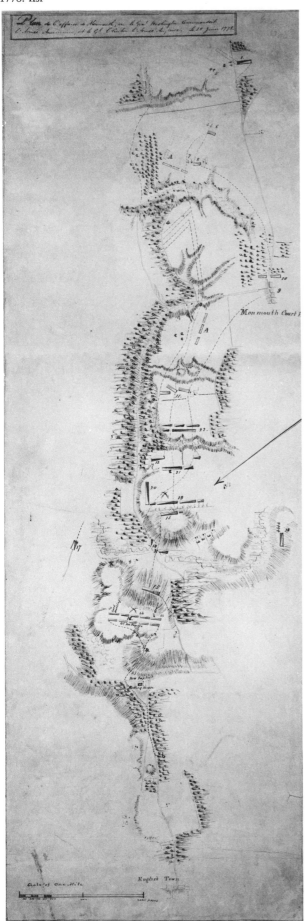

In the middle of June in 1778 Clinton moved his army of ten thousand men out of Philadelphia by land. Washington's men stopped momentarily in the city and then followed the enemy into New Jersey. In the face of strong staff opposition, Washington attacked the British at Monmouth. Recently exchanged after more than a year as a prisoner of war, General Charles Lee was given command of the first wave of the attack. His contact with the enemy was confused, and he retreated. Washington moved up with the main force to fight off the British counterattack and met and berated Lee, taking from him his command. The battle was still being fought when night came. Clinton used the darkness to cover his march back into New York City.

Anthony Wayne.
Letter to Richard Peters, Paramus, July 12, 1778. HSP

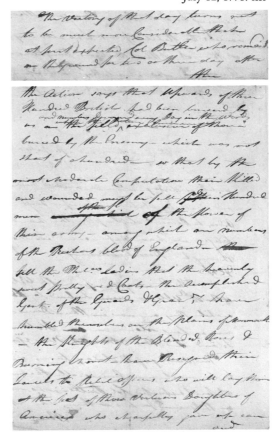

The next days brought the slowly dawning realization that "the Victory of that day turns out to be much more Considerable" than had appeared at first. Anthony Wayne rejoiced over the British loss of "full fifteen Hundred men of the flower of their army," and in biting reference to the Meschianza remarked that many of the defeated were but recently the darlings of the Philadelphia ladies. "The Knights of the Blended Roses & Burning Mount have Resigned the Laurel to *Rebel* Officers who will lay them at the feet of those Virtuous Daughters of America who chearfully gave up ease and affluence in a City for Liberty and peace of mind in a Cottage."

Israel Shreve. *Letter to his wife,*
Englishtown, July 2, 1778.
HSP

Anthony Wayne. *Letter to
Sharp Delany,* Camp near
White Plains, July 20,
1778. HSP

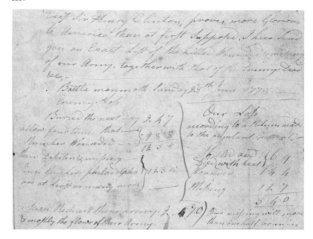

In a happy letter home one survivor of the battle
of Monmouth made a grim reckoning, calculating
nearly 2,500 English casualties to only 340 for the
Americans. He thought it the greatest victory won
by Americans since the beginning of the war and
was not shy in the telling of his part in it.

Thaddeus Kosciusko.
*Caricature of General
Charles Lee.*
ca. 1778. HSP

This contemporary view by the Polish engineer in
the American Army was not flattering to Lee,
nor was it intended to be. Whatever judgment
might be made of him as a military commander,
Lee was an eccentric character whose personal
behavior before and after the war displayed
bizarre habits and tastes.

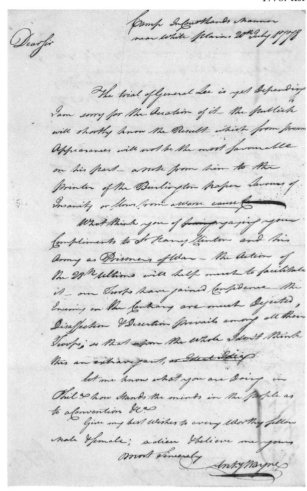

General Lee's equivocal conduct in the battle of
Monmouth was widely criticized. In response he
demanded an apology for Washington's words
addressed to him in heat of battle, and made
charges against brother officers, accusing Wayne of
"temerity, folly, and contempt of orders," until
Wayne replied that Lee's conduct "Savours of
Insanity." Lee called for a court of inquiry; he got
a court martial. He was found guilty of disobedience
of orders, misbehavior before the enemy, and
disrespect to the Commander-in-Chief. He was
ordered suspended from the army, and retired to
his Virginia home soon afterward. (Lee was
English-born and not related to the patriot family
of Virginia of the same name.)

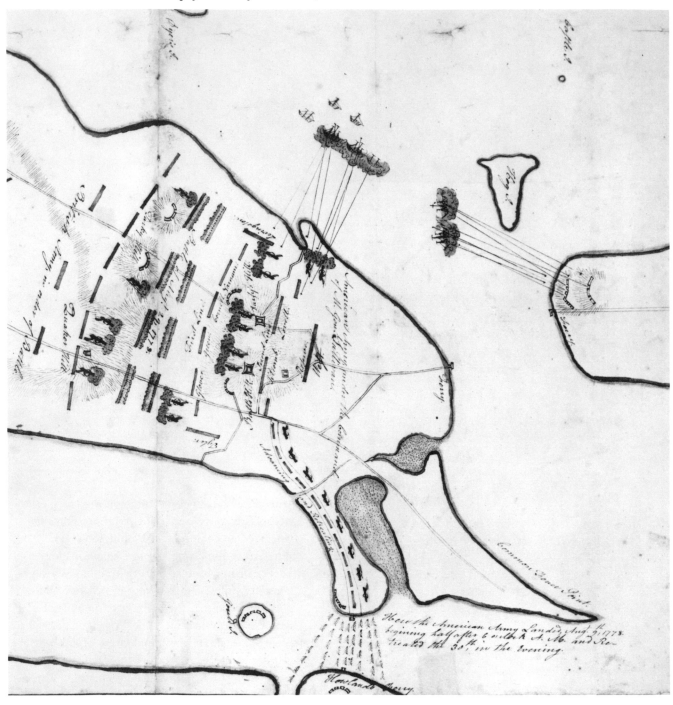

In the summer of 1778 New York and Newport were
in British hands. Washington had gained the approval of
Admiral Comte d'Estaing for a French naval squadron
to attack New York City, but a sandbar prevented the
vessels' entry into the harbor. The allies decided then on
a joint land and sea attack on Newport, where the British
had more than three thousand men. The plans for a
concerted attack broke down in the execution.

General John Sullivan. *Letter to General John Hancock*, Camp before Newport, August 23, 1778. HSP

George Washington. *Letter to Anthony Wayne*, White Plains, September 1, 1778. HSP

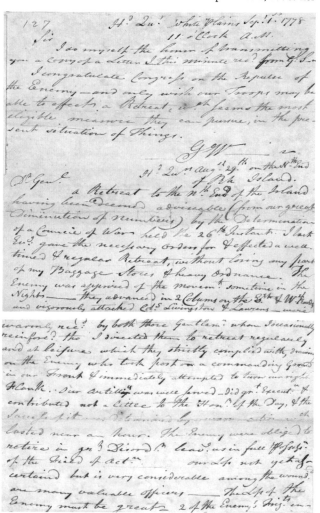

Sullivan's retreat at Newport was orderly until the British, learning of it, attacked, with great losses on both sides. The British retired, General Sullivan reported, "in great Disorder leaving us in full Possession of the Field of Action."

...amenting that the French admiral had "abandoned us ...the present Enterprize," General Sullivan asks ...ancock's advice on alternatives: should the siege of ...ewport be continued, should the investing force attack ...he place, or should the army withdraw? Hancock, no ...nger a member of Congress, was now a major general ...f Massachusetts militia.

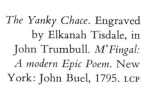

The Yanky Chace. Engraved by Elkanah Tisdale, in John Trumbull. *M'Fingal: A modern Epic Poem.* New York: John Buel, 1795. LCP

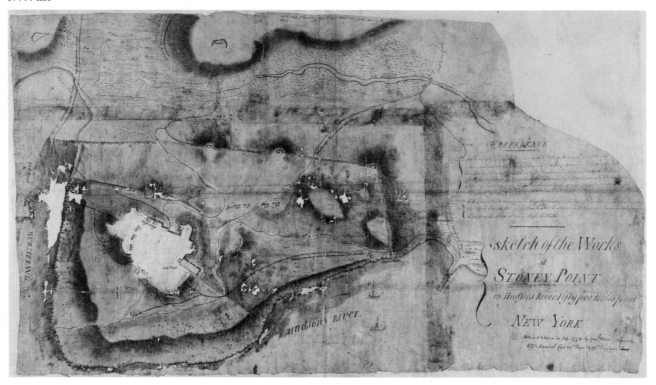

Newport was the last major action of 1778, and the larger part of the American forces under Washington were camped at White Plains. The Commander-in-Chief continued to plan a decisive blow in cooperation with the French fleet. His defense system around New York City centered on West Point. Clinton tried to tempt Washington into open field battle by advancing in force toward West Point at such spots as Stony Point. In this purpose he failed. Washington remained in place, Clinton withdrew to New York, but left a small garrison at Stony Point, whose defenses were sketched by an engineer of the 63rd Regiment.

Anthony Wayne. [*Draft of the Order of battle for Stony Point*], July 15, 1779. HSP

Washington determined to attack and destroy the British garrison at Stony Point, and chose Wayne to lead the action. Wayne's draft of his orders for the attack reveal his careful attention to detail and his determination that his orders be followed: "Should there be any Soldier so lost to every feeling of Honor, as to attempt to Retreat one Single foot or Sculk in the face of danger, the Officer next to him is Immediately to put him to death, that he may no longer disgrace the Name of a Soldier, or the Corps or State he belongs to."

Extract from General Orders, Headquarters, New Windsor, July 16, 1779. HSP

Head Quarters, New Windsor, July 16
1779

The Commander in Chief is happy to congratulate the Army, on the success of ~~[illegible]~~ under Brigadier General Wayne, who last night with the Corps of Light Infantry, surprised and took the enemy's post at Stony point, with the whole Garrison, Cannon & Stores, with very inconsiderable loss on our side — The General has not yet received the particulars of the affair, but He has the satisfaction to learn, that the officers and men in general, gloriously distinguished themselves in the attack —

He requests the Brigadier and his whole Corps to accept his warmest thanks, for the good conduct and signal bravery, manifested upon the occasion —

Extract from General Orders

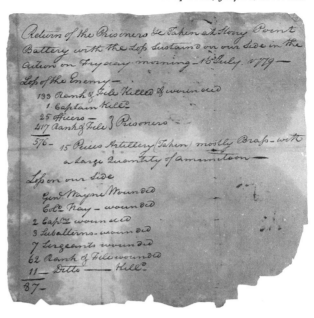

On the night of July 15, 1779, Wayne's elite "Corps of Light Infantry, surprised and took the enemy's post at Stony point, with the whole Garrison, Cannon & Stores, with very inconsiderable loss on our side." The success of the action won Washington's warm praise and heartened the American Army.

Return of the Prisoners &c Taken at Stony Point, July 16, 1779. HSP

Return of the Prisoners &c Taken at Stony Point Battery with the Loss sustaind on our side in the action on Fryday morning 15 July. 1779 —

Loss of the Enemy —
133 Rank & File Killed & wounded
1 Captain Killd
25 officers —
417 Rank & File } Prisoners
576 — 15 Peices Artillery (Taken) mostly Brass — with a Large Quantity of ammunition —

Loss on our side
Genl Wayne Wounded
Col. Hay — wounded
2 Captns wounded
3 Subalterns — wounded
7 Sergeants wounded
62 Rank & File wounded
11 Ditto —— Killd
87 —

Inventory of Baggage taken from the British Officers Viz.

Superfine Scarlet Cloth (suppose) a Pattern for a Coat of narrow Cloth.
1 Small piece do. 3/4 Yards
2 1/2 Yds. White Shalloon or thereabt.
pr. Buckram, 2 Sticks red & White Twist
some red and White Silk
1 Spy Glass Elegant of Dollands make
2 Red Silk Sashes & 2 Black Leather Belts
1 fur Cap
3 pr. Breeches 1 pr. Overalls & 1 Jacket
2 pr. Worsted 2 pr. Silk 1 pr. Thread & 1 pair of Buckskin Stockgs. —
1 Table Cloth
1 pillow Case
1 Pocket Handkf.
1 Towell
2 night Caps 1 Woollen do.
Bundle of Flints
1 pr. Boots —
1 pr. Gaiters & 1 odd one
1 Candlestick
1 Powder Bag.

Inventory of Baggage taken From the British Officers [Stony Point, July 16, 1779]. HSP

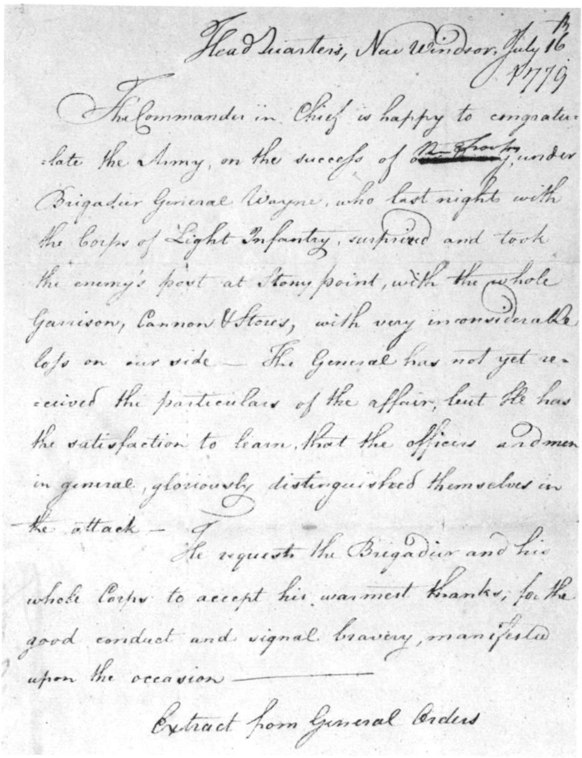

The American victory at Stony Point was complete, as these two lists tell clearly. The enemy lost 576 to the Americans' 87. The list of the baggage of the officers does not include what must have been more precious to the proud prisoners than night caps, gaiters, or silk sashes—their pride and confidence in ultimate victory.

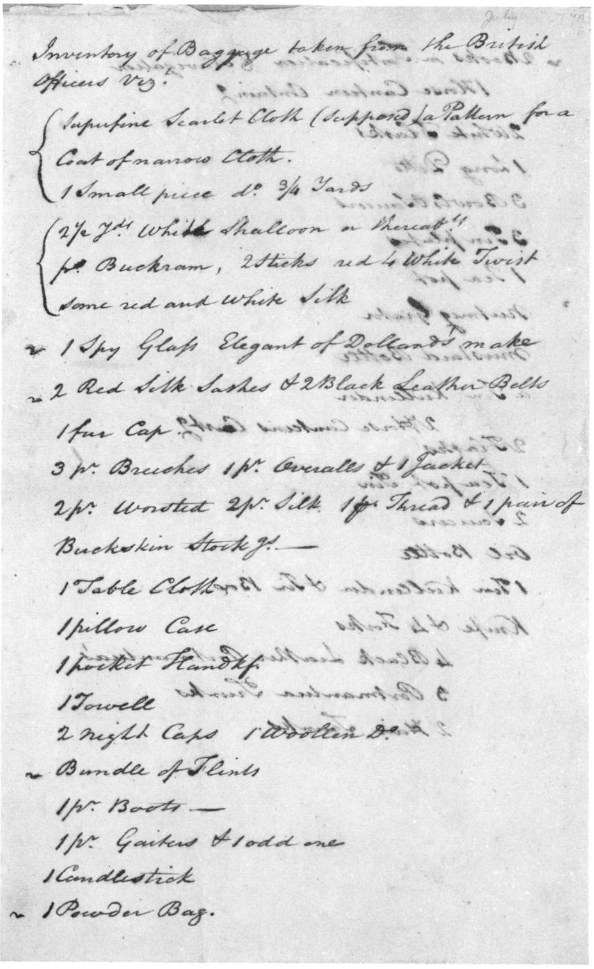

Throughout the conventional war along the seaboard, a frontier war was being waged in the West. British and Loyalists at Fort Niagara and Detroit incited the Indians to scalp and to kill the white settlers. The Mohawk and Wyoming valleys were burned-over targets of their wrath. This poem in 29 stanzas tells the gory tale of battle, defeat, and torture at Forty Fort in Pennsylvania. It was but one of many sad tales of the wilderness.

Taking advantage of the inaction of Clinton's army quartered in New York, Washington sent General Sullivan with a picked force of Continentals to the New York frontier to put a stop to the Indian raids.

John Ross. *Order of March of Maj. Gen. Sullivan's Army on the Western Expedition,* July 30, 1779. LCP

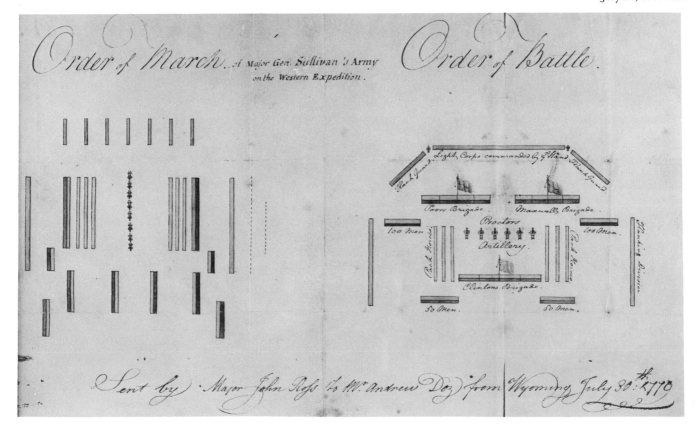

Thayendanegea
(baptized *Joseph Brant*).
Artist unknown. Oil
on wood. HSP

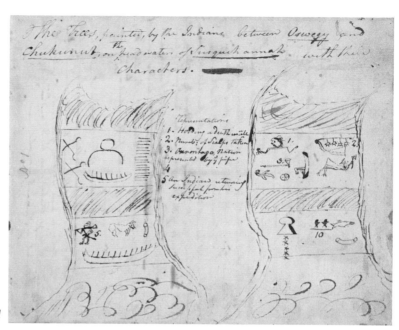

Adam Hubley. [*Journal on the Western Expedition*], 1779. HSP

Lieutenant Colonel Hubley of Pennsylvania, commander of a regiment and a good observer of the country, sketched in his journal the plan of the encampment at Wyoming and the designs and symbols the Indians painted on the forest trees.

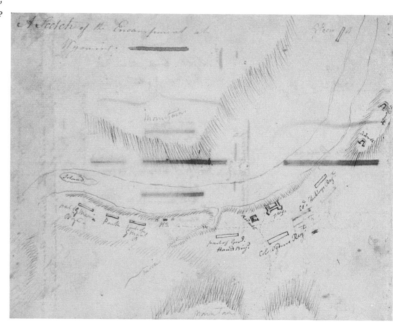

Zebulon Butler. *Letter to General Nathanael Greene*, Wyoming, November 6, 1779. HSP

From Wyoming, Sullivan's expedition went on, continued its advance into the Indians' country, defeated Indians and Loyalists at Newtown in New York in late August, but, because of difficulties with supplies, could not attack and destroy Fort Niagara, which was the headquarters from which the Indians were directed. However, as this letter points out, Sullivan's activities did bring a lessening in Indian attacks.

At sea John Paul Jones, whose successful raids on British shipping and harbors had won him in England the epithet of pirate, now led his little fleet of *Bon Homme Richard,* 40 guns, *Alliance,* 36 guns, *Pallas,* 30 guns, a cutter, an armed brig, and two French privateers against the Baltic fleet, which was protected by the *Serapis* and her squadron. In the "dreadful" engagement that ensued off Flamborough Head Jones gave the enemy a reply that passed into American history and tradition: "I have not begun to fight." The Americans carried the battle.

Captain John Paul Jones. Engraved by Daniel-Nicholas Chodowiecki in *Historisch-genealogischer Calender, oder Jahrbuch der merkwürdigsten neuen Welt.* Leipzig, 1784. LCP

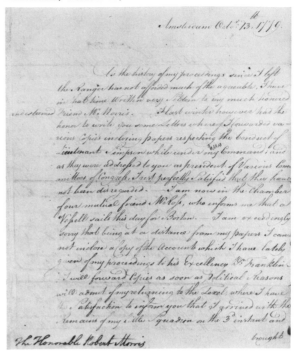

In this report Jones vividly describes the action between the *Bonhomme Richard* and the *Serapis,* which lasted two and a half hours, during which both ships were burning, and his flagship was actually fired upon by one of his own vessels. The *Bonhomme Richard* sank; that and the loss of life made the victory "too dear."

Marquis de Lafayette. *Letter to Benjamin Franklin,* [Paris], October 6, 1779. APS

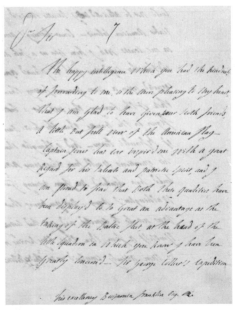

Jones's victory over the Baltic fleet inspired Lafayette "with a great Regard for his talents and patriotic Spirit," and encouraged the latter in the plans then being made to launch an attack on England from France, under his command. Nothing came of this project.

Comte d'Estaing. *Letter to General Augustine Prevost,* Camp before Savannah, September 16, 1779. HSP

Augustin Dupré. *Libertas Americana.* Reverse of the medal. Engraving in *Historisch-genealogischer Calender, oder Jahrbuch der merkwürdigsten neuen Welt.* Leipzig, 1784. LCP

During the summer of 1779, the American theater of war moved to the South, where the British occupied coastal ports, including Savannah. There French forces under d'Estaing joined American troops under General Benjamin Lincoln in a siege. In this letter to the commander of the English garrison d'Estaing called on him to surrender his force "to the Army of his Majesty the King of France." Prevost rejected the summons, and as a result saved Savannah for the British.

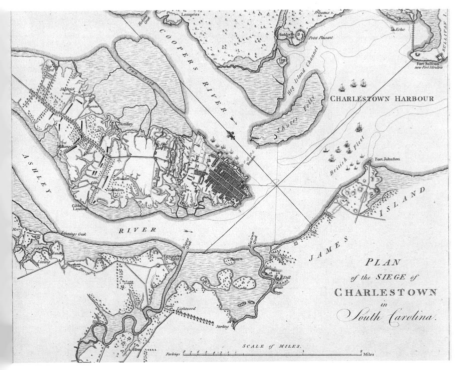

Chevalier Dussauts. *Relation du Siège de Charlestown,* [1780]. Manuscript. HSP

Plan of the Siege of Charlestown in South Carolina. London: [William Faden], 1787. HSP

After the failure to take Savannah in concert with the French, Lincoln and the American troops moved to Charleston, where in early 1780 he was besieged by a concentrated British force drawn from Savannah and from New York. In traditional 18th-century tactics the siege proceeded to its inevitable result—the surrender of Lincoln's force of 5500 men, including some of their French allies.

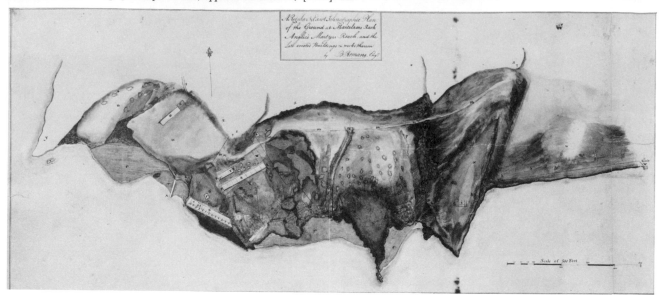

Proceedings of a General Court Martial . . . of Major General Arnold
Philadelphia: Francis Bailey, 1780. LCP
Benedict Arnold. *Letter to Colonel James Livingston,*
Head Quarters, Robinson's House, August 5, 1780. HSP

Henry Lee, Jr. [*Account of Benedict Arnold's Treason*], October 4, 1780. HSP

General Arnold had distinguished himself early and often as a field commander in the American army, first at Quebec, then at Saratoga. But his conduct as military governor of Philadelphia in 1778 led to a court martial, which sentenced him to be reprimanded by Washington. Smarting under this mild disgrace, Arnold opened treasonous negotiations with the enemy. To further his intentions, he obtained command of the important American fort at West Point. In view of the design he was contemplating, this call on the commander of the garrisons at Stony Point and Verplanck's Point for "every information in your power" can be thought to have an ominous undertone.

A month after Arnold wrote Colonel Livingston from West Point, his treason was uncovered by the capture of Major John André, who was carrying messages from Arnold to Sir Henry Clinton in New York. With Arnold's fall, facts and suppositions about his character and activities were gathered. Colonel "Light Horse Harry" Lee was outraged to realize that "Mr. Arnold has been a villain on the small scale as well as the great. He had established lucrative connexions with sutlers & sutlers' wifes, and had made them the instruments of converting into money, his embezzlement of public stores." What is more, he had deceived his wife and betrayed his friend André.

*Marquis de Lafayette. Letter to Benjamin Franklin,
Camp on the Passaic, November 19, 1780.* APS

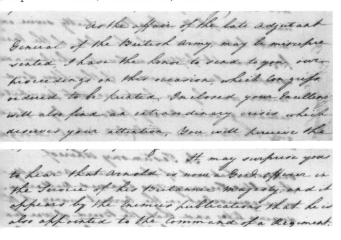

The outrage Lafayette and others in the American Army
felt at Arnold's behavior and at his being rewarded
with a major general's commission in the British Army,
was coupled with sympathy for André, an honorable
and attractive person. To put the facts about his
court-martial and execution before the world, Congress
ordered that the proceedings of the court-martial be
published. Such was the interest in the case that the
pamphlet, a copy of which Lafayette sent to Franklin,
was reprinted in several American cities and in Europe
as well.

PROCEEDINGS
OF A
BOARD
OF
GENERAL OFFICERS,

HELD BY ORDER OF

His Excellency Gen. WASHINGTON,

Commander in Chief of the Army of the United States
of AMERICA.

RESPECTING

Major *JOHN ANDRÉ,*

Adjutant General of the British Army.

SEPTEMBER 29, 1780.

PHILADELPHIA:
Printed by FRANCIS BAILEY, in Market-Street

M,DCC,LXXX.

*Proceedings of a Board of
General Officers, . . .
respecting Major John André.*
Philadelphia: Francis
Bailey, 1780. APS

James Burd.
Letter to Edward Burd,
Tinian, November 20,
1780. HSP

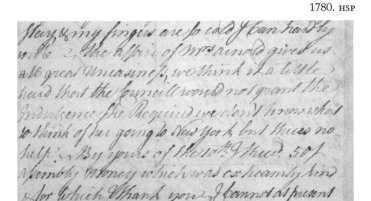

[Charles Willson Peale].
[*Arnold in Effigy drawn
through the Streets*].
[Philadelphia, 1780].
Woodcut. HSP

Benedict Arnold.
Engraved by Pierre E.
Du Simitière. London:
W. Richardson,
1783. LCP

The Capture of Major André. Engraved by
Daniel-Nicholas Chodowiecki in
*Historisch-genealogischer Calender,
oder Jahrbuch der merkwürdigsten neuen
Welt.* Leipzig, 1784. LCP

Arnold's treason produced public anger
and scorn, and personal tragedies for
many who were close to him.

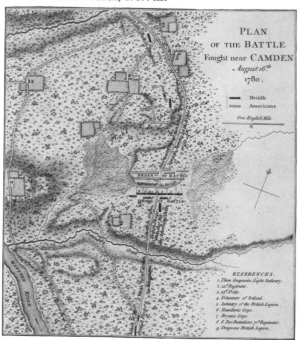

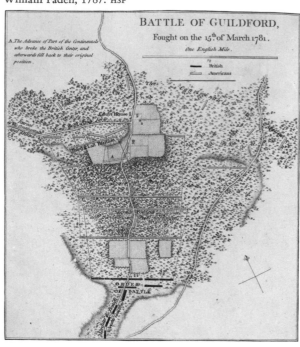

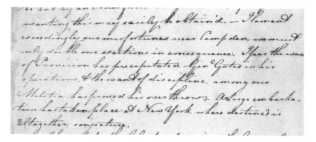

The British under Cornwallis marched north from
Charleston with relentless purpose, taking victories
along the way. Camden on August 16, 1780, was
a disaster for General Gates and his Continentals,
who fled before the British bayonets all the way
160 miles back to Hillsborough. "We must only
double our exertions in consequence," was General
Weedon's comment.

Gates was removed from command after his defeat
at Camden. General Nathanael Greene succeeded
him as commander of the American Army in the
South. Still more defeats were in store for the
Americans, however, like that at Guildford Court
House, where the militia crumpled before Lord
Cornwallis's attack. But Greene continued his
retreat, drawing the British ever farther from their
bases on the coast.

Marquis de Lafayette. *Letter to General George Weedon,*
Deep Creek, June 16, 1781. APS

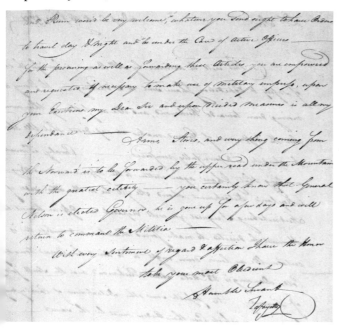

George Weedon. *Letter to Marquis de Lafayette,*
Fredericksburg, June 17, 1781. APS

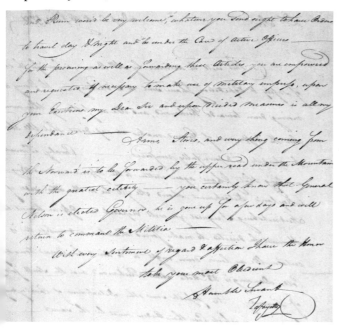

Thomas Nelson, Jr.
*Printed letter concerning
French Forces,* Richmond,
September 2, 1781. HSP

RICHMOND, SEPTEMBER 2, 1781.

SIR,

THE arrival of a French fleet of twenty eight ships of the line, and
six frigates, with three thousand troops, at this critical period,
must give the highest satisfaction to every man interested in the happiness
of his country. Vigorous exertions on our part will insure to us the
conquest of the British army. There is not, I hope, a man in Virginia
who will not step forth to improve this favourable opportunity of relieving
his country from the distresses of an invading army. On you, Sir, I call,
as the head of the militia of your county, to send into the field every
man, who can be furnished with a gun of any sort. Expedition is the
life of all military operations. Let it be remembered that the destruction
of Burgoyne's army was in a great measure effected by the manly behaviour of the northern militia: And Virginia has now a most glorious opportunity of signalizing herself.

A number of horses, saddles, and bridles will be wanted. Some of
the best sort for the General and field officers; others of an inferiour
quality for the artillery and to mount 100 dragoons which the Count de
Grasse has brought with him. As the services of these horses will be required only for a short time, I expect that Gentlemen will lend them most
cheerfully, after having them appraised in specie for fear of losses.

I would beg your attention to another object of much importance. For
so large an army large supplies of provisions and liquors will be necessary.
I wish you to press the commissioners of your county to procure flour,
spirits and cattle, to be brought to some particular place in the country,
ready to be delivered to the order of the Commissary General; but particularly flour and spirits. I hope every person who has wheat will prepare
part of it immediately for the mills. Waggons are also exceedingly wanted;
endeavour to procure as many of them as possible on hire for this expedition, the hire at ten shillings per day and depreciation. I could wish
them to be loaded with liquors for the use of the army. It is not in my
power to ascertain the depreciation that will be allowed for the specie
prices at which the different supplies will be valued; but the Assembly
will undoubtedly act with generosity on this occasion.

I am, with much respect,
Your most obedient servant,

Cornwallis's campaign had left him a decimated army
and very few supplies; accordingly he retreated to the
coast, where he might be provisioned by the British
Navy. The Continental Army was also in need of
materiel, especially if they were to maintain pressure on
the enemy. Lafayette was in desperate need for supplies
of all kinds ("We are in the greatest want of Shoes.
For Gods sake my dear friend, if it is possible try to
collect a supply of them, and send them to me with the
greatest dispatch.") Weedon promised to do what he
could—but there would be no shoes, for they had been
sent away to keep them from the British.

The arrival of the French fleet with regular
troops was something to cheer about and the
Governor of Virginia applauded the prospects,
all the while calling on the heads of the county
militia to provide men and supplies promptly.
"Expedition is the life of all military
operations."

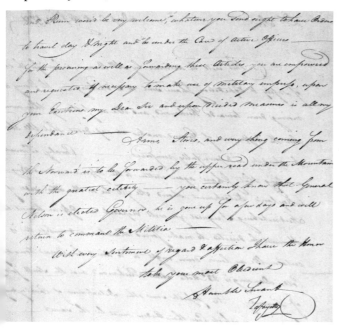

169

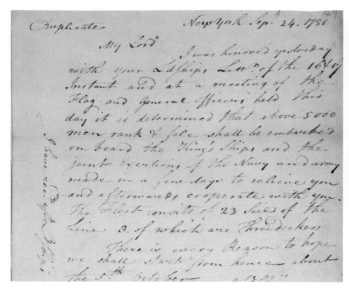

In late September Clinton in New York promised British troops to an apprehensive Cornwallis in Virginia. The convoy would leave about October 5.

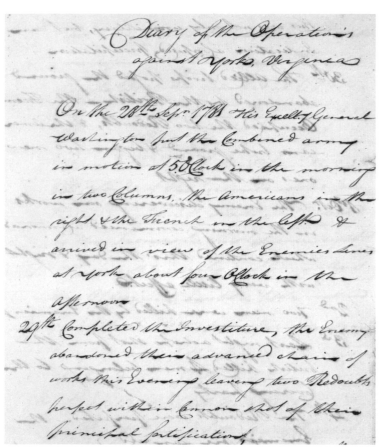

Anthony Wayne. *Diary of the Operations against York, Virginia,* [September 28– October 17, 1781]. HSP

Troops on both sides in great numbers moved by sea and over the land to the Virginia theater of war. Lafayette waited cautiously outside Yorktown, where Cornwallis had withdrawn his army, hoping for relief by sea. Soon the besieging forces were strengthened by additional American and French troops. At 5 o'clock in the morning of September 28 General Washington put his combined army in motion; they reached Yorktown at 4 o'clock that afternoon. Next day the investment was completed, and the siege began.

Sebastian Bauman. *Plan of the Investment of York and Gloucester.* [1781]. LCP

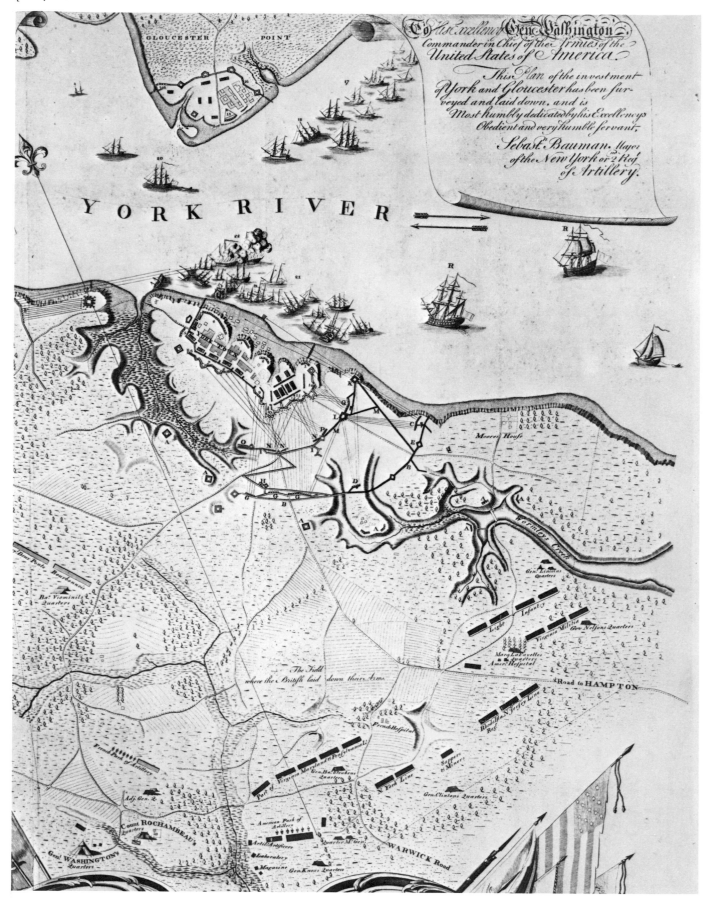

The defense of Yorktown depended upon control of the river by the British.

[manuscript letter, Arthur Lee]

The theme of the war had been shortage of supplies, and Yorktown was no exception. Lee wrote of the compelling need for regular and orderly provision of supplies. The alternative was that bodies of armed men roamed the countryside searching for food and clothing for the army, with the result that the citizens were frightened and concealed what they had. Lee warned that "force, in the manner it is exercised, defeats itself."

[manuscript letter, Thomas McKean to George Washington]

Washington was informed that the British fleet planned a move to relieve Cornwallis at Yorktown. All were aware of the overriding necessity for coordination between the army under Washington and the French fleet under Comte de Grasse.

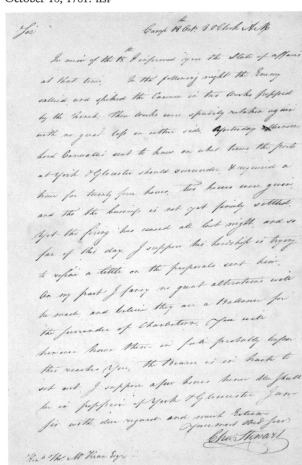

By October 18 it was clear to Cornwallis that his army would not be saved by the British navy. He asked for the terms of surrender and 24 hours to consider them. He was allowed two. Already the guns were falling silent and all knew what the outcome of the siege would be.

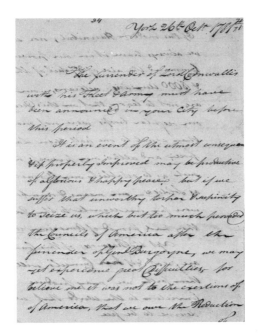

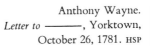

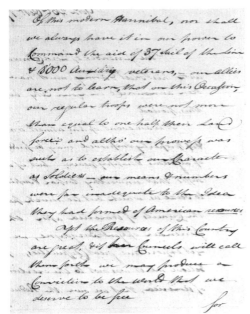

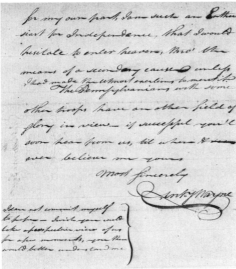

The surrender was negotiated, the Americans took possession of Yorktown, the British forces laid down their arms. They appeared to be, an American soldier noticed, "much in Liquor"—drunk, possibly, to dull their feelings. The British band played "The World Turned Upside Down"—as indeed it must have seemed on both sides.

The Surrender of Cornwallis at Yorktown.
Engraved by Daniel-Nicholas
Chodowiecki in *Historisch-genealogischer
Calender, oder Jahrbuch der merkwürdigsten
neuen Welt.* Leipzig, 1784. LCP

It was not certain that the battle of Yorktown had ended the war. Another spring might see another army in the field. General Wayne, who had seen six years of action, pointed out that "we owe the Reduction of this modern Hannibal" [Cornwallis] to the French, that such aid might not be forthcoming at some future time, and that therefore Americans must beware of "unworthy torpor & supinity," by which they would lose the benefits of the victory.

Surrender of Earl Cornwallis. HSP

John Jay. *Letter to George Washington,* Madrid, December 9, 1781. HSP

Madrid 9th December 1781

Sir

on the 7th Inst. I had the Honor of receiving your Excellency's favor of the 22d. of October last, with the Copies of the articles of Capitulation, Returns, & of General Greene's letter, mentioned in it. I also rec'd. on the same Day, Duplicates of each.

The Reasons which induced your Excellency to transmit these Papers, will I am persuaded, appear no less proper to Congress, than the speedy Reception of such welcome & interesting Intelligence, is agreable to me.

I congratulate your Excellency and my Country, on this important Event, & permit me to assure you, that its having been achieved under the immediate Direction of the Commander in chief, adds to the Satisfaction I feel on the Occasion. General Greene's Conduct merits the Commendation & Thanks of his Country - He

Lord Cornwallis. *Letter to Anthony Wayne,* Yorktown, November 1, 1781. HSP

Lord Cornwallis presents his Compliments to General Wayne and is sorry he cannot have the pleasure of waiting upon him to morrow, being engaged to dine with Count de Saint-Maime.

Thomas Jefferson. *Letter to George Washington,* Monticello. October 28, 1781. HSP

Monticello Oct. 28. 1781.

Sir

I hope it will not be unacceptable to your Excellency to receive the congratulations of a private individual on your return to your native country, & above all things on the important success which has attended it. great as this has been however, it can scarcely add to the affection with which we had looked up to you, and if in the minds of any the motives of gratitude to our good allies were not sufficiently apparent the part they have borne in this action, must amply evince them. notwithstanding the state of perpetual decrepitude to which I am unfortunately reduced, I should certainly have done myself the honour of paying my respects to you personally, but that I apprehend those visits which are meant by us as marks of our attachment to you must interfere with the regulations of a camp, and be particularly inconvenient to one whose time is too precious to be wasted in ceremony.

I beg you to believe me among the sincerest of those who subscribe themselves.

Your Excellency's
most obed t.
& most humble serv t.

Th: Jefferson

In the aftermath of military victory the President of Congress offered congratulations to Washington "on this important Event;" Cornwallis was invited to dinner by his erstwhile enemy General Wayne, but declined because of a prior engagement; and Thomas Jefferson, a private citizen again, congratulated his fellow-Virginian and, indirectly, the French allies.

175

George the Third by the Grace of God King of Great Britain, France and Ireland, Defender [of the Faith]... and Lüneburg, Arch Treasurer and Prince Elector of the Holy Germain Empire &c &c To all to wh[om]...

Whereas for the perfecting and establishing the Peace Friendship and good Understanding so ha[ppily]... Articles signed at Paris the Thirtieth Day of November last by the Commissioners of Us and Our Good [Friends the United States of] America viz New Hampshire, Massachusets Bay, Rhode Island, Connecticut, New York, New [Jersey, Pennsylvania, the Three] Counties on Delaware, Maryland, Virginia, North Carolina, South Carolina, and Georgia, in North [America and for] promoting and regulating ... the mutual Intercourse of Trade and Commerce between Our Kin[gdoms and the] United States We have thought fit ... to cause some fit Person with full Power on our Part to meet [with the Commissioners of the] said United States now residing at Paris duly authorized for the accomplishing of such laudable ...

... that We reposing especial Trust and Confidence in the Wisdom Loyalty Diligence and Circumspe[ction of our trusty and well beloved] David Hartley Esquire ... on whom We have therefore conferred the Rank of Our Minister Plenipotentiary ... and appoint ... and by these Presents do nominate constitute and appoint him Our true certain and undoubted ... and Plenipotentiary, Giving and granting to him all and all Manner of Faculty Power and Auth[ority] ... special Order or ... derogate from the special nor the special ... for ... the action ... with the Power to Him to ... furnished with sufficient Power on the Part of Our said Good Friends ... concerning all such Matters and Things as may be requisite and necessary for accomplishing and comp[leting the Matters] herein before mentioned and also for Us and in Our Name to sign such Treaty or Treaties, Conven[tion or Conventions] whatsoever as may be agreed upon In the Premises and mutually to deliver and receive the same ... all such other Acts Matters and Things as may be any ways proper and conducive to the Purposes ... and ... and ... the ... Faculty as though We Ourself if We were present could do ... ... that We will accept ratify and confirm in the most effectual Manner all such Act[s] ... transacted and concluded by Our aforesaid Commissioner Procurator and Plenipotentiary, and ... violate the same In the Whole or in Part, or to act contrary thereto. In Testimony and Confirm[ation whereof We have caused the] Great Seal of Great Britain to be affixed to these Presents signed with Our Royal Hand. Give[n at ...] Fourteenth Day of May in the Year of Our Lord One Thousand Seven Hundred and Eighty [Three ...] of Our Reign ...

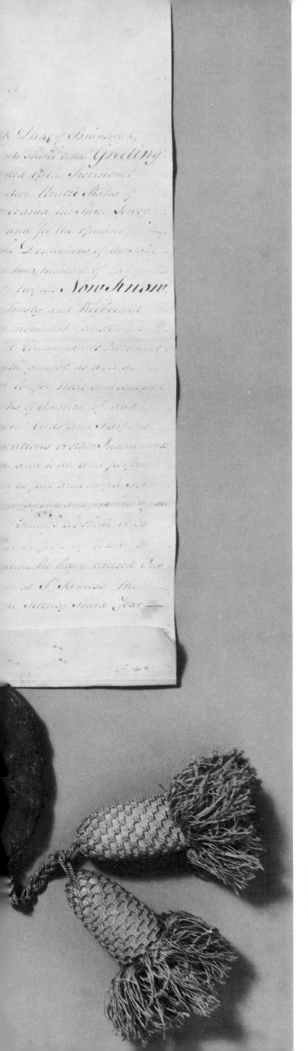

Peace-Making, 1782-1783

"There never was a good war or a bad peace."—Benjamin Franklin. Letter to David Hartley, July 27, 1783

George III. *Commission to David Hartley*, St. James's, London, May 14, 1783. APS

Josiah Bartlett. *Letter to General Nathaniel Folsom,* York Town, Pa., June 12, 1778. HSP

The British offer of conciliation through General Howe, made soon after the Declaration of Independence in 1776, failed. So did their second offer, made by a commission headed by the Earl of Carlisle when the British Army was being forced from Philadelphia. Bartlett, a member of Congress from New Hampshire, describes Washington's characteristic punctiliousness—refusal to receive any communication on military matters except in writing, or to receive any political communication at all.

Even before receiving Carlisle's proposals, Congress reacted coolly, instructing their president, in Bartlett's words, to inform the British emissaries "that when the King of England was seriously inclined to put an end to the cruel and unprovoked war he had waged against the United States they would readily concur in all proper measures consistent with the Rights of Independant Nations, the Intrest of their Constituents & the Sacred Regard they owed to Treaties."

John Banister. *Letter to [Theodorick Bland],* York, Pa., June 19, 1778. HSP

A member of Congress, commenting on the rejection of the Earl of Carlisle's proposals for reconciliation, is puzzled why the British had so misunderstood the Americans as to believe they would accept any proposals "short of Independence." He suggests the British made the peace offer for the purpose of "Reconciling their own People, & to give a colouring to their own Conduct in the Eyes of the Powers of Europe."

Augustin Dupré. *America offering the Laurel.* Sketch for the obverse of a medal to General Daniel Morgan, 1789. APS

Letters and other Papers relating to the Proceedings of his Majesty's Commissioners, &c.

By the Earl of CARLISLE, Sir HENRY CLINTON, WILLIAM EDEN, Esquire, and GEORGE JOHNSTONE, Esquire, Commissioners appointed by his Majesty, in pursuance of an Act of Parliament, to treat, consult and agree upon the means of quieting the disorders now subsisting in certain of the Colonies, Plantations, and Provinces of North-America.

PROCLAMATION.

WHEREAS the King in Parliament being desirous to restore the blessings of reconciliation and peace to Great-Britain and her colonies, did in the course of last session repeal certain acts, which were found to have excited jealousies, and given apprehensions of danger to liberty in the said colonies. And being further desirous, in the most speedy and effectual manner, to remove every obstruction to the re-establishment of peace, did appoint us his Commissioners to act on this Continent, and by our presence in America to prevent the delays that must have attended the passage and return of messages to and from Europe, on every subject of discussion that might arise. Be it known to all whom it may concern, that we being met at Philadelphia, on the tenth of June, did from thence dispatch the following letter, with the inclosures hereto annexed, to Henry Laurens, Esq; President of the Congress, and have received the answer subjoined.

COPY of a Letter to the President of the Congress.

GENTLEMEN,

WITH an earnest desire to stop the farther effusion of blood and the calamities of war, we communicate to you, with the least possible delay, after our arrival in this city, a copy

The British Commissioners publish a record of their efforts at reconciliation and of Congress' rejection.

Earl of Carlisle and other Commissioners. *Letters and other Papers relating to the Proceedings of his Majesty's Commissioners, &c.* [New York, 1778]. Broadside. LCP

MANIFESTO AND PROCLAMATION.

in making our appeal to those constituents and to the free inhabitants of this continent in general, have determined to give to them what in our opinion should have been the first object of those who appeared to have taken the management of their interests; and adopt this mode of carrying the said authorities and powers into execution. WE ACCORDINGLY HEREBY GRANT AND PROCLAIM A PARDON OR PARDONS OF ALL, AND ALL MANNER OF, TREASONS OR MISPRISIONS OF TREASONS, BY ANY PERSON OR PERSONS, OR BY ANY NUMBER OR DESCRIPTION OF PERSONS WITHIN THE SAID COLONIES, PLANTATIONS, OR PROVINCES, COUNSELLED, COMMANDED, ACTED, OR DONE, ON OR BEFORE THE DATE OF THIS MANIFESTO AND PROCLAMATION.

Earl of Carlisle and other Commissioners. *Manifesto and Proclamation.* [New York, 1778]. LCP

Having failed in their mission to offer peace and reconciliation to the American States within the Empire, the Carlisle Commission make a final appeal to individual Americans, including the promise of pardon. Nothing came of this. It was too late.

Samuel Huntington, president of Congress. *Letter to Benjamin Franklin,* Philadelphia, June 19, 1781. Copy. HSP

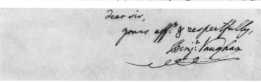

Dear sir; London, Midnight March 30th, 1782.

I am desired by Lord Shelburne to send to you to acquaint you that his lordship wishes to see "you without delay." — I have executed my com-mission without delay; and as far as health...

dear sir,
yours aff. & respectfully,
Benj. Vaughan

Benjamin Vaughan, *Letter to Henry Laurens,* London, "Midnight" March 30, 1782. HSP

The first step toward negotiating peace is taken. Lord Shelburne asks Henry Laurens, an American commissioner recently released from an English prison, to see him "without delay." Note that the invitation is dated "Midnight." Obviously Shelburne's secretary had just left the Minister and was not losing a minute.

Congress sends Franklin new instructions to negotiate peace, in conjunction with John Adams, minister in Paris, and John Jay, minister to Spain; and also with Henry Laurens, minister to The Netherlands but then a prisoner in the Tower of London, and Thomas Jefferson, who did not leave Virginia.

This copy is docketed by Franklin himself.

Benjamin Franklin, *Letter to David Hartley,* Passy, March 31, 1782. HSP

Throughout the war Franklin in France kept open a channel of communication with his friend David Hartley in London that was useful to both countries. Hartley, who confessed he was "not unambitious of the office of a peace-maker," kept Franklin informed of the change in the ministry from North to Rockingham and in the mood of British authorities toward peace with America.

Samuel Huntington, president of Congress. *Letter to Benjamin Franklin,* Philadelphia, July 5, 1781. HSP

Henry Laurens, formerly president of Congress, was commissioned to negotiate a commercial treaty with Holland. His vessel was captured by the British and he was committed to the Tower of London in 1780 "on suspicion of high treason." Despite claims to diplomatic immunity and the protests of Franklin and others, Laurens was held in prison for more than a year, often subjected to physical hardships and pressure to renounce his allegiance. Congress authorized Franklin to negotiate his exchange. Laurens was released on parole after the battle of Yorktown, was finally exchanged in 1782, and served as one of the peace negotiators in Paris in 1783.

Samuel Huntington, president of the Continental Congress. Drawn from life by Pierre E. Du Simitière and engraved by B. L. Prevost, 1781. APS

Conditions of the Exchange of Prisoners with America
8th May 1782.

The American Prisoners now in Forton and Mill Prisons are to be sent forthwith to America in Transports provided for that purpose, and to be supplied with Provisions for their Subsistence during the Passage at the Expence of Government. The Prisoners who belong to Massachusets Bay and to the Colonies adjacent to be conveyed to Boston, and those belonging to the Southern Colonies to be conveyed to the Chesapeak or Philadelphia. The Prisoners are not upon any Account to be allowed to proceed from hence to any other Country but America, and in case they should take

William Carmichael. *Letter to ——*, Madrid, June 24, 1781. HSP

Madrid 24th June 1781

25th The Letters rec'd from France to Day talk much of Peace I can say nothing positive on this Subject, but were I in your Case I would regulate my Conduct in such Manner as not to suffer in the Commercial Way should it take place soon — Depend Friend Adieu Yours Sincerely Wm. Carmichael

he prospect of peace, which seemed to open in the
mmer of 1781, led commercial firms to alter their
olicies accordingly. In this letter, John Jay's secretary,
ho remained in Madrid after his principal left, advises
s correspodent to regulate his conduct "in such Manner
not to Suffer in the Commercial Way should it
eace] take place soon."

Stephen Sayre. *Letter to Benjamin Franklin*, Paris, June 12, 1782. HSP

Paris 12th June 1782

Sir
As the English Commissioners of peace may probably demand the Island of Porto Rico, either as a preliminary article, or endeavour to obtain it in the course of negotiation; I beg leave to offer the following Idea to your Excellency's consideration.

Excellency's most obedient Servant
Stephen Sayre

his Excellency Benjamin Franklin Esq. &c &c

e expectation that the forthcoming treaty of peace
ould reorganize the world and its empires produced
ne bizarre proposals, among them one that Puerto Rico,
e island possession of a power friendly to the United
tes, should be separated from Spain and made "free &
en to a commerce with all the world." Franklin's
itioner hopes he will be made an officer in the new state.

With the effective conclusion of fighting in 1782, one of Franklin's first concerns was for "those poor brave men, who, with so much public virtue," had "endured four or five years' hard imprisonment rather than serve against their country." These were the captured American seamen, confined in the infamous Mill and Forton naval prisons. As a result of Franklin's initiative and the passage of an act of Parliament, the exchange of American and British prisoners began in the summer of 1782.

eorge the Third

King of Great Britain France and Ireland ... Defender of the Faith ... to ... London Esquire **Greeting Whereas** by virtue of an Act passed in the last session ... True with certain Colonies in North America therein mentioned ... It is cited "That it ... Colonies or plantations of New Hampshire Massachusetts Bay Rhode Island Conn ... Maryland Virginia North Carolina South Carolina and Georgia in North Amer ... them" ... **Therefore** and for a full manifestation of our earnest wish and desire and of that ... it should and might be lawful for us to treat consult of agree and conclude with any ... plantations or with any body or bodies Corporate or politic or any Assembly or Assem ... or a Truce with the said Colonies or plantations or any of them or any part or part ... in any wise notwithstanding **Now Know Ye** that we reposing especial Trust ... of the Affairs to be thereby committed to your charge **Have** nominated and appoin ... appoint constitute and assign you the said Richard Oswald to be our Commissioner ... authorities thereby entrusted and committed to you the said Richard Oswald and to ... and committed to your care during our will and pleasure and no longer according to ... pleasure And we do hereby authorize empower and require you the said Richard ... Commissioners named or to be named by the said Colonies or plantations and any ... Description of Men or any person or persons whatsoever a peace or a Truce with ... thereof any Law Act or Acts of parliament Matter or Thing to the contrary in any wi ... every regulation provision Matter or thing which shall have been agreed upon ... Commissioners Body or Bodies Corporate or politic Assembly or Assemblies Description ... ... and sufficient to enter into such agreement shall be fully and distinctly

... York New Jersey Pensylvania the three lower Counties on Delaware Maryland ... ... course Trade and Commerce should be restored between them **Therefore** and for a ... ment to put an end to the Calamities of war It is enacted that it should and might ... ...missioner or Commissioners named or to be named by the said Colonies or planta ... ... ate or politic or any Assembly or Assemblies or description of Men or any person or ... ... tions or any of them or any part or parts thereof any Law Act or Acts of parliame ... **Know Ye** that we reposing especial Trust in your wisdom Loyalty Diligence and ... ... to your charge **Have** nominated and appointed constituted and assigned and by ... ... the said Richard Oswald to be our Commissioner in that behalf to use and exercise ... ... committed to you the said Richard Oswald and to do perform and execute all other ... ... our will and pleasure and no longer according to the tenor of these our Letters pate ... ...orize empower and require you the said Richard Oswald to treat consult of and ... ... by and on the part of the thirteen United States of America Viz! New Hampshire M ... ... Pensylvania the three lower Counties on Delaware Maryland Virginia North C ... ... thirteen United States any Law Act or Acts of parliament Matter or Thing to the co ... ... pleasure that every Regulation provision Matter or thing within shall have b ... ...missioners or persons as aforesaid with whom you shall have judged meet and s ... ... in writing and authenticated by your hand and Seal on one side and by the hand ... ...trument so authenticated shall be by you transmitted to us through one of our pr ...

George III. *Commissions to Richard Oswald to negotiate peace,* July 25, September 21, 1782. APS

The instructions first given to the British commissioner to negotiate peace with the Americans authorized him to treat with any commissioner or commissioner of the *"colonies or plantations."* Though Franklin would have overlooked mere words, his colleagues John Adams and John Jay were adamant that Oswald must be empowered to negotiate with representatives of *"the thirteen United States of America."* Accordingly Oswald had to obtain a new commission; and peace negotiations were opened with American *independence* accepted as a fact by all parties.

Boston Septr. 12. 1782.

Sir,

Knowing how important it is that your Excellency should receive the latest and most authentic advices from our friends in Europe, particularly upon the great Point of Peace, I have taken the Liberty to send you a Transcript of a Letter lately received from our minister to State of Holland, Mr Adams, dated at the Hague July 25. 1782. His Words are —

Samuel Cooper.

His Excellency Genl. Washington.

Samuel Cooper. *Letter to George Washington*, Boston, September 12, 1782. HSP

Perhaps rather officiously, a Boston minister sends the Commander-in-Chief the latest news "upon the great Point of Peace"—an extract from a private letter to him from John Adams in Holland.

Augustin Dupré. *Minerva*. Sketch for the reverse of a medal for Benjamin Franklin, 1784. APS

Jonathan Williams. *Letter to Benjamin Franklin*, Nantes, December 6, 1782. HSP

Dear hond Sir   Nantes Decem 6. 1782.

The Day before yesterday there were a number of Letters in Town announcing a Peace. The News came from the Secretary of the Duc d'orleans who 'tis said informed that the King had announced it to the Duc. Such respectable Information prevented every Doubt and I among the Rest believed it. I immediately set myself to work to get a little fast sailing Brig I have here ready to sail at 24 Hours Notice supposing you wanted an Express Boat. The foolish Public always think I am in the Secret when anything happens that regards America and immediately on this news one cried out "M. Williams doit savoir cela". "Oui" says another & peut être il a reçu un exprès de M. Franklin" — the third left the peutêtre out of the Question, & it was established

established as a Fact that an Express had arrived to me in 36 hours, nay some knew the matter so well as to describe whether the Express wore a green or a blue Jacket. —

affectionately Yours.

Jon Williams

Upon receiving a report that a preliminary treaty of peace between Britain and the United States had been signed on November 30, 1782, Jonathan Williams, United States commercial agent at the French port of Nantes and Franklin's nephew, readied a fast-sailing vessel to carry the news to America.

eat Britain. *A Proclamation, declaring the Cessation of Arms, as well by Sea as Land,*
reed upon between His Majesty, the Most Christian King, the King of Spain, the States
neral of the United Provinces, and the United States of America. . . .
ndon: Charles Eyre and William Strahan, 1783. Broadside. LCP

By the KING.

A PROCLAMATION,

Declaring the Ceſſation of Arms, as well by Sea as Land, agreed upon between His Majeſty, the Moſt Chriſtian King, the King of *Spain*, the States General of the *United Provinces*, and the United States of *America*, and enjoining the Obſervance thereof.

GEORGE R.

HEREAS Proviſional Articles were ſigned at *Paris*, on the Thirtieth Day of *November* laſt, between Our Commiſſioner for treating of Peace with the Commiſſioners of the United States of *America* and the Commiſſioners of the ſaid States, to be inſerted in and to conſtitute the Treaty of Peace propoſed to be concluded between Us and the ſaid United States, when Terms of Peace ſhould be agreed upon between Us and His Moſt Chriſtian Majeſty: And whereas Preliminaries for reſtoring Peace between Us and His Moſt Chriſtian Majeſty were ſigned at *Verſailles* on the Twentieth Day of *January* laſt, by the Miniſters of

Given at Our Court at *Saint James's*, the Fourteenth Day of *February*, in the Twenty-third Year of Our Reign, and in the Year of Our Lord One thouſand ſeven hundred and eighty-three.

God ſave the King.

LONDON:

Printed by CHARLES EYRE and WILLIAM STRAHAN, Printers to the King's moſt Excellent Majeſty. 1783.

King George III formally
proclaims the cessation of
hostilities between Great Britain
and France, Spain, Holland, and
the United States.

John Adams. Engraved from
life by Reinier Vinkeles,
1782. APS

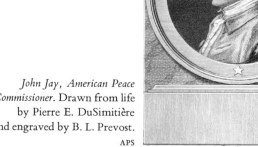

*John Jay, American Peace
Commissioner.* Drawn from life
by Pierre E. DuSimitière
and engraved by B. L. Prevost.
APS

Elias Boudinot, president of Congress. *Letter to General George Washington*, Philadelphia, March 23, 1783. HSP

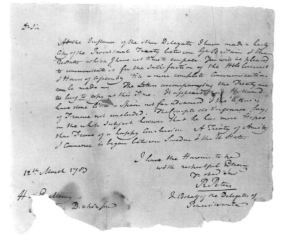

Richard Peters, Jr. *Letter to Governor John Dickinson*, [Philadelphia], March 12, 1783. LCP

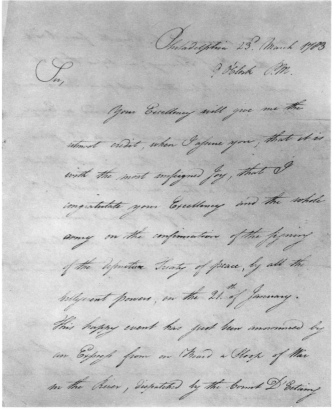

Elias Boudinot. *Letter to Lewis Pintard*, Philadelphia, March 12, 1783. HSP

The president of Congress, "with the most unfeigned Joy," informs General Washington and the Army that war between Britain and France, Spain, Holland and the United States has ended with the signing of preliminary treaties on January 20.

Eleazar McComb. *Letter to Caesar Rodney*, Philadelphia, March 12, 1783. HSP

General George Washington. Drawn from life by Pierre E. DuSimitière and engraved by B. L. Prevost. APS

News of the signing of the Preliminary Treaty of Peace between Britain and the United States reached Philadelphia on March 12, and was carried rapidly through the country. A copy was prepared for the information of the Supreme Executive Council of Pennsylvania. "The Compte de Virgennes says . . . that he has more Hopes than Fears of a happy Conclusion." And members of Congress, on hearing the great news, informed friends and colleagues of the terms.

By the UNITED STATES of America
In Congreſs Aſſembled.

A PROCLAMATION,

Declaring the Ceſſation of Arms, as well by Sea as by Land, agreed upon between the United States of America and His Britannic Majeſty; and enjoining the Obſervance thereof.

WHEREAS Proviſional Articles were ſigned at Paris on the Thirtieth Day of November laſt, between the Miniſters Plenipotentiary of the United States of America for treating of Peace, and the Miniſter Plenipotentiary of His Britannic Majeſty, to be inſerted in and to conſtitute the Treaty of Peace propoſed to be concluded between the United States of America and his Britannic Majeſty, when Terms of Peace ſhould be agreed upon between their Moſt Chriſtian and Britannic Majeſties: And Whereas Preliminaries for reſtoring Peace between their Moſt Chriſtian and Britannic Majeſties were ſigned at Verſailles, on the Twentieth Day of January laſt, by the Miniſters of their Moſt Chriſtian and Britannic Majeſties : And Whereas Preliminaries for reſtoring Peace between the ſaid King of Great Britain and the King of Spain were alſo ſigned at Verſailles, on the ſame Twentieth Day of January laſt.

By which ſaid Preliminary Articles it hath been agreed, That as ſoon as the ſame were ratified, Hoſtilities between the ſaid Kings, their Kingdoms, States and Subjects, ſhould Ceaſe in all Parts of the World; and it was farther agreed, That all Veſſels and Effects that might be taken in the Channel and in the North Seas, after the Space of Twelve Days from the Ratification of the ſaid Preliminary Articles, ſhould be reſtored; that the Term ſhould be One Month from the Channel and North Seas as far as the Canary Iſlands incluſively, whether in the Ocean or the Mediterranean, Two Months from the ſaid Canary Iſlands as far as the Equinoctial Line or Equator; and laſtly, Five Months in all other Parts of the World, without any Exception or more particular Deſcription of time or Place : And Whereas it was Declared by the Miniſter Plenipotentiary of the King of Great Britain, in the Name and by the expreſs Order of the King his Maſter, on the ſaid Twentieth day of January laſt, that the ſaid United States of America, their Subjects and their Poſſeſſions ſhall be compriſed in the above mentioned Suſpenſion of Arms, at the ſame Epochs, and in the ſame manner, as the three Crowns above mentioned, their Subjects and Poſſeſſions reſpectively; upon Condition that on the Part, and in the Name of the United States of America, a ſimilar Declaration ſhall be Delivered, expreſſly Declaring their Aſſent to the ſaid Suſpenſion of Arms, and containing an Aſſurance of the moſt perfect Reciprocity on their Part: And Whereas the Miniſters Plenipotentiary of theſe United States, did, on the ſame Twentieth Day of January, in the Name and by the Authority of the ſaid United States, accept the ſaid Declaration, and declare, that the ſaid States ſhould cauſe all Hoſtilities to Ceaſe againſt His Britannic Majeſty, his Subjects and his Poſſeſſions, at the Terms and Epochs agreed upon between His ſaid Majeſty the King of Great-Britain, His Majeſty the King of France, and His Majeſty the King of Spain, ſo, and in the ſame Manner, as had been agreed upon between thoſe Three Crowns, and to produce the ſame Effects: And Whereas the Ratifications of the ſaid Preliminary Articles between their Moſt Chriſtian and Britannic Majeſties were exchanged by their Miniſters on the Third Day of February laſt, and between His Britannic Majeſty and the King of Spain on the Ninth Day of February laſt: And Whereas it is Our Will and Pleaſure that the Ceſſation of Hoſtilities between the United States of America and his Britannic Majeſty, ſhould be conformable to the Epochs fixed between their Moſt Chriſtian and Britannic Majeſties.

WE have thought fit to make known the ſame to the Citizens of theſe States, and we hereby ſtrictly Charge and Command all our Officers, both by Sea and Land, and others, Subjects of theſe United States, to Forbear all Acts of Hoſtility, either by Sea or by Land, againſt His Britannic Majeſty or his Subjects, from and after the reſpective Times agreed upon between their Moſt Chriſtian and Britannic Majeſties as aforeſaid.

AND We do further require all Governors and others, the Executive Powers of theſe United States reſpectively, to cauſe this our Proclamation to be made Public, to the end that the ſame be duly obſerved within their ſeveral Juriſdictions.

DONE in Congreſs, at Philadelphia, this Eleventh Day of April, in the Year of our Lord One Thouſand Seven Hundred and Eighty-Three, and of our Sovereignty and Independence the Seventh.

United States. *A Proclamation, Declaring the Cessation of Arms, as well by Sea as by Land, agreed upon between the United States of America and His Britannic Majesty.* [Philadelphia, 1783]. Broadside. LCP

Congress formally announces the cessation of hostilities.

"The Business of Peace is done, in substance, and will be compleated formally in the definitive Treaty in a few Days." So believing, Adams wanted to be sent as United States Minister to England. But he was too sanguine. The definitive treaty was not signed for seven months; and he did not go to London until 1785.

Thomas FitzSimons. *Letter to the President of the Supreme Executive Council of Pennsylvania,* [Philadelphia], April 12, 1783. HSP

The end of hostilities meant the resumption of trade. "The Commercial people" were anxious to know whether British vessels might now freely enter American ports, and British goods be imported. The answer "may be of Considerable Consequence to the Commerce of the state."

John Adams. *Letter to Robert R. Livingston,* Paris, June 27, 1783. HSP

Benjamin Franklin. *Letter to Henry Laurens,* Passy, July 6, 1783. HSP

Calling on Laurens to come to Paris to help with the business of the American Commission, Franklin informs him that the British commander-in-chief in America, in violation of the Preliminary Articles of Peace, has sent away a large number of slaves, to whom Britain had promised freedom. This was the beginning of the colony of Sierra Leone in Africa.

Though trade between England and the United States resumed in the wake of the Preliminary Treaty of Peace, one of the ministers in Paris was not certain whether this was wise. John Adams preferred to have a treaty of commerce *before* opening trade, especially because otherwise American vessels might be barred from the West Indian trade. One American minister in London, with proper instructions, he assures the American Secretary for Foreign Affairs, could negotiate the definitive treaty. "For it is not merely mercantile Profit and Convenience that is at Stake, future Wars, long and bloody Wars may be either avoided or intailed upon our Posterity, as We conduct wisely or otherwise the present Negotiation with Great Britain."

This endorsement is by Mr. Oswald himself

Reparation of Damages, Devastations plunder — &ca—

This paper certainly passed from Dr. Franklin to Mr. Oswald, as it has on it the hand writing of both. The body of it I believe is written by Dr. Franklin's Secretary his grandson W. Temple Franklin. BV.

This therefore was an original document used in the Negotiation for peace. BV.

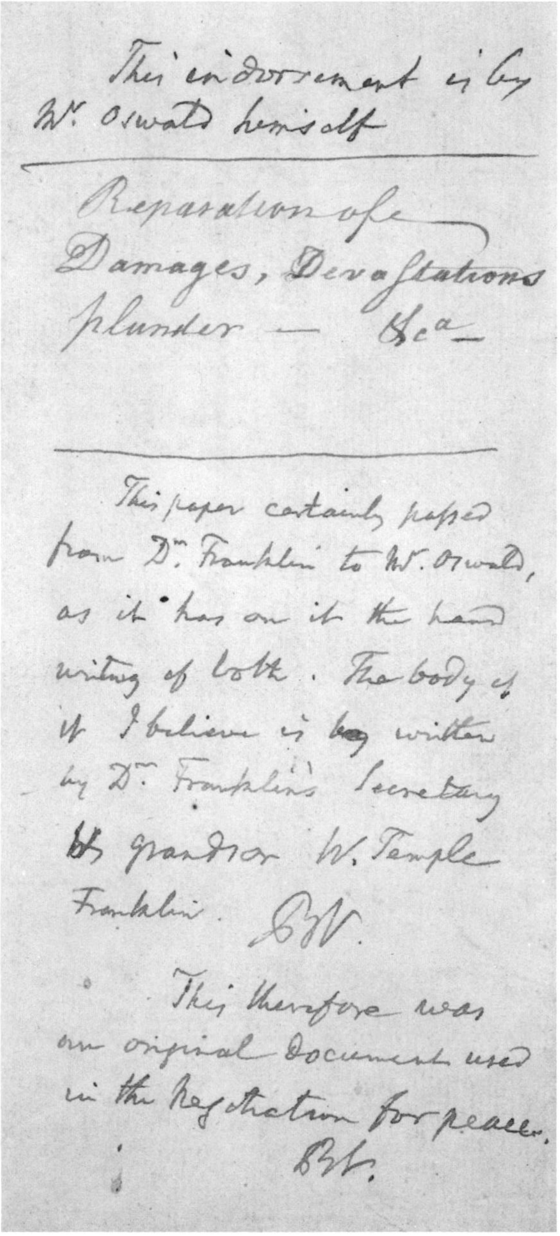

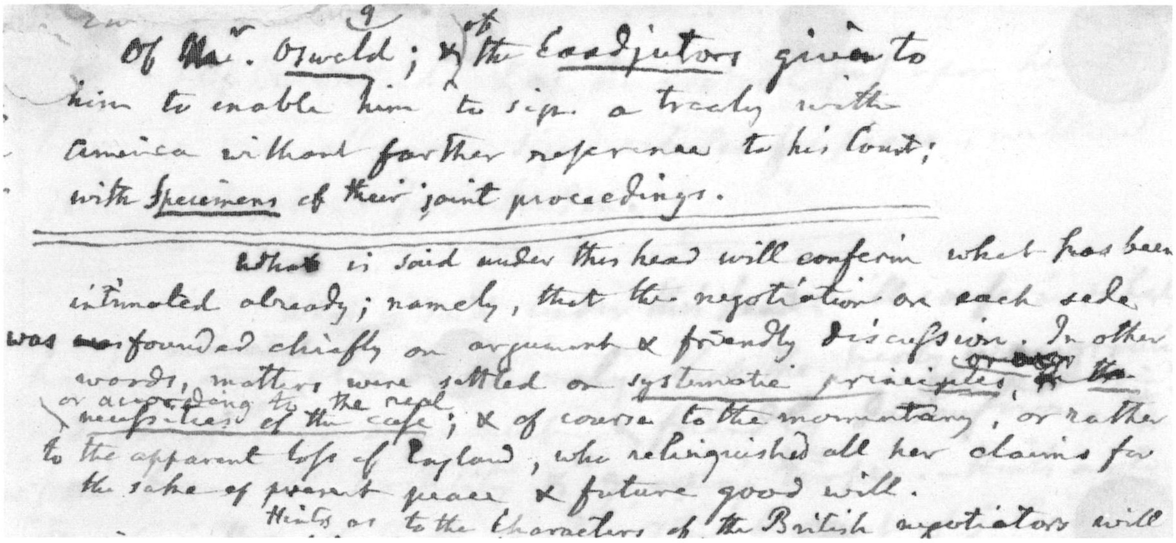

United States Peace Commissioners. *Article Proposed,* [Versailles] November 29, 1782. APS

Compensation for losses American towns and citizens suffered at the hands of the British Army was an issue in the peace negotiations. This actual memorandum was delivered by Dr. Franklin to the British commissioner Richard Oswald. On the other hand, the British sought compensation for the damages Loyalists suffered from the rebels. In the resulting standoff the article was dropped.

A strong advocate for the American cause during the Revolution, a friend and admirer of Franklin (whose *Political, Miscellaneous, and Philosophical Pieces* he edited in 1779), Benjamin Vaughan was employed as confidential agent by the Earl of Shelburne and played an important part in promoting confidence between the American commissioner and the British Government and in reconciling differences over the terms of the peace treaty. In 1796 Vaughan moved to the United States, where he lived at Hallowell, Maine. This is a historical account of preliminary negotiations for peace, written about 1830 by Vaughan, who participated in them.

Of Mr. Oswald; & of the Coadjutors given to him to enable him to sign a treaty with America without farther reference to his Court; with Specimens of their joint proceedings.

What is said under this head will confirm what has been intimated already; namely, that the negotiation on each side was founded chiefly on argument & friendly discussion. In other words, matters were settled on systematic principles, or according to the real necessities of the case; & of course to the momentary, or rather to the apparent loss of England, who relinquished all her claims for the sake of present peace & future good will.

Hints as to the Characters of the British negotiators will

Benjamin Vaughan. *Memoranda on Peace Negotiations in 1782–83.* APS

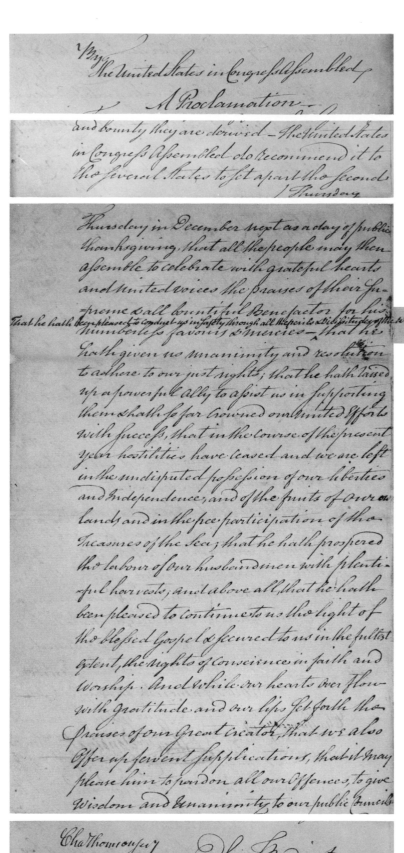

In gratitude for the cessation of hostilities by the preliminary treaties of peace, Congress calls on the several States to proclaim a day of thanksgiving and prayer that God might "give Wisdom and Unanimity to our public Councils . . . cement all our Citizens in the bonds of affection . . . enable them to improve the days of prosperity by every good work and to be lovers of peace and tranquillity . . . bless us in our husbandry, our commerce and navigation . . . smile upon our seminaries & means of Education . . . cause pure religion & virtue to flourish . . . give peace to all nations . . . ."

The Definitive Treaty between Great Britain, and the United States of America. [Passy], 1783. APS

This handsomely designed publication of the Treaty of Peace was printed in Franklin's private printing shop in his house at Passy.

United States Congress. *Proclamation of a Day of Thanksgiving.* Signed by Elias Boudinot, president of Congress, October 18, 1783. HSP

The Definitive Treaty, between
reat-Britain and the United States
of America, signed at Paris, the
3d day of September 1783.
hiladelphia: David C. Claypoole,
1783. Broadside. HSP

her copies of the Definitive
Treaty reached New York
November. On November
19 John Adams arrived,
aring a copy of the Treaty,
hich he carried at once to
Philadelphia. This
Philadelphia broadside is
taken from a New York
oadside, which was taken
om a London publication
of September 30.

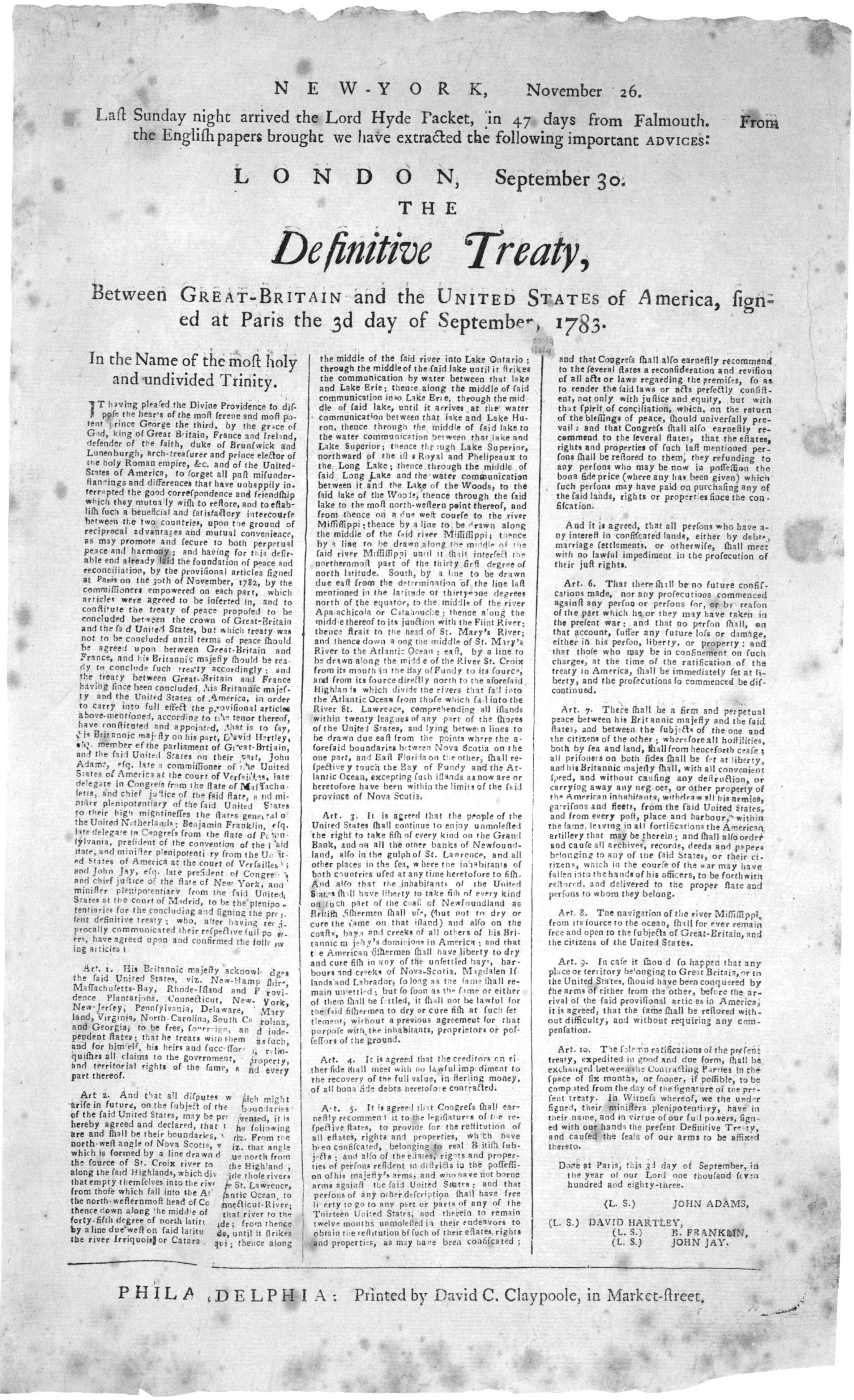

N E W - Y O R K, November 26.

Laſt Sunday night arrived the Lord Hyde Packet, in 47 days from Falmouth. From the Engliſh papers brought we have extracted the following important ADVICES:

L O N D O N, September 30.

THE

Definitive Treaty,

Between GREAT-BRITAIN and the UNITED STATES of America, ſign-ed at Paris the 3d day of September, 1783.

In the Name of the moſt holy and undivided Trinity.

IT having pleaſed the Divine Providence to diſpoſe the hearts of the moſt ſerene and moſt potent prince George the third, by the grace of God, king of Great Britain, France and Ireland, defender of the faith, duke of Brunſwick and Lunenburgh, arch-treaſurer and prince elector of the holy Roman empire, &c. and of the United-States of America, to forget all paſt miſunderſtandings and differences that have unhappily interrupted the good correſpondence and friendſhip which they mutually wiſh to reſtore, and to eſtabliſh ſuch a beneficial and ſatisfactory intercourſe between the two countries, upon the ground of reciprocal advantages and mutual convenience, as may promote and ſecure to both perpetual peace and harmony; and having for this deſirable end already laid the foundation of peace and reconciliation, by the proviſional articles ſigned at Paris on the 30th of November, 1782, by the commiſſioners empowered on each part, which articles were agreed to be inſerted in, and to conſtitute the treaty of peace propoſed to be concluded between the crown of Great-Britain and the ſaid United States, but which treaty was not to be concluded until terms of peace ſhould be agreed upon between Great-Britain and France, and his Britannic majeſty ſhould be ready to conclude ſuch treaty accordingly: and the treaty between Great-Britain and France having ſince been concluded, his Britannic majeſty and the United States of America, in order to carry into full effect the proviſional articles above-mentioned, according to the tenor thereof, have conſtituted and appointed, that is to ſay, his Britannic majeſty on his part, David Hartley, eſq. member of the parliament of Great-Brtiain, and the ſaid United States on their part, John Adams, eſq. late a commiſſioner of the United States of America at the court of Verſailles, late delegate in Congreſs from the ſtate of Maſſachuſetts, and chief juſtice of the ſaid ſtate, and miniſter plenipotentiary of the ſaid United States to their high mightineſſes the ſtates general of the United Netherlands; Benjamin Franklin, eſq. late delegate in Congreſs from the ſtate of Pennſylvania, preſident of the convention of the ſaid ſtate, and miniſter plenipotentiary from the United States of America at the court of Verſailles; and John Jay, eſq. late preſident of Congreſs, and chief juſtice of the ſtate of New York, and miniſter plenipotentiary from the ſaid United States at the court of Madrid, to be the plenipotentiaries for the concluding and ſigning the preſent definitive treaty; who, after having reciprocally communicated their reſpective full powers, have agreed upon and confirmed the following articles:

Art. 1. His Britannic majeſty acknowledges the ſaid United States, viz. New-Hampſhire, Maſſachuſetts-Bay, Rhode-Iſland and Providence Plantations, Connecticut, New-York, New-Jerſey, Pennſylvania, Delaware, Maryland, Virginia, North-Carolina, South Carolina, and Georgia, to be free, ſovereign, and independent ſtates; that he treats with them as ſuch, and for himſelf, his heirs and ſucceſſors, relinquiſhes all claims to the government, property, and territorial rights of the ſame, and every part thereof.

Art 2. And that all diſputes which might ariſe in future, on the ſubject of the boundaries of the ſaid United States, may be prevented, it is hereby agreed and declared, that the following are and ſhall be their boundaries, viz. From the north-weſt angle of Nova Scotia, viz. that angle which is formed by a line drawn due north from the ſource of St. Croix river to the Highland; along the ſaid Highlands, which divide thoſe rivers that empty themſelves into the river St. Lawrence, from thoſe which fall into the Atlantic Ocean, to the north-weſternmoſt head of Connecticut-River; thence down along the middle of that river to the forty-fifth degree of north latitude; from thence by a line due weſt on ſaid latitude, until it ſtrikes the river Irriquois or Cataraqui; thence along the middle of the ſaid river into Lake Ontario; through the middle of the ſaid lake until it ſtrikes the communication by water between that lake and Lake Erie; thence along the middle of ſaid communication into Lake Erie, through the middle of ſaid lake, until it arrives at the water communication between that lake and Lake Huron, thence through the middle of ſaid lake to the water communication between that lake and Lake Superior; thence through Lake Superior, northward of the iſles Royal and Phelipeaux to the Long Lake; thence through the middle of ſaid Long Lake and the water communication between it and the Lake of the Woods, to the ſaid lake of the Woods, thence through the ſaid lake to the moſt north-weſtern point thereof, and from thence on a due weſt courſe to the river Miſſiſſippi; thence by a line to be drawn along the middle of the ſaid river Miſſiſſippi; thence by a line to be drawn along the middle of the ſaid river Miſſiſſippi until it ſhall interſect the northernmoſt part of the thirty firſt degree of north latitude. South, by a line to be drawn due eaſt from the determination of the line laſt mentioned in the latitude of thirty-one degrees north of the equator, to the middle of the river Apalachicola or Catahouche; thence along the middle thereof to its junction with the Flint River; thence ſtrait to the head of St. Mary's River; and thence down along the middle of St. Mary's River to the Atlantic Ocean; eaſt, by a line to be drawn along the middle of the River St. Croix from its mouth in the Bay of Fundy to its ſource, and from its ſource directly north to the aforeſaid Highlands which divide the rivers that fall into the Atlantic Ocean from thoſe which fall into the River St. Lawrence, comprehending all iſlands within twenty leagues of any part of the ſhores of the United States, and lying between lines to be drawn due eaſt from the points where the aforeſaid boundaries between Nova Scotia on the one part, and Eaſt Florida on the other, ſhall reſpectively touch the Bay of Fundy and the Atlantic Ocean, excepting ſuch iſlands as now are or heretofore have been within the limits of the ſaid province of Nova Scotia.

Art. 3. It is agreed that the people of the United States ſhall continue to enjoy unmoleſted the right to take fiſh of every kind on the Grand Bank, and on all the other banks of Newfoundland, alſo in the gulph of St. Lawrence, and all other places in the ſea, where the inhabitants of both countries uſed at any time heretofore to fiſh. And alſo that the inhabitants of the United States ſhall have liberty to take fiſh of every kind on ſuch part of the coaſt of Newfoundland as Britiſh fiſhermen ſhall uſe, (but not to dry or cure the ſame on that iſland) and alſo on the coaſts, bays and creeks of all others of his Britannic majeſty's dominions in America; and that the American fiſhermen ſhall have liberty to dry and cure fiſh in any of the unſettled bays, harbours and creeks of Nova-Scotia, Magdalen Iſlands and Labrador, ſo long as the ſame ſhall remain unſettled; but ſo ſoon as the ſame or either of them ſhall be ſettled, it ſhall not be lawful for the ſaid fiſhermen to dry or cure fiſh at ſuch ſettlement, without a previous agreement for that purpoſe with the inhabitants, proprietors or poſſeſſors of the ground.

Art. 4. It is agreed that the creditors on either ſide ſhall meet with no lawful impediment to the recovery of the full value, in ſterling money, of all bona fide debts heretofore contracted.

Art. 5. It is agreed that Congreſs ſhall earneſtly recommend it to the legiſlatures of the reſpective ſtates, to provide for the reſtitution of all eſtates, rights and properties, which have been confiſcated, belonging to real Britiſh ſubjects; and alſo of the eſtates, rights and properties of perſons reſident in diſtricts in the poſſeſſion of his majeſty's arms, and who have not borne arms againſt the ſaid United States; and that perſons of any other deſcription ſhall have free liberty to go to any part or parts of any of the Thirteen United States, and therein to remain twelve months unmoleſted in their endeavors to obtain the reſtitution of ſuch of their eſtates, rights and properties, as may have been confiſcated; and that Congreſs ſhall alſo earneſtly recommend to the ſeveral ſtates a reconſideration and reviſion of all acts or laws regarding the premiſes, ſo as to render the ſaid laws or acts perfectly conſiſtent, not only with juſtice and equity, but with that ſpirit of conciliation, which, on the return of the bleſſings of peace, ſhould univerſally prevail: and that Congreſs ſhall alſo earneſtly recommend to the ſeveral ſtates, that the eſtates, rights and properties of ſuch laſt mentioned perſons ſhall be reſtored to them, they refunding to any perſons who may be now in poſſeſſion the bona fide price (where any has been given) which ſuch perſons may have paid on purchaſing any of the ſaid lands, rights or properties ſince the confiſcation.

And it is agreed, that all perſons who have any intereſt in confiſcated lands, either by debts, marriage ſettlements, or otherwiſe, ſhall meet with no lawful impediment in the proſecution of their juſt rights.

Art. 6. That there ſhall be no future confiſcations made, nor any proſecutions commenced againſt any perſon or perſons for, or by reaſon of the part which he or they may have taken in the preſent war: and that no perſon ſhall, on that account, ſuffer any future loſs or damage, either in his perſon, liberty, or property: and that thoſe who may be in confinement on ſuch charges, at the time of the ratification of the treaty in America, ſhall be immediately ſet at liberty, and the proſecutions ſo commenced be diſcontinued.

Art. 7. There ſhall be a firm and perpetual peace between his Britannic majeſty and the ſaid ſtates, and between the ſubjects of the one and the citizens of the other; wherefore all hoſtilities, both by ſea and land, ſhall from henceforth ceaſe; all priſoners on both ſides ſhall be ſet at liberty, and his Britannic majeſty ſhall, with all convenient ſpeed, and without cauſing any deſtruction, or carrying away any negroes, or other property of the American inhabitants, withdraw all his armies, garriſons and fleets, from the ſaid United States, and from every poſt, place and harbour, within the ſame, leaving in all fortifications the American artillery that may be therein; and ſhall alſo order and cauſe all archives, records, deeds and papers belonging to any of the ſaid States, or their citizens, which in the courſe of the war may have fallen into the hands of his officers, to be forthwith reſtored, and delivered to the proper ſtate and perſons to whom they belong.

Art. 8. The navigation of the river Miſſiſſippi, from its ſource to the ocean, ſhall for ever remain free and open to the ſubjects of Great-Britain, and the citizens of the United States.

Art. 9. In caſe it ſhould ſo happen that any place or territory belonging to Great Britain, or to the United States, ſhould have been conquered by the arms of either from the other, before the arrival of the ſaid proviſional articles in America, it is agreed, that the ſame ſhall be reſtored without difficulty, and without requiring any compenſation.

Art. 10. The ſolemn ratifications of the preſent treaty, expedited in good and due form, ſhall be exchanged between the Contracting Parties in the ſpace of ſix months, or ſooner, if poſſible, to be computed from the day of the ſignature of the preſent treaty. In Witneſs whereof, we the underſigned, their miniſters plenipotentiary, have in their name, and in virtue of our full powers, ſigned with our hands the preſent Definitive Treaty, and cauſed the ſeals of our arms to be affixed thereto.

Done at Paris, this 3d day of September, in the year of our Lord one thouſand ſeven hundred and eighty-three.

(L. S.) JOHN ADAMS,
(L. S.) DAVID HARTLEY,
(L. S.) B. FRANKLIN,
(L. S.) JOHN JAY.

PHILADELPHIA: Printed by David C. Claypoole, in Market-ſtreet.

Thomas Mifflin. *Letter to John Dickinson*, Annapolis, January 14, 1784. HSP

The President of Congress notifies the President of Pennsylvania that Congress has this day unanimously ratified the Treaty of Peace. The American *War* was over, Dr. Benjamin Rush was to say—but not the American *Revolution*.

By the United States in Congress Assembled, A PROCLAMATION.

WHEREAS in pursuance of a plenipotentiary commission, given on the 29th day of September, 1782, to the honorable Benjamin Franklin, a treaty of amity and commerce between his majesty the king of Sweden and the United States of America, was on the 3d day of April, 1783, concluded by the said Benjamin Franklin, with a minister plenipotentiary, named for that purpose, by the said king: and whereas the said treaty hath been duly approved and ratified by the United States in Congress assembled, and a translation thereof made in the words following, to wit:

By the United States in Congress Assembled, A Proclamation. Baltimore: Hay and Killen, 178[ ]. Broadside. LCP

Sweden, which had shown no great sympathy for America but had joined the Armed Neutrality of 1780, was the first European power to recognize American independence and make a treaty of amity and commerce. It was signed at Paris (by Franklin on behalf of the United States) on April 3, 1783, ratified by Congress on July 29, and published in September in this form to all citizens and officers of government.

The smaller illustration is the official Swedish publication of the treaty with the United States.

Wanskaps och Handels Tractat, Traité d'Amitié de Commerce. Stockholm: Ro[ ] Printing Office 1785. LCP

Pennsylvania
Assembly.
*In Assembly,
Tuesday,
December 2d,
1783, A.M.*
Broadside. HSP

In ASSEMBLY,

Tuesday, December 2d, 1783, A. M.

THE Report of the Committee, read November 29th, relative to the Preparations to be made for Public Demonstrations of Joy, was read the second Time, and adopted as follows, viz.

The Committee appointed to confer with Council concerning the Public Demonstrations of Joy it may now be proper to authorise in this State, upon the Definitive Treaty of Peace between The United States and Great-Britain, beg Leave to report, as the joint Opinion of that Board and your Committee—

That a Triumphal Arch be erected at the Upper End of High or Market Street, between Sixth and Seventh Streets, to be embellished with illuminated Paintings and suitable Inscriptions; and that some Fireworks be prepared for the Occasion:

That such an Exhibition, in Point of Elegance, as well as in Regard to the Convenience and Safety of the Spectators, will prove most generally acceptable; it being intended there should be no other Illumination in the City: That these Preparations may be completed in three or four Weeks, and will require, by the most exact Computation they could at present make, about Five or at most Six Hundred Pounds: And therefore,

RESOLVED, *That a Sum not exceeding Six Hundred Pounds be, and is hereby appropriated for the Purpose of enabling The Supreme Executive Council to make Public Demonstrations of Joy upon the Definitive Treaty of Peace between The United States and Great-Britain.*

As these Demonstrations of Joy are prescribed and regulated by the Directions and at the Expence of the State, it is expected, that no Person or Persons whatever will presume, in Defiance of the Authority of the Commonwealth, to require or to make any other Demonstrations of Joy upon the Occasion, than those directed and authorised as aforesaid.

A Description of the Triumphal Arch and its Ornaments.

THE Arch is fifty Feet and six Inches wide, and thirty-five Feet and six Inches high, exclusive of the Ballustrade, which is three Feet and nine Inches in Height. The Arch is fourteen Feet wide in the clear, and each of the smaller Arches nine Feet. The Pillars are of the *Ionic* Order. The Entablature, all the other Parts, and the Proportions, correspond with that Order; and the whole Edifice is finished in the Style of Architecture proper for such a Building, and used by the *Romans.* The Pillars are adorned with spiral Festoons of Flowers in their natural Colours.

The following Devices and Inscriptions are distributed in the several Parts appropriated by the Antients to such Ornaments.

I.
Over the Centre Arch, the Temple of *Janus* shut—
NUMINE FAVENTE
MAGNUS AB INTEGRO SÆCULORUM NASCITUR ORDO.
By the Divine Favor
A great and new Order of Ages commences.

II.
On the South Side of the Balluftrade, a Buft of *Lewis* the XVIth,
MERENDO MEMORES FACIT.
His Merit makes us remember him.

III.
On the other Side of the Balluftrade, a Pyramidal Cenotaph to the Memory of those brave Men who have died for their Country in the late War,
OB PATRIAM PUGNANDO VULNERA PASSI.
These received their Wounds for their Country.

IV.
On the South Side of the Frize, Three Lilies, the Arms of *France,*
GLORIAM SUPERANT.
They exceed Glory.

V.
On the left of the former, a Plough, Sheaves of Wheat, and a Ship under sail, the Arms of *Pennsylvania,*
TERRA SUIS CONTENTA BONIS.
A Land contented with its own Blessings.

VI.
On the left of the preceding, a Sun, the Device of *France*—and Thirteen Stars, the Device of *The United States,*
CÆLO SOCIATI.
Allied in the Heavens.

VII.
On the left of the last, two Hands joined holding Branches of Olive and the Caduceus of Commerce,
CONCORDIA GENTIUM.
The Concord of Nations.

VIII.
On the South Pannel, Confederated *America* leaning upon a Soldier, military Trophies on each Side of them,
FIDES EXERCITUS.
The Fidelity of the Army.

IX.
On the other Pannel, *Indians* building Churches in the Wilderness,
PONUNT FEROCIA CORDA.
Their savage Hearts become mild.

X.
On the Dye of the South Pedestal, a Library, with Instruments and Emblems of Arts and Sciences,
EMOLLIUNT MORES.
These soften Manners.

XI.
On the Dye of the next Pedestal, a large Tree bearing *thirteen* principal and distinct Branches loaded with Fruit,
ROBORE STIPITIS MATURABUNT.
By the Strength of the Body these will ripen.

XII.
On the Dye of the Pedestal, upon the right Hand in passing through the Centre Arch, *Cincinnatus,* crowned with Laurel, returning to his Plough—The Plough adorned with a Wreath of the same—The Countenance of *Cincinnatus* is a striking Resemblance of General *Washington,*
VICTRIX VIRTUS.
Victorious Virtue.

XIII.
On the Dye of the next Pedestal, Militia exercising,
PROTEGENTES GAUDEBUNT.
Protecting they shall enjoy.

On the Spandrels of the Centre Arch these Letters, S. P. Q. P. *The Senate and People of Pennsylvania.*

The Top of the Balluftrade is embellished with Figures representing the Cardinal Virtues, Justice, Prudence, Temperance, and Fortitude.

The whole Building illuminated by about twelve hundred Lamps.

Directions will be put up in *Market* Street near *Fifth* Street, for having the following Regulations observed, in order that the Citizens may have an Opportunity of viewing and examining the Exhibition with the greatest Convenience and Satisfaction to themselves:

1st. Persons walking will please to advance towards the Exhibition by the Ways on the Outside of the Foot-pavements, which lead in straight Lines from *Fifth* Street through the Side Arches. Those that advance on the South Side, after passing the South Arch, will turn on the left Hand down *Market* Street on the Foot-pavement to *Fifth* Street. Those who advance on the North Side, after passing the North Arch, will turn on the right Hand down *Market* Street on the Foot-pavement to *Fifth* Street. In this Manner they may pass and return as often as they chuse.

2d. Persons on Horseback or in Carriages are to advance in the Middle of *Market* Street, and passing through the Centre Arch, continue on to *Seventh* Street; then turning to the right or left return by *Arch* Street or *Chesnut* Street to *Fifth* Street, and so pass and return as often as they please.

Any Boys or others, who disturb the Citizens by throwing Squibs or Crackers, or otherwise, will be immediately apprehended and sent to the Work-house.

The Definitive Treaty of Peace was celebrated in Philadelphia with "Public Demonstrations of Joy." The artist Charles Willson Peale was commissioned to design and erect a great triumphal arch 50 feet wide and 35 high, decorated with symbols and mottoes worthy of patriot heroes and citizens. On January 22, 1784, the ratification of the treaty was proclaimed and celebrated. But a careless bombardier discharged his gun too soon or aimed too low, sparks fell on Peale's arch of triumph and peace, and moments before it was to be illuminated in victory, it was consumed in fiery conflagration.

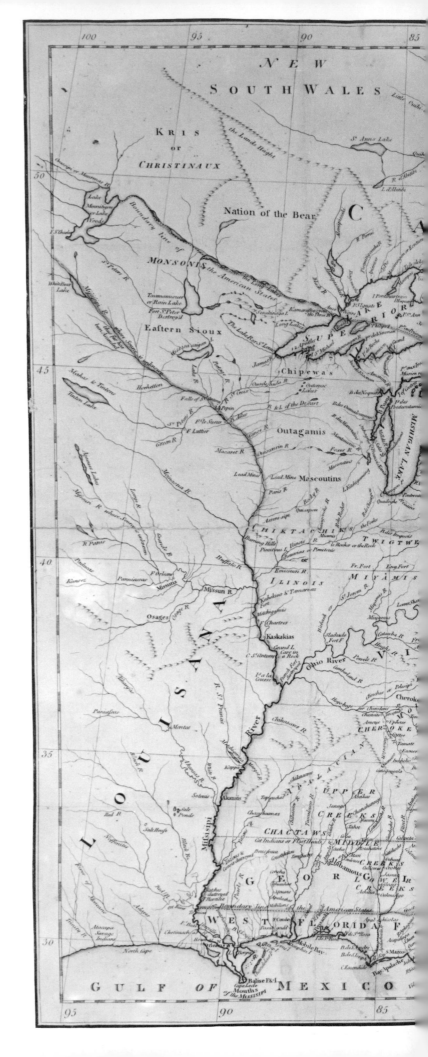

The United States of America laid down from the best Authorities agreeable to the Peace of 1783. HSP

Behold Columbia's empire rise,
On Freedom's solid base to stand;
Supported by propitious skies,
And seal'd by her deliverer's hand.

—A Federal Song. *Albany* (N.Y.) *Journal,* August 4, 1788.

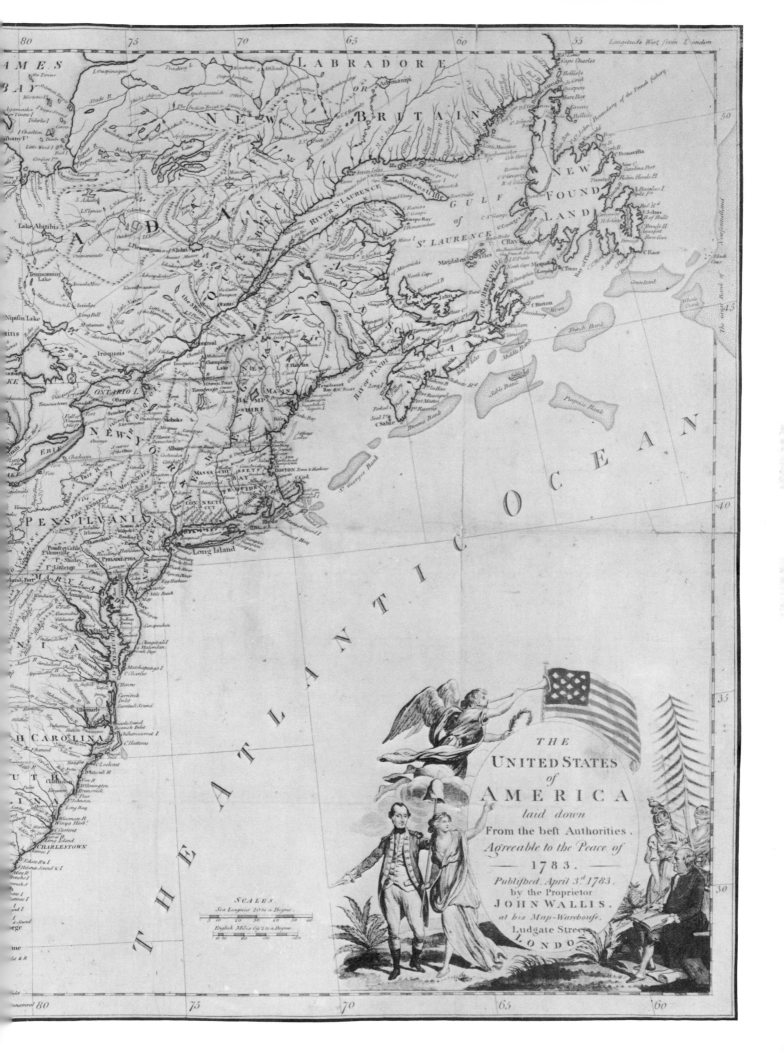

THE
UNITED STATES
of
AMERICA
laid down
From the best Authorities,
Agreeable to the Peace of
——— 1783. ———
Published April 3d 1783.
by the Proprietor
JOHN WALLIS,
at his Map-Warehouse,
Ludgate Street
LONDON

To the people of the united ſtates

THERE is nothing mo
common than to confoun
the terms of the American r
volution with thoſe of the la

"We have . . . yet to effect a
revolution in our principles,
opinions, and manners."—Benjamin
Rush. Letter to Richard Price,
May 25, 1786

American war. The American
war is over : but this is far from
being the cafe with the American revolution. On the contrary, nothing but the firft act of
the great drama is clofed. It remains yet to eftablifh and perfect our new forms of govern-

Benjamin Rush. "To the
people of the united
states." *American Museum*,
I (1787), 9-13. APS

Benjamin Rush. "To the
people of the united
states." *American Museum*,
I (1787), 9–13. APS

To the people of the united states.

THERE is nothing more common than to confound the terms of the American revolution with those of the late American war. The American war is over : but this is far from being the cafe with the American revolution. On the contrary, nothing but the firft act of the great drama is clofed. It remains yet to eftablish and perfect our new forms of government ; and to prepare the principles, morals, and manners of our citizens, for thefe forms of government, after they are eftablifhed and brought to perfection.

Benjamin Rush. "A Discourse delivered
before the College of Physicians of
Philadelphia . . . on the Objects of
their Institution." *Transactions of the
College of Physicians of Philadelphia*,
I, pt. 1 (1793), xxi–xxxi. APS

A DISCOURSE

DELIVERED BEFORE THE

COLLEGE OF PHYSICIANS

OF PHILADELPHIA, FEB. 6th, 1787.

ON THE OBJECTS OF THEIR INSTITUTION.

BY BENJAMIN RUSH, M.D. &c. &c.

MR. PRESIDENT AND GENTLEMEN,

I FEEL peculiar pleafure in reflecting, that the late revolution, which has given fuch a fpring to the mind in objects of philofophical and moral enquiry, has at laft extended itfelf to medicine, and in lefs than five years after the peace, before the human faculties had contracted to their former dimenfions, a college of phyficians, formed upon principles accommodated to the prefent ftate of fociety and government in America, has been eftablifhed in the capital of the United States.

INTRODUCTION

TO VOL. THE THIRD.

An Effay on thofe inquiries in Natural Philofophy, which at prefent are moft beneficial to the UNITED STATES OF NORTH AMERICA. By DR. NICHOLAS COLLIN, Rector of the Swedifh Churches in Pennfylvania.

Read before the Society the 3d of April, 1789.

PHILOSOPHERS are citizens of the world; the fruits of their labours are freely diftributed among all nations; what they fow is reaped by the antipodes, and blooms through future generations. It is, however, their duty to cultivate with peculiar attention thofe parts of fcience, which are moft beneficial to that country in which Providence has appointed their earthly ftations. Patriotic affections are in this, as in other inftances, conducive to the general happinefs of mankind, becaufe we have the beft means of inveftigating thofe objects, which are moft interefting to us. In the prefent circumftances of the United States fome problems of natural philofophy are of peculiar importance; a furvey of thefe may contribute to the moft ufeful direction of our own inquiries, and thofe of our ingenious fellow citizens. I fubmit, gentlemen, my reflections on this fubject to your candid indulgence and enlightened judgment.

Nicholas Collin. "An Essay on those
inquiries in Natural Philosophy, which
at present are most beneficial to the
United States of North America."
*Transactions of the American
Philosophical Society*, III (1793),
iii–xxvii. APS

The American *war* and the American *revolution*, Dr. Benjamin Rush liked to declare, were different events. The latter gave "a spring to the mind in objects of philosophical and moral inquiry," established new forms of government, and required citizens to reform their principles, morals and manners to support those forms. In an address written in anticipation of the Federal Convention, he summons his fellow-citizens to the unfinished work of the revolution. In more specific terms, he calls on his fellow-physicians to investigate American diseases, identify American drugs, and study the effect of American conditions on human beings. In similar spirit, the Reverend Mr. Nicholas Collin of Philadelphia prepares a list of inquiries which American scientists have the opportunity and obligation to make for the benefit of their own country and of mankind.

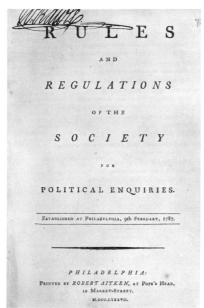

Government, too, was to be examined rationally in the light of the conditions of American society. "The revolution can only be said to be compleat, when we shall have freed ourselves, no less from the indulgence of foreign prejudice than from the fetters of foreign power."

Benjamin Franklin was president (the Society met at his house), and members included John Dickinson, Robert Morris, James Madison, James Wilson (the two latter influential members of the Federal Convention), and Thomas Paine.

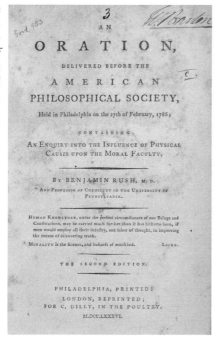

This was the best known American statement of the philosophical undergirding of the reforms of the post-Revolutionary years. Rational yet hopeful, Rush believed that men and societies might both be improved if the material reasons for their shortcomings were removed or altered. Men's duty to practice charity, he declared, "is enforced by motives drawn from science, as well as from the precepts of Christianity."

Benjamin Rush. By Charles B. J. F. de Saint-Mémin. Engraving. APS

Benjamin Rush. *Travels through Life.* APS

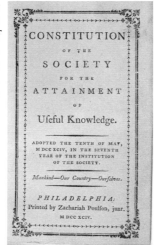

One of many hopeful, even naive, enterprises of improvement, this Society aimed, among other things, "to investigate the means of promoting the happiness of mankind," discover defects in the laws and recommend amendments and new laws, watch for invasions of the people's rights by state and national governments, and "strengthen those benevolent ties which bind us together." With only 30 members, the Society cannot be said to have had a discernible influence.

Antibiastes, *pseud. Observations on the Slaves and the Indented Servants, inlisted in the Army, and in the Navy of the United States.* [Philadelphia]: Styner and Cist, [1777]. LCP

Not least among the many anomalies of the systems of slavery and indented service in the American colonies and states was that both slaves and servants were enlisted to fight for the liberties of America. "Can it be much longer suffered," this pamphleteer indignantly demands, "in this land of freedom, thus to sport with human nature?"

A Dialogue Concerning the Slavery of the Africans. Norwich: Judah P. Spooner, 1776. Reprinted New York: Robert Hodge, 1785. APS

The Constitution of the New-Jersey Society for Promoting the Abolition of Slavery. Burlington: Isaac Neale, 1793. APS

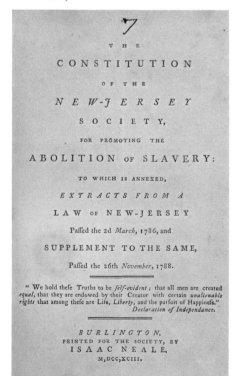

[Anthony Benezet]. *A Serious Address to the Rulers of America, on . . . their Conduct respecting Slavery.* Trenton: Isaac Collins, 1783. APS

That men who fought for liberty for themselves should keep other men in bondage was, to say the least, inconsistent; and the conduct did not pass unnoticed, as these pamphlets show. Note that the New Jersey abolitionists boldly quote the Declaration of Independence in support of their cause.

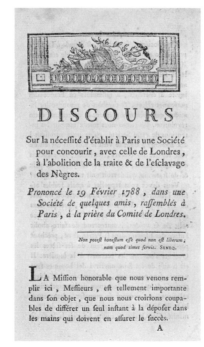

To the Representatives of the FREEMEN of the Commonwealth of PENNSYLVANIA, *in General Assembly met*,

The Representation and Petition of the SUBSCRIBERS, Citizens of *Pennsylvania.*

YOUR Petitioners have observed, with great satisfaction, the salutary effects of the Law of this State, passed on the first day of March, 1780, for the "gradual abolition of slavery."—They have also seen, with equal satisfaction, the progress which the humane and just principles of that Law have made in other States.

THEY, however, find themselves called upon, by the interesting nature of those principles, to suggest to the General Assembly, that vessels have been publicly equipt in this Port for the Slave Trade, and that several other practices have taken place which they conceive to be inconsistent with the spirit of the Law abovementioned; and that these, and other circumstances relating to the afflicted Africans, do, in the opinion of your Petitioners, require the further interposition of the Legislature.

YOUR Petitioners, therefore, earnestly request that you will again take this subject into your serious consideration, and that you will make such additions to the said Law, as shall effectually put a stop to the Slave Trade being carried on directly or indirectly in this Commonwealth, and to answer other purposes of benevolence and justice to an oppressed part of the human species.

To the Representatives of the Freemen of the Commonwealth of Pennsylvania. [Philadelphia, 1788]. HSP

Pennsylvania in 1780 enacted a law for the gradual abolition of slavery. But the law was evaded. Some owners sent their slaves out of the state for sale at high prices; while a few engaged in the slave trade. Citizens to the number of 1688 here petition the legislature to check such abuses by strengthening the law—which was done in 1788.

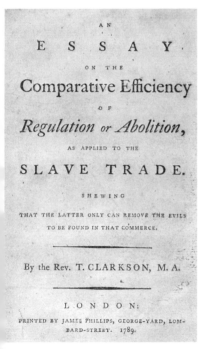

AN ESSAY ON THE Comparative Efficiency OF Regulation or Abolition, AS APPLIED TO THE SLAVE TRADE. SHEWING THAT THE LATTER ONLY CAN REMOVE THE EVILS TO BE FOUND IN THAT COMMERCE. By the Rev. T. CLARKSON, M. A. LONDON: PRINTED BY JAMES PHILLIPS, GEORGE-YARD, LOMBARD-STREET. 1789.

Thomas Clarkson. *An Essay on the Comparative Efficiency of Regulation or Abolition, as applied to the Slave Trade.* London: James Phillips, 1789. LCP

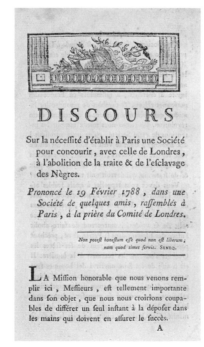

DISCOURS Sur la nécessité d'établir à Paris une Société pour concourir, avec celle de Londres, à l'abolition de la traite & de l'esclavage des Nègres. Prononcé le 19 Février 1788, dans une Société de quelques amis, rassemblés à Paris, à la prière du Comité de Londres.

Non potest honestum esse quod non est liberum; nam quod timet servit. SENEQ.

LA Mission honorable que nous venons remplir ici, Messieurs, est tellement importante dans son objet, que nous nous croirions coupables de différer un seul instant à la déposer dans les mains qui doivent en assurer le succès.

A

[J. P. Brissot de Warville]. *Discours sur la Nécessité d'établir à Paris une Société pour concourir . . . à l'abolition de la traite & de l'esclavage des Nègres.* [Paris, 1788]. APS

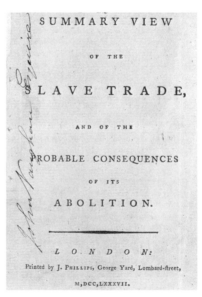

SUMMARY VIEW OF THE SLAVE TRADE, AND OF THE PROBABLE CONSEQUENCES OF ITS ABOLITION. LONDON: Printed by J. PHILLIPS, George-Yard, Lombard-street, M,DCC,LXXXVII.

A Summary View of the Slave Trade and of the Probable Consequences of its Abolition. London: J. Phillips, 1787. APS

The American abolition movement was part of an international movement. The Americans provided European reformers with detailed information; the Europeans gave the Americans encouragement, support, and arguments, like those of Thomas Clarkson. Before long, the several national societies were linked in a network of correspondence, publications, and personal visitations.

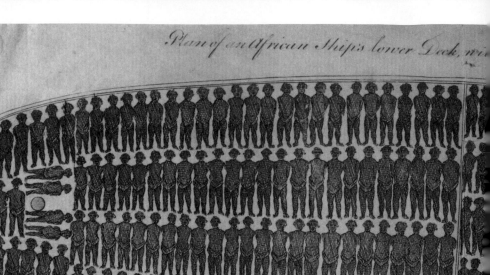

Plan of an African Ship's lower Deck, wi...

Men's room

REMARKS on the

Extracted from the AMERICAN

IT muſt afford great pleaſure to every true friend to liberty, to find the caſe of the unhappy Africans engroſſes the general attention of the humane, in many parts of Europe : but we do not recollect to have met with a more ſtriking illuſtration of the barbarity of the ſlave trade, than in a ſmall pamphlet lately publiſhed by a ſociety at Plymouth, in Great Britain ; from which the Pennſylvania ſociety for promoting the abolition of ſlavery have taken the following extracts, and have added a copy of the plate, which accompanied it. Perhaps a more powerful mode of conviction could not have been adopted, than is diſplayed in this ſmall piece. Here is preſented to our view, one of the moſt horrid ſpectacles—a number of human creatures, packed, ſide by ſide, almoſt like herrings in a barrel, and reduced nearly to the ſtate of being buried alive, with juſt air enough to preſerve a degree of life ſufficient to make them ſenſible of all the horrors of their ſituation. To every perſon, who has ever been at ſea, it muſt preſent a ſcene of wretchedneſs in the extreme ; for, with every comfort, which room, air, variety of nouriſhment, and careful cleanlineſs can yield, it is ſtill a weariſome and irkſome ſtate. What then muſt it be to thoſe, who are not only deprived of the neceſſaries of life, but confined down, the greater part of the voyage, to the ſame poſture, with ſcarcely the privilege of turning from one painful ſide to the other, and ſubjected to all the nauſeous conſequences ariſing from ſea-ſickneſs, and other diſorders, unavoidable amongſt ſuch a number of forlorn wretches ? Where is the human being, that can picture to himſelf this ſcene of woe, without at the ſame time execrating a trade, which ſpreads miſery and deſolation wherever it appears ? Where is the man of real benevolence, who will not join heart and hand, in oppoſing this barbarous, this iniquitous traffic ?

Philadelphia, May 29, 1789.

"THE above plate repreſents the lower deck of an African ſhip, of two hundred and ninety-ſeven tons burden, with the ſlaves ſtowed on it, in the proportion of not quite one to a ton.

"In the men's apartment, the ſpace, allowed to each, is ſix feet in length, by ſixteen inches in breadth. The boys are each allowed five feet, by fourteen inches. The women, five feet ten inches, by ſixteen inches ; and the girls, four feet by one foot, each. The perpendicular height, between the decks, is five feet eight inches.

"The men are faſtened together, two and two, by handcuffs on their wriſts, and by irons rivetted on their legs—they are brought up on the main deck every day, about eight o'clock, and, as each pair aſcend, a ſtrong chain, faſtened by ring-bolts to the deck, is paſſed through their ſhackles ; a precaution abſolutely neceſſary, to prevent inſurrections. In this ſtate, if the weather is favourable, they are permitted to remain about one third part of the twenty-four hours, and during this interval they are fed, and their apartment below is cleaned ; but when the weather is bad, even theſe indulgences cannot be granted them, and they are only permitted to come up in ſmall companies of about ten at a time, to be fed, where, after remaining a quarter of an hour, each meſs is obliged to give place to the next, in rotation.

"It may perhaps be conceived, from the crouded ſtate, in which the ſlaves appear in this plate, that an unuſual and exaggerated inſtance has been produced ; this, however, is ſo far from being the caſe, that no ſhip, if her intended cargo can be procured, ever carries a leſs number than one to a ton, and the uſual practice has been, to carry nearly double that number. The bill, which has paſſed this laſt ſeſſion of parliament, only reſtricts the carriage to five ſlaves for three tons : and the Brooks, of Liverpool, a capital ſhip, from which the above ſketch was proportioned, did, in one voyage, actually carry ſix

PHILADELPHIA: PRINTED BY MATHEW CAREY, FOR THE NE

First used to illustrate an English tract, the diagram of the frightful accommodations in a typical slave ship was often reprinted and became one of the most familiar and effective articles in the abolitionists' propaganda.

202

Remarks on the Slave Trade. Philadelphia: Printed by Mathew Carey for the New Society for Promoting the Abolition of Slavery, 1789. HSP

es, in the proportion of not quite one to a Ton.

Store room

Girls room

Store room

Women's room

AVE TRADE,

, for May, 1789.

slaves, which is more than double the number
e plate. The mode of stowing them was as
ns, or wide shelves, were erected between the
fo far from the fides towards the middle of
e capable of containing four additional rows
ch means the perpendicular height above each
ng for the beams and platforms, was reduced
ches, so that they could not even sit in an erect
which, in the men's apartment, inftead of four
owed, by placing the heads of one between
ther. All the horrors of this fituation are still
fmaller veffels. The Kitty, of one hundred
tons, had only one foot ten inches; and the
ndred and forty-fix tons, only one foot nine
lar height, above each layer.

node of carrying the flaves, however, is only
ufand other miferies, which thofe unhappy
ures fuffer, from this difgraceful traffic of
s, which, in every part of its progrefs, exhibits
us with horror and indignation. If we re-
e of it, on the continent of Africa, we find,
oufand flaves are annually produced there for
greateft part of whom confifts of innocent per-
eir deareft friends and connexions, fometimes
etimes by treachery. Of thefe, experience
rty-five thoufand perifh, either in the dread-
yance before defcribed, or within two years
at the plantations, before they are feafoned
hofe who unhappily furvive thefe hardfhips,
oeafts of burden, to exhauft their lives in the
s of flavery, without recompenfe, and with-

he well-wifhers to this trade, that the fup-
l deftroy a great nurfery for feamen, and

annihilate a very confiderable fource of commercial profit. In
anfwer to thefe objections, mr. Clarkfon, in his admirable
treatife on the impolicy of the trade, lays down two pofitions,
which he has proved from the moft inconteftible authority—
Firft, that fo far from being a nurfery, it has been conftantly
and regularly a grave for our feamen; for, that in this traffic
only, more men perifh in one year, than in all the other trades
of Great Britain in two years:

"And, fecondly, that the balance of the trade, from its extreme precarioufnefs and uncertainty, is fo notorioufly againft
the merchants, that if all the veffels, employed in it, were the
property of one man, he would infallibly, at the end of their
voyages, find himfelf a lofer.

"As then the cruelty and inhumanity of this trade muft be
univerfally admitted and lamented, and as the policy or impolicy
of its abolition is a queftion, which the wifdom of the legiflature muft ultimately decide upon, and which it can only be enabled to form a juft eftimate of, by the moft thorough invefiga-
tion of all its relations and dependencies; it becomes the indif-
penfable duty of every friend to humanity, however his fpecu-
lations may have led him to conclude on the political tendency
of the meafure, to ftand forward, and affift the committees, either by producing fuch facts as he may himfelf be acquainted
with, or by fubfcribing, to enable them to procure and tranf-
mit to the legiflature, fuch evidence as will tend to throw the
neceffary lights on the fubject. And people would do well to
confider, that it does not often fall to the lot of individuals, to
have an opportunity of performing fo important a moral and
religious duty, as that of endeavouring to put an end to a
practice, which may, without exaggeration, be ftiled one of the
greateft evils at this day exifting upon the earth.

"By the Plymouth committee,
"W. ELFORD, chairman."

Rules for the Regulation of the Society for the Relief of Free Negroes, and others, unlawfully held in Bondage. Philadelphia: Joseph Crukshank, 1784. LCP

Pennsylvania Society for promoting the Abolition of Slavery and the relief of Free Negroes unlawfully held in Bondage. *Constitution and Minutes,* April 23, 1787. HSP

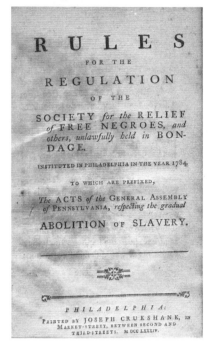

RULES
FOR THE
REGULATION
OF THE
SOCIETY *for the* RELIEF *of* FREE NEGROES, *and others, unlawfully held in* BONDAGE.

INSTITUTED IN PHILADELPHIA IN THE YEAR 1784,

TO WHICH ARE PREFIXED,

The ACTS of the GENERAL ASSEMBLY of PENNSYLVANIA, respecting the gradual

ABOLITION OF SLAVERY.

PHILADELPHIA:
PRINTED BY JOSEPH CRUKSHANK, IN MARKET-STREET, BETWEEN SECOND AND THIRD-STREETS. M DCC LXXXIV.

The Constitution

It having pleased the Creator of the World to make of one flesh all the Children of men, it becomes them to consult & promote each others happiness as Members of the same family, however diversified they may be by color, situation, religion, or different states of Society. It is more especially the Duty of those Persons, who profess to maintain for themselves the rights of human nature, & who acknowlege the obligations of Christianity, to use such means as are in their power, to extend the blessings of freedom to every part of the human race, & in a more particular manner, to such of their fellow creatures, as are entitled to freedom by the laws & Constitutions of any of the United States, & who notwithstanding, are detained in Bondage, by fraud or violence — From a full conviction of the truth & obligation of these Principles — from a desire to diffuse them, wherever the miseries & vices of Slavery exist, & in humble confidence of the favor & support of the Father of Mankind, the Subscribers have associated themselves under the title of the Pennsylvania Society "for promoting the abolition of Slavery, & the relief of "free Negroes unlawfully held in Bondage" —

For effecting these purposes, they have adopted the

AN ADDRESS
TO THE PUBLIC,
FROM THE

Pennsylvania Society for promoting the Abolition of Slavery, and the Relief of Free Negroes, unlawfully held in Bondage.

It is with peculiar satisfaction we assure the friends of humanity, that in prosecuting the design of our association, our endeavours have proved successful, far beyond our most sanguine expectations.

Encouraged by this success, and by the daily progress of that luminous and benign spirit of liberty, which is diffusing itself throughout the world; and humbly hoping for the continuance of the divine blessing on our labors, we have ventured to make an important addition to our original plan, and do therefore, earnestly solicit the support and assistance, of all who can feel the tender emotions of sympathy and compassion, or relish the exalted pleasure of beneficence.

Slavery is such an atrocious debasement of human nature, that its very extirpation, if not performed with solicitous care, may sometimes open a source of serious evils.

The unhappy man who has long been treated as a brute animal, too frequently sinks beneath the common standard of the human species. The galling chains that bind his body, do also fetter his intellectual faculties, and impair the social affections of his heart. Accustomed to move like a mere machine, by the will of a master, reflection is suspended; he has not the power of choice; and reason and conscience, have but little influence over his conduct: because he is chiefly governed by the passion of fear. He is poor and friendless—perhaps worn out by extreme labor, age and disease.

Under such circumstances, freedom may often prove a misfortune to himself, and prejudicial to society.

Attention to emancipated black people, it is therefore to be hoped, will become a branch of our national police; but as far as we contribute to promote this emancipation, so far that attention is evidently a serious duty, incumbent on us, and which we mean to discharge to the best of our judgment and abilities.

To instruct; to advise; to qualify those who have been restored to freedom, for the exercise and enjoyment of civil liberty. To promote in them habits of industry; to furnish them with employments suited to their age, sex, talents, and other circumstances; and to procure their children an education calculated for their future situation in life. These are the great outlines of the annexed plan, which we have adopted, and which we conceive will essentially promote the public good, and the happiness of these our hitherto too much neglected fellow creatures.

A Plan so extensive cannot be carried into execution, without considerable pecuniary resources, beyond the present ordinary funds of the society. We hope much from the generosity of enlightened and benevolent freemen, and will gratefully receive any donations or subscriptions for this purpose, which may be made to our treasurer, James Starr, or to James Pemberton, chairman, of our committee of correspondence.

Signed by order of the Society,

B. FRANKLIN, *President.*

Philadelphia, 9th of *November,* 1789.

These three documents show the progressively enlarging scope of the Pennsylvania Abolition Society, the oldest, strongest, and most influential in the country before 1820. Originally, the Society contented itself with helping free blacks; then it added active effort to abolish slavery entirely; finally, as the *Address* signed by Benjamin Franklin, its president, shows, it undertook "to instruct, to advise, to qualify those who have been restored to freedom, for the exercise and enjoyment of civil liberty."

Pennsylvania Society for promoting the Abolition of Slavery. *An Address to the Public.* [Philadelphia, 1789]. LCP

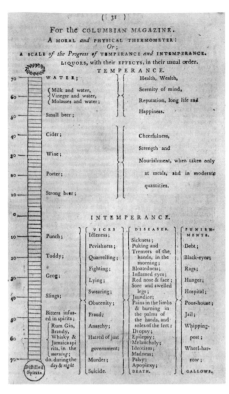

(31)

For the COLUMBIAN MAGAZINE.

A MORAL *and* PHYSICAL THERMOMETER.
Or;
A SCALE *of the Progress of* TEMPERANCE *and* INTEMPERANCE.
LIQUORS, with their EFFECTS, in their usual order.

TEMPERANCE.

	WATER;	Health, Wealth,
70		Serenity of mind,
60	Milk and water, Vinegar and water, Molasses and water;	Reputation, long life and
	Small beer;	Happiness.
50		
40	Cider;	Cheerfulness,
30	Wine;	Strength and
		Nourishment, when taken only
20	Porter;	at meals, and in moderate
10		quantities.
	Strong beer;	
0		

INTEMPERANCE.

		VICES.	DISEASES.	PUNISHMENTS.
10	Punch;	Idleness;	Sickness; Puking and Tremors of the hands, in the morning;	Debt;
20	Toddy;	Peevishness; Quarreling;	Black-eyes;	
	Grog;	Fighting; Lying;	Bloatedness; Inflamed eyes; Red nose & face; Sore and swelled legs; Jaundice;	Rags; Hunger; Hospital;
30	Slings;	Swearing; Obscenity;	Pains in the limbs & burning in the palms of	Poor-house;
40		Fraud;	the hands, and soles of the feet; Dropsy;	Jail;
50	Bitters infused in spirits;	Anarchy; Hatred of just government;	Epilepsy; Melancholy; Idiotism; Madness;	Whipping-post; Wheel-bar-
60	Rum Gin, Brandy, Whisky & Jamaica spirits, in the morning;	Murder;	Palsy; Apoplexy;	row;
70	do. during the day & night	Suicide.	DEATH.	GALLOWS.

Distilled Spirits.

A Moral and Physical Thermometer. Engraving. *Columbian Magazine*, III (1789), 31. LCP

Plan of the Philadelphia Dispensary for the Medical Relief of the Poor [Philadelphia, 1786]. LCP

PLAN

OF THE

PHILADELPHIA DISPENSARY

FOR THE

Medical Relief of the Poor.

To the CITIZENS *of* PHILADELPHIA.

IN all large cities there are many poor persons afflicted by diseases, whose former circumstances and habits of independence will not permit them to expose themselves as patients in a public hospital. There are also many diseases and accidents, of so acute and dangerous a nature, that the removal of patients afflicted by them is attended with many obvious inconveniences. And there are some diseases of such a nature, that the air of an hospital, crowded with patients, is injurious in them. A number of gentlemen, having taken these things into consideration, have proposed to establish a PUBLIC DISPENSARY in the city of Philadelphia, for the medical relief of the poor.

The particular advantages of this institution will be as follow : 1st.

The economic and physiological arguments of advocates of temperance in the 1780s were clearly represented in the Moral Thermometer, in which liquors are ranked from water to gin, with their attendant moral consequences from health, wealth and happiness to suicide, death, and the gallows.

The Moral Thermometer was invented by Dr. John Coakley Lettsom of London, and promoted in America by his friend Dr. Benjamin Rush.

In the enlightened humanitarian feeling that followed the war, the sick poor received thoughtful attention. Dispensaries—the first was in Philadelphia in 1786—provided a sort of out-patient care, including care in one's own home. It is a significant commentary on hospitals of the day—even the Pennsylvania Hospital, one of Philadelphia's glories —that admission to them was considered in many cases "injurious" to the patient.

SUNDAY SCHOOLS.

[Society for the Institution and Support of First Day or Sunday Schools]. *Sunday Schools.* [Philadelphia, 1796]. LCP

WHEREAS the good education of youth is of the first importance to Society—and numbers of children, the offspring of indigent parents, have not proper opportunities of instruction, previously to their being apprenticed to trades :—and whereas among the youth of every large city, various instances occur, of the first day of the week, called Sunday, a day which ought to be devoted to religious improvement, being employed to the worst of purposes, the depravation of morals and manners : It is therefore the opinion of sundry persons, that the establishment of First Day or Sunday Schools, in this city, would be of essential advantage to the rising generation : and for effecting that benevolent purpose, they have formed themselves into a Society by the name of " The Society for the institution and support of First Day or Sunday Schools, in the city of Philadelphia, and the districts of Southwark and the Northern-Liberties :" and have adopted the following

The Sunday School movement, begun in England in the 1780s, had educational and social purposes—to instruct the children of the poor and keep them usefully occupied on Sundays, instead of letting them waste their time in amusements, sport, and other depraving activities.

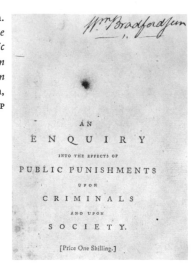

The Pennsylvania Legislature in 1786 reduced the number of capital offenses and substituted "continued hard labor, publicly and disgracefully imposed," for capital and corporal punishments. The sight of chained prisoners working in the city streets induced second thoughts. Speaking both as a humanitarian and as a physician and psychologist, Benjamin Rush questioned the new practice in a paper read to the Society for Political Inquiries, then developed his arguments further in this pamphlet, which was frequently reprinted and became a principal title in the propaganda of prison reform.

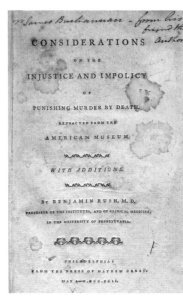

Rush continued his campaign against capital punishments, using arguments from reason, religion, and historical experience. He particularly relished refuting "Old Testament saints" who found arguments for capital punishment in the Bible.

Rush's pamphlet led directly to the formation of the Prison Society, which occurred two weeks after the publication. Asserting that the "Obligations of Benevolence . . . are not cancelled by the follies or crimes of our fellow-creatures," the Society, which was composed principally of Quakers, addressed itself to such practical matters as the institution of solitary confinement (instead of public punishment), the separation of sexes, and the prohibition of spirituous liquors in jail. The Society achieved results principally by peaceful persuasion of the warden and public authorities.

RULES, ORDERS, AND REGULATIONS

FOR THE

GAOL OF THE CITY AND COUNTY OF PHILADELPHIA.

Rules, Orders, and Regulations for the Gaol of the City and County of Philadelphia. Philadelphia: D. Humphreys, 1792. LCP

XIV.

The Prifon fhall be white-wafhed at leaft twice in the year, and oftener, if occafion requires; the floors fhall be fwept every morning, and wafhed on Wednefdays and Saturdays, from 20th of May to the 1ft of October, and once a week for the remainder of the year.

XV.

The fweepings of the Prifon fhall be collected and depofited in a place for the purpofe, and removed once in every two weeks; the neceffaries fhall alfo be cleanfed daily.

XVI.

The yards of the Prifon fhall be kept free from Cows, Hogs, Dogs, and Fowls.

XVII.

The Phyfician for the time being fhall keep a regifter of the fick, their diforders, and his prefcriptions; and fhall render his accounts for the examination and allowance of the Infpectors at each of their quarterly meetings.

XVIII.

At the performance of divine worfhip, all the Prifoners fhall attend, except fuch as may be fick.

Walnut Street Jail. By J. G. Malcolm. Print. APS

The Walnut Street Prison, built in 1792, embodied most of the reforms the Pennsylvania Prison Society sought. As a result it was for many years a famous resort for travellers and observers, who were much impressed by the prevailing order and decency, in striking contrast to conditions in European jails at the time. "I do not believe," wrote a Polish visitor, "that there is in the world an establishment conceived with better judgment and more humanity."

An Address, from the
Philadelphia Society
for Promoting
Agriculture.
[Philadelphia], 1785.
HSP

Philadelphia Society
for Promoting
Agriculture. *Notice of
Election of Thomas
McKean to
Membership*, May
2, 1785. HSP

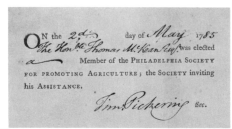

The second association of the kind in the United States, the Philadelphia Society for Promoting Agriculture encouraged American farmers to employ better methods in cultivation, spread knowledge of English agricultural improvements, and fostered the ideal of the independent freeholder as the bulwark of the republic. Though none were "dirt farmers," the Philadelphians had considerable influence, and their example was followed elsewhere in the country.

John Beale Bordley.
*Essays and Notes on
Husbandry and Rural
Affairs.*
Philadelphia: Budd
and Bartram, for
Thomas Dobson,
1799. APS

John Beale Bordley.
*A Summary View
of the Courses of
Crops.* Philadelphia:
Charles Cist,
1784. APS

Judge Bordley, one of the most intelligent and successful farmers in America, shared his experience with his fellow-citizens in a series of letters and essays on the benefits of crop rotation, fertilizing fields, use of machinery, even the proper principles on which to build a country house secure from fire and house-breakers.

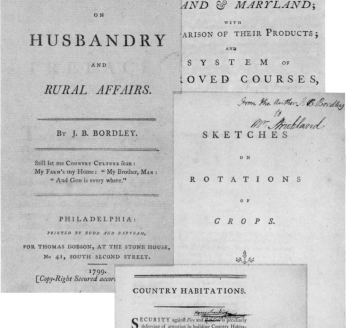

John Beale
Bordley. *Sketches
on Rotation of
Crops.*
Philadelphia:
Charles Cist,
1792. APS

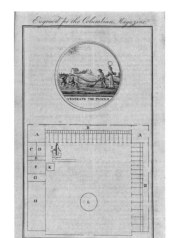

*The Plan of a Farm
Yard.* Engraving.
Columbian Magazine.
I (1786), facing
p. 77. APS

"A well-ordered farm-yard being the foundation of all good husbandry," the Philadelphia Society for Promoting Agriculture offered a gold medal for the best plan. The prize was won by George Morgan of Princeton, N. J. The motto on the Society's seal, shown here, was taken from James Thomson's popular poem *The Seasons.*

John Beale Bordley. *Country Habitations.*
[Philadelphia: Charles Cist, 1798]. LCP

Managers of the Society for Promoting the Manufacture of Sugar from the Sugar Maple Tree. *Address to the Members*. Philadelphia, November 9, 1795. HSP

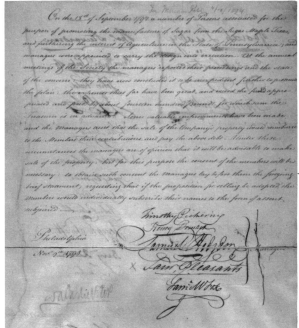

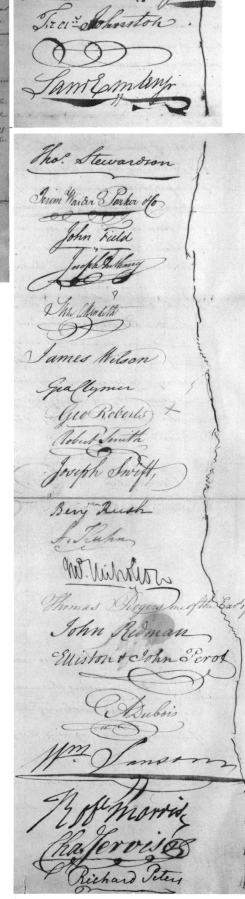

The Maple Sugar Society embodied several reforming ideas: maple sugar would relieve the United States of dependence on West Indian sugar; by reducing the demand for West Indian sugar, it would strike a blow at slavery in those islands; and it seemed a more honest, simple, and therefore desirably "republican," commodity. But the cost of making maple sugar in quantity was too great. Three years after its foundation, the Society disbanded.

The Plan of the Pennsylvania Society for the Encouragement of Manufactures and the Useful Arts. Philadelphia: R. Aitken & Son, 1787. HSP

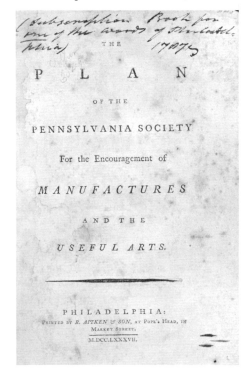

No less than agriculture were manufactures to be encouraged, that the new republic might be economically as well as politically independent. The Manufacturing Society resorted to a time-tested method of raising capital for their textile factory—small quarterly payments from a large number of private persons. "Many a mickle makes a muckle," as Poor Richard had said.

Benjamin Rush. [*Notes on Education*], 1789. LCP

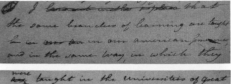

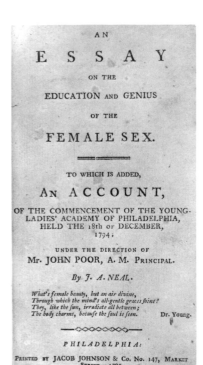

One of the most tireless advocates of *American* education, Rush urged that colleges reform existing curricula and methods of instruction. In his own University of Pennsylvania, where he was professor of medicine, he recommended that the system of education be accommodated to the new form of republican government "and the many national duties and Objects of knowledge, that have been imposed upon us by the American Revolution." Rush particularly deplored that so much time was spent on Latin and Greek, so little on the arts and sciences.

The Rise and Progress of the Young-Ladies' Academy of Philadelphia. Philadelphia: Stewart & Cochran, 1794. LCP

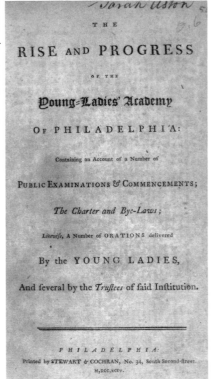

J. A. Neal. *An Essay on the Education and Genius of the Female Sex.* Philadelphia: Jacob Johnson & Co., 1795. LCP

The example of Abigail Adams, Mercy Warren and the English Catherine Macaulay, not to say simple justice and good sense, encouraged schemes for the education of women. Here, as in other educational reforms, Dr. Benjamin Rush was a leader. He was one of the trustees of the Young Ladies' Academy of Philadelphia, founded in 1786.

210

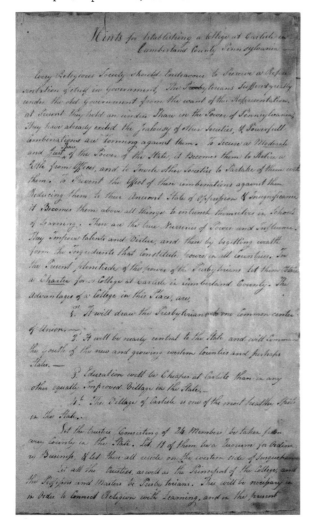

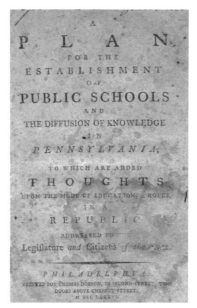

PLAN of a FEDERAL UNIVERSITY.

"YOUR government cannot be executed. It is too extensive for a republic. It is contrary to the habits of the people," say the enemies of the constitution of the United States.— However opposite to the opinions and wishes of a majority of the citizens of the United States these declarations and predictions may be, they will certainly come to pass, unless the people are prepared for our new form of government by an education adapted to the new and peculiar situation of our country. To effect this great and necessary work, let one of the first acts of the new Congress be, to establish within the district to be allotted for them, a FEDERAL UNIVERSITY, into which the youth of the United States shall be received after they have finished their studies, and taken their degrees in the colleges of their respective states. In this University, let those branches of literature only be taught, which are calculated to prepare our youth for civil and public life. These branches should be taught by means of lectures, and the

In thirty years after this university is established, let an act of Congress be passed to prevent any person being chosen or appointed into power or office, who has not taken a degree in the federal university. We require certain qualifications in lawyers, physicians and clergymen, before we commit our property, our lives or our souls to their care. We even refuse to commit the charge of a ship to a pilot, who cannot produce a certificate of his education and knowledge in his business. Why then should we commit our country, which includes liberty, property, life, wives and children, to men who cannot produce vouchers of their qualifications for the important trust? We are restrained from injuring ourselves by employing quacks in law; why should we not be restrained in like manner, by law, from employing quacks in government? Should this plan of a federal university or one like it be adopted, then will begin the golden age of the United States. While the business of education in Europe consists in lectures upon the ruins of Palmyra and the antiquities of Herculaneum, or in disputes about Hebrew points, Greek particles, or the accent and quantity of the Roman language, the youth of America will be employed in acquiring those branches of knowledge which increase the conveniencies of life, lessen human misery, improve our country, promote population, exalt the human understanding, and establish domestic, so-

Few subjects absorbed thoughtful Americans in the years after the American Revolution as much as education. What kind of education was best for citizens of a republic? Benjamin Rush had an answer. Learning, he asserted unequivocally, "is favourable to liberty. A free government can only exist in an equal diffusion of literature. Without learning men become Savages or Barbarians, and where learning is confined to a *few* people, we always find monarchy, aristocracy and slavery."

Dickinson College, chartered in 1783, was the first fruit of Rush's efforts, "the best bulwark," he declared, "of the blessings obtained by the Revolution." He chose Carlisle as its location because the town was a county seat and students could therefore easily observe the courts and local government in action, thus preparing themselves for responsible citizenship.

In 1786 Rush developed his educational system still further. In each state there should be a university to train men for the professions. Below this there should be colleges (four in Pennsylvania) to provide grounding in the liberal arts and the usual duties of a farmer, manufacturer, and citizen. In every county there should be an academy.

Ultimately Rush proposed that the federal government establish a national university to train public officials. "We require certain qualifications in lawyers, physicians and clergymen, before we commit our property, our lives or our souls to their care. . . . Why then should we commit our country, which includes liberty, property, life, wives and children, to men who cannot produce vouchers of their qualifications for the important trust?"

Why indeed?

Jedidiah Morse. *The American Gazetteer.* Boston:
S. Hall, and Thomas & Andrews, 1797. LCP

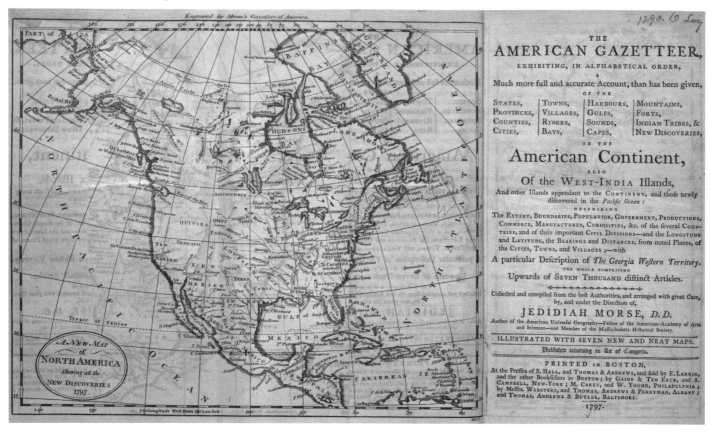

The newly independent country needed its own
school books. Jedidiah Morse, a young New England
Congregational clergyman, beginning with
Geography Made Easy in 1784, wrote several texts.
They were phenomenally successful and virtually
monopolized the field until the second third of the
nineteenth century. Morse's fame and influence are
comparable to those of Noah Webster, author of
English spellers, grammars, and dictionary.

Elizabeth Hewson, who owned this copy of
The American Geography, was the daughter of
Benjamin Franklin's close friend, Mrs. Mary
Stevenson Hewson.

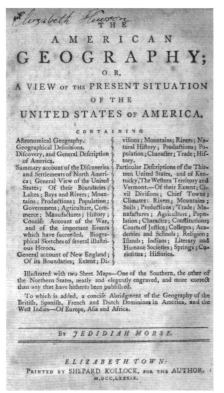

Jedidiah Morse. *The American
Geography.* Elizabethtown, N.J.:
Shepard Kollock, 1789. LCP

Noah Webster, Jr. Frontispiece (woodcut)
in Noah Webster, Jr. *An American Selection
of Lessons in Reading and Speaking . . .
Being the Third Part of a Grammatical
Institute of the English Language.* Boston:
Isaiah Thomas and Ebenezer T.
Andrews, 1796. LCP

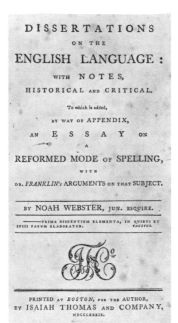

Best known for his dictionary, Noah Webster throughout life was a tireless and imaginative advocate of Americanism in culture. In this book he predicted the development of an American English, "as different from the future language of England as the modern Dutch, Spanish, and Swedish are from the German or from one another." This copy of the *Dissertations* belonged to Benjamin Franklin, to whom it was dedicated.

Noah Webster, Jr. *Dissertations on the English Language*. Boston: Isaiah Thomas and Company, 1789. LCP

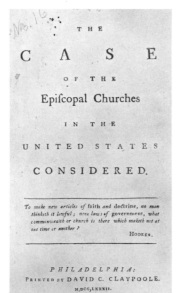

The political independence of the United States created problems for the Anglican Church in America. With no bishop in America, for example, Americans had to go to England for ordination. And there was the troublesome matter of prayers for the King! Reverend Mr. William White took a lead in making the changes which established the Protestant Episcopal Church in the United States in 1785; and he was himself consecrated bishop in 1787—thus making the church independent.

[William White]. *The Case of the Episcopal Churches in the United States Considered*. Philadelphia: David C. Claypoole, 1782. LCP

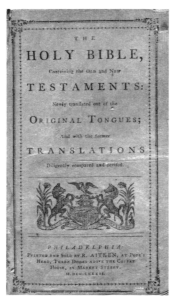

The Holy Bible. Philadelphia: R. Aitken, 1782. LCP

Americans were determined that even the *Bible* should be their own. An enterprising Philadelphia printer, Robert Aitken, published an edition with the endorsement of Congress, which regarded it as an "instance of the progress of the arts in this country." Aitken's *Bible* was the first printed in the United States.

William Cullen. *First Lines of the Practice of Physic*. Philadelphia: Steiner and Cist, 1781. LCP

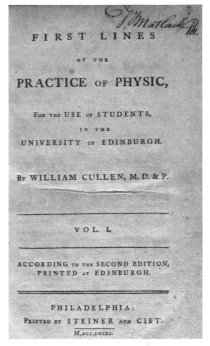

The heaviest "tax" American physicians paid during the Revolution, Benjamin Rush told his Edinburgh professor William Cullen, was the interruption in the supply of books from Europe. Cullen's *First Lines of the Practice of Physic* was almost the only book that came in. Rush had it published; it sold well and had considerable influence on American military physicians and surgeons. "Thus, sir, you . . . have had a hand in the Revolution by contributing indirectly to save the lives of the officers and soldiers of the American army."

Ebenezer Hazard. *Historical Collections; Consisting of State Papers, and other Authentic Documents; intended as Materials for an History of the United States of America.* 2 volumes. Philadelphia: T. Dobson, 1792-94. APS

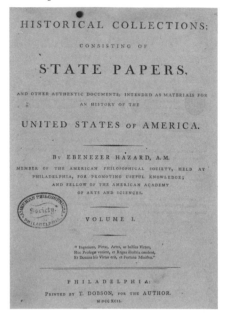

Jeremy Belknap. *The History of New Hampshire.* 3 volumes. Philadelphia: Robert Aitken, 1784-92. APS

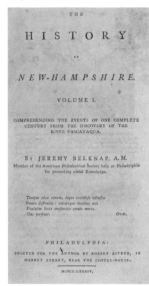

David Ramsay. *The History of the Revolution of South-Carolina.* 2 volumes. Trenton: Isaac Collins, 1785. APS

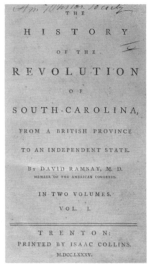

Samuel Miller. *A Brief Retrospect of the Eighteenth Century.* 2 volumes. New York: T. and J. Swords, 1803. LCP

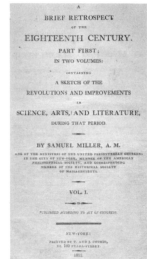

American historians, whose work was indispensable to the citizens of a republic, in Hazard's view produced books of only limited scope and value. One reason was that the records were widely scattered and not easily accessible. "To remove this Obstruction from the Path of Science, and, at the same Time, to lay the Foundation of a good American History, is the Object of the following Compilation." The *Historical Collections* were the first of many documentary publications which are the foundations of "a good American History."

Thoughtful Americans appreciated that the American Revolution closed an era of American history even as it opened another. Histories of the colonial period of several states were published—of Pennsylvania by Robert Proud, of New England by Hannah Adams. Belknap received the praise of William Cullen Bryant as the first writer "to make American history attractive."

Historians of the American Revolution, one of whom was Dr. Ramsay, who has served in Congress, generally agreed that the American system of government was new in the world and that the federal republic was an experiment. They tried to show how the experiment began and to suggest what might be required to make it succeed.

A magisterial survey of intellectual achievements of the 18th century, the *Brief Retrospect* was initially a sermon delivered by a New York clergyman at the close of the century. In a long section devoted to "nations lately become literary"—Sweden, Russia, and the United States—Miller predicted of the latter "that we shall soon be able to make some return to our transatlantic brethren, for the rich stores of useful knowledge which they have been pouring upon us for nearly two centuries."

Edward Savage.
Liberty. Engraving.
Philadelphia:
E. Savage, 1796. HSP

Liberty, in the form of a youthful
goddess, nourishes America,
represented by the bald eagle.

Note at Liberty's feet the shattered
scepter and crushed insignia
of aristocracy.

London Jan: 18: 1779

Dr Price returns his best thanks to the Honourable Benjamin Franklin, Arthur Lee, and John Adams Esquires, for conveying to him the resolution of Congress of the 6th of October last, by which he is invited to become a member of the united States; and to give his assistance in regulating their Finances. It is not possible for him to express the sense he has of the honour which this resolution does him, and the satisfaction with which he reflects on the favourable opinion of him which has occasioned it. But he knows himself not to be sufficiently qualified for giving such assistance; and he is so connected in this country, and also advancing so fast into the evening of life, that he cannot think of a removal. He requests the favour of the honourable Commissioners to transmit this reply to Congress, with assurances that Dr Price feels the warmest gratitude for the notice taken of him, and that he looks to the American States as now the hope, and likely soon to become the refuge of mankind.

The Continental Congress on October 6, 1778, formally offered American citizenship to Dr. Richard Price, an eminent economist and an outstanding English friend to America. This was done out of respect and gratitude and because Congress hoped that Price could put the Continental finances in order. Price declined the extraordinary invitation, assuring the American representatives in Paris that he nonetheless regarded America "as *now* the hope, and likely *soon* to become the refuge of mankind."

Seal of Pennsylvania.
Title-page of
Laws of Pennsylvania.
Philadelphia:
B. Franklin,
1749. HSP

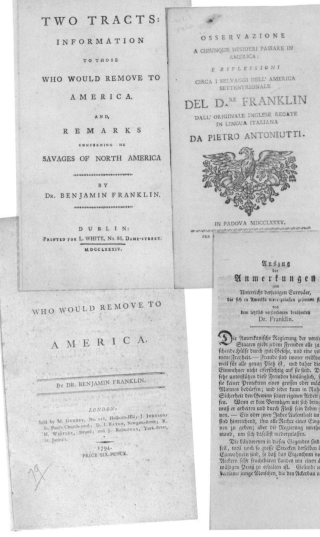

Benjamin Franklin. *Two Tracts: Information to those who would remove to America.* Dublin: L. White, 1784. APS

Information to those who would remove to America. London, 1794. APS

Osservazione a chiunque desideri passare in America. Padua: Gio: Antonio Conzatti, 1785. APS

Auszug der Anmerkungen zum Unterricht derjenigen Europäer, die sich in Amerika niederzulassen gesonnen sind. 1791. APS

Importuned by Europeans wishing to settle in America, many of them of large expectations but few qualifications, Franklin wrote and printed in Paris a little pamphlet of practical advice, which he sent in reply. Birth had its value in Europe, he pointed out, "but it is a Commodity that cannot be carried to a worse Market than to that of America, where People do not enquire of a Stranger, *What is he?* but *What can he do?*" Useful in Franklin's day—the pamphlet was frequently reprinted, as is seen here—the *Advice* is appealing today because of the picture it sketches of a country of honest, industrious, self-respecting free men.

Many Europeans of education and talent were attracted to America after the Revolution, some by the lure of profits, many by dreams of liberty. Among those who made lasting contributions to the new republic were:

*FIGURES 1 AND 2

Mathew Carey (1760-1839). From Ireland, 1784. He had been involved in Irish revolutionary activity. In America he became a leading publisher and, after 1815, an eloquent advocate of protectionism.

FIGURES 3 AND 4

Peter S. Du Ponceau (1760-1844). From France, 1777. Coming to America as secretary to General Steuben, he remained to become America's outstanding authority on international law and, in Philadelphia, founder or president of a host of cultural institutions, including two of the three sponsors of this exhibition.

FIGURE 5

Albert Gallatin (1761-1849). From Switzerland, 1780. As Secretary of the Treasury, 1801-1814, he believed the Federal Government should employ its surplus revenues in national projects for education and internal improvements. He was himself a pioneer in the study of American ethnology.

FIGURE 6

Benjamin Latrobe (1764-1820). From England, 1796. An engineer and architect. Latrobe provided the new republic with a score of distinguished public buildings worthy of the national ideals.

FIGURE 7

Peter Le Gaux (1748-1827). From France, 1785. He planted vineyards near Philadelphia and endeavored to introduce viniculture into the United States. He also kept daily records of the weather for half a century.

FIGURE 8

Friedrich V. Melsheimer (1749-1814). From Germany, 1777. A chaplain to Brunswick troops in Burgoyne's army, he was made prisoner, sent to Pennsylvania, where he became minister to several small German churches, then professor in the new Franklin College, and author of the first work on entomology published in the United States.

FIGURE 9

Walter Minto (1753-1796). From Scotland, 1786. He was professor of mathematics and natural philosophy in the College of New Jersey (Princeton), 1787-1796.

FIGURE 10

Charles Nisbet (1736-1804). From Scotland, 1785. A Scottish clergyman who had been sympathetic to the American cause, he was invited by Dr. Benjamin Rush to become president of Dickinson College, which he served until his death.

FIGURES 11 AND 12

Joseph Priestley (1733-1804). From England, 1794. The discoverer of oxygen, an imaginative educator, and a fearless theologian, he was the correspondent and friend of Franklin, Jefferson, Rush, and other political and religious liberals. Driven from England as a result of sympathy with the French Revolution, he came to the United States, where he settled at Northumberland, Pa., writing steadily and making occasional visits to Philadelphia.

FIGURE 13

William Thornton (1759-1828). From the West Indies, 1787. By profession a physician, by avocation an architect, Thornton designed the hall of the Library Company of Philadelphia and the United States Capitol. He wrote on language, promoted the education of the deaf and the work of the American Colonization Society, and was Commissioner of Patents, appointed by President Jefferson.

*See figures on following two pages.

Figure 1. *Mathew Carey.* Engraving by Samuel Sartain of a portrait by John Neagle. APS

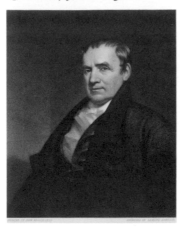

Figure 3. *Peter S. Du Ponceau.* Pencil sketch. 1822. APS

[THIRD EDITION.]

PHILADELPHIA, March 14, 1834.

SOCIETIES FOR PROMOTING MANUAL LABOR IN LITERARY INSTITUTIONS.

Among the numerous and valuable institutions which the benevolence of late years has called into existence, there is a class which has not as yet attracted much notice, but which gives fair promise of vieing in point of utility with most of those which have preceded it—I mean, " Societies for the promotion of manual labor in literary institutions."

The principal object with most of those liberal citizens to whose patronage the world is mainly indebted for this invaluable system, was, to facilitate to young men in confined circumstances, the means of procuring a liberal education. The world had witnessed the fact, that hundreds of the brightest geniuses that ever reflected honor on human nature, had never, in their early days, had any advantage of education beyond the first rudiments, and some of them not even that small advantage; whereby society has been in a great measure debarred of the benefit which their talents were calculated to confer on mankind—and some of those bright geniuses, through the want of proper education, and the misdirection of their talents, had become the curses of their age; whereas by proper cul-

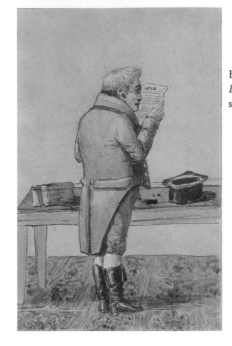

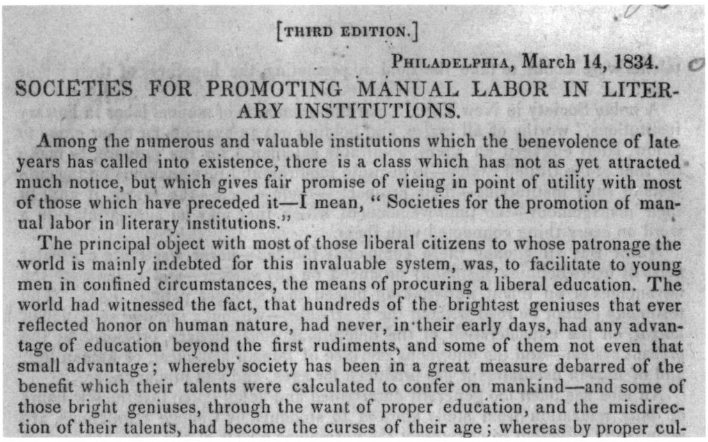

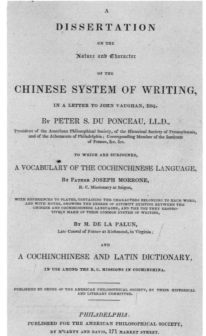

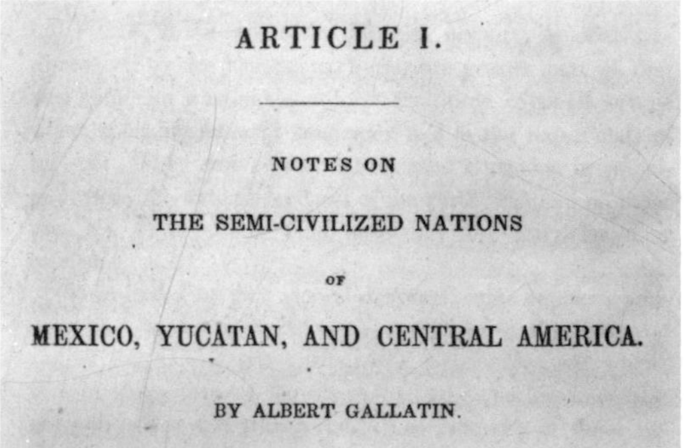

Figure 2. Mathew Carey. *Societies for Promoting Manual Labor in Literary Institutions.* Philadelphia, 1834. APS

A

DISSERTATION

ON THE

Nature and Character

OF THE

CHINESE SYSTEM OF WRITING,

IN A LETTER TO JOHN VAUGHAN, ESQ.

BY PETER S. DU PONCEAU, LL.D.,

President of the American Philosophical Society, of the Historical Society of Pennsylvania, and of the Athenæum of Philadelphia; Corresponding Member of the Institute of France, &c. &c.

TO WHICH ARE SUBJOINED,

A VOCABULARY OF THE COCHINCHINESE LANGUAGE,

BY FATHER JOSEPH MORRONE,

R. C. Missionary at Saigon,

WITH REFERENCES TO PLATES, CONTAINING THE CHARACTERS BELONGING TO EACH WORD, AND WITH NOTES, SHOWING THE DEGREE OF AFFINITY EXISTING BETWEEN THE CHINESE AND COCHINCHINESE LANGUAGES, AND THE USE THEY RESPECTIVELY MAKE OF THEIR COMMON SYSTEM OF WRITING,

BY M. DE LA PALUN,

Late Consul of France at Richmond, in Virginia;

AND

A COCHINCHINESE AND LATIN DICTIONARY,

IN USE AMONG THE R. C. MISSIONS IN COCHINCHINA.

PUBLISHED BY ORDER OF THE AMERICAN PHILOSOPHICAL SOCIETY, BY THEIR HISTORICAL AND LITERARY COMMITTEE.

PHILADELPHIA:

PUBLISHED FOR THE AMERICAN PHILOSOPHICAL SOCIETY,

BY M'CARTY AND DAVIS, 171 MARKET STREET.

1838.

Figure 4. Peter Du Ponceau. *The Chinese System of Writing.* Philadelphia: American Philosophical Society, by M'Carty and Davis, 1838. APS

ARTICLE I.

NOTES ON

THE SEMI-CIVILIZED NATIONS

OF

MEXICO, YUCATAN, AND CENTRAL AMERICA.

BY ALBERT GALLATIN.

Figure 5. Albert Gallatin. *Notes on the Semi-Civilized Nations of Mexico, Yucatan, and Central America.* New York, 1845. APS

Figure 6. Benjamin Latrobe. *An Answer . . on the Subject of a Plan for Supplying the City with Water, &c.* [Philadelphia, 1799]. APS

AN

ANSWER

TO THE

JOINT COMMITTEE

OF THE

SELECT AND COMMON COUNCILS

OF

PHILADELPHIA,

ON THE SUBJECT OF A PLAN FOR

Supplying the City with Water, &c.

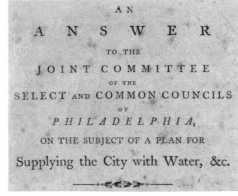

Figure 7. Peter Le Gaux. *Extracts of a Journal of Meteorological Observations*, Spring Mill, February 1789. Manuscript. APS

This is Le Gaux's copy of the original Journal sent to Benjamin Franklin on April 2, 1789.

Figure 8. Friedrich V. Melsheimer. *A Catalogue of Insects of Pennsylvania.* Hanover: W. D. Lepper, 1806. APS

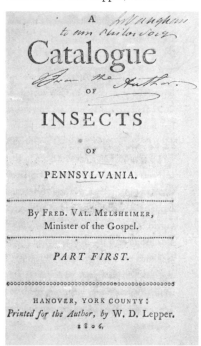

This volume was presented by the author to the naturalist Benjamin Smith Barton of Philadelphia.

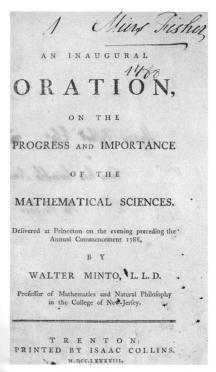

Figure 9. Walter Minto. *An Inaugural Oration, on the Progress and Importance of the Mathematical Sciences.* Trenton: Isaac Collins, 1788. APS

Figure 11. *Joseph Priestley.* Engraving by W. Bromley in *European Magazine*, 1791. APS

Figure 10. *Charles Nisbet.* Engraving by John Sartain from an oil painting by a Scottish artist. APS

Figure 12. Joseph Priestley. *Réflexions sur la Doctrine du Phlogistique et la Décomposition de l'Eau.* Philadelphia: Moreau de Saint-Méry, 1797. APS

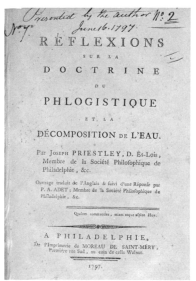

A French translation, printed in Philadelphia by a refugee from San Domingo, presented by the author to the American Philosophical Society, to which the printer also belonged.

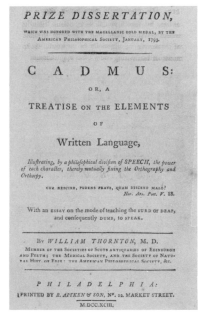

Figure 13. William Thornton. *Cadmus: or, a Treatise on the Elements of Written Language.* Philadelphia: Robert Aitken & Son, 1793. APS

The Triumph of
Liberty. By John
Francis Renault.
Engraved by Peter
C. Verger. New
York, 1796. LCP

Drawn by J. F. Renault N.º York

By a Column raised to Liberty, is a Monument sacred to the memory of
the American Heroes, fallen in defence of their Country. While
Liberty is Crowning them, America under the figure of Minerva sacrifices to their
Manes, and a Priest of that Deity sings their glorious actions. The Hydra of
Despotism mortally wounded by those great men expires in frightful convulsions.

Engraved by P. C. Roger January 1796

of Liberty

Defenders in America

Peace and Justice hand in hand, join with America in her homage to Liberty.
Plenty reclining on her emblematical Horn, reposes on American ground. The Genius
of Liberty points out the declaration of Independence, and a Book of the American
Constitution. From the dreadful Sight, a group of Kings turn away with horror
and dismay.

John Dickinson.
*Preliminary Draft of the
Articles of Confederation
and perpetual Union*
[Philadelphia, July 1776].
Manuscript. HSP

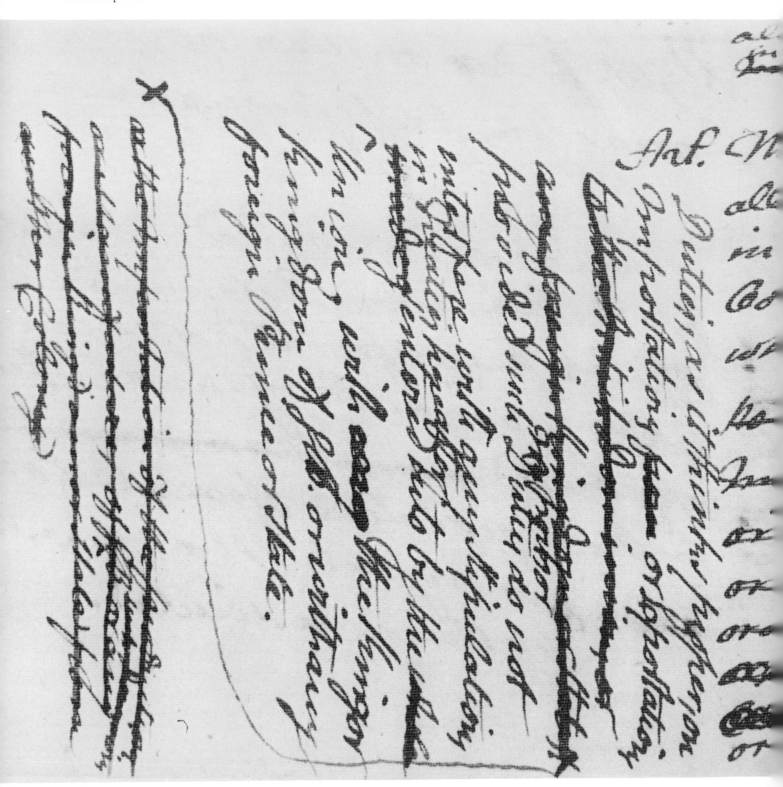

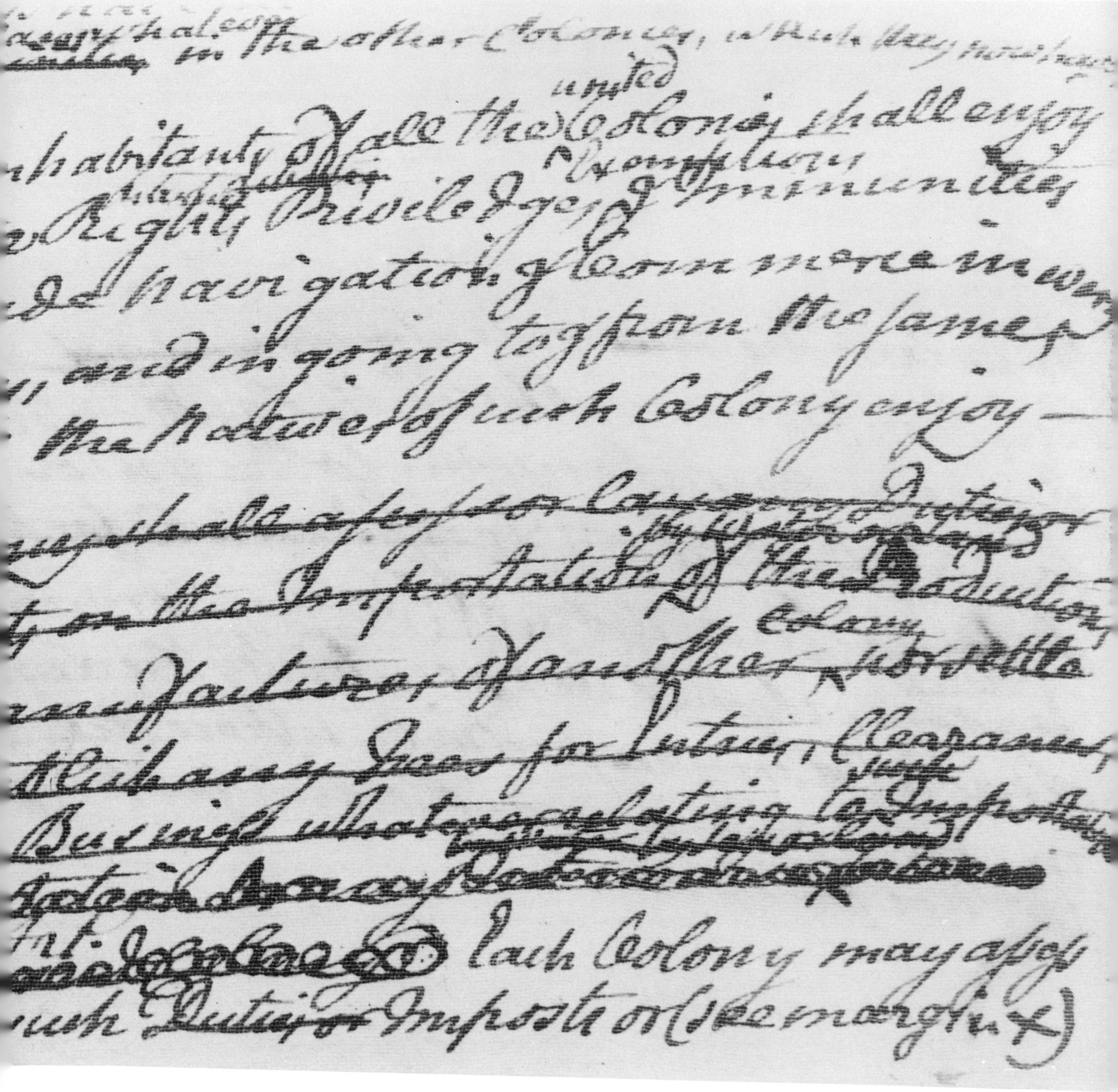

in the other Colonies, which they now have

inhabitants of all the ~~united~~ Colony shall enjoy

Rights Priviledges & immunities

navigation of commerce in

and in going to & upon the James

the Natives of such Colony enjoy —

shall lay no

upon the Importation of the production

manufactures of another Colony

nor any fees for entries, Clearances

But will whatever relating to Import

Each Colony may assess

such Duties or Imposts or (see margin x)

South Carolina. *A Constitution,*
or Form of Government.
[Charleston: Peter Timothy.
1776]. HSP

In Congress, May 15,1776. Whereas his Britannic Majesty,
in conjunction with the Lords and Commons of Great-Britain,
has, by a late Act of Parliament, excluded the inhabitants of
these United Colonies from the protection of his crown.
Philadelphia: John Dunlap, [1776]. LCP

South Carolina was the second colony to take
action on a separate instrument of government. In
a stirring preamble it listed the actions of Parliament
which reduced its citizens "from the rank of
Freemen to a state of the most abject Slavery," a
recital which Jefferson included in the Declaration
of Independence. This hastily drawn document
was superseded when a carefully drafted constitution
was adopted in its place early in 1777.

Even before Congress declared itself independent, it
recommended that each of the colonies "adopt such
Government as shall in the opinion of the
Representatives of the People best conduce to the
happiness and safety of their Constituents in
particular, and America in general." This was the
call for the British colonies to throw off their
provincial governments and become American
states.

The Protest Of divers of the Inhabitants of this Province, in behalf of themselves and others. [Philadelphia, 1776]. LCP

Philadelphia May 20. 1776.

The PROTEST

Of divers of the Inhabitants of this Province, in behalf of themselves and others.

To the Honorable the REPRESENTATIVES of the Province of PENNSYLVANIA,

GENTLEMEN,

WE the underfigned, in behalf of ourfelves, and others, the Inhabitants of Pennfylvania, until the fenfe of the majority of the fame can be more fully known, concieve it our duty to reprefent unto this houfe as followeth;

THAT whereas the Hon. CONTINENTAL CONGRESS hath by a refolve bearing date the 15th Inft. recommending the taking up, and *eftablifhing* new Governments throughout all the United Colonies, under the " AUTHORITY of the PEOPLE," and as the chartered power of this Houfe is derived from our Mortal Enemy the King of *Great-Britain*, and the members thereof were elected by fuch perfons *only*, as were, either, in real or fuppofed allegiance to the faid King, to the exclufion of many of the worthy inhabitants, whom the aforefaid refolve of Congrefs hath now rendered electors, and as this houfe, *in its Prefent ftate*, is in immediate intercourfe with a Governor bearing the faid King's Commiffion, and who is his fworn reprefentative, holding, and by oath obliged to hold official correfponednce with the Minifters of the faid King, and is not within the reach of any act of ours to be abfolved therefrom. We therefore in this folemn manner, in behalf of ourfelves and others, do hereby renounce and proteft againft the authority of this Houfe, and againft all thofe who act officially under the faid King.

Extracts from the Proceedings of the Provincial Conference of Committees for the Province of Pennsylvania. Held at Carpenter's Hall, Philadelphia, June 18, 1776. Philadelphia: Styner and Cist, [1776]. LCP

PROCEEDINGS

OF THE

PROVINCIAL CONFERENCE

OF

COMMITTEES,

OF THE

PROVINCE OF PENNSYLVANIA;

Held at the CARPENTER's HALL,

AT

PHILADELPHIA.

Began *JUNE* 18th, and continued by adjournments to *JUNE* 25, 1776.

PHILADELPHIA:

Printed by W. & T. BRADFORD.

Proceedings of the Provincial Conference of Committees, of the Province of Pennsylvania. Philadelphia: W. & T. Bradford, [1776]. LCP

[1]

EXTRACTS from the PROCEEDINGS of the PROVINCIAL CONFERENCE of COMMITTEES for the Province of *Pennfylvania*,

Held at CARPENTER's HALL, Philadelphia, *June* 18, 1776.

JUNE 19, 1776.

On Motion, *Refolved, N. C. D.*

THAT it is neceffary that a PROVINCIAL CONVENTION be called by this Conference, for the exprefs Purpofe of forming a NEW GOVERNMENT in this Province, *on the Authority of the People only.*

Refolved,

That every Affociator in the Province fhall be admitted to a Vote for Members of the Convention in the City or County in which he refides; Provided fuch Affociator be of the Age of Twenty-one Years, and fhall have lived One Year in the Province immediately preceding the Election; and fhall have contributed at any Time, before the Paffing of this Refolve, to the Payment of either Provincial or County Taxes, or fhall have been rated or affeffed towards the fame.

Refolved,

That every Perfon qualified by the Laws of this Province to vote for Reprefentatives in Affembly, fhall be admitted to vote for Members of the intended Convention; Provided he fhall firft take the following Teft, if thereunto required by any one of the Judges or Infpectors of the Election, *viz.*

" I ―― do fwear, (or affirm) That I do not hold myfelf bound to bear Allegiance to
" George the Third, *King of Great-Britain, &c.* and that *I will not by any Means*
" *directly or indirectly oppofe the Eftablifhment of a free Government in this Province by*
" *the Convention now to be chofen; nor the Meafures adopted by the Congrefs againft the*
" *Tyranny attempted to be eftablifhed in thefe Colonies by the Court of Great-Britain.*"

On Motion, *Refolved,*

That whereas the County of *Weftmoreland* has been exempted from Taxes for Three Years laft paft, and thereby many Perfons may be excluded from a Vote at the enfuing Election in confequence of the foregoing Regulations, contrary to the Intention thereof, therefore every Perfon of Twenty-one Years of Age, being a Freeman, refiding in faid County, fhall be admitted to vote, he being an Affociator, and having lived One Year in this Province next preceding the Election, and taking the Teft aforefaid, if thereunto required.

Refolved,

The reaction in Pennsylvania to the call of Congress to establish state governments was swift. On May 20 a group of citizens declared that they no longer considered themselves under the authority of the Assembly. A Provincial Conference was convened on June 18 "for the express Purpose of forming a NEW GOVERNMENT in this Province, *on the Authority of the People only.*" It provided qualifications for the election of delegates to a convention to frame a new constitution, set the places for that election and appointed July 15 as the time of meeting for a convention to frame a constitution for the new state. And on June 24 the most significant action was taken: "We the Deputies of the People of Pennsylvania," the Conference agreed, "UNANIMOUSLY declare our willingness to concur in a Vote of the Congress, declaring the United Colonies free and independent States."

[John Adams]. *Thoughts on Government: applicable to The Present State of the American Colonies.* Philadelphia: John Dunlap, 1776. LCP

IN A GENERAL CONVENTION.

Begun and holden at the CAPITOL, in the city of WILLIAMSBURG, on MONDAY the sixth day of MAY, one thousand seven hundred and seventy six, and continued, by adjournment, to the day of JULY following.

The CONSTITUTION, or FORM of GOVERNMENT, agreed to and resolved upon by the Delegates and Representatives of the several counties and corporations of VIRGINIA.

WHEREAS George the third, king of Great Britain and Ireland, and elector of Hanover, heretofore intrusted with the exercise of the kingly office in this government, hath endeavoured to pervert the same into a detestable and insupportable tyranny, by putting his negative on laws the most wholesome and necessary for the publick good;

By denying his governours permission to pass laws of immediate and pressing importance, unless suspended in their operation for his assent, and, when so suspended, neglecting to attend to them for many years;

By refusing to pass certain other laws, unless the persons to be benefited by them would relinquish the inestimable right of representation in the legislature;

By dissolving legislative assemblies repeatedly and continually, for opposing with manly firmness his invasions of the rights of the people;

When dissolved, by refusing to call others for a long space of time, thereby leaving the political system without any legislative head;

By endeavouring to prevent the population of our country, and, for that purpose, obstructing the laws for the naturalization of foreigners;

By keeping among us, in times of peace, standing armies and ships of war;

By affecting to render the military independent of, and superiour to, the civil power;

By combining with others to subject us to a foreign jurisdiction, giving his assent to their pretended acts of legislation:

For quartering large bodies of armed troops among us:

For cutting off our trade with all parts of the world:

For imposing taxes on us without our consent:

For depriving us of the benefits of trial by jury:

For transporting us beyond seas, to be tried for pretended offences:

For suspending our own legislatures, and declaring themselves invested with power to legislate for us in all cases whatsoever:

By plundering our seas, ravaging our coasts, burning our towns, and destroying the lives of our people:

By inciting insurrections of our fellow subjects, with the allurements of forfeiture and confiscation:

By prompting our negroes to rise in arms among us, those very negroes whom, by an inhuman use of his negative, he hath refused us permission to exclude by law:

By endeavouring to bring on the inhabitants of our frontiers the merciless Indian savages, whose known rule of warfare is an undistinguished destruction of all ages, sexes, and conditions of existence:

By transporting, at this time, a large army of foreign mercenaries, to complete the works of death, desolation, and tyranny, already begun with circumstances of cruelty and perfidy unworthy the head of a civilized nation:

By answering our repeated petitions for redress with a repetition of injuries:

And finally, by abandoning the helm of government, and declaring us out of his allegiance and protection.

By which several acts of misrule, the government of this country, as formerly exercised under the crown of *Great Britain*, is TOTALLY DISSOLVED:

We therefore, the delegates and representatives of the good people of Virginia, having maturely considered the premises, and viewing with great concern the deplorable condition to which this once happy country must be reduced, unless some regular adequate mode of civil polity is speedily adopted, and in compliance with a recommendation of the General Congress, do ordain and declare the future form of government of Virginia to be as followeth:

The legislative, executive, and judiciary departments, shall be separate and distinct, so that neither exercise the powers properly belonging to the other; nor shall any person exercise the powers of more than one of them at the same time, except that the justices of the county courts shall be eligible to either House of Assembly.

The legislative shall be formed of two distinct branches, who, together, shall be a complete legislature. They shall meet once, or oftener, every year, and shall be called the GENERAL ASSEMBLY OF VIRGINIA.

One of these shall be called the HOUSE OF DELEGATES, and consist of two representatives to be chosen for each county, and for the district of *West Augusta*, annually, of such men as actually reside in and are freeholders of the same, or duly qualified according to law, and also one delegate or representative to be chosen annually for the city of *Williamsburg*, and one for the borough of *Norfolk*, and a representative for each of such other cities and boroughs as may hereafter be allowed particular representation by the legislature; but when any city or borough shall so decrease as that the number of persons having right of suffrage therein shall have been for the space of seven years successively less than half the number of voters in some one county in *Virginia*, such city or borough thenceforward shall cease to send a delegate or representative to the Assembly.

The other shall be called the SENATE, and consist of twenty four members, of whom thirteen shall constitute a House to proceed on business, for whose election the different counties shall be divided into twenty four districts, and each county of the respective district, at the time of the election of its delegates, shall vote for one Senator, who is actually a resident and freeholder within the district, or duly qualified according to law, and is upwards of twenty five years of age; and the sheriffs of each county, within five days at farthest after the last county election in the district, shall meet at some convenient place, and from the poll so taken in their respective counties return as a Senator the man who shall have the greatest number of votes in the whole district. To keep up this Assembly by rotation, the districts shall be equally divided into four classes, and numbered by lot. At the end of one year after the general election, the six members elected by the first division shall be displaced, and the vacancies thereby occasioned supplied from such class or division, by new election, in the manner aforesaid. This rotation shall be applied to each division, according to its number, and continued in due order annually.

The right of suffrage in the election of members for both Houses shall remain as exercised at present, and each House shall choose its own speaker, appoint its own officers, settle its own rules of proceeding, and direct writs of election for supplying intermediate vacancies.

All laws shall originate in the House of Delegates, to be approved or rejected by the Senate, or to be amended with the consent of the House of Delegates; except money bills, which in no instance shall be altered by the Senate, but wholly approved or rejected.

A Governour, or chief magistrate, shall be chosen annually, by joint ballot of both Houses, to be taken in each House respectively, deposited in the conference room, the boxes examined jointly by a committee of each House, and the numbers severally reported to them, that the appointments may be entered (which shall be the mode of taking the joint ballot of both Houses in all cases) who shall not continue in that office longer than three years successively, nor be eligible until the expiration of four years after he shall have been out of that office. An adequate, but moderate salary, shall be settled on him during his continuance in office; and he shall, with the advice of a Council of State, exercise the executive powers of government according to the laws of this commonwealth; and shall not, under any pretence, exercise any power or prerogative by virtue of any law, statute, or custom, of *England*: But he shall, with the advice of the Council of State, have the power of granting reprieves or pardons, except where the prosecution shall have been carried on by the House of Delegates, or the law shall otherwise particularly direct; in which cases no reprieve or pardon shall be granted, but by resolve of the House of Delegates.

Either House of the General Assembly may adjourn themselves respectively. The Governour shall not prorogue or adjourn the Assembly during their sitting, nor dissolve them at any time; but he shall, if necessary, either by advice of the Council of State, or on application of a majority of the House of Delegates, call them before the time to which they shall stand prorogued or adjourned.

A Privy Council, or Council of State, consisting of eight members, shall be chosen by joint ballot of both Houses of Assembly, either from their own members or the people at large, to assist in the administration of government. They shall annually choose out of their own members a president, who, in case of the death, inability, or necessary absence of the Governour from the government, shall act as Lieutenant-Governour. Four members shall be sufficient to act, and their advice and proceedings shall be entered of record, and signed by the members present (to any part whereof any member may enter his dissent) to be laid before the General Assembly, when called for by them. This Council may appoint their own clerk, who shall have a salary settled by law, and take an oath of secrecy in such matters as he shall be directed by the board to conceal. A sum of money appropriated to that purpose shall be divided annually among the members, in proportion to their attendance; and they shall be incapable, during their continuance in office, of sitting in either House of Assembly. Two members shall be removed by joint ballot of both Houses of Assembly at the end of every three years, and be ineligible for the three next years. These vacancies, as well as those occasioned by death or incapacity, shall be supplied by new elections, in the same manner.

The delegates for *Virginia* to the Continental Congress shall be chosen annually, or superseded in the mean time by joint ballot of both Houses of Assembly.

The present militia officers shall be continued, and vacancies supplied by appointment of the Governour, with the advice of the Privy Council, on recommendations...

In a General Convention. . . . The Constitution, or Form of Government . . . of Virginia. [Williamsburg: Alexander Purdie, 1776]. LCP

THOUGHTS

ON

GOVERNMENT:

APPLICABLE TO

THE PRESENT STATE

OF THE

AMERICAN COLONIES.

In a LETTER from a GENTLEMAN To his FRIEND.

PHILADELPHIA:
PRINTED BY JOHN DUNLAP.
M,DCC,LXXVI.

The composition of Virginia's first constitution was a complicated matter, and the ideas and the text are the result of several men's contributions. As early as November 15, 1775, Adams had outlined his thoughts on state constitutions for Richard Henry Lee. The printed version was prepared at the request of George Wythe, and copies went to a number of Virginians. On May 15, 1776, in convention they adopted a resolution calling for independence and appointed a committee to draft a plan of government. Jefferson made three drafts, including a preamble spelling out malevolent actions of the King's government, a list of charges which was also used in the Declaration of Independence. George Mason also supplied a plan. Some of Adams's ideas were incorporated. The committee then revised all the material available and on June 28 ordered that the constitution be fairly transcribed. A copy was sent to Purdie, the publisher of the *Virginia Gazette,* who printed it in this broadside form and also as a supplement, using the same type, to the issue of July 5, 1776.

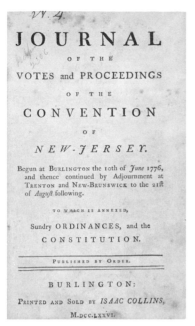

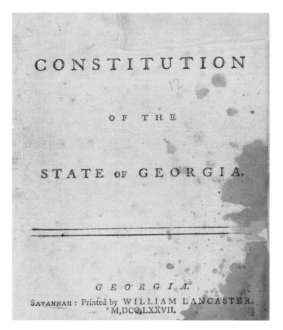

Journal of the Votes and Proceedings of the Convention of New-Jersey. . . . To which is annexed, Sundry Ordinances, and the Constitution. Burlington: Isaac Collins, 1776. HSP

The Constitution of the State of Georgia. Savannah: William Lancaster, 1777. LCP

New Jersey was one of the four states which acted upon a constitution before July 4, 1776. The document was passed by the convention on July 2. Most unusual, and indicative of the comparatively conservative character of the delegates to that convention, was the final clause stating that if a reconciliation should be effected with Great Britain, "this charter shall be null and void, otherwise to remain firm and inviolable." It is a commentary upon the relaxed manners of librarians in the past, that this copy was first given by descendants of its printer to the American Antiquarian Society, then passed into the collection of Samuel Latham Mitchill Barlow, and thence to the Historical Society of Pennsylvania.

Button Gwinnett, who had arrived in Philadelphia as a delegate from Georgia in May 1776, stayed only long enough to sign the Declaration, returning home in August. He took with him a copy of the new constitution of Pennsylvania, on the basis of which he drafted the constitution of Georgia. Its first printing is one of the rarest of the state constitutions. Not long after its adoption Gwinnett was killed in a duel.

The Constitution and Form of Government proposed for the Consideration of the Delegates of Maryland. [Annapolis: Frederick Green, 1776]. HSP

The Declaration and Charter of Rights. [Annapolis: Frederick Green, 1776]. HSP

On August 14, 1776, Marylanders assembled in a convention to draw up instruments of state government. As in many states both a constitution and a bill of rights were drafted. These two printings, both of which belonged to John Dickinson and both of which are the only copies known, represent the drafts which were submitted to the convention. In the *Declaration* there is a strong flavor of the old English Whigs or Commonwealthmen in such as statement as the first: "That all government of right originates from the people, is founded in compact only, and instituted solely for the good of the whole."

That all government of right originates from the people,

An Essay of a Declaration of Rights, Brought in by the Committee appointed for that Purpose, and now under the Consideration of the Convention of the State of Pennsylvania. [Philadelphia: 1776]. LCP

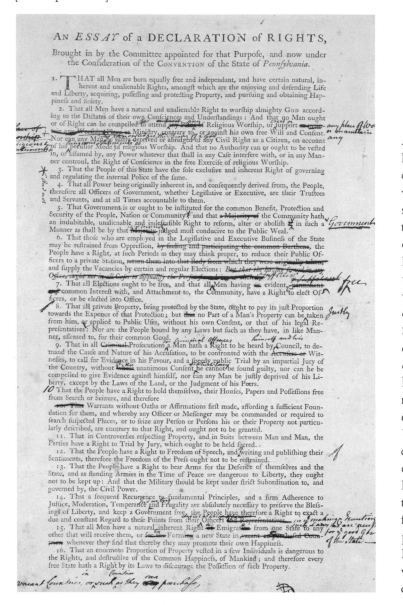

As a preamble to a frame of government for Pennsylvania, the Convention ordered a Declaration of Rights to be drafted. A committee for that purpose was appointed on July 18 and a week later a draft was submitted. The exact wording proved difficult. While the Convention considered it, Franklin, the president of the Convention, and Dickinson, then with the Flying Camp in New Jersey, revised it, as this copy with their autograph changes indicates. In this form it was adopted on August 16. Then came consideration of the constitution, which was finally approved on September 28. It provided for a single legislative body elected annually, a supreme executive council, and a council of censors to oversee the execution of the laws. Dickinson did not approve of it; in an attempt to rewrite the instrument he covered his copy with emendations. Rush did not like it either; in his letter to Wayne, telling of the defection from the patriot camp of William Allen, Jr., and deploring the American evacuation of New York, he remarks that the new Pennsylvania constitution was "tho't by many people to be rather too much upon the democratical Order, for liberty is as apt to degenerate into licentiousness, as power is to become arbitrary." The following year Rush wrote a reasoned critique of the constitution which he published anonymously, but in this copy, his own, he added his name on the title.

Benjamin Rush. *Letter to Colonel Anthony Wayne,* Philadelphia, September 24, 1776. HSP

The Constitution of the Common-wealth of Pennsylvania,
as established by The General Convention Elected *for*
that Purpose. Philadelphia: John Dunlap, 1776. HSP

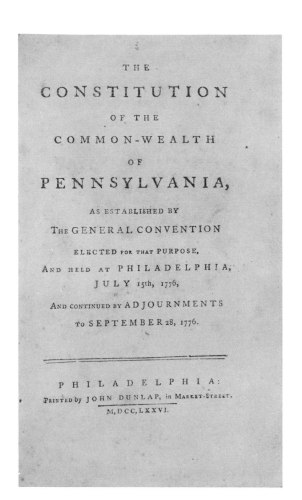

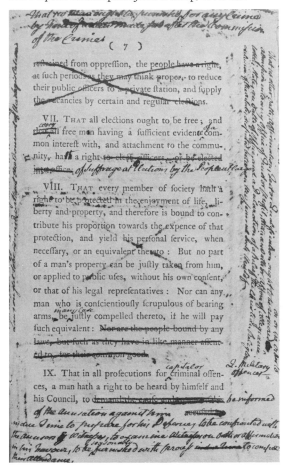

Benjamin Rush.
By Thomas Sully.
Oil on canvas. APS

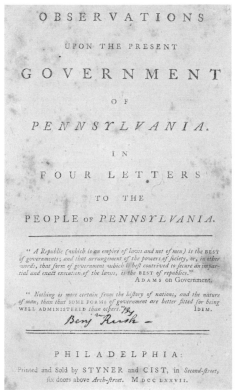

[Benjamin Rush].
Observations upon the
present Government of
Pennsylvania.
Philadelphia: Styner
and Cist, 1777. LCP

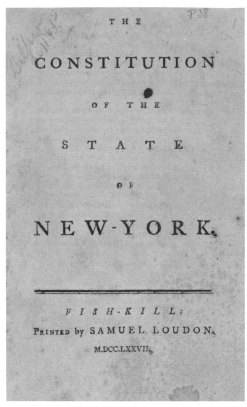

In Convention, At New-Castle, For the Delaware State, . . . The Constitution or System of Government. Wilmington: James Adams, 1776. LCP

The Constitution of the State of New-York. Fishkill: Samuel Loudon, 1777. HSP

By its constitution the old colonial name, the Counties of New-Castle, Kent and Sussex, upon Delaware, was changed to Delaware State. It is interesting that, as in most of the states, a prefatory bill of rights guaranteed liberties which the colonies had been deprived of by the English government. Only two other copies of this rare official printing of Delaware's Declaration of Rights and Constitution are known.

With the British occupying New York city, the state of New York was forced to move its temporary capital west to Fishkill. There on April 20, 1777, a convention approved a constitution drafted by John Jay. The preamble was a lengthy one, incorporating within it the full text of the Declaration of Independence.

Although the constitution of North Carolina was adopted at Halifax by a state congress which opened on December 18, 1776, no separate printing of it was issued until this edition of 1779. This copy belonged to Col. John Laurens of South Carolina, who was sent to France by Congress as an envoy extraordinary to obtain military supplies for the army. There he worked with Franklin and may then have given him this copy, which is bound into one of Franklin's pamphlet volumes.

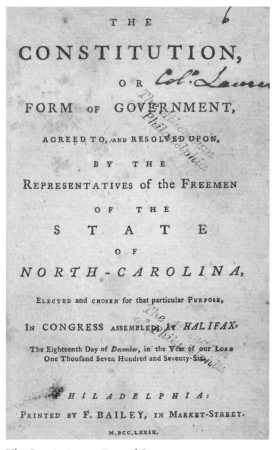

The Constitution, or Form of Government, agreed to, and resolved upon, by the Representatives of the Freemen of the State of North-Carolina. Philadelphia: F. Bailey, 1779. HSP

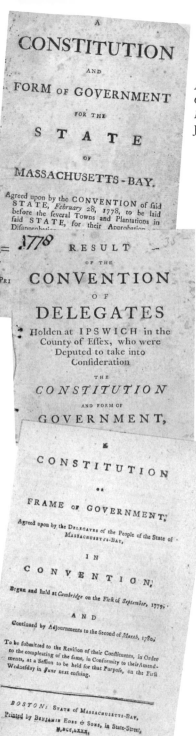

A Constitution and Form of Government for the State of Massachusetts-Bay. Boston: J. Gill, 1778. LCP

Result of the Convention of Delegates Holden at Ipswich in the County of Essex, who were Deputed to take into Consideration the Constitution and Form of Government, proposed by the Convention of the State of Massachusetts-Bay. Newburyport: John Mycall, 1778. LCP

A Constitution or Frame of Government, Agreed upon by the Delegates of the People of the State of Massachusetts-Bay, in Convention, Begun and held at Cambridge on the First of September, 1779. Boston: Benjamin Edes & Sons, 1780. LCP

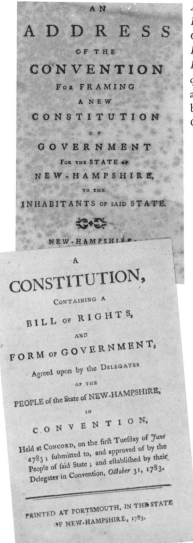

An Address of the Convention For Framing a new Constitution of Government For the State of New-Hampshire, to the Inhabitants of said State. Portsmouth and Exeter: "Printed, and to be Sold, at the Printing-Offices," 1781. LCP

A Constitution, Containing a Bill of Rights, and Form of Government, Agreed upon by the Delegates of the People of the State of New-Hampshire, in Convention, Held at Concord, on the first Tuesday of June 1783. Portsmouth: [Daniel Fowle], 1783. LCP

Hurriedly on January 5, 1776, the colony of New Hampshire adopted a constitution by act of the General Assembly. It was not carefully prepared. In 1779 a more formal Declaration of Rights and Plan of Government was submitted to popular ratification, but failed to obtain approval. It was try, try again. It took conventions in 1781, 1782 and 1783 to come up with a constitution which the people of New Hampshire were willing to accept.

Massachusetts had trouble drafting a constitution which met the desires of its citizens. After one document had been agreed upon early in 1778, a convention in Essex County met to debate its adoption. There the young lawyer Theophilus Parsons, greatly influenced by John Adams's *Thoughts on Government*, pointed out the weakness of the executive in the proposed plan and suggested other principles. In the face of the expressed opposition, the first constitution was abandoned and a second convention was held in 1779-80, which finally adopted a frame of government drafted by Adams, which included much of the change advocated by Parsons.

Recueil des Loix Constitutives des Colonies Angloises, confédérées sous la Dénomination d'États-Unis de l'Amérique-Septentrionale. Paris: Chez Cellot & Jombert, 1778. LCP

The Constitutions of the Several Independent States of America; The Declaration of Independence; The Articles of Confederation between the said States; The Treaties between His Most Christian Majesty and the United States of America. Philadelphia: Francis Bailey, 1781. HSP

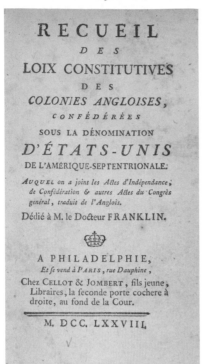

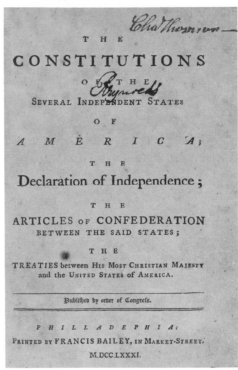

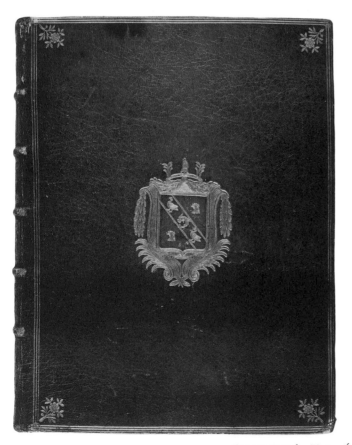

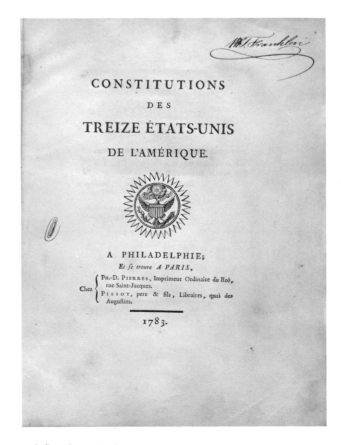

Constitutions des Treize États-Unis de l'Amérique. Paris: Chez Ph.-D. Pierres [&] Pissot, père et fils, 1783. APS

[Gerard van de Brantsen]. *Letter to
Benjamin Franklin*, Paris, July 25, 1783. APS

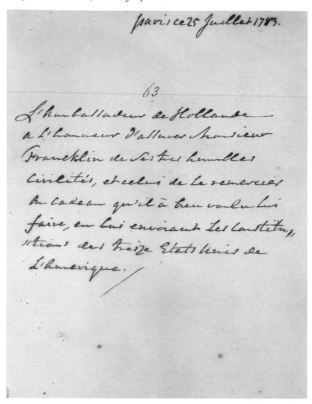

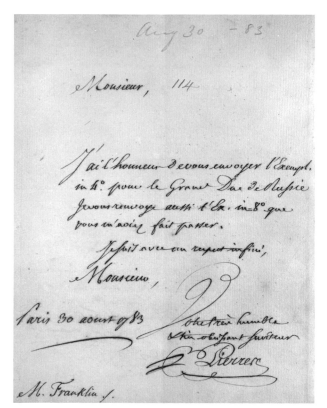

Philippe-Denis Pierres. *Letter to Benjamin Franklin*,
Paris, August 30, 1783. APS

One of the results of the enthusiasm with which the
French people hailed the American alliance was the
translation and publication of some of the state
constitutions, the Declaration of Independence, the
Articles of Confederation and other official documents.
The work was dedicated to Franklin, and this is his
copy. On December 29, 1780, Congress authorized
the compilation and publication of a similar volume;
only two hundred copies were ordered printed,
presumably for official circulation only. This was the
first time the constitutions of the thirteen states had
been issued together within the covers of a single
volume. Charles Thomson, the perennial secretary of
Congress, owned this copy. In the euphoria of the
formal and final ending of the war with agreement on
a definitive peace treaty with Great Britain, Franklin
in Paris sponsored the publication of still another
collection of state constitutions, this one translated
into French by his friend the Duc de La Rochefoucauld
d'Enville. The title-page bore the earliest
representation of the new arms of the United States.
Such examples of democratic ideals and procedures,
Franklin thought, should be made known widely. A
number of special copies, printed in quarto and some
handsomely bound in morocco, were distributed to
statesmen and monarchs throughout Europe. The
Dutch ambassador in Paris thanked Franklin for his
copy, and the printer Pierres sent along another for the
Grand Duke of Russia. One even went to King
George, and Franklin kept one of the large paper copies
for himself and had the sides decorated grandly with
the Franklin family coat-of-arms.

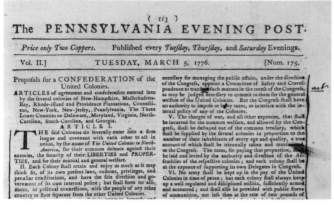

Proposals for a Confederation of the United Colonies. *The Pennsylvania Evening Post,* March 5, 1776. HSP

As early as July 21, 1775, Benjamin Franklin submitted to Congress "Articles of Confederation and Perpetual Union." The moderate delegates, fearful that the establishment of a central government would cut off any hope of reconciliation with Britain, prevented serious consideration of the plan. Although no debate on the subject took place in Congress for over a year, Towne's *Evening Post* printed these Proposals, the first appearance in print of any tentative form of government for the United Colonies. Much of the newspaper printing is similar to Franklin's suggestion, although its author submitted it to draw the attention of the public to the subject rather than to offer it "as a perfect *model.*" Was this issued by, or with the consent of, Franklin?

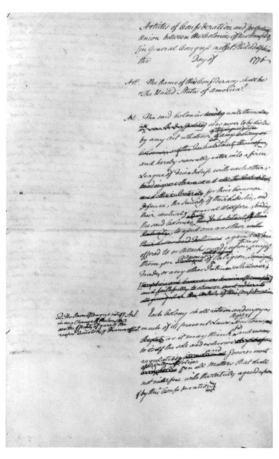

John Dickinson. *Preliminary Draft of the Articles of Confederation and perpetual Union,* [Philadelphia, July 1776 Manuscript. HSP

On June 11, 1776, Congress appointed a committee to draft Articles of Confederation. John Dickinson, who opposed the idea of forming an independent government, was nonetheless charged with writing the instrument. His draft, which began in much the same language as had Franklin's, was elaborated, and included a full description of the powers and limitations of the authority of Congress. Dickinson's first thoughts, as here set down, were over-long and over-complicated. The corrections, eliminations and annotations, showing much care and hard work, are typical of most of Dickinson's official writings. One of the articles, giving Congress broad powers over western lands, was bitterly opposed by some states. The whole document, after Dickinson withdrew from Congress on July 4, was argued over and revised for weeks.

The debate on Dickinson's draft of the Articles of Confederation occupied Congress on and off during much of July and August. Chase, a delegate from Maryland, wrote of the problems which made a decision difficult. "I hurried to Congress," he told Lee, "to give my little assistance to the framing a *Confederacy* and a plan for a foreign alliance, both of them Subjects of the utmost Importance, and which in my Judgment demand immediate Dispatch. The *Confederacy* has engaged our close attention for a Week. Three great Difficulties occur. *Representation, The Mode of Voting, and the Claims to the South Sea*. The whole might in my opinion be settled if Candor, Justice and the real Interests of America were attended to." The day he wrote this letter Chase moved that each state's quota of taxes be based on the number of white inhabitants only.

For over a month after the revised Dickinson draft was presented, Congress argued and re-argued the controversial points. It was finally agreed that taxes should be assessed to each state "in proportion to the number of inhabitants of every age, sex and quality," which meant that slaves were to be counted; that Congress should have to right to settle any boundary disputes; and that the Articles should be sent to the legislatures of all the states for approval. The small states won an important battle: each state was to have one vote. On August 20, 1776, it was resolved that eighty copies of the new revision of the Articles be printed for the use of the members of Congress only, who were enjoined "not to disclose, either directly or indirectly, the contents of the said confederation." With the printed document in the hands of the delegates, the whole matter of Confederation was thrust into limbo. This is Benjamin Franklin's copy of the August printing, with a minor correction and a docket title in his hand.

Benjamin Rush. *Notes on Debates
in Congress*, February 14, 1777. LCP

Benjamin Rush. *Characters of the Revolutionary
Patriots*, [Philadelphia, ca. 1778-79]. APS

Dr. Rush kept several commonplace books in which he set down the record of events, recollections, observations and anecdotes. In one notebook he chronicled in detail the debate on the resolution to regulate prices and wages. He was against it, as were Wilson, Witherspoon and others. Richard Henry Lee and Chase were among its supporters. The New England states had already adopted such control; Congress was unsure concerning the extent of state and federal powers. After several days of inconclusive argument, with the delegates evenly divided, the action of the New Englanders was mildly approved and the other states were asked to consider the problem. In another set of notes Rush wrote thumbnail sketches of all the signers of the Declaration, most of them quite favorable. Bartlett of New Hampshire was described as "a practitioner of physic, of excellent character, and warmly attached to the liberties of his country." Samuel Adams "was near sixty years of age when he took his seat in Congress, but possessed all the vigor of mind of a young man of five and twenty." Sherman of Connecticut was "a plain man of slender education." Rush's father-in-law Stockton "was timid where bold measures were required, but was at all times sincerely devoted to the liberties of his country." Witherspoon was "a well informed statesman and remarkably luminous and correct in all his speeches." He called his colleague Taylor from Pennsylvania "a respectable country gentleman, but not much distinguished in any way in Congress." Paca of Maryland had "a sound understanding which he was too indolent to exercise, and hence his reputation in public life was less than his talents." And Jefferson "possessed a genius of the first order." Of himself Rush said only that "he aimed well."

Samuel Adams. *Letter to
Richard Henry Lee,*
Philadelphia, June 26,
1777. APS

Though nominally "united," the states, through their representatives in Congress, wished to retain certain powers they had long held. Claims to land under their colonial charters was one of the most serious obstacles to agreement. Adams wrote his friend Lee: "A Thousand little Matters too often thrust out greater ones—A kind of Fatality still prevents our proceeding a Step in the important affair of Confederation—Yesterday and the day before was wholly spent in passing Resolutions to gratify N Y or as they say to prevent a civil War between that State and the Green Mountains Men."

William Clingan and Daniel Roberdeau. *Letter to Thomas Wharton, Jr.*, York Town, November 13, 1777. HSP

Articles of Confederation and Perpetual Union between the States of New-Hampshire, Massachusetts-Bay, Rhode Island and Providence Plantations, Connecticut, New-York, New-Jersey, Pennsylvania, Delaware, Maryland, Virginia, North-Carolina, South-Carolina and Georgia. Lancaster: Francis Bailey, 1777. HSP

Legislative Council and General Assembly of New Jersey. *Representation and Remonstrance to the United States in Congress assembled,* December 29, 1780. Copy. LCP

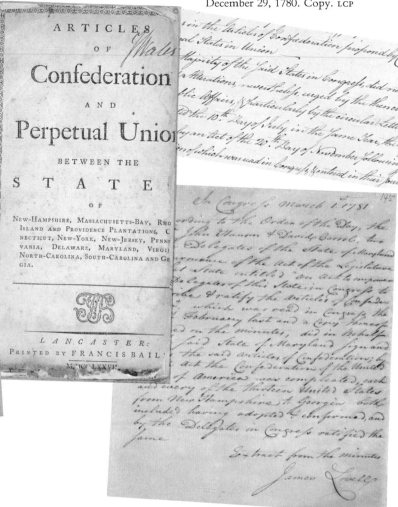

George Clinton. *Letter to the House of Representatives of New York,* Poughkeepsie, January 16, 1778. HSP

James Lovell. *Extract from the Minutes of Congress,* March 1, 1781. HSP

Congress finally approved the Articles of Confederation on November 15, 1777, and sent them to the states for ratification. The accompanying circular letter described them conservatively as "the best which could be adapted to the circumstances of all," and speedy approval was expected. But the road to ratification was tortuous. Pennsylvania ratified the Articles on July 22, 1778. New Jersey acted favorably on November 26, 1778, but two years later expressed its continuing concern over the unresolved question of western lands. Virginia had begun to consolidate its claims by offering lands for sale. In the circumstances New Jersey represented "that they acknowledge no Tribunal but that of Congress, competent to the Redress of such a Grievance, as the setting up by any State, an exclusive Claim to any of the said Lands, in whatever Part of the Union they may be situated." Maryland was the last to accept the Articles, delaying action until the French Minister La Luzerne let it be known that failure to establish a general government might jeopardize the French Alliance. As of March 1, 1781, the nation finally had a frame of government under which to operate.

C A

Lake of the Woods

Long Lake

Red R.

SYLVANIA

St Lewis R.

Red Lake.

White Bear L.

I. Royal Lake

Supe - rior

St Mary

45

Chippeway

Ottawas

LAKE

Maudowessie

Ottigamies

MICHIGANIA

CHERO

Falls of St Ant.

R. St Croix

L. Pepin

Sawkies

Fort Michillimackinac

Lake Michigan

R. St Pierre

Fox R.

Detroit

River Ouisconsin

Illinois R.

METROPOTAMIA

40

Head of the Oregon which runs W. to the Pacific Ocean.

ASSENISIPIA

Wabash R.

SARATOGA

Miamys R.

Delaw

ILLINOIA

Missouri T. & R.

POLY-POTAMIA

PELI-SIPIA

L. Shawan

Ohio

Kentucke

Cuttawa R.

Louisiana

Mississippi Forks

VIRGIN

35

Cherokees

E. PLURIBUS

UNUM

NORTH CARO

Chicasaws

SOUTH CAROLI

Yasous R.

Creek Indians

A MAP of the

GEORGIA

United States

Chactaws

30

of N. AMERICA

WEST FLORIDA

EAST

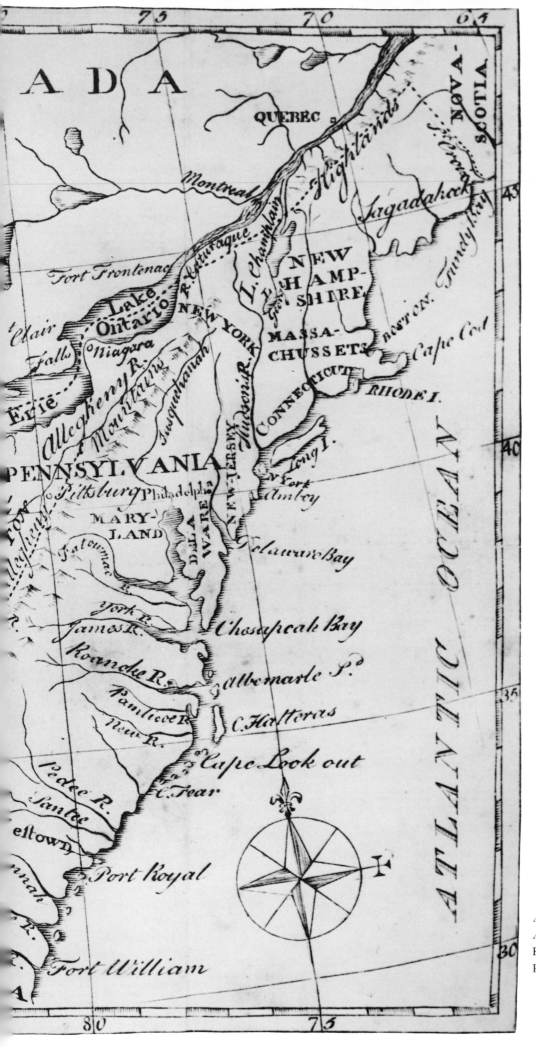

In Congress Assembled, 1777-1784

"The subject . . . is nothing less than . . . the fate of an empire."—*The Federalist*, No. 1, 1787

A Map of the United States of N. America. Philadelphia: "Engraved by H. D. Pursell for F. Bailey's Pocket Almanac," [1786]. LCP

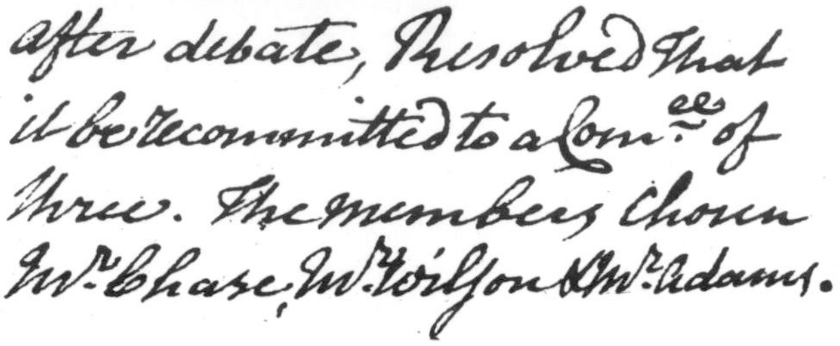

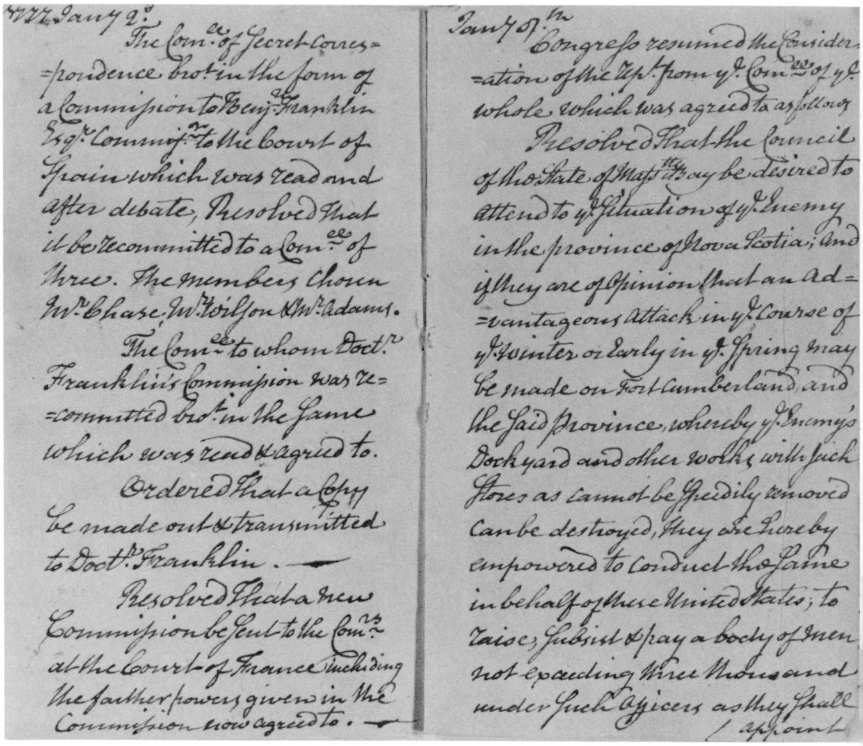

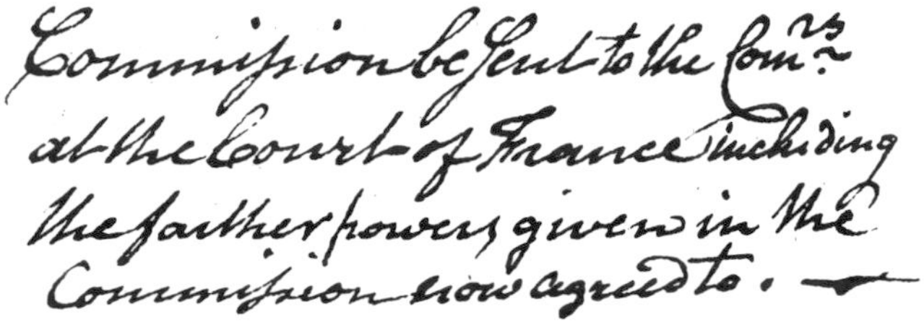

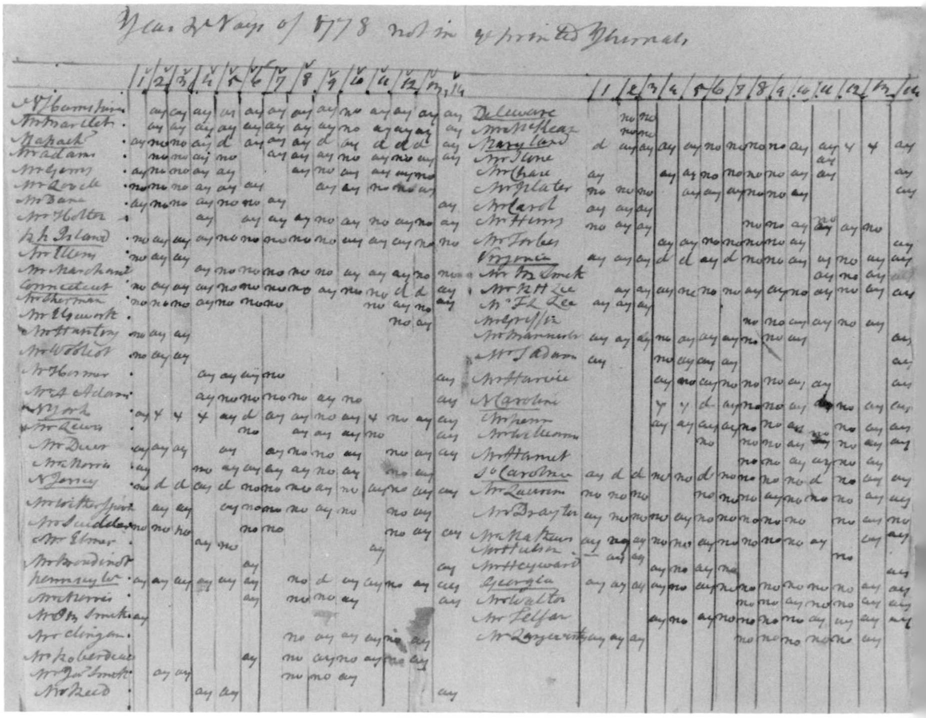

Charles Thomson and Elbridge Gerry. *Secret Journal of Congress,* Philadelphia and York, October 14, 1774, to May 20, 1780. HSP

1777 Jany 9th.
The Comee of Secret Correspondence brot in the form of a Commission to Benjn Franklin Esqr Commisr to the Court of Spain which was read and after debate, Resolved that it be recommitted to a Comee of three. The members chosen Mr Chase, Mr Wilson & Mr Adams.
The Comee to whom Doctr Franklin's Commission was recommitted brot in the same which was read & agreed to.
Ordered that a Copy be made out & transmitted to Doctr Franklin. —
Resolved that a new Commission be sent to the Comrs at the Court of France including the farther powers given in the Commission now agreed to. —

Jany 9th
Congress resumed the consideration of the Rept from ye Comee of ye whole which was agreed to as follows
Resolved that the Council of the State of Massts Bay be desired to attend to ye situation of ye Enemy in the province of Nova Scotia; and if they are of opinion that an advantageous attack in ye course of ye winter or early in ye spring may be made on Fort Cumberland and the said province, whereby ye Enemy's Dockyard and other works with such stores as cannot be speedily removed can be destroyed, they are hereby empowered to conduct the same in behalf of these United States; to raise, subsist & pay a body of men not exceeding three thousand under such officers as they shall / appoint

Yeas & Nays of 1778 not in ye printed Journal.

the said province, whereby y.ᵉ Enemy's Dock yard and other works, with such Stores as cannot be speedily removed Can be destroyed, They are hereby

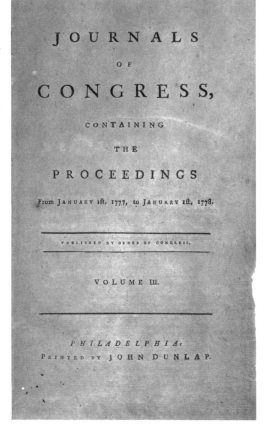

Journals of Congress, containing the Proceedings From January 1st, 1777, to January 1st, 1778. Philadelphia: John Dunlap, [1778]. LCP

The Journals of Congress were faithfully kept by its secretary, Charles Thomson. Periodically they were published in an edited form, for certain actions, resolutions and orders were deemed of a secret nature. These included such matters as negotiations with foreign powers and military plans. A secret journal was, however, kept which recorded all such matters. Two pages of it written by Thomson in 1777 include action taken on Franklin's appointment as commissioner to the Courts of Spain and France and the suggestion of an attack on Nova Scotia. A chart of the votes in Congress during 1778 is in the hand of Elbridge Gerry; these were not listed in the printed Journals, nor was an account of plans for the reception of Monsieur Gérard, the French Minister, nor, indeed, an estimate of troops needed in South Carolina. What was printed in the official *Journal* was sent to Franklin in France. This is his copy of the proceedings during the year 1777.

Elbridge Gerry. Engraving by J. B. Longacre after a drawing by John Vanderlyn, in James T. Austin, *Life of Elbridge Gerry.* Boston: Wells and Lilly, 1828. LCP

By His Excellency JOSEPH REED, *Esq;* President, *and the* Supreme Executive Council *of the Commonwealth of* Pennsylvania,

A PROCLAMATION.

WHEREAS the unhappy Difputes which have fubfifted between this State and that of *Virginia,* touching the Weftern Boundary of this State, have been hitherto fufpended, fo as to afford a juft and reafonable Expectation that they might be terminated in perfect Confiftency with the general Interefts of the common Union, and the mutual Friendfhip between the contending States: For the Attainment of this defirable End, Propofitions were heretofore made on the Part of this State to appoint Commiffioners to adjuft the faid Boundary Line, which were acceded to on the Part of *Virginia,* and the faid Commiffioners, having met on the Thirty-firft of *Auguft* laft, entered into the following Agreement:

" We, *George Bryan, John Ewing* and *David Rittenhoufe,* Commiffioners from the State of *Pennfylvania,* and we, *James*
" *Madifon* and *Robert Andrews,* Commiffioners for the State of *Virginia,* do hereby mutually, in Behalf of our refpective
" States, ratify and confirm the following Agreement, *viz.* To extend *Mafon* and *Dixon's* Line due Weft five Degrees of
" Longitude, to be computed from the River *Delaware,* for the Southern Boundary of *Pennfylvania,* and that a Meredian,
" drawn from the Weftern Extremity thereof to the Northern Limit of the faid State, be the Weftern Boundary of *Penn-*
" *fylvania* for ever."

By His Excellency Joseph Reed, Esq; President, and the Supreme Executive Council of the Commonwealth of Pennsylvania, A Proclamation. [Philadelphia]: Hall and Sellers, 1779. LCP

Edmund Randolph. Engraving by H. B. Hall. HSP

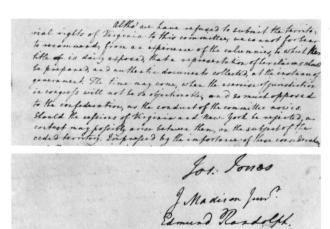

Joseph Jones, James Madison and Edmund Randolph. *Letter to Thomas Nelson, Governor of Virginia,* Philadelphia, October 16, 1781. HSP

The boundaries between the states were for many years sources of friction and dispute. At the end of December 1779, Congress had to intervene between Pennsylvania and Virginia. Congress ordered all parties to withdraw to the pre-war boundaries. Just before the surrender at Yorktown, the Virginia delegates in Congress informed the governor that the matter of the western lands and the claims of the Illinois and Wabash and Indiana Companies was being discussed. By March 26, 1783, the Pennsylvania-Virginia line had been agreed upon, and John Dickinson, president of Pennsylvania, issued a proclamation ordering the inhabitants of a tract placed in that state to "pay due obedience" to its laws. North Carolina faced trouble, according to its delegate, when a group of inhabitants of frontier counties declared themselves "an independent State by the Title of 'The State of Franklin,'" and asked Congress to accept North Carolina's cession of the land and admit them into the Union. As late as the autumn of 1786 agents from New York were setting up a meeting with agents from Massachusetts to work out a boundary compromise.

By the PRESIDENT *and the* SUPREME EXECUTIVE COUNCIL *of the Commonwealth of* Pennsylvania,

A PROCLAMATION.

WHEREAS the General Assembly of this commonwealth, by their resolution of the twenty second day of this present month, did approve and confirm the line lately run by messieurs M'Clean and Nevil, as the boundary between this state and that of Virginia, until the final settlement thereof be obtained: We have thought fit to make known the same; and we do hereby charge, enjoin, and require, all persons whatsoever residing within that tract of country, situate between the meridian line run by messieurs Sinclair and M'Clean, and that lately run by messieurs Nevil and M'Clean, bounded southward by an extension of Mason's and Dixon's line, and northward by the Ohio river; and also all others residing to the eastward of the said line run by messieurs Sinclair and M'Lean, who heretofore may have supposed themselves to be there settled within the state of Virginia, to take notice of the proceedings aforesaid, and to pay due obedience to the laws of this commonwealth.

GIVEN in Council, under the hand of the President and the seal of the state, at Philadelphia, this twenty sixth day of March, one thousand seven hundred and eighty three.

JOHN DICKINSON.

ATTEST:

JOHN ARMSTRONG, Jun. SECRETARY:

GOD SAVE THE COMMONWEALTH!

By the President and the Supreme Executive Council of the Commonwealth of Pennsylvania, A Proclamation. [Philadelphia]: Francis Bailey, [1783]. LCP

James Duane, John Haring, Melancton Smith and Egbert Benson. *Letter to Robert Yates and John Lansing,* New York, September 22, 1786. HSP

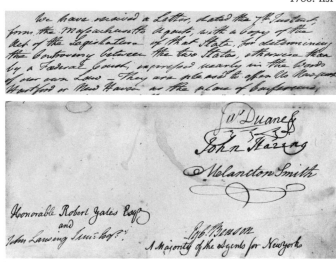

Richard D. Spaight. *Letter to Richard Caswell, Governor of North Carolina,* New York, June 5, 1785. HSP

In order to buttress the finances of the new nation, which he noted were "not the most flourishing," Jefferson suggested that the money of the Genoese merchants on deposit in London be withdrawn and loaned to the United States. That would be "doubly beneficial by supplying our wants, and perhaps rendering our Enemies bankrupt by sudden & large calls on them." The Virginia governor believed that his Tuscan friend Mazzei, "a zealous whig from the beginning," would be able to convince the Grand Duke of Tuscany to carry out the plan if Congress would advance £600 to him. Nothing came of the ingenious scheme.

Honorable Sir   Albemarle in Virginia Octob. 19. 1778.

In a late conversation with mr T. Adams since his return from Congress I find, what indeed might have been well supposed that the state of the Continental finances is not the most flourishing. the establishment of banks in Europe for the purpose of maintaining our credit there, as well as here, and by that means of en-larging our supplies by way of loan may perhaps meet with the attention of Congress. as it is probable this cannot be done to a sufficient extent in any one place in Eu-rope, the procuring credit in several places tho' to no great amount in any one of them, will answer the same end. an acquaintance with two Italian gentlemen who have settled in my neighborhood has been the means of my becoming acquainted with some facts which may perhaps be of some use to the general cause. the Grand duke of Tuscany by great oeconomy & a particular attention to the affairs of his treasury has I understand a very large sum in ready money which it is thought he would readily put out to interest, more especially if it was proposed not to carry it out of his state, but to invest it in necessaries there. having also established at his own expence public manu-factures for the employment of his poor, it is said he has immense magazines of these which he would without doubt gladly furnish on credit. — the Genoese are among the richest people in Europe. being principally commercial they make great sums of money, which their sumptuary laws put it out of their power to expend. the consequence is that for a long time they have put their money into the banks of Europe for 3 and 3½ per cent. they have immense sums in the London bank, the state of which has for some time alarmed them: & nothing has prevented their drawing it out but the im-possibility of disposing of it elsewhere. were they indeed to go pretty generally on the plan of selling out, it is probable they must sell to considerable loss, yet the high interest we pay would make amends for that, more especially when they contemplate the certain loss of their principal at no very distant period if suffered to remain there. there seems therefore reason to hope we might do something clever with them, which would be doubly beneficial by supplying our wants, and perhaps rendering our Enemies bankrupt by sudden & large calls on them. I throw out these things for your contemplation. if

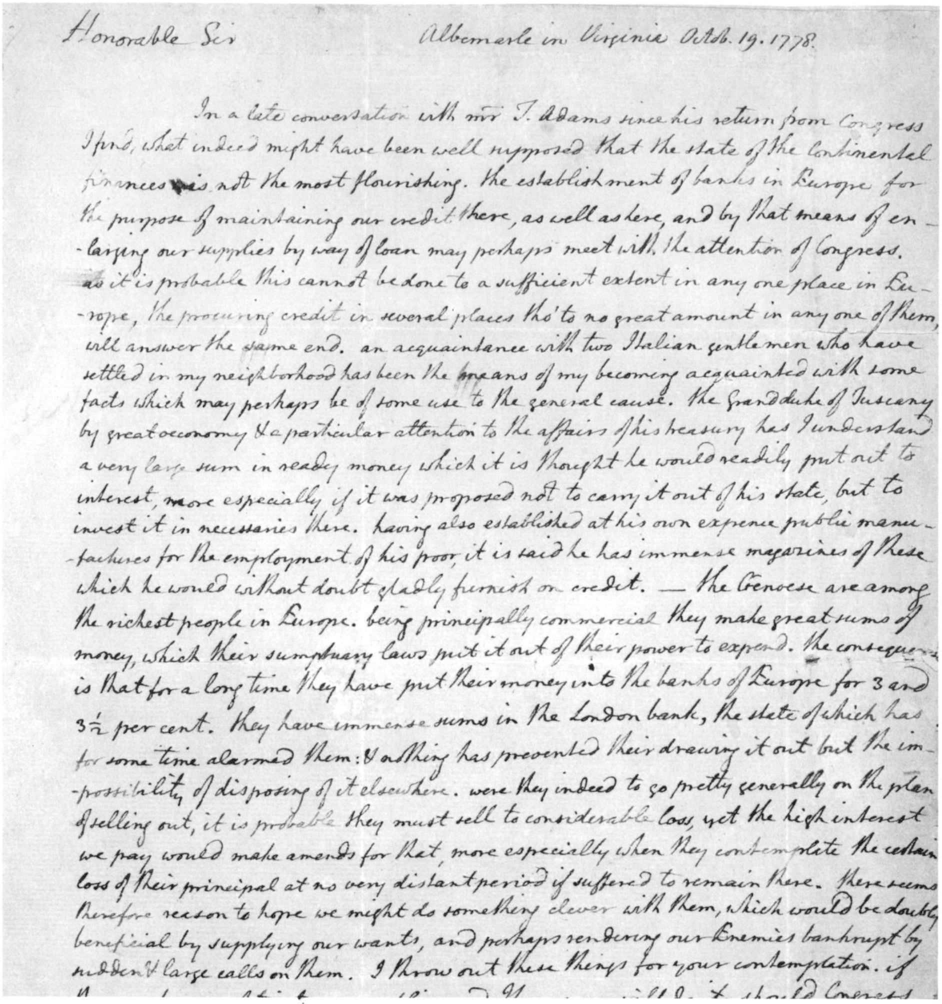

Thomas Jefferson. *Letter to John Hancock*, Albemarle in Virginia, October 19, 1778. HSP

In desperation Congress ordered that a lottery be held in order to raise vitally needed funds for the prosecution of the war. Aaron Levy, as his note in Hebrew characters indicates, bought some tickets. It is a commentary on the times that "the managers are instructed to sell the tickets for money only."

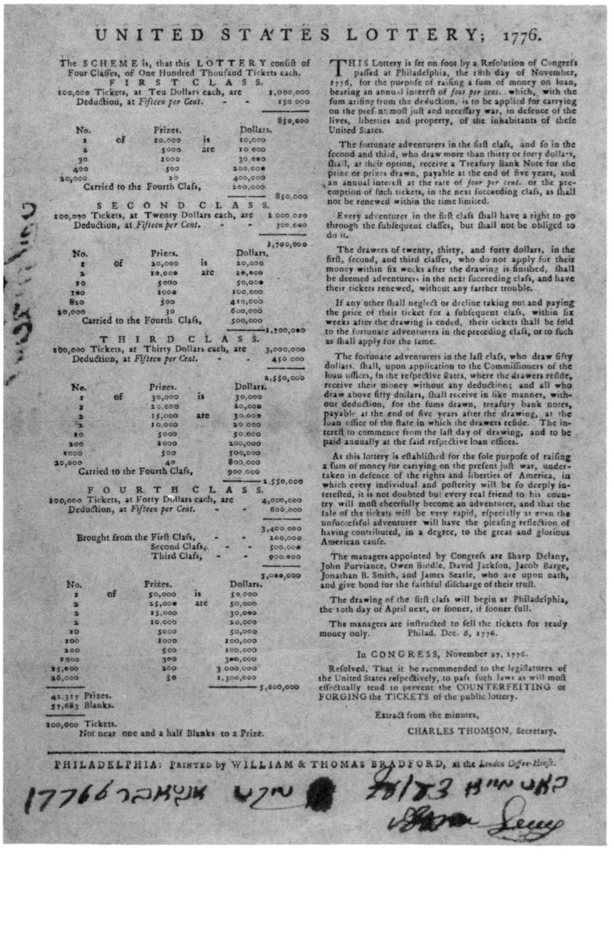

UNITED STATES LOTTERY; 1776.

The SCHEME is, that this LOTTERY consist of Four Classes, of One Hundred Thousand Tickets each.

FIRST CLASS.

100,000 Tickets, at Ten Dollars each, are - 1,000,000
Deduction, at *Fifteen per Cent.* - - 150,000
850,000

No.		Prizes.		Dollars.
1	of	10,000	is	10,000
2		5000	are	10,000
30		1000		30,000
400		500		200,000
20,000		20		400,000
Carried to the Fourth Class,				200,000
				850,000

SECOND CLASS.

100,000 Tickets, at Twenty Dollars each, are 2,000,000
Deduction, at *Fifteen per Cent.* - - 300,000
1,700,000

No.		Prizes.		Dollars.
1	of	20,000	is	20,000
2		10,000	are	20,000
10		5000		50,000
100		1000		100,000
820		500		410,000
20,000		30		600,000
Carried to the Fourth Class,				500,000
				1,700,000

THIRD CLASS.

100,000 Tickets, at Thirty Dollars each, are 3,000,000
Deduction, at *Fifteen per Cent.* - - 450,000
2,550,000

No.		Prizes.		Dollars.
1	of	30,000	is	30,000
1		20,000		20,000
2		15,000	are	30,000
2		10,000		20,000
10		5000		50,000
200		1000		200,000
1000		500		500,000
20,000		40		800,000
Carried to the Fourth Class,				900,000
				2,550,000

FOURTH CLASS.

100,000 Tickets, at Forty Dollars each, are 4,000,000
Deduction, at *Fifteen per Cent.* - - 600,000
3,400,000
Brought from the First Class, - - 100,000
Second Class, - - 500,000
Third Class, - - 900,000
5,000,000

No.		Prizes.		Dollars.
1	of	50,000	is	50,000
2		25,000	are	50,000
2		15,000		30,000
2		10,000		20,000
10		5000		50,000
100		1000		100,000
200		500		100,000
1000		300		300,000
15,000		200		3,000,000
26,000		50		1,300,000
				5,000,000

42,317 Prizes.
57,683 Blanks.

100,000 Tickets.
Not near one and a half Blanks to a Prize.

THIS Lottery is set on foot by a Resolution of Congress passed at Philadelphia, the 18th day of November, 1776, for the purpose of raising a sum of money on loan, bearing an annual interest of *four per cent.* which, with the sum arising from the deduction, is to be applied for carrying on the present most just and necessary war, in defence of the lives, liberties and property, of the inhabitants of these United States.

The fortunate adventurers in the first class, and so in the second and third, who draw more than thirty or forty dollars, shall, at their option, receive a Treasury Bank Note for the prize or prizes drawn, payable at the end of five years, and an annual interest at the rate of *four per cent.* or the pre-emption of such tickets, in the next succeeding class, as shall not be renewed within the time limited.

Every adventurer in the first class shall have a right to go through the subsequent classes, but shall not be obliged to do it.

The drawers of twenty, thirty, and forty dollars, in the first, second, and third classes, who do not apply for their money within six weeks after the drawing is finished, shall be deemed adventurers in the next succeeding class, and have their tickets renewed, without any farther trouble.

If any other shall neglect or decline taking out and paying the price of their ticket for a subsequent class, within six weeks after the drawing is ended, their tickets shall be sold to the fortunate adventurers in the preceding class, or to such as shall apply for the same.

The fortunate adventurers in the last class, who draw fifty dollars, shall, upon application to the Commissioners of the loan offices, in the respective states, where the drawers reside, receive their money without any deduction; and all who draw above fifty dollars, shall receive in like manner, without deduction, for the sums drawn, treasury bank notes, payable at the end of five years after the drawing, at the loan office of the state in which the drawers reside. The interest to commence from the last day of drawing, and to be paid annually at the said respective loan offices.

As this lottery is established for the sole purpose of raising a sum of money for carrying on the present just war, undertaken in defence of the rights and liberties of America, in which every individual and posterity will be so deeply interested, it is not doubted but every real friend to his country will most cheerfully become an adventurer, and that the sale of the tickets will be very rapid, especially as even the unsuccessful adventurer will have the pleasing reflection of having contributed, in a degree, to the great and glorious American cause.

The managers appointed by Congress are Sharp Delany, John Purviance, Owen Biddle, David Jackson, Jacob Barge, Jonathan B. Smith, and James Searle, who are upon oath, and give bond for the faithful discharge of their trust.

The drawing of the first class will begin at Philadelphia, the 10th day of April next, or sooner, if sooner full.

The managers are instructed to sell the tickets for ready money only. Philad. Dec. 6, 1776.

In CONGRESS, November 27, 1776.

Resolved, That it be recommended to the legislatures of the United States respectively, to pass such laws as will most effectually tend to prevent the COUNTERFEITING or FORGING the TICKETS of the public lottery.

Extract from the minutes,
CHARLES THOMSON, Secretary.

PHILADELPHIA: PRINTED by WILLIAM & THOMAS BRADFORD, at the *London Coffee-House.*

United States Lottery; 1776. Philadelphia: William & Thomas Bradford, [1776]. HSP

COMMITTEE - ROOM,

June 26, 1779.

AGREEABLE to the refolution of the laft General Town-Meeting, for lowering the prices month by month, the following lift of feveral articles, and the prices they bore on the firft day of April laft, is publifhed for the guidance of buyer and feller, for the month of July, and to commence on the firft day thereof.

And the feveral dealers and others are likewife defired to take notice, that if any article or articles, whether mentioned in this lift or not, fhall, after the firft of July, be charged higher than the fame was charged on the firft day of April laft, that fuch perfon or perfons will, on detection, be proceeded againft in the fame manner as if fuch article or articles was herein mentioned and limited.

And it is furthermore intended that the regulations do take place as well in the Markets as the fhops, of which all perfons, as well buyers and fellers, are defired to take notice, and abide the confequences.

And whereas murmurings and difcontents have arifen, refpecting the price of butter. Therefore,

Refolved, That if any inhabitant of this city fhall give more than Fifteen Shillings for a pound of butter, fuch perfon or perfons fo purchafing, whether man or woman, fhall either be fummoned to appear at the next Town Meeting, or pay Twenty Shillings into the hands of this Committee, to be aplied to the relief of the poor; one half thereof to the poor of this city, and the other half to the poor of the townfhip where the feller of fuch butter fhall live.

PRICES of the following Articles on the firft of April, which are to continue for the month of July.

WHOLESALE.				RETAIL.			WHOLESALE.		RETAIL.
Coffee per lb.	0	15	0	per lb. 0 16 0			Cotton, from 40f. to 55 f.	45f. to 60/p.lb.	
Chocolate, do.	1	17	6	do. 2 0 0			Hemp	8f.	
Bohea Tea, do.	4	10	0	do. 4 15 0			Candles	14/6 15f.	
Com. Green do.	5	10	0	from 6l. to7 10 0			Beft Hard Soap	10/6 12/6	
Beft Hyfon do.	18	0	0	20 0 0			Butter	15f.	
WeftIndia Rum per gallon,	6	5	0	6 12 6			Blomety Bar Iron per. ton,50l. p. cwt.28l.		
Country do.	4	10	0	4 15 0			Refined do. 700l. 38l.		
French do.	4	10	0	4 15 0			Nail Rod Iron 1000l. 55l.		
Madeira Wine, per gal.		10	0 0				Sheet Iron, per lb. 12f. per lb. 15f.		
Mufcovado Sugar, from 15f. to 20f. 7ol. to 95l. per cwt.				per lb.			Beft dintle foal leather, per pound, 20f.		
Loaf Sugar, from 42/6 to 50f. per lb.				from 47/6 to 52/6 per lb.			Neats leather, by the fide 150f.		
							A calf-fkin that will cut 4 pair of fhoes,150f.		
Rice				3f. p.lb.			Beft boot legs, per pair 180f.		
French Indigo, per lb.	2	15	0	60f.			Harnefs Leather, per pound, 20f.		
Carolina do.	2	0	0	45f.			Bridle ditto, per fide, 150f.		
Black Pepper,	1	17	6	42/6			Boots, per pair, from 37l. to 40l.		
							Men's beft leather fhoes,from 135f. to 150f.		
							Womens fhoes 120f.		

The Committee have continued the price of flour, middlings, &c. the fame as on the laft month, and are happy to inform the public, that the price of molaffes and the various kinds of falt are at prefent lower than on the firft of April, and the committee expect they will not be raifed higher than at prefent.

Signed by order of the Committee,

WILLIAM HENRY, *Chairman.*

COMMITTEE-ROOM, *June 26, 1779.*

WHEREAS, under pretence of fupplying our fellow citizens in the country, great quantities of goods are daily removed from this city, and there is reafon to believe, with a defign of concealment, in order to produce a fcarcity. Therefore,

Refolved, That if any goods, exceeding the value of one hundred pounds, be removed or offered to be removed from this city, without firft obtaining a permit from this committee; fuch goods fo removed or offered to be removed, fhall, on detection, be detained under the care of the Committee, until the next Town Meeting; and the owner to abide the confequences.

Signed by order of the Committee,

WILLIAM HENRY, *Chairman.*

PHILADELPHIA, *Printed by* FRANCIS BAILEY, *in Market-Street.*

With the people pinched by the shortage of supplies caused by the war, measures were taken to prevent speculators from hoarding or benefiting from situation. Prices were fixed, profits limited, and removal of goods from the city prohibited.

M.

VOUS êtes prié de la part du Miniftre Plenipotentiaire de France, d'affifter au TE DEUM, qu'il fera chanter Dimanche 4 de ce Mois, à midi dans la Chapelle Catholique neuve pour celebrer l'Anniverfaire de l'Independance des Etats Unis de l'Amerique.

A Philadelphie, le 2 Juillet, 1779.

A PHILADELPHIE, De l'Imprimeri de FRANÇOIS BAILEY, Rue de Marche,

A bright spot in the gloom of the drawn-out war, the shortage of supplies and the lack of money was the French Alliance. It offered hope that funds, arms and military assistance would be forthcoming. Conrad Alexandre Gérard de Rayneval had been sent to Philadelphia by Louis XVI as minister plenipotentiary. On the third anniversary of the Declaration of Independence he invited Americans to join with him in a prayerful celebration in the Catholic church.

Thomas Rodney. *Letter to John Dickinson,* Dover, July 28, 1779. HSP

Thomas Cushing. *Letter to Oliver Ellsworth,* Boston, November 17, 1779. HSP

William C. Houston. *"What are the Kinds of Property in the State of New Jersey which ought, more particularly, to be subject to Taxation,"* [Trenton], May 14, 1781. HSP

James Monroe. *Letter to John F. Mercer,* Richmond, May 16, 1783. HSP

Money was a crying need for both national and state use; taxes were as unpopular as they have always been. With inflation rife, Rodney suggested to Dickinson, representing Delaware in Congress, a scheme to reduce the supply of currency by taxation, which, he believed, could be raised, because "America is in the most flourishing Circumstances now than it has been in since the war began." Cushing informed Ellsworth that Massachusetts had voted to levy £2,800,000 in taxes to prevent the further depreciation of its currency, but he was not optimistic about the maintenance of price control. Houston, a member of Congress from New Jersey, suggested that the most logical taxables were "the Superfluities, Extravagancies, Luxuries, Follies, or by whatever other name Things unnecessary may be described." The resistance to taxation was noted by Monroe, who, writing to Mercer in Philadelphia, expressed doubt that the legislature would pass a tax bill, "for the complaints of the people are great agnst those measures wh. induce the necessity of taxes."

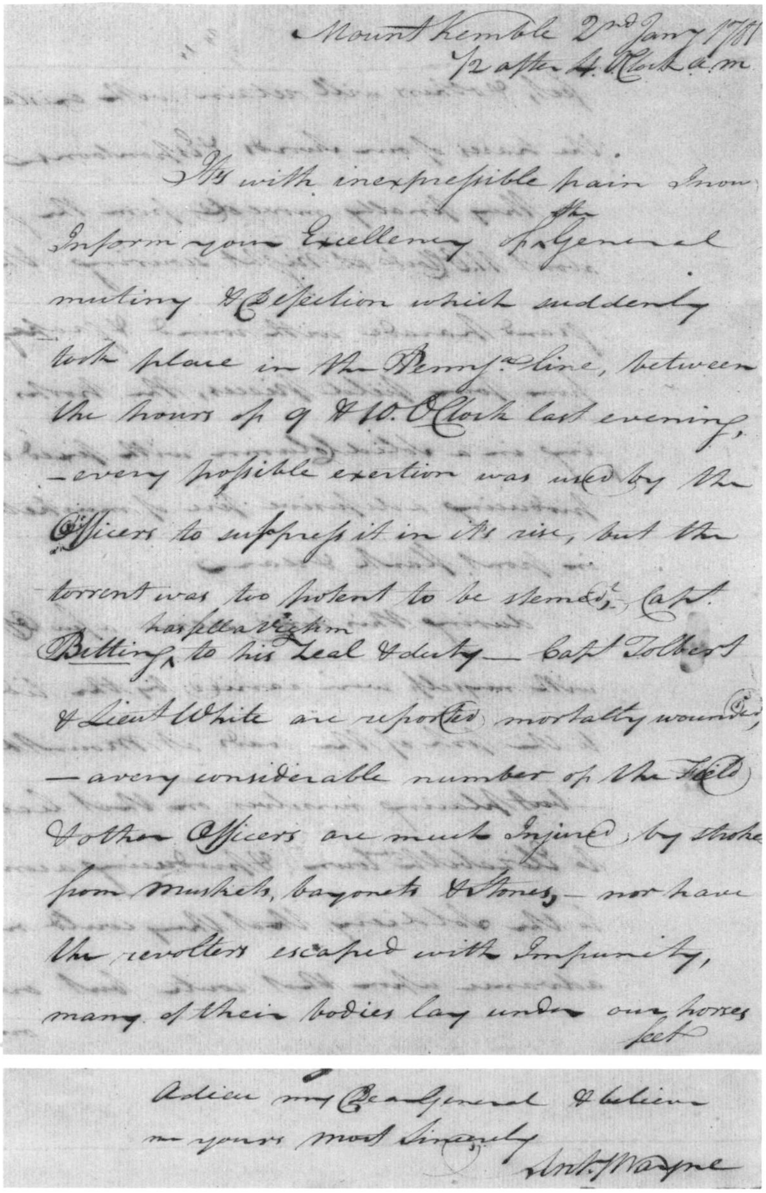

Mount Kemble 2nd Jany 1781
½ after 4 OClock A.M.

It's with inexpressible pain I now Inform your Excellency of the General mutiny & Defection which suddenly took place in the Pennsa line, between the hours of 9 & 10 OClock last evening, —every possible exertion was used by the Officers to suppress it in its rise, but the torrent was too potent to be stemed, Capt. Bettin, fell a Victim to his Zeal & duty — Capt Tolbert & Lieut White are reported mortally wounded, —a very considerable number of the Field & other Officers are much Injured by strokes from muskets, bayonets & Stones — nor have the revolters escaped with Impunity, many of their bodies lay under our horses feet

Adieu my Dear General & believe me yours most Sincerely
Ant. Wayne

Anthony Wayne. *Letter to George Washington,* Mount Kemble, January 2, 1781. HSP

General Anthony Wayne. Engraved frontispiece by G. J. Warner in Charles Smith. *The Monthly Military Repository,* II. New York: John Buel, 1797. LCP

On New Year's Day, 1781, troops of the Pennsylvania Line mutinied, complaining that they had been kept in service beyond an agreed-upon three-year term and that they had not received their promised pay or clothing. The soldiers put themselves under a committee of sergeants and marched upon Congress at Princeton. Wayne sent news of the uprising to his commander-in-chief: "It's with inexpressible pain I now Inform your Excellency of the General mutiny & Defection which suddenly took place in the Pennsa. line, between the hours of 9 & 10 OClock last evening—every possible exertion was used by the Officers to suppress it in its rise, but the torrent was too potent to be stemed." Both officers and men were wounded in the melee. Proposals were submitted by the mutineers, including release of men in the army since 1776, bounties for others, and pay and clothing for all. The chief executives of Pennsylvania agreed with almost all the "reasonable Grievances": discharge for those who qualified, back pay and "A Pair of Shoes, Overalls & Shirt," as well as amnesty. The *Proposals* as printed were identical with the signed manuscript. Sir Henry Clinton had hoped to get the mutineers to defect, but the American soldiers rejected such action as treason. He was mocked in the amusing satire printed as a broadside.

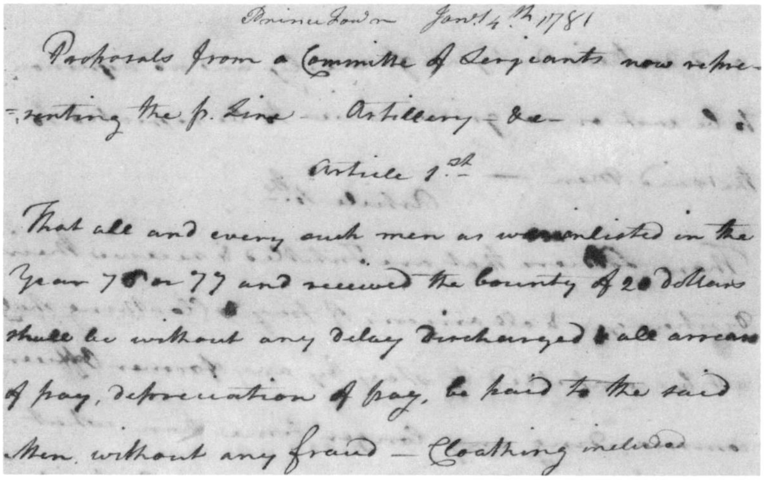

Princeton Jany 4th 1781
Proposals from a Committee of Serjeants now representing the P. Line Artillery &c—

Article 1st

That all and every such men as were inlisted in the Year 76 or 77 and received the bounty of 20 dollars shall be without any delay discharged & all arrears of pay, depreciation of pay, be paid to the said Men without any fraud — Cloathing included

"Proposals from a Committee of Serjeants now representing the p[ennsylvania] Line—Artillery—&c.," Princeton, January 4, 1781. Copy. HSP

Regular Pennsylvania Infantryman.
Engraved by Daniel-Nicholas
Chodowiecki in *Historisch-
genealogischer Calender, oder
Jahrbuch der merkwürdigsten neuen
Welt.* Leipzig, 1784. LCP

Joseph Reed, President of the
Supreme Executive Council, and
James Potter. *Proposals made to the
Pennsylvania Line,* [Princeton,
January 7, 1781]. HSP

*Proposals Made to the
non-commissioned Officers
and Soldiers of the
Pennsylvania Line, at
Trenton, January 7,
1781. [Philadelphia ?:
1781]. Broadside.* HSP

Philadelphia, January 22, 1781. Extract of a letter from Trenton, dated Jan. 20, 1781. [Philadelphia: 1781]. Broadside. HSP

Extract of a letter from Trenton, dated Jan. 20. 1781.

MILITARY systems, in general, are founded on long experience; and the operations of armies, in various ages and countries, under the conduct of great commanders, have displayed the most brilliant exertions of genius and magnanimity. To such a degree of certainty and sublimity has the art of war been advanced, that few generals dare presume so much upon their own importance as to deviate materially from the beaten tract. A Frederic indeed may contend with impossibilities, and a Washington add new lustre to the military science; but where is the Briton who is encircled with laurels uncommon to other nations? In the contest with the United States, the British operations have displayed a mixture of cruelty, blunders and indecision. In the petite guerre, however, some instances of gallantry have been exhibited, which a generous enemy will admire; but nothing of the sublime has ever descended upon their grand manoeuvres.—Their defects have uniformly resulted from superior conduct in the opposite commanders; their successes have flowed from decided superiority of numbers; and instead of being directed to the much wished for object of their master, the subduction of America, they have universally terminated in robbery, plunder, and desolation. Repeated disappointments have produced a variety of succeeding commanders; but despairing of conquest in the usual manner of conducting war, administration have finally given to the world an unparalleled instance of their wisdom, in the appointment of Sir Henry Clinton. This officer, remarkable only for the flights of a bewildered imagination, which the British ministry, in a fit of political phrenzy, construed into the rare sallies of a sublime genius, has adopted a system entirely new to the military world; a system founded partly in treason, partly in intrigue, and partly in necromancy.— The " crimen læsæ majestatis" may apply as well to the laws of nations and of arms as to the municipal laws of any particular country. The infamous attempts of sir Henry upon the posts of West Point and its vicinity, through that sink of pollution, Arnold, are fully evincive of the two first ingredients of this system. How different was the conduct of the Roman consul, when receiving an information from the chief Physician of King Pyrrhus that for an adequate reward he would poison his master: inflamed with indignation at the monster of villainy, the magnanimous consul execrated the proposal, and informed the king, declaring that the Romans, conquered by valor, not through treason.

Sir Henry places much confidence in the certainty of dreams; for in that interval between sleeping and waking, he is perfuaded that his conversation is with familiar spirits, from whom he receives infallible information. These genii, he supposes, are composed of different corps of demons, recruited nearly to their full establishment, from the straggling ghosts of Tories, deserters from this globe, during the present war. As he finds himself and his nation in the closest league with these invisible infernals, he omits no opportunity of availing himself of their assistance and pays the most obsequious deference to their suggestions.—For some time since he has indulged himself in the most profound reveries: he has frequently started from table, quitted his guests, thrown himself upon a couch, and by his foaming, frothing, and writing, discovered all the incomprehensible agitations of the pseudomanthetic fury. One day recovering in a moment from an extraordinary paroxism, he declared to his generals, that on the first day of January, anno domini 1781, the rebel army would universally mutiny, renounce their allegiance to the United States, and proffer their service to the king his master. Elated at a prospect so flattering to his views, he immediately gave orders for the necessary dispositions to receive his intended allies. Staten-Island he appointed as a place well situated, on which he could assemble a large detachment of his army, from whence he could easily cross over to the state of New-Jersey, and there form a junction with the Pennsylvania line. Armed vessels and boats were accordingly collected in the Sound. Our brave and vigilant general Wayne having undoubted intelligence of the intentions and movements of the aerial Briton, was determined to fix the delusion, and, if possible, turn the comic into a tragic scene, communicated the whole to his troops; and changing uniforms between officers and serjeants, threw the line into the real appearance of a most serious insurrection.—In order to draw the romantic hero as far into the country as possible, and prevent his retreat, the new made serjeants marched the troops from Morristown to Princeton, and from Princeton to Trenton; there manoeuvring in such a manner, that any but those really in the plan, would have conceived an absolute revolt. The serjeants in officers uniform, took quarters in Penny-town, apparently soliciting a return to duty. In the mean time the Jersey militia were collecting in the vicinity of Staten-Island, in order to attack the rear of sir Henry, should he direct his rout towards Trenton. Great were our expectations upon this rare occasion. The descent was almost realized, when a strange whim came into sir Henry's head, that as these insurgents had condescended to put themselves upon a par with his troops, it was absolutely necessary to receive from them the rout they intended, in order to form a junction, previous to any farther movements of his army. To this end an ambassador and a courier extraordinary were dispatched; they arrived in camp, and, as their characters rendered their persons sacred, a strong guard was posted at their quarters, to prevent any violence that might possibly be offered them. In the mean time, beholding the militia in force upon the Jersey shore, Macbeth's moving forest occurred to the mind of sir Henry, with all its horrors: He immediately changed his resolution and determined to return to New-York, as a place of greater security.—Our general finding that no farther advantage could be taken of this military phænomenon, hung the ambassador and courier as spies, and re-assumed his usual order and discipline.

State of Pennsylvania. In General Assembly, Tuesday, February 26, 1782. . . . To the Public. . . . Plan for establishing a National Bank, for the the United States of North-America. [Philadelphia]: Hall & Sellers, [1781]. Broadside. HSP

The state of Pennsylvania herewith officially printed the resolution of Congress establishing the Bank of North America, together with its sponsor Robert Morris's explanation of the scheme. It was the setting up of this, the first national bank, which was the major step taken by Morris as Superintendant of the Office of Finance to control the credit of the nation. Capital was to be obtained from the issuance of stock, and notes against that capital were to have the value of specie when used for the payment of duties and taxes.

The credit of the United States was shattered; merchants who had accepted government paper for goods sold were desperate for lack of capital; the states had not complied with the resolutions of Congress levying payments upon them. Robert Morris was trying frantically to get the needed money in any way he could. In this letter, virtually a treatise on public credit, loans and taxes, filling 22 pages, Morris delivered a lecture in economics. His thesis was a simple one: constructive loans could be obtained once public credit was re-established; that could be done if taxes were obtained to fund the loans and pay the interest on them; taxes could be raised by the states from a land tax, a poll tax and an impost on strong liquors. Further, if the states would agree, funds could be obtained from the sale of public lands ceded to the federal government. It took a long while until the financial situation was improved.

[Peletiah Webster]. *An Essay on Free Trade and Finance.* Philadelphia: Thomas Bradford, 1779. LCP

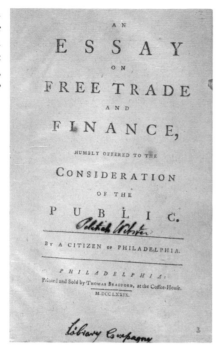

[Nathaniel Hazard]. *Observations On the peculiar Case of the Whig Merchants, Indebted to Great-Britain At the Commencement of the Late War.* New York: 1785. LCP

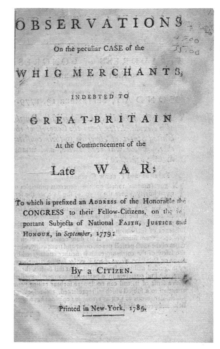

[Peletiah Webster]. *Reasons for Repealing the Act of the Legislature of Pennsylvania, Of September 13, 1785, For Repealing their Acts of March 18, and April 1, 1782, For Supporting and Incorporating the Bank of North-America.* Philadelphia: Eleazer Oswald, 1786. LCP

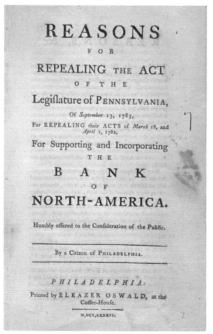

[William Barton]. *The True Interest of the United States, and particularly of Pennsylvania, considered; with respect to the advantages resulting from a State Paper-Money.* Philadelphia: Charles Cist, 1786. LCP

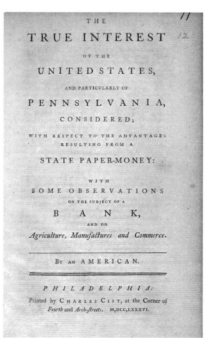

Webster, who over a period of years wrote seven essays on free trade and finance, was an economic conservative. He favored support of the war by taxation rather than by loans, advocated a strong central control of money, believed in free trade and opposed the issuance of paper money, particularly by the states. The problem of the payment of internal and external debts, intensified by the lack of a stable currency and the shaky credit of both the states and the nation, brought forth a spate of pamphlets proposing one or another solution.

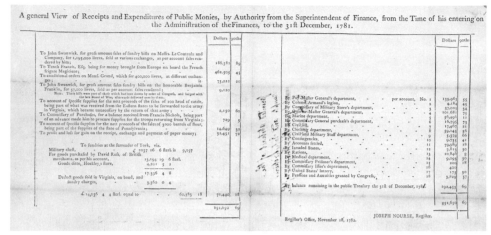

A general View of Receipts and Expenditures of Public Monies, by Authority from the Superintendent of Finance, from the Time of his entering on the Administration of theFinances, to the 31st December, 1781.

A general View of Receipts and Expenditures of Public Monies, by Authority from the Superintendent of Finance, from the Time of his entering on the Administration of the Finances, to the 31st December, 1781. [Philadelphia, 1782]. LCP

Robert Morris. *Note of Exchange payable by Haym Salomon,* Philadelphia, January 15, 1783. HSP

Haym Salomon. Advertisement. *Pennsylvania Packet,* July 20, 1782. LCP

With Morris as the Superintendant of Finance and the French loans pouring into the coffers of the United States, there was at least a temporary easing of the critical financial affairs of the nation. To turn the French *livres Tournois* into American currencies to pay for governmental expenses, the services of a broker experienced in foreign exchange were needed. Morris turned to Haym Salomon, who was willing to handle the funds at an extremely low rate. In July 1782, Salomon was officially appointed "Broker to the Office of Finance."

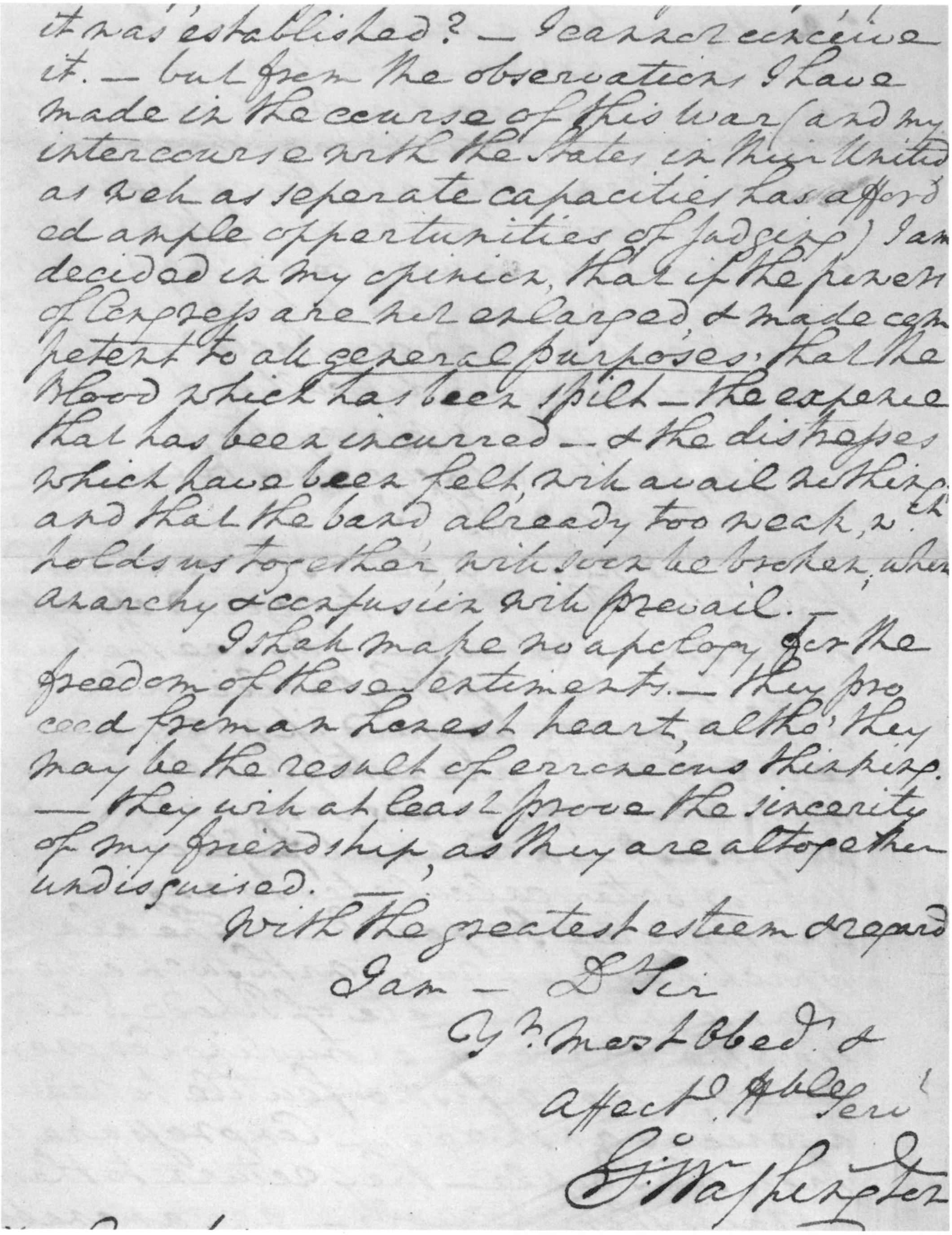

Much of Washington's letter is concerned with his thoughts on the imminence of peace, for no official word of the preliminary peace treaty had yet reached America. But he was particularly concerned with the hesitance of Virginia and the other states in raising funds for the federal government. "I cannot conceive it," he wrote, "but from the observations I have made in the course of this War . . . I am decided in my opinion, that if the powers of Congress are not enlarged, & made competent to all *general purposes*, that the Blood which has been spilt—the expence that has been incurred—& the distresses which have been felt, will avail nothing; and that the band, already too weak, wch. holds us together, will soon be broken; when anarchy & confusion will prevail."

On June 13, 1783, some
Pennsylvania troops awaiting
discharge demanded the pay
due them from Congress.
That body temporized and
peaceful petitions gave way to
threatening demonstrations.
Fearful for their safety,
Congress, in accordance with
this proclamation, removed
to Princeton. Philadelphia did
not again become the seat of
government until 1790.

By His EXCELLENCY

Elias Boudinot, Esquire,

Prefident of the United States in Congrefs Affembled.

Joseph Parker Norris. 1783

A PROCLAMATION.

WHEREAS a body of armed Soldiers in the fervice of the United States, and quartered in the Barracks of this City, having mutinoufly renounced their obedience to their Officers, did, on Saturday the Twenty-Firft Day of this inftant, proceed, under the direction of their Serjeants, in a hoftile and threatning manner, to the Place in which Congrefs were affembled, and did furround the fame with Guards: And whereas Congrefs in confequence thereof, did on the fame Day, refolve, " That the Prefident and Supreme Executive Council of this State " fhould be informed, that the authority of the United States having been, that Day, grofsly infulted by the " diforderly and menacing appearance of a body of armed Soldiers, about the Place within which Congrefs were affem- " bled; and that the Peace of this City being endangered by the mutinous Difpofition of the faid Troops then in the " Barracks; it was, in the Opinion of Congrefs, neceffary, that effectual Meafures fhould be immediately taken for " fupporting the public Authority:" And alfo whereas Congrefs did at the fame Time appoint a Committee to con- fer with the faid Prefident and Supreme Executive Council on the practicability of carrying the faid Refolution into due effect: And alfo whereas the faid Committee have reported to me, that they have not received fatisfactory Affurances for expecting adequate and prompt exertions of this State for fupporting the Dignity of the fœderal Government: And alfo whereas the faid Soldiers ftill continue in a ftate of open Mutiny and Revolt, fo that the Dignity and Authority of the United States would be conftantly expofed to a repetition of Infult, while Congrefs fhall continue to fit in this City, I do therefore, by and with the Advice of the faid Committee, and according to the Powers and Authorities in me veft- ed for this Purpofe, hereby fummon the honourable the Delegates compofing the Congrefs of the United States, and every of them, to meet in Congrefs on Thurfday the Twenty-Sixth Day of June inftant, at Princeton, in the ftate of New-Jerfey, in order that further and more effectual Meafures may be taken for fuppreffing the prefent Revolt, and maintaining the Dignity and Authority of the United States, of which all Officers of the United States, civil and military, and all others whom it may concern, are defired to take Notice and govern themfelves accordingly.

GIVEN under my Hand and Seal at Philadelphia, in the ftate of Pennfylvania, this Twenty-Fourth Day of June, in the Year of Our Lord One Thoufand Seven Hundred and Eighty-Three, and of our Sovereignty and Inde- pendence the feventh.

ELIAS BOUDINOT.

Atteft.

SAMUEL STERETT, *Private Secretary.*

Philadelphia, Printed by DAVID C. CLAYPOOLE.

'79

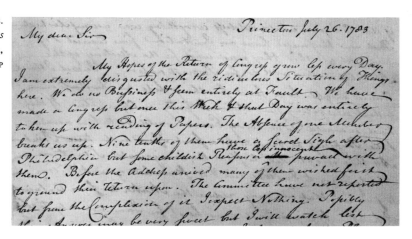

After Congress was forced to leave Philadelphia, it
settled uncomfortably in Princeton, where the attendance
of delegates fell off. Peters wrote of the dissatisfaction.
"My Hopes of the Return of Congress grow less every
Day. . . . We do no Business & seem entirely at Fault.
. . . The Absence of one Member breaks us up. Nine
tenths of them have a secret Sigh after Philadelphia
but some childish Reasons or those less innocent prevail
with them." Congress, after wandering on to Annapolis
and New York, returned only in 1790.

By the United States in Congreſs Assembled,

A PROCLAMATION.

WHEREAS by the ninth of the Articles of Confederation, it is among other Things declared, that "the United States in Congreſs aſſembled have the ſole and excluſive Right and Power of regulating the Trade, and managing all Affairs with the Indians not Members of any of the States; Provided, that the Legiſlative Right of any State within its own Limits be not infringed or violated." And whereas, it is eſſential to the Welfare and Intereſt of the United States, as well as neceſſary for the Maintenance of Harmony and Friendſhip with the Indians, not Members of any of the States, that all Cauſe of Quarrel or Complaint between them and the United States, or any of them, ſhould be removed and prevented: Therefore the United States in Congreſs aſſembled have thought proper to iſſue their Proclamation, and they do hereby prohibit and forbid all Perſons from making Settlements on Lands inhabited or claimed by Indians without the Limits or Juriſdiction of any particular State, and from purchaſing or receiving any Gift or Ceſſion of ſuch Lands or Claims, without the expreſs Authority and Directions of the United States in Congreſs aſſembled:

And it is moreover declared, that every ſuch Purchaſe or Settlement, Gift or Ceſſion, not having the Authority aforeſaid, is null and void, and that no Right or Title will accrue in conſequence of any ſuch Purchaſe, Gift, Ceſſion or Settlement.

John Montgomery and Richard Peters. *Letter to George Gray, Speaker of the Assembly of Pennsylvania,* Princeton, September 25, 1783. HSP

ARTICLES of a TREATY,

Concluded at HOPEWELL, on the Keowee, near Seneca Old Town, between Benjamin Hawkins, Andrew Pickens and Joseph Martin, COMMISSIONERS PLENIPOTENTIARY of the United States of America of the one part ; and Yockonahoma, great Medal Chief of Soonacoha, Yockahoopoie, leading Chief of Bugtoogoloo, Mingohoopoie, leading Chief of Haskooqua, Tobocoh, great Medal Chief of Congetoo, Pooshemastubie, Gorget Captain of Senayazo, and thirteen small Medal Chiefs of the first Class, twelve Medal and Gorget Captains, COMMISSIONERS PLENIPOTENTIARY, of all the Choctaw Nation of the other part.

THE Commissioners Plenipotentiary of the United States of America give peace to all the Choctaw nation, and receive them into the favor and protection of the United States of America, on the following conditions:

Art. 1. The Commissioners Plenipotentiary of all the Choctaw nation, shall restore all the prisoners, citizens of the United States, or subjects of their allies, to their entire liberty, if any there be in the Choctaw nation. They shall also restore all the negroes, and all other property taken during the late war, from the citizens, to such person, and at such time and place, as the commissioners of the United States of America shall appoint, if any there be in the Choctaw nation.

Art. 2. The Commissioners Plenipotentiary of all the Choctaw nation, do hereby acknowledge the tribes and towns of the said nation, and the lands within the boundary allotted to the said Indians, to live and hunt on, as mentioned in the third article, to be under the protection of the United States of America, and of no other sovereign whosoever.

Art. 3. The boundary of the lands, hereby allotted to the Choctaw nation to live and hunt on, within the limits of the United States of America is, and shall be the following, viz. Beginning at a point on the

IN WITNESS of all, and every thing herein determined, between the United States of America and all the Choctaws, we their underwriten commissioners, by virtue of our full powers have signed this definitive treaty, and have caused our seals to be hereunto affixed. ——— DONE at Hopewell, on the Keowee, this third day of January, in the year of our Lord one thousand seven hundred and eighty-six

(Signed)	BENJAMIN HAWKINS,	(L.S.)	
	ANDW. PICKENS,	(L.S.)	
	JOS. MARTIN,	(L.S.)	
	YOCKENAHOMA,	his × mark.	( )
	YOCKEHOOPOIE,	his × mark.	( )
	MINGOHOOPOIE,	his × mark.	( )
	TOBOCOH,	his × mark.	( )
	POOSHEMASTUBY,	his × mark.	( )
	POOSHAHOOMA,	his × mark.	
	TUSCOONOOHOOPOIE,	his × mark.	( )
	SHINSHEMASTUBY,	his × mark.	( )

[Signers caried forward.]   YOOPAKOOMA,

YOOPAKOOMA,	his × mark.	( )
STOONOKOOHOOPOIE,	his × mark.	( )
TEHAKUHBAY,	his × mark.	( )
POOSHEMASTUBY,	his × mark.	( )
TUSKKAHOOMOCH,	his × mark.	( )
TUSHKAHOOMOCH,	his × mark.	( )
YOOSTENOCHHA,	his × mark.	( )
TOOTEHOOMA,	his × mark.	( )
TOOBENOHOOMOCH,	his × mark.	( )
CSHECOOPOOHOOMOCH,	his × mark.	( )
STONAKOOHOOPOIE,	his × mark.	( )
TUSHKOHEEGOHTA,	his × mark.	( )
TESHUHENOCHLOCH,	his × mark.	
POOSHONALTLA,	his × mark.	( )
OKANCONNOOBA,	his × mark.	( )
UTOONACHUBAA,	his × mark.	( )
PANGEKOOLOCH,	his × mark.	( )
STEABEE,	his × mark	( )
TENCTEHENNA,	his × mark.	( )
TUSHKEMENTAHOCK,	his × mark.	( )
TUSHTALLAY,	his × mark	( )
CSHNAANGCHABBA,	his × mark.	( )
CUNNOPOIE,	his × mark.	( )

Witness·

WM. BLOUNT,
JOHN WOODS,
SAML. TAYLOR,
ROBERT ANDERSON,
BENJN. LAWRENCE.
JOHN PITCHLYNN, } Interpreters.
JAMES COLE,

Articles of a Treaty, Concluded at Hopewell, on the Keowee, near Seneca Old Town, between . . . Commissioners Plenipotentiary of the United States of America of the one part; and . . . Commissioners Plenipotentiary, of all the Choctaw Nation of the other part. [New York, 1786]. HSP

As Congress began to concern itself with the future of the unsettled lands in the west acquired under the peace treaty with Great Britain, some settlement with the Indians who lived there and had been hostile, became important. One of the rights which Congress took for itself under the Articles of Confederation was that of treating with them. By the proclamation of September 22, 1783, persons were forbidden to settle on Indian land, and states were enjoined from buying or selling that land. News of this was promptly sent by two Pennsylvania delegates in Congress to the state Assembly, telling them not to go ahead with a planned purchase of land from Indians "inhabiting or claiming Part of the Territory of Pennsilvania." In furtherance of the Congressional resolution, commissioners began to make treaties with the Indian tribes who lived in the unsettled lands to the west and south. On January 3, 1786, this treaty of peace, similar to others negotiated earlier and later, was entered into with the Choctaws. It guaranteed them full rights within the lands designated for their tribes and towns, and prohibited others from settling thereon. A week later a similar treaty with the same stipulations was made with the Chickasaws, the text of which is included in this four-page printing, possibly the only copy known. These were among the Indian treaties which the United States later shamefully dishonored.

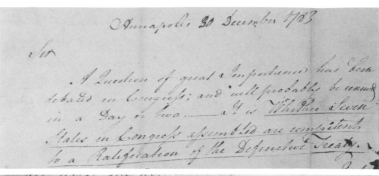

Thomas Mifflin, Cadwalader Morris and Edward Hand. *Letter to John Dickinson, president of Pennsylvania*, Annapolis, December 30, 1783. HSP

Thomas Mifflin. Engraving by E. Wellmore after a painting by Gilbert Stuart. LCP

Thomas Mifflin. *Letter to John Dickinson, president of Pennsylvania*, Annapolis, February 20, 1784. HSP

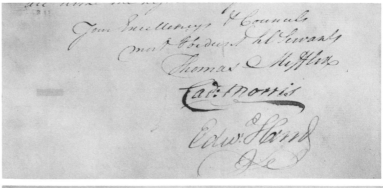

No sooner had the Articles of Confederation officially become the national frame of government, than Congress found itself unable to function for lack of attending delegates. Although the Definitive Treaty of Peace had arrived in America in November, Congress had been unable to act upon it for want of a quorum of states. The Pennsylvania delegates reported that an attempt was being made to permit seven, rather than nine, states to ratify the treaty, and asked for instructions. Briefly, in January, nine states did assemble, but shortly thereafter congressional business was once more held up by absences. In this strong letter Mifflin, as president of Congress, stressed the importance of the matters awaiting decision. He noted "that the members present are dissatisfied with attending to no purpose." A list of the states not represented was appended.

One of the more important concessions which Franklin won from Great Britain in the Peace Treaty was the right of navigation on the Mississippi. However, as Congress met in exile in Trenton, a dispute arose with Spain, which claimed sole jurisdiction over that waterway as she "was possessed of the Territory on each side of it, by Conquest, prior to the date of the Treaty with G. B." Other news from Congress included the election of Richard Henry Lee as president; but nothing had been done, Spaight reported, concerning North Carolina's cession of its western lands.

Richard D. Spaight. *Letter to Alexander Martin, governor of North Carolina,* Trenton, December 6, 1784. HSP

John Filson. *The Discovery, Settlement And present State of Kentucke: . . . To which is added, An Appendix, Containing, I. The Adventures of Col. Daniel Boon, one of the first Settlers.* Wilmington: James Adams, 1784. LCP

The push toward the West was one of first manifestations of American expansionism. Even during the war consolidation of the area east of the Mississippi was taking place. The entry of Daniel Boone into Kentucky and the settlement of that area paved the way for the acceptance of Kentucky into the Union as a state. Filson's narrative of the pioneer's exploits established Boone as a great American folk hero.

Daniel Boone. Engraving by J. B. Longacre after a painting by Chester Harding. HSP

THE
DISCOVERY, SETTLEMENT
And present State of
K E N T U C K E:
A N D
An ESSAY towards the TOPOGRAPHY, and NATURAL HISTORY of that important Country:
To which is added,
An A P P E N D I X,
CONTAINING,
I. The ADVENTURES of Col. *Daniel Boon,* one of the first Settlers, comprehending every important Occurrence in the political History of that Province.
II The MINUTES of the *Piankafhaw* council, held at *Poft St. Vincents, April* 15, 1784.
III. An ACCOUNT of the *Indian* Nations inhabiting within the Limits of the Thirteen United States, their Manners and Cuftoms, and Reflections on their Origin.
IV. The STAGES and DISTANCES between *Philadelphia* and the Falls of the *Ohio*; from *Pittfburg* to *Penfacola* and feveral other Places. —The Whole illuftrated by a new and accurate MAP of *Kentucke* and the Country adjoining, drawn from actual Surveys.

By *J O H N F I L S O N.*

Wilmington, Printed by JAMES ADAMS, 1784.

*The Committee appointed to prepare a Plan
for the temporary Government of the Western
Territory, have agreed to the following
Resolutions.* [Annapolis: John Dunlap,
1784]. HSP

As soon as Virginia's cession of its claim to western lands was received in Congress on March 1, 1784, Jefferson submitted his plan for the formation of federal territories. Julian P. Boyd has called the document "the foundation stone of American territorial policy." It provided for a temporary government, the privilege of becoming a state under certain conditions, and the division of the land into ten fancifully named separate territories. Jefferson prepared a map showing the bounds of such governmental units as Assenisipia, Metropotamia, Saratoga and Washington. After reconsideration by the committee, a revised report was submitted on March 22. The specific names and boundaries proposed by Jefferson for the new territories were removed. The amended plan specified that when a territory acquired 20,000 inhabitants, it could apply for statehood and that slavery would be abolished in all the western territories after 1800. In the ensuing debate the slavery clause was deleted. All the delegates from states including and north of Pennsylvania voted for the exclusion of slavery, while all those to the southward, except for Jefferson and Hugh Williamson, voted to maintain it. All the changes were written on the printed broadside by Edward Hand, a delegate from Pennsylvania. The final instrument, known as the "Ordinance of 1784", was adopted by Congress on April 23.

The COMMITTEE appointed to prepare a PLAN for the temporary Government of the WESTERN TERRITORY, have agreed to the following RESOLUTIONS.

RESOLVED,

THAT the territory ceded, or to be ceded by individual states, to the United States, shall be formed into distinct states, bounded in the following manner, as nearly as such cessions will admit; that is to say, northwardly and southwardly by parallels of latitude, so that each state shall comprehend from south to north two degrees of latitude, beginning to count from the completion of thirty-one degrees north of the equator: but any territory northwardly of the 47th degree, shall make part of the state next below. And eastwardly and westwardly they shall be bounded, those on the Missisippi by that river on one side, and the meridian of the lowest point of the rapids of Ohio on the other; and those adjoining on the east, by the same meridian on their western side, and on their eastern, by the meridian of the western cape of the mouth of the Great Kanhaway. And the territory eastward of this last meridian, between the Ohio, lake Erie, and Pennsylvania, shall be one state.

That the settlers within any of the said states shall, either on their own petition, or on the order of Congress, receive authority from them, with appointments of time and place for their free males of full age to meet together for the purpose of establishing a temporary government, to adopt the constitution and laws of any one of these states, so that such laws nevertheless shall be subject to alteration by their ordinary legislature; and to erect, subject to a like alteration, counties or townships for the election of members for their legislature.

That such temporary government shall only continue in force in any state, until it shall have acquired twenty thousand free inhabitants; when giving due proof thereof to Congress, they shall receive from them authority, with appointments of time and place to call a convention of representatives to establish a permanent constitution and government for themselves.

Provided that both the temporary and permanent governments be established on these principles as their basis. 1. That they shall for ever remain a part of the United States of America. 2. That in their persons, property and territory they shall be subject to the government of the United States in Congress assembled, and to the articles of confederation in all those cases in which the original states shall be so subject. 3. That they shall be subject to pay a part of the federal debts contracted or to be contracted, to be apportioned on them by Congress, according to the same common rule and measure, by which apportionments thereof shall be made on the other states. 4. That their respective governments shall be in republican forms, and shall admit no person to be a citizen who holds any hereditary title. 5. That after the year 1800 of the christian æra, there shall be neither slavery nor involuntary servitude in any of the said states, otherwise than in punishment of crimes, whereof the party shall have been duly convicted to have been personally guilty.

The COMMITTEE to whom was recommitted the Report of a PLAN for a temporary Government of the WESTERN TER-RITORY, have agreed to the following RESOLUTIONS.

RESOLVED,

THAT so much of the territory ceded, or to be ceded by individual states, to the United States, as is already purchased or shall be purchased of the Indian inhabitants, and offered for sale by Congress, shall be divided into distinct states, in the following manner, as nearly as such cessions will admit; that is to say, by parallels of latitude, so that each state shall comprehend from ~~south to~~ north *to South* two degrees of latitude, beginning to count from the completion of ~~thirty-one degrees~~ *45 degrees* north of the equator; and by meridians of longitude, one of which shall pass through the lowest point of the rapids of Ohio, and the other through the western cape of the mouth of the Great Kanhaway. But the territory eastward of this last meridian, between the Ohio, lake Erie, and Pennsylvania, shall be one state, whatsoever may be its comprehension of latitude. That which may lie beyond the completion of the 45th degree, between the said meridians, shall make part of the state adjoining it on the south, and that part of the Ohio which is between the same meridians, coinciding nearly with the parallel of 39° shall be substituted so far in lieu of that parallel as a boundary line.

That the settlers on any territory so purchased and offered for sale, shall, either on their own petition, or on the order of Congress, receive authority from them, with appointments of time and place, for their free males of full age, within the limits of their state, to meet together for the purpose of establishing a temporary government, to adopt the constitution and laws of any one of the original states; so that such laws nevertheless shall be subject to alteration by their ordinary legislature; and to erect, subject to a like alteration, counties ~~or~~ townships *or other divisions* for the election of members for their legislature.

That ~~such temporary government shall only continue in force in~~ *Such* any state, ~~until it~~ shall have acquired twenty thousand free inhabitants; ~~when~~ *on* giving due proof thereof to Congress, they shall receive from them authority, with appointments of time and place to call a convention of representatives to establish a permanent constitution and government for themselves.

Provided that both the temporary and permanent governments be established on these principles as their basis. 1. That they shall for ever remain a part of this confederacy of the United States of America. 2. That ~~in their persons, property and territory~~ they shall be subject ~~to the government of the United States in Congress assembled, and~~ to the articles of confederation in all those cases in which the original states shall be so subject. *and to all the acts & ordinances of the U.S. in Congress Assembled conformable thereto* ⁴ That they shall be subject to pay a part of the federal debts contracted or to be contracted, to be apportioned on them by Congress, according to the same common rule and measure, by which apportionments thereof shall be made on the other states. ⁶ That their respective governments shall be ~~in~~ republican ~~forms, and shall admit no person to be a citizen who holds any hereditary title~~. ~~5. That after the year 1800 of the christian æra, there shall be neither slavery nor involuntary servitude in any of the said states, otherwise than in punishment of crimes, whereof the party shall have been convicted to have been personally guilty.~~

3. That they in no case shall interfere with the primary disposal of the Soil by the U.S. in Congress assembled nor with the ordinances & regulations which Congress may find necessary for securing the title in such Soil to the bona fide purchasers

 # the consent of so many states in Congress is first obtained as may at the time be competent

⁴ from & after the Sale of any part of the territory of such State pursuant to this resolve

That whensoever any of the said states shall have, of free inhabitants, as many as shall then be in any one the least numerous of the thirteen original states, such states shall be admitted by it's delegates into the Congress of the United States, on an equal footing with the said original states; Provided ~~nine states agree~~ to such admission, ~~according to the reservation of the eleventh of the articles of confederation~~. And in order to adopt the said articles of confederation, to the state of Congress, when its numbers shall be thus encreased, it shall be proposed to the legislatures of the states originally parties thereto, to require the assent of two-thirds of the United States in Congress assembled, in all those cases wherein by the said articles, the assent of nine states is now required; which being agreed to by them, shall be binding on the new states. Until such admission by their delegates into Congress, any of the said states, after the establishment of their temporary government, shall have authority to keep a ~~sitting~~ member in Congress, with a right of debating, but not of voting.

5th that no tax shall be imposed on lands the property of the U.S.

6ty That the lands of non-resident proprietors shall in no case be taxed higher than those of residents within any new State before the admission thereof to a vote by its delegates in Congress

That the preceding articles shall be formed into a charter of compact, shall be duly executed by the president of the United States in Congress assembled, under his hand and the seal of the United States, shall be promulgated, and shall stand as fundamental constitutions between the thirteen original states, and each of the several states now newly described, unalterable but by the joint consent of the United States in Congress assembled, and of the particular state within which such alteration is proposed to be made.

8 That measures not inconsistent with the principles of the confederation & necessary for the preservation of peace & good order among the settlers in any of the said new States until they shall assume a temporary government as aforesaid may from time to time be taken by the U.S. in Congress assembled —

The Committee to whom was recommitted the Report of a Plan for a temporary Government of the Western Territory, have agreed to the following Resolutions. [Annapolis: John Dunlap, 1784]. HSP

We, the People of the United States, in order to
form a more perfect union . . . do ordain and
establish this Constitution for the United States of
America. [Philadelphia]: Dunlap & Claypoole,
[1787]. (With marginal notes by
Benjamin Franklin). APS

WE, the People of the United S

a more perfect union, establish justice, in

for the common defence, promote the genera

of liberty to ourselves and our posterity, do ordain an

United States of America.

A R T I C L E

Sect. 1. ALL legiflative powers herein granted fhall be
States, which fhall confift of a Senate and Houfe of Reprefe

Sect. 2. The Houfe of Reprefentatives fhall be compofed
by the people of the feveral ftates, and the electors in each
fice for electors of the moft numerous branch of the ftate le

No perfon fhall be a reprefentative who fhall not have atta
been feven years a citizen of the United States, and who fh
of that ftate in which he fhall be chofen.

Reprefentatives and direct taxes fhall be apportioned amo
cluded within this Union, according to their refpective numl
ing to the whole number of free perfons, including thofe l
and excluding Indians not taxed, three-fifths of all other p

"To secure the
blessings of liberty"
—Preamble to
The Constitution, 1787

the Rev. Mr Lothrop ⸺

from B. Franklin ⸺

es, in order to form

domeſtic tranquility, provide

fare, and ſecure the bleſſings

bliſh this Conſtitution for the

ed in a Congreſs of the United
es.

:mbers choſen every ſecond year
all have the qualifications require.

o the age of twenty-five years, and
t, when elected, be an inhabitant

e ſeveral ſtates which may be in-
which ſhall be determined by add-
to ſervice for a term of years,
. The actual enumeration ſhall

Congreſs

Houſe of Rep^s.

Qualif^n of Electors

— of Repreſent:

*Proportion of
Repreſentatives
of Direct Taxes*

263

Nicholas Van Dyke. *Letter to Governor Samuel Huntington*, New Castle, July 12, 1786. HSP

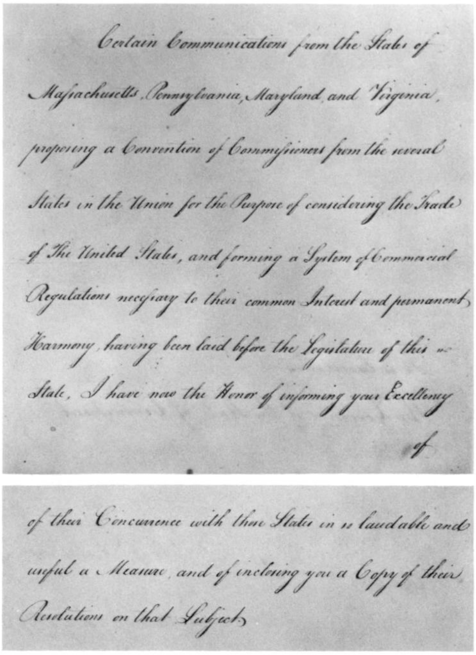

John Dickinson. *Letter to the Legislatures of Virginia, Delaware, Pennsylvania, New-Jersey and New York*, Annapolis, September 14, 1786. HSP

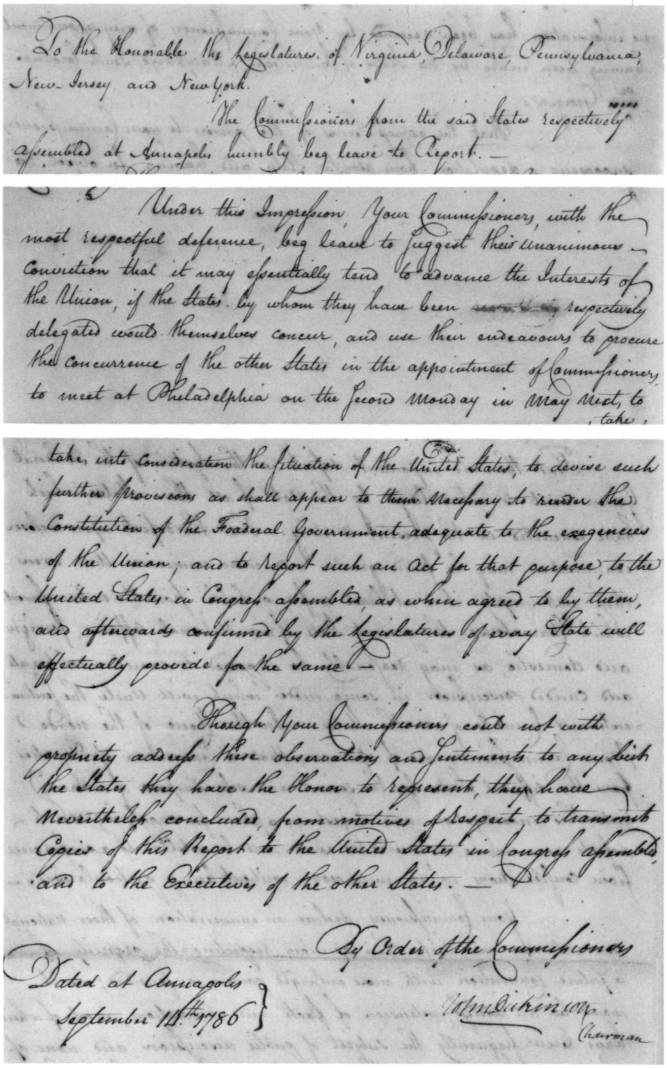

George Read. *Letter to Charles Thomson*, New Castle, October 7, 1786. HSP

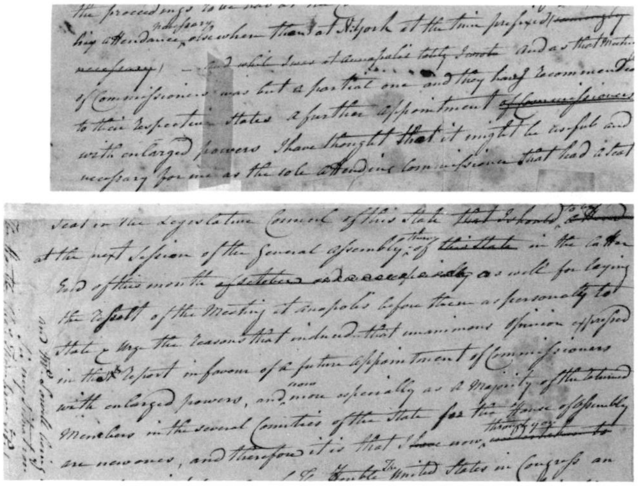

AN ORDINANCE for the GOVERNMENT of the TERRITORY of the UNITED STATES, North-West of the RIVER OHIO.

BE IT ORDAINED by the United States in Congress assembled, That the said territory, for the purposes of temporary government, be one district; subject, however, to be divided into two districts, as future circumstances may, in the opinion of Congress, make it expedient.

Be it ordained by the authority aforesaid, That the estates both of resident and non-resident proprietors in the said territory, dying intestate, shall descend to, and be distributed among their children, and the descendants of a deceased child in equal parts; the descendants of a deceased child or grand-child, to take the share of their deceased parent in equal parts among them: And where there shall be no children or descendants, then in equal parts to the next of kin, in equal degree; and among collaterals, the children of a deceased brother or sister of the intestate, shall have in equal parts among them their deceased parents share; and there shall in no case be a distinction between kindred of the whole and half blood; saving in all cases to the widow of the intestate, her third part of the real estate for life, and one third part of the personal estate; and this law relative to descents and dower, shall remain in full force until altered by the legislature of the district. —— And until the governor and judges shall adopt laws as herein after mentioned, estates in the said territory may be devised or bequeathed by wills in writing, signed and sealed by him or her, in whom the estate may be, (being of full age) and attested by three witnesses; —— and real estates may be conveyed by lease and release, or bargain and sale, signed, sealed, and delivered by the person being of full age, in whom the estate may be, and attested by two witnesses, provided such wills be duly proved, and such conveyances be acknowledged, or the execution thereof duly proved, and be recorded within one year after proper magistrates, courts, and registers shall be appointed for that purpose; and personal property may be transferred by delivery, saving, however, to the French and Canadian inhabitants, and other settlers of the Kaskaskies, Saint Vincent's, and the neighbouring villages, who have heretofore professed themselves citizens of Virginia, their laws and customs now in force among them, relative to the descent and conveyance of property.

Be it ordained by the authority aforesaid, That there shall be appointed from time to time, by Congress, a governor, whose commission shall continue in force for the term of three years, unless sooner revoked by Congress; he shall reside in the district, and have a freehold estate therein, in one thousand acres of land, while in the exercise of his office.

There shall be appointed from time to time, by Congress, a secretary, whose commission shall continue in force for four years, unless sooner revoked, he shall reside in the district, and have a freehold estate therein, in five hundred acres of land, while in the exercise of his office; it shall be his duty to keep and preserve the acts and laws passed by the legislature, and the public records of the district, and the proceedings of the governor in his executive department; and transmit authentic copies of such acts and proceedings, every six months, to the secretary of Congress: There shall also be appointed a court to consist of three judges, any two of whom to form a court, who shall have a common law jurisdiction, and reside in the district, and have each therein a freehold estate in five hundred acres of land, while in the exercise of their offices; and their commissions shall continue in force during good behaviour.

The governor and judges, or a majority of them, shall adopt and publish in the district, such laws of the original states, criminal and civil, as may be necessary, and best suited to the circumstances of the district, and report them to Congress, from time to time, which laws shall be in force in the district until the organization of the general assembly therein, unless disapproved of by Congress; but afterwards the legislature shall have authority to alter them as they shall

Article the Fifth. There shall be formed in the said territory, not less than three nor more than five states; and the boundaries of the states, as soon as Virginia shall alter her act of cession and consent to the same, shall become fixed and established as follows, to wit: The western state in the said territory, shall be bounded by the Mississippi, the Ohio and Wabash rivers; a direct line drawn from the Wabash and Post Vincent's due north to the territorial line between the United States and Canada, and by the said territorial line to the lake of the Woods and Mississippi. The middle state shall be bounded by the said direct line, the Wabash from Post Vincent's to the Ohio; by the Ohio, by a direct line drawn due north from the mouth of the Great Miami to the said territorial line, and by the said territorial line. The eastern state shall be bounded by the last mentioned direct line, the Ohio, Pennsylvania, and the said territorial line: Provided however, and it is further understood and declared, that the boundaries of these three states, shall be subject so far to be altered, that if Congress shall hereafter find it expedient, they shall have authority to form one or two states in that part of the said territory which lies north of an east and west line drawn through the southerly bend or extreme of lake Michigan. And whenever any of the said states shall have sixty thousand free inhabitants therein, such state shall be admitted by its delegates into the Congress of the United States, on an equal footing with the original states in all respects whatever; and shall be at liberty to form a permanent constitution and state government: Provided the constitution and government so to be formed, shall be republican, and in conformity to the principles contained in these articles; and so far as it can be consistent with the general interest of the confederacy, such admission shall be allowed at an earlier period, and when there may be a less number of free inhabitants in the state than sixty thousand.

Article the Sixth. There shall be neither slavery nor involuntary servitude in the said territory, otherwise than in punishment of crimes whereof the party shall have been duly convicted: Provided always, that any person escaping into the same, from whom labor or service is lawfully claimed in any one of the original states, such fugitive may be lawfully reclaimed and conveyed to the person claiming his or her labor or service as aforesaid.

Be it ordained by the authority aforesaid, That the resolutions of the 23d of April, 1784, relative to the subject of this ordinance, be, and the same are hereby repealed and declared null and void.

DONE by the UNITED STATES in CONGRESS assembled, the 13th day of July, in the year of our Lord 1787, and of their sovereignty and independence the 12th.

Cha Thomson sec'y

On September 11, 1786, commissioners from New York, New Jersey, Pennsylvania, Delaware and Virginia met at Annapolis in an attempt to unravel the tangle caused by the restrictions placed upon interstate commerce by the individual states, one of the many problems of the loose federal government under the Articles of Confederation. Van Dyke, the president of the state of Delaware, informed the governor of Connecticut that his state had agreed to attend. The specific matters brought before the convention were not resolved, but it was the opinion of all who attended that a further, expanded convention should be convened. Dickinson, as chairman of the Annapolis Convention, issued the call for that meeting: "Your Commissioners, with the most respectful deference, beg leave to suggest their Unanimous Conviction that it may essentially tend to advance the Interests of the Union, if the States by whom they have been respectively delegated would themselves concur, and use their endeavours to procure the concurrence of the other States in the appointment of Commissioners to meet at Philadelphia on the second Monday in May next, to take into consideration the situation of the United States, to devise such further provisions as shall appear to them necessary to render the Constitution of the Foederal [!] Government adequate to the exegencies of the Union." Read, a delegate at Annapolis, told the secretary of Congress that he considered his presence in Delaware essential and wished to be excused from his attendance at the Court of Appeals until action was taken by the state on the proposed Constitutional Convention.

The most important single act of Congress between the approval of the Declaration of Independence and the ratification of the Constitution by the states was the passage of the Northwest Ordinance. It established a form of government for the almost vacant land in what is now the Middle West. Among its provisions was one that "there shall be neither slavery nor involuntary servitude in said territory." The ordinance set a pattern for the administration of lands later acquired by territorial expansion.

Edmund Randolph. *Letter to Benjamin Franklin,* Richmond, December 6, 1786. APS

James Madison. *Letter to George Washington,* Richmond, December 7, 1786. HSP

George Washington. *Letter to Edmund Randolph,* Mount Vernon, March 28, 1787. HSP

It having been decided that a Constitutional Convention should be held, the states began appointing their delegates. Randolph hoped that Franklin would "give a zealous attention to the present American crisis," and informed him that Washington, Henry, Wythe, Blair, Madison and himself had been appointed to represent Virginia at Philadelphia. Madison impressed upon Washington the importance of his attendance at the Convention. He wrote that "it was the opinion of every judicious friend whom I consulted that your name could not be spared from the Deputation to the Meeting in May in Philada." Washington, suffering from "a rheumatic complaint in my shoulder," had at first declined to accept the appointment. However, he informed Governor Randolph that "as my friends . . . seem to wish my attendance on this occasion, I have come to a resolution to go, if my health will permit."

Thomas McKean. *Letter to John Adams,*
Philadelphia, April 30, 1787. HSP

A Convention of the several States will be held here next week, for the purpose of revising the Confederation, and giving greater powers to Congress. I have heard of Appointments from each State, except Rhode-island; and from the characters delegated to this service, most of them having been old members of Congress in 1776, or 1777, I have some hopes that public utility may be derived from it; tho' the present popular opinion is, that we should be very jealous of conferring power on any man or any body of men. Indeed we seem afraid to enable any one to do good, lest he should do evil. Please to present my compliments to Mr. Cutting when you

Jacob Broom. *Letter to John Dickinson,*
Wilmington, May 13, 1787. LCP

Wilmington May 13th: 1787.

Sir,
this day I returned from Philada. where I have been since Tuesday last. I had the pleasure to find Mr. Read there, who is very anxious for your arrival.—Several Gentlemen of the Convention have been enquiring for you.—The illustrious Washington left here this morning, on his way to Philada.—nothing but the importance of the business could have induced him to come forward——Capt. Strong from

I am Sir with the Greatest respect and esteem, Your most Obedt. & most Hble Servt.

Jacob Broom

The Honble John Dickinson Esquire.

Thomas McKean.
Engraving by
C. Tiebout. HSP

There was excitement in the air as the delegates began to assemble in
Philadelphia. McKean, writing to John Adams, then serving as envoy to the
Court of St. James, thanked him for Adams' thorough study of the constitutions
of the various states, and went on speak of the convention that was to open
the following week: "from the characters delegated to this service, most of
them having been old members of Congress in 1776, or 1777, I have hopes that
public utility may be derived from it; tho' the present popular opinion is, that
we should be very jealous of conferring power on any man or body of men."
Broom, a delegate from Delaware, told Dickinson that his arrival in Philadelphia
was anxiously awaited and that "the illustrious Washington left here this
morning, on his way to Philada.—nothing but the importance of the business
could have induced him to come forward."

The Gent. who came here early particularly from Virginia that had a Quorum on the first day express much uneasiness at the backwardness of individuals in giving attendance — it is meant to Organise the body as soon as seven States Quorum's attend — I could wish you were here.

I am in possession of a copied Draught of a federal System intended to be proposed if something nearly similar shall not precede it — some of its principal features are taken from the N. York System of their Govt. — A house of delegates & Senate for a genl. Legislature as to the great business of the Union

Member in Eighty — I suspect it of importance to the small States that their deputies keep a strict watch upon the Movements & Propositions from the larger States who will probably combine to swallow up the smaller ones by addition division or impoverishment — and if you have any wish to assist in guarding against such attempts you will be speedy in your attendance —

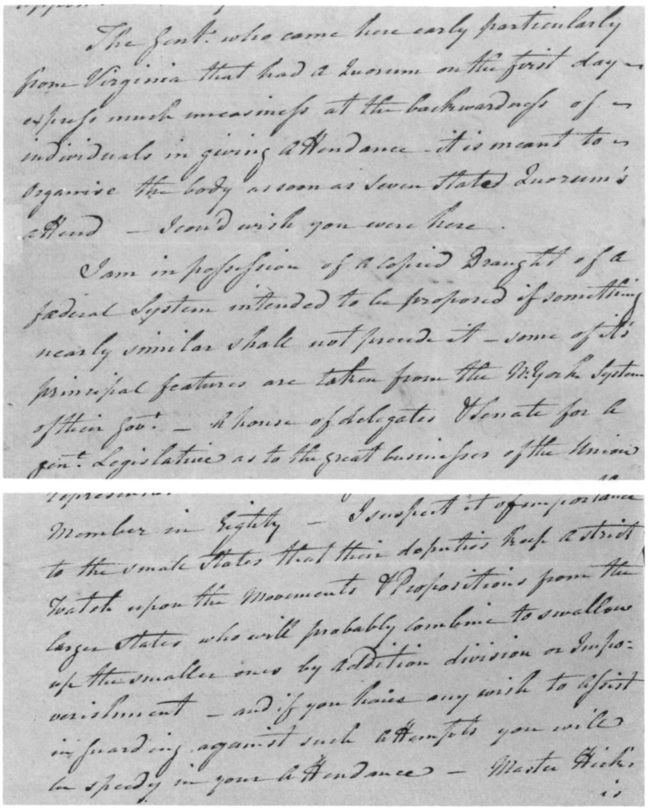

George Read. *Letter to John Dickinson,* Philadelphia, May 21, 1787. HSP

Jacob Broom. "*Resolutions offered by Mr. [Edmund] Randolph in Convention, May 29th, 1787*" (with additional notes by Richard Bassett and John Dickinson). Manuscript. LCP

Resolutions offered by Mr. Randolph in Convention May 29th 1787.

1st. Resolved that the articles of the Confederation ought to be so corrected & enlarged as to accomplish the objects proposed by their institution; namely "common defence, security of liberty & general welfare."

2d. Resolved therefore, that the rights of suffrage in the national legislature ought to be proportioned to the quota's of contribution or to the number of free inhabitants as the one or the other Rule may seem best in different cases.

3. Resolved that the National Legislature ought to consist of two branches

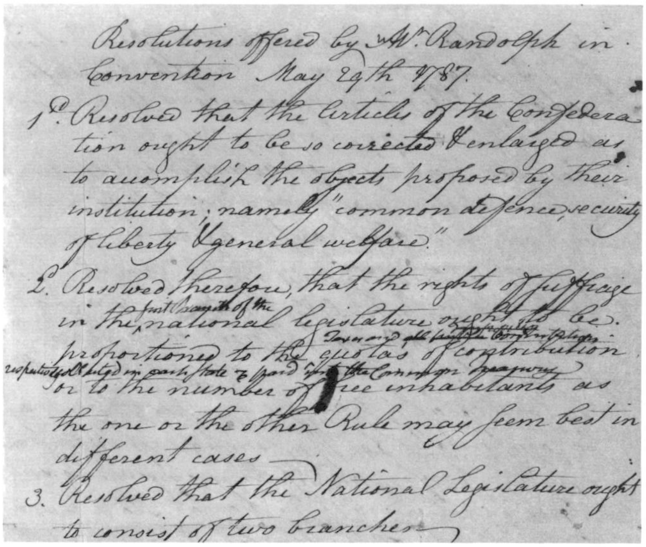

John Dickinson. *Revision of the Virginia Plan,* [May 30, 1787]. Manuscript. LCP

Resolved —

1 That the articles of Confederation ought to be revised and amended, so as to render the Government of the United States adequate to the Exigencies, the preservation, & the prosperity of the Union

2 That this Government ought to consist of a Legislative, Executive and Judiciary

3 That the Legislature ought to be composed of two Branches

4 That the Members of the first Branch ought to be chosen as they are by the existing Confederation, that is by the Legislatures of the several States, each State having an equal Vote

that immediately after the first Election they be divided into seven Classes, as equal as possible, & numbered 1 2 3 4 5 6 7 that the seats of the Members of the first Class shall be vacated at the End of the first Year, of the second Class at the End of the second Year, and so on continually, to the End that the part of the Branch, as nearly as possible, may be annually chosen —

that if any Member dies, the person elected in his place shall serve only for the Residue of the Term for which the deceased was elected

	Quota of Tax	Delegates	
Virginia	512, 974	16	4
Massachusetts	448, 854	14	4
Pennsylvania	410, 378	12 3/4	4
Maryland	283, 034	8 3/4	3
Connecticut	264, 182	8	3
New York	256, 406	8	3
North Carolina	218, 012	6 3/4	2
South Carolina	192, 366	6	2
New Jersey	166, 316	5	2
New-Hampsh.e	105, 416	3 1/4	2
Rhode Island	64, 636	2	1
Delaware	44 886	1 1/4	1
Georgia	32, 060	1.	
		90	

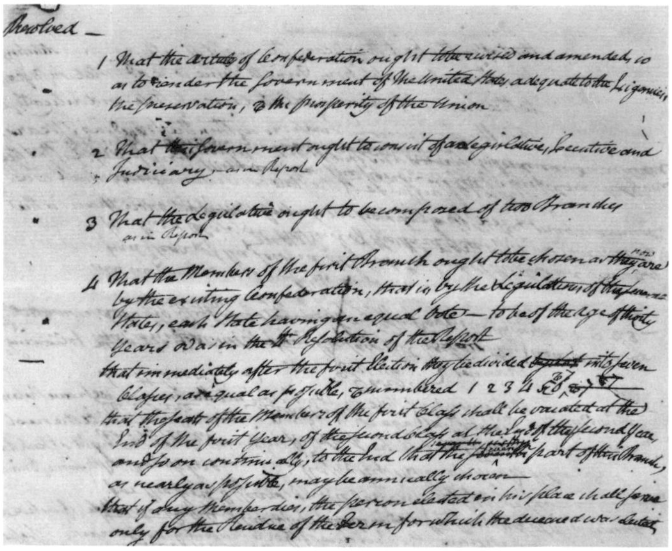

Read informed his fellow-delegate Dickinson of the state of affairs in Philadelphia as the members of the Convention gathered. There was concern at the slowness with which they were arriving. The Virginia delegates, however, were already prepared to offer a plan for a new constitution. "I am in possession of a copied Draught of a foederal System," Read wrote, "intended to be proposed if something nearly similar shall not precede it." He was worried that the provision for representation proportional to taxes and population would be unfair to the smaller states. On May 29, 1787, Edmund Randolph presented his delegation's plan, in the framing of which James Madison had played a leading role. The calculations by Bassett of Delaware on the last page of Broom's copy indicated how representation by wealth favored the large states. Below, Dickinson added some points made by James Wilson in the course of debate, as well as some notes, presumably for one of his own speeches. Dickinson's own revision was carefully written out. The second is of great significance: "That this Government ought to consist of a Legislative, Executive and Judiciary."

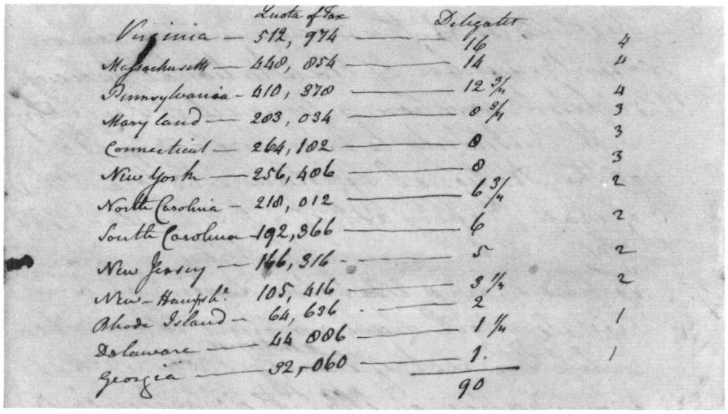

William Paterson. *"Propositions
pr[oposed] from New Jersey by
Mr. Paterson,"* June 15, 1787. Manuscript
of George Read and Jacob Broom. LCP

Charles Pinckney. *Observations on the
Plan of Government submitted to the
Federal Convention, in Philadelphia, on
the 28th of May, 1787.* New York:
Francis Childs, [1787]. HSP

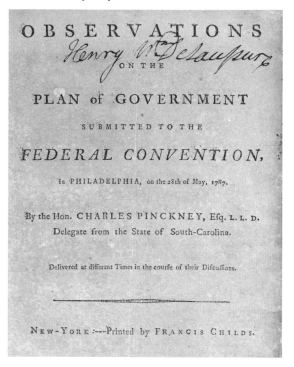

Among the different plans submitted to the Convention
during the extended debate was one offered by the New
Jersey delegates. As its preamble indicated, it was merely
a tightening up of the Articles of Confederation. Though
it gave Congress the right to impose taxes in proportion
to population and to control foreign relations, it was not
in essence a new frame of government. This copy, made
by two Delaware delegates, was turned over to
John Dickinson.

As the debate continued alternative plans,
modifications and compromises were suggested
by the delegates. One of the most important was
that of Pinckney. Although its text has not survived,
research has shown that it contained over 30
provisions which were finally accepted. In presenting
his ideas Pinckney made a speech, which he later
printed in full. Less influential were the somewhat
monarchical propositions of Hamilton, who
proposed that senators and a chief executive be
elected for life, "to serve during good behaviour,"
and that governors of the states be appointed by
the federal government.

Charles Pinckney.
Engraving by
Max Rosenthal. HSP

Alexander Hamilton. *"Propositions by Col. Hamilton,"* June 18, 1787. Manuscript of George Read. HSP

David Brearley. *Letter to Jonathan Dayton,* Philadelphia, July 27, 1787. HSP

One compromise after another was offered to obtain the support of one state after another with a special interest. It was finally agreed that in a house of representatives members would be elected in proportion to population, while in a senate all states would be equally represented. To conciliate the South, three-fifths of the slave population would be counted in the apportionment, and foreign slave trade would not be prohibited until 1808. The compromise then went to committee for drafting, as Brearley reported.

James Wilson. Engraving by Albert Rosenthal, in John Bach McMaster and Frederick D. Stone, *Pennsylvania and the Federal Constitution, 1787-1788.* [Philadelphia]: Historical Society of Pennsylvania, 1888. LCP

The hot summer of debate came to an end when a committee was charged with drafting a plan of government which would be acceptable to almost all the delegates. James Wilson, called by Bryce "one of the deepest thinkers and most exact reasoners" in the convention, was on that committee and wrote out the document, which was submitted on August 7. His two drafts show the definition of language worked out in the last stage before presentation to the Convention.

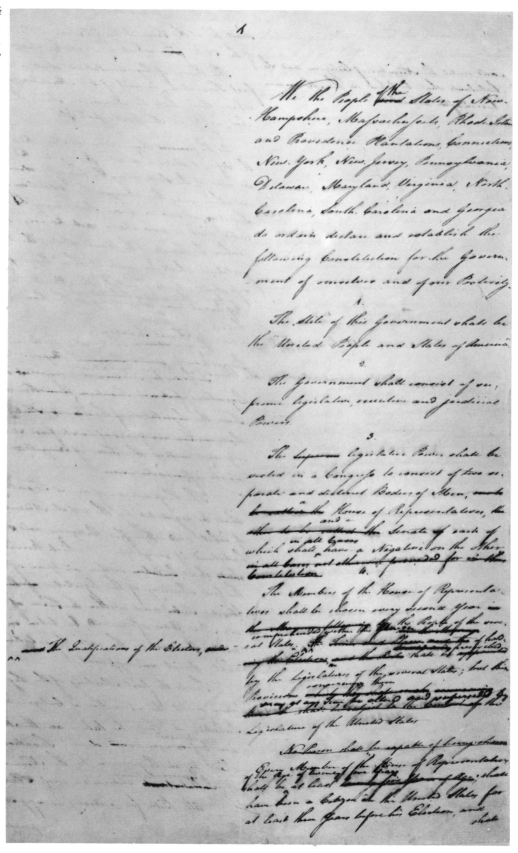

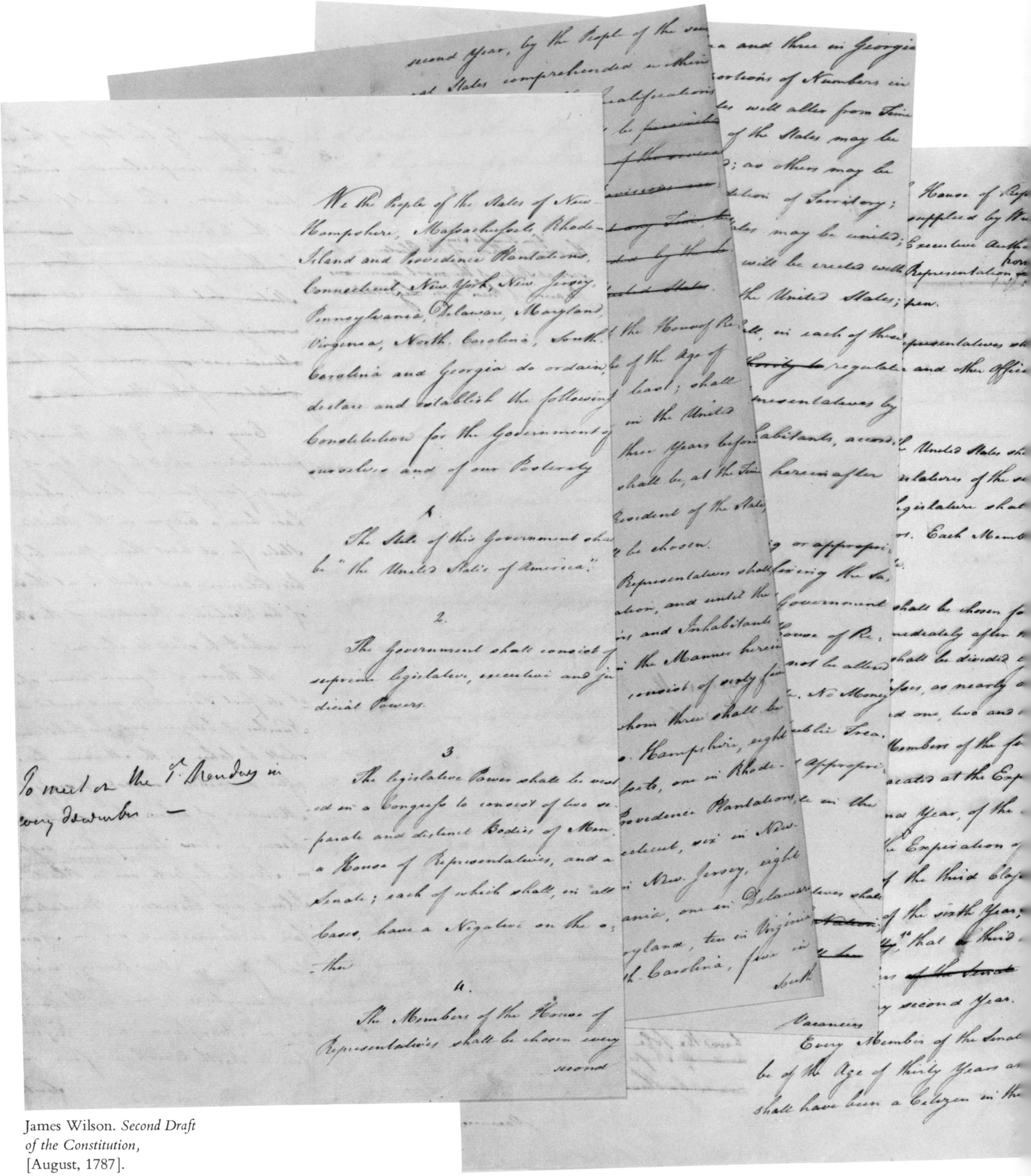

We the People of the States of New-
Hampshire, Massachusetts, Rhode-
Island and Providence Plantations,
Connecticut, New-York, New-Jersey,
Pennsylvania, Delaware, Maryland,
Virginia, North-Carolina, South-
Carolina and Georgia do ordain
declare and establish the following
Constitution for the Government of
ourselves and of our Posterity

1.

The Stile of this Government shall
be "the United States of America."

2.

The Government shall consist of
supreme legislative, executive and judicial Powers.

3.

The legislative Power shall be vested in a Congress to consist of two separate and distinct Bodies of Men,
a House of Representatives, and a
Senate; each of which shall, in all
cases, have a Negative on the o-
ther

4.

The Members of the House of
Representatives shall be chosen every
second

To meet on the 1st Monday in
every December. —

James Wilson. *Second Draft
of the Constitution,*
[August, 1787].
Manuscript. HSP

We the people of the States . . . do ordain, declare and establish the following Constitution for the Government of Ourselves and our Posterity. [Philadelphia: Dunlap and Claypoole, 1787]. (With corrections of Edmund Randolph). HSP

We the People of the States . . . do ordain, declare and establish the following Constitution for the Government of Ourselves and our Posterity. [Philadelphia: Dunlap and Claypoole, 1787]. (With emendations by John Dickinson). LCP

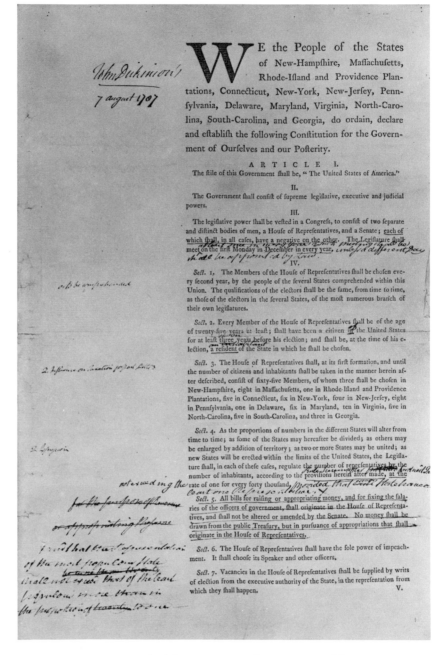

On August 7 the committee's draft was printed so that the delegates could properly consider it. Since the proceedings of the convention were secret, the edition was limited and never published in a public sense; one copy went to each delegate. A proof was corrected by Randolph. On his copy Dickinson inserted the changes agreed upon in the course of debate, and made further notes in the margin.

WE, the People of the United States, in order to form

a more perfect union, to establish justice, insure domestic tranquility, provide for the common defence, promote the general welfare, and secure the blessings of liberty to ourselves and our posterity, do ordain and establish this Constitution for the United States of America.

ARTICLE I.

Sect. 1. ALL legislative powers herein granted shall be vested in a Congress of the United States, which shall consist of a Senate and House of Representatives.

Sect. 2. The House of Representatives shall be composed of members chosen every second year by the people of the several states, and the electors in each state shall have the qualifications requisite for electors of the most numerous branch of the state legislature.

No person shall be a representative who shall not have attained to the age of twenty-five years, and been seven years a citizen of the United States, and who shall not, when elected, be an inhabitant of that state in which he shall be chosen.

Representatives and direct taxes shall be apportioned among the several states which may be included within this Union, according to their respective numbers, which shall be determined by adding to the whole number of free persons, including those bound to servitude for a term of years, and excluding Indians not taxed, three-fifths of all other persons. The actual enumeration shall be made within three years after the first meeting of the Congress of the United States, and within every subsequent term of ten years, in such manner as they shall by law direct. The number of representatives shall not exceed one for every forty thousand, but each state shall have at least one representative: and until such enumeration shall be made, the state of New-Hampshire shall be entitled to chuse three, Massachusetts eight, Rhode-Island and Providence Plantations one, Connecticut five, New-York six, New-Jersey four, Pennsylvania eight, Delaware one, Maryland six, Virginia ten, North-Carolina five, South-Carolina five, and Georgia three.

When vacancies happen in the representation from any state, the Executive authority thereof shall issue writs of election to fill such vacancies.

The House of Representatives shall choose their Speaker and other officers; and ~~they~~ shall have the sole power of impeachment.

Sect. 3. The Senate of the United States shall be composed of two senators from each state, chosen by the legislature thereof, for six years: and each senator shall have one vote.

Immediately after they shall be assembled in consequence of the first election, they shall be divided as equally as may be into three classes. The seats of the senators of the first class shall be vacated at the expiration of the second year, of the second class at the expiration of the fourth year, and of the third class at the expiration of the sixth year, so that one-third may be chosen every second year: and if vacancies happen by resignation, or otherwise, during the recess of the Legislature of any state, the Executive thereof may make temporary appointments until the next meeting of the Legislature, *which shall then fill such vacancies.*

No person shall be a senator who shall not have attained to the age of thirty years, and been nine years a citizen of the United States, and who shall not, when elected, be an inhabitant of that state for which he shall be chosen.

The Vice-President of the United States shall be, ~~ex officio,~~ President of the senate, but shall have no vote, unless they be equally divided.

The Senate shall choose their other officers, and also a President pro tempore, in the absence of the Vice-President, or when he shall exercise the office of President of the United States.

The Senate shall have the sole power to try all impeachments. When sitting for that purpose, they shall be on oath. When the President of the United States is tried, the Chief Justice shall preside: And no person shall be convicted without the concurrence of two-thirds of the members present.

Judgment in cases of impeachment shall not extend further than to removal from office, and disqualification to hold and enjoy any office of honor, trust or profit under the United States: but the party convicted shall nevertheless be liable and subject to indictment, trial, judgment and punishment, according to law.

Sect. 4. The times, places and manner of holding elections for senators and representatives, shall be prescribed in each state by the legislature thereof: but the Congress may at any time by law make or alter such regulations, *except as to the place of choosing Senators.*

The Congress shall assemble at least once in every year, and such meeting shall be on the first Monday in December, unless they shall by law appoint a different day.

Sect. 5. Each house shall be the judge of the elections, returns and qualifications of its own members, and a majority of each shall constitute a quorum to do business: but a smaller number may adjourn from day to day, and may be authorised to compel the attendance of absent members, in such manner, and under such penalties as each house may provide.

Each house may determine the rules of its proceedings; punish its members for disorderly behaviour, and, with the concurrence of two-thirds, expel a member.

Each house shall keep a journal of its proceedings, and from time to time publish the same, excepting such parts as may in their judgment require secrecy; and the yeas and nays of the members of either house on any question shall, at the desire of one-fifth of those present, be entered on the journal.

Neither house, during the session of Congress, shall, without the consent of the other, adjourn for more than three days, nor to any other place than that in which the two houses shall be sitting.

Sect. 6. The senators and representatives shall receive a compensation for their services, to be ascertained by law, and paid out of the treasury of the United States. They shall in all cases, except treason, felony and breach of the peace, be privileged from arrest during their attendance at the session of their respective houses, and in going to and returning from the same; and for any speech or debate in either house, they shall not be questioned in any other place.

No senator or representative shall, during the time for which he was elected, be appointed to any civil office under the authority of the United States, which shall have been created, or the emoluments

We, the People of the United States, in order to form a more perfect union . . . do ordain and establish this Constitution for the United States of America. [Philadelphia: Dunlap and Claypoole, 1787]. (With changes in the hand of Jacob Broom). HSP

William Paterson. Lithograph portrait by Albert Rosenthal. HSP

William Paterson. *Letter to William Ellsworth,* New Brunswick, August 23 1787. HSP

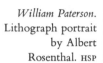

The world outside the State House in Philadelphia wondered what was taking so long. There was fear that the delegates might wind up their deliberations drowned in words without accomplishing anything. No news came out of the convention; "it is said, that you are afraid of the very Windows, and have a Man planted under them to prevent Secrets and Doings from flying out." "I hope," Paterson continued, "you will not have as much Altercation upon the Detail, as there was in settling the Principles of the System."

On September 13 the last stage had almost been reached. Extensive alterations of the earlier draft had been agreed upon. A new preamble, stronger and more dramatic, was written. But there were still a few minor points which had to be amended. Broom wrote these in his copy of the second privately printed draft.

Sept. 1787.

For the Rev.d M.r Lothrop from B. Franklin

WE, the People of the United States, in order to form

a more perfect union, establish justice, insure domestic tranquility, provide for the common defence, promote the general welfare, and secure the blessings of liberty to ourselves and our posterity, do ordain and establish this Constitution for the United States of America.

ARTICLE I.

Sect. 1. ALL legislative powers herein granted shall be vested in a Congress of the United States, which shall consist of a Senate and House of Representatives.

Sect. 2. The House of Representatives shall be composed of members chosen every second year by the people of the several states, and the electors in each state shall have the qualifications requisite for electors of the most numerous branch of the state legislature.

No person shall be a representative who shall not have attained to the age of twenty-five years, and been seven years a citizen of the United States, and who shall not, when elected, be an inhabitant of that state in which he shall be chosen.

Representatives and direct taxes shall be apportioned among the several states which may be included within this Union, according to their respective numbers, which shall be determined by adding to the whole number of free persons, including those bound to service for a term of years, and excluding Indians not taxed, three-fifths of all other persons. The actual enumeration shall be made within three years after the first meeting of the Congress of the United States, and within every subsequent term of ten years, in such manner as they shall by law direct. The number of representatives shall not exceed one for every thirty thousand, but each state shall have at least one representative; and until such enumeration shall be made, the state of New-Hampshire shall be entitled to chuse three, Massachusetts eight, Rhode-Island and Providence Plantations one, Connecticut five, New-York six, New-Jersey four, Pennsylvania eight, Delaware one, Maryland six, Virginia ten, North-Carolina five, South-Carolina five, and Georgia three.

When vacancies happen in the representation from any state, the Executive authority thereof shall issue writs of election to fill such vacancies.

The House of Representatives shall chuse their Speaker and other officers; and shall have the sole power of impeachment.

Sect. 3. The Senate of the United States shall be composed of two senators from each state, chosen by the legislature thereof, for six years; and each senator shall have one vote.

Immediately after they shall be assembled in consequence of the first election, they shall be divided as equally as may be into three classes. The seats of the senators of the first class shall be vacated at the expiration of the second year, of the second class at the expiration of the fourth year, and of the third class at the expiration of the sixth year, so that one-third may be chosen every second year; and if vacancies happen by resignation, or otherwise, during the recess of the Legislature of any state, the Executive thereof may make temporary appointments until the next meeting of the Legislature, which shall then fill such vacancies.

No person shall be a senator who shall not have attained to the age of thirty years, and been nine years a citizen of the United States, and who shall not, when elected, be an inhabitant of that state for which he shall be chosen.

The Vice-President of the United States shall be President of the senate, but shall have no vote, unless they be equally divided.

The Senate shall chuse their other officers, and also a President pro tempore, in the absence of the Vice-President, or when he shall exercise the office of President of the United States.

The Senate shall have the sole power to try all impeachments. When sitting for that purpose, they shall be on oath or affirmation. When the President of the United States is tried, the Chief Justice shall preside: And no person shall be convicted without the concurrence of two-thirds of the members present.

Judgment in cases of impeachment shall not extend further than to removal from office, and disqualification to hold and enjoy any office of honor, trust or profit under the United States; but the party convicted shall nevertheless be liable and subject to indictment, trial, judgment and punishment, according to law.

Sect. 4. The times, places and manner of holding elections for senators and representatives, shall be prescribed in each state by the legislature thereof; but the Congress may at any time by law make or alter such regulations, except as to the places of chusing Senators.

The Congress shall assemble at least once in every year, and such meeting shall be on the first Monday in December, unless they shall by law appoint a different day.

Sect. 5. Each house shall be the judge of the elections, returns and qualifications of its own members, and a majority of each shall constitute a quorum to do business; but a smaller number may adjourn from day to day, and may be authorised to compel the attendance of absent members, in such manner, and under such penalties as each house may provide.

Each house may determine the rules of its proceedings, punish its members for disorderly behaviour, and, with the concurrence of two-thirds, expel a member.

Each house shall keep a journal of its proceedings, and from time to time publish the same, excepting such parts as may in their judgment require secrecy; and the yeas and nays of the members of either house on any question shall, at the desire of one-fifth of those present, be entered on the journal.

Neither house, during the session of Congress, shall, without the consent of the other, adjourn for more than three days, nor to any other place than that in which the two houses shall be sitting.

Sect. 6. The senators and representatives shall receive a compensation for their services, to be ascertained by law, and paid out of the treasury of the United States. They shall in all cases, except treason, felony and breach of the peace, be privileged from arrest during their attendance at the

[marginal notes by Benjamin Franklin:]
Congress
House of Rep.s
Qualif.n of Electors
— of Representat.s
Proportion of Representatives & of Direct Taxes
Number of Rep.
Vacancies how to be filled
House of Rep. to chuse their Officers & impt
Senate
Of Rotation
Of Vacancies
Qualification of Senators
Vice Presid.t
Senate to chuse their Officers & one Presid.t pro tempore
Powers of Senate
Limitation of Judgm.t
Times &c of Election
Meeting of Congress
Power of each House
Journal
Adjournments
Wages of Senators & Rep.s and the Privileges

The Pennsylvania Packet, *and*

[Price Four-Pence.]   WEDNESDAY, SEPTEMB

WE, the People of the United
a more perfect Union, establ
Tranquility, provide for th
mote the General Welfare, a
Liberty to Ourfelves and our Pofterity, d
Conftitution for the United States of Ame

Nathaniel Gorham. Lithograph portrait by Albert Rosenthal. HSP

aily Advertifer.

1787.   [No. 2690.]

tes, in order to form
uftice, infure domeftic
ommon Defence, pro-
fecure the Bleffings of
dain and eftablifh this

At long last, on September 17, 1787, the Constitution of the United States was adopted by the Convention and sent to the states for ratification. Franklin put marginal keys on a copy of the first official printing and sent it to the Reverend John Lathrop of the Second Church of Boston. The Constitution first appeared in a newspaper on September 19, and thereafter it was reprinted all over the new nation. Franklin throughout the discussions had played the role of the elder statesman, urging moderation, compromise and agreement. In his speech at the close of the convention he said: "I confess, that I do not entirely approve of this Constitution at present; but, Sir, I am not sure I shall never approve it." From Gorham, a delegate to the Convention from Massachusetts, he received a request for a copy of the speech and permission to publish it. "The speech you made in Convention just before the close of the business," he wrote, "I think the last day of our siting, was in the opinion of every one who heard you—exceedingly well calculated to correct that possitive attachment which men are too apt to have for their own ideas."

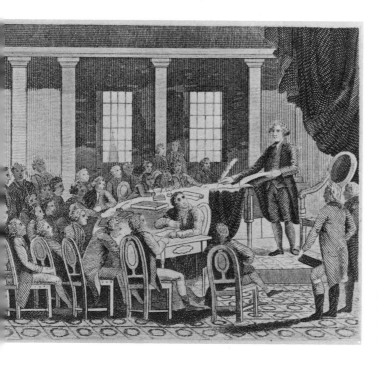

Convention at Philadelphia, 1787. In: Charles A. Goodrich. *A History of the United States of America.* Hartford: Huntington & Hopkins, 1823. HSP

Charles Willson Peale. *Eagles.*
Pencil sketch, 1813. APS

"The streams of power . . . we trace . . . to one great and noble source, THE PEOPLE."
—James Wilson. Speech in the Pennsylvania Convention, November 24, 1787

We the People, of the United States. . . . Hartford: Nathaniel Patten, 1787, HSP

The Federal Constitution for the United States of America, &c. Richmond: Augustine Davis, [1787]. HSP

The Constitution of the United States of America. Trenton: Isaac Collins, 1787. HSP

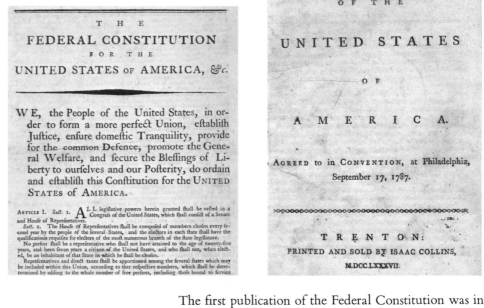

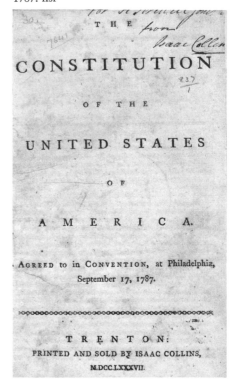

The first publication of the Federal Constitution was in the *Pennsylvania Packet* of September 19. In the following days and weeks other newspapers printed it, and printers throughout the country published it in pamphlet form with various titles and in various formats

Robert Milligan, *Letter to William Tilghman,* Talbot County Court House, September 20, 1787. HSP

With the publication of the Constitution, speculation and debate over its purposes and provisions commenced. Sentiment was by no means unanimous, and even many of those who favored the new frame of government had reservations about it. As in the years before the Revolution, correspondence was a principal means of conveying political intelligence, arguments, and propaganda. Three days after the Convention rose one observer, probably seeing in the plan what he wanted to see, remarks that it was "applauded . . . for its moderation," condemns George Mason, Edmund Randolph, and Elbridge Gerry for refusing to sign the Constitution, and conveys the reassuring report that Washington is willing to serve as President.

[Alexander Hamilton, James Madison, and John Jay]. *The Federalist: a Collection of Essays, written in favour of the New Constitution.* Two volumes. New York: J. and A. M'Lean, 1788. HSP

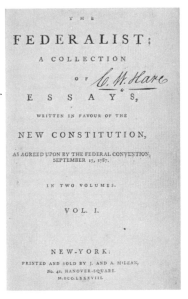

THE

FEDERALIST;

A COLLECTION

OF *C. H. Hare*

E S S A Y S,

WRITTEN IN FAVOUR OF THE

NEW CONSTITUTION,

AS AGREED UPON BY THE FEDERAL CONVENTION, SEPTEMBER 17, 1787.

IN TWO VOLUMES.

VOL. I.

NEW-YORK:

PRINTED AND SOLD BY J. AND A. M'LEAN, No. 41, HANOVER-SQUARE. M.DCC.LXXXVIII.

John Vaughan. *Letter to John Dickinson,* Philadelphia, April 9, 1788. LCP

THE *S.P. Tyson*

L E T T E R S

O F

F A B I U S,

IN 1788,

ON THE FEDERAL CONSTITUTION;

AND

IN 1797,

ON THE PRESENT SITUATION

OF

PUBLIC AFFAIRS.

Copy-Right Secured.

FROM THE OFFICE OF THE DELAWARE GAZETTE, WILMINGTON, BY W. C. SMYTH.

1797.

[John Dickinson]. *The Letters of Fabius, in 1788, on the Federal Constitution.* Wilmington: Office of the Delaware Gazette, 1797. HSP

Supporters of the Constitution lost no time in recommending it to the public. On October 27, under the pseudonym "Publius," the first of the Federalist Papers appeared in a New York newspaper; it had been composed by Alexander Hamilton in the cabin of a small vessel bringing him home from an appearance in court in Albany. In the ensuing months he, James Madison, and John Jay, all members of the Federal Convention, wrote 84 more essays explaining the philosophy of the new Constitution, the reasons and expectations behind each clause. The Federalist Papers quickly became and, published in book form, have remained the clearest and fullest exposition of American constitutional government. This copy was presented by Hamilton to William Bingham, who was to become one of Pennsylvania's first senators in the new government.

A copy of the first volume of the Federalist Papers—"Publius Letters"—came into the hands of John Vaughan, a Philadelphia merchant but recently arrived from England, who sent it on at once to his friend John Dickinson.

Dickinson wrote nine letters for the local press in support of the new Federal Constitution. Because they were not published in book form until 1797, their influence was limited. Vaughan brought them to the notice of Washington, who praised the author as "a master of his subject; he treats it with dignity, and at the same time expresses himself in such a manner as to render it intelligible to every capacity." Dickinson was only one leader of the revolutionary movement before 1776 who helped establish the post-revolutionary government. Unlike many such movements elsewhere, the American Revolution was completed by men who began it.

Alexander Hamilton   John Jay   James Madison
Engravings by William S. Leney after portraits from life, in Alexander Hamilton and others. *The Federalist.* Philadelphia: Benjamin Warner, 1818. LCP

FRIENDS and FELLOW-CITIZENS,

THE late Convention have submitted to your consideration a plan of a new federal government—The subject is highly interesting to your future welfare—Whether it be calculated to promote the great ends of civil society, viz. the happiness and prosperity of the community; it behoves you well to consider, uninfluenced by the authority of names. Instead of that frenzy of enthusiasm, that has actuated the citizens of Philadelphia, in their approbation of the proposed plan, before it was possible that it could be the result of a rational investigation into its principles; it ought to be dispassionately and deliberately examined, and its own intrinsic merit the only criterion of your patronage. If ever free and unbiassed discussion was proper or necessary, it is on such an occasion.—All the blessings of liberty and the dearest privileges of freemen, are now at stake and dependent on your present conduct. Those who are competent to the task of developing the principles of government, ought to be encouraged to come forward, and thereby the better enable the people to make a proper judgment; for the science of government is so abstruse, that few are able to judge for themselves; without such assistance the people are too apt to yield an implicit assent to the opinions of those characters, whose abilities are held in the highest esteem, and to those in whose integrity and patriotism they can confide; not considering that the love of domination is generally in proportion to talents, abilities, and superior acquirements, and that the men of the greatest purity of intention may be made instruments of despotism in the hands of the *artful and designing*. If it were not for the stability and attachment which time and habit gives to forms of government, it would be in the power of the enlightened and aspiring few, if they should combine, at any time to destroy the best establishments, and even make the people the instruments of their own subjugation.

The late revolution having effaced in a great measure all former habits, and the present institutions are so recent, that there exists not that great reluctance to innovation, so remarkable in old communities, and which accords with reason, for the most comprehensive mind cannot foresee the full operation of material changes on civil polity; it is the genius of the common law to resist innovation.

The wealthy and ambitious, who in every community think they have a right to lord it over their fellow creatures, have availed themselves, very successfully, of this favourable disposition; for the people thus unsettled in their sentiments, have been prepared to accede to any extreme of government; all the distresses and difficulties they experience, proceeding from various causes, have been ascribed to the impotency of the present confederation, and thence they have been led to expect full relief from the adoption of the proposed system of government; and in the other event, immediate ruin and annihilation as a nation. These characters flatter themselves that they have lulled all distrust and jealousy of their new plan, by gaining the concurrence of the two men in whom America has the highest confidence, and now triumphantly exult in the completion of their long meditated schemes of power and aggrandisement. I would be very far from insinuating that the two illustrious personages alluded to, have not the welfare of their country at heart; but that the unsuspecting goodness and zeal of the one, has been imposed on, in a subject of which he must be necessarily inexperienced, from his other arduous engagements; and that the weakness and indecision attendant on old age, has been practised on in the other.

Therefore, as different orders in government will not produce the good of the whole, we must recur to other principles. I believe it will be found, that the form of government, which holds those entrusted with power, in the greatest responsibility to their constituents, the best calculated for freemen. A republican, or free government, can only exist where the body of the people are virtuous, and where property is pretty equally divided, in such a government the people are the sovereign and their sense or opinion is the criterion of every public measure; for when this ceases to be the case, the nature of the government is changed, and an aristocracy, monarchy or despotism will rise on its ruin. The highest responsibility is to be attained, in a simple structure of government, for the great body of the people never steadily attend to the operations of government, and for want of due information are liable to be imposed on.—If you complicate the plan by various orders, the people will be perplexed and divided in their sentiments about the source of abuses or misconduct, some will impute it to the senate, others to the house of representatives, and so on, that the interposition of the people may be rendered imperfect or perhaps wholly abortive. But if, imitating the constitution of Pennsylvania, you vest all the legislative power in one body of men, (separating the executive and judicial) elected for a short period, and necessarily excluded by rotation from permanency, and guarded from precipitancy and surprise by delays imposed on its proceedings, you will create the most perfect responsibility, for then, whenever the people feel a grievance they cannot mistake the authors, and will apply the remedy with certainty and effect, discarding them at the next election. This tie of responsibility will obviate all the dangers apprehended from a single legislature, and will the best secure the rights of the people.

It will not be controverted that the legislative is the highest delegated power in government, and that all others are subordinate to it. The celebrated *Montesquieu* establishes it as a maxim, that legislation necessarily follows the power of taxation. By sect. 8 of the 1st. article of the proposed plan of government "the Congress are to have power to lay and collect taxes, duties, imposts and excises, to pay the "debts and provide for the common defence and *general welfare* of the United States; but all duties, "imposts and excises shall be uniform throughout the United States." Now what can be more comprehensive than these words; not content by other sections of this plan, to grant all the great executive powers of a confederation, and a STANDING ARMY IN TIME OF PEACE, that grand engine of oppression, and moreover the absolute controul over the commerce of the United States and all external objects of revenue, such as unlimited imposts upon imports, &c.—they are to be vested with every species of *internal* taxation;——whatever taxes, duties and excises that they may deem requisite for the *general welfare*, may be imposed on the citizens of these states, levied by the officers of Congress, distributed through every district in America; and the collection would be enforced by the standing army, however grievous or improper they may be. The Congress may construe every purpose for which the state legislatures now lay taxes, to be for the *general welfare*, and thereby seize upon every object of revenue.

If the foregoing be a just comment—if the United States are to be melted down into one empire, it becomes you to consider, whether such a government, however constructed, would be eligible in so extended a territory; and whether it would be practicable, consistent with freedom? It is the opinion of the greatest writers, that a very extensive country cannot be governed on democratical principles, on any other plan, than a confederation of a number of small republics, possessing all the powers of internal government, but united in the management of their foreign and general concerns.

It would not be difficult to prove, that any thing short of despotism, could not bind so great a country under one government; and that whatever plan you might, at the first setting out, establish, it would issue in a despotism.

If one general government could be instituted and maintained on principles of freedom, it would not be so competent to attend to the various local concerns and wants, of every particular district; as well as the peculiar governments, who are nearer the scene, and possessed of superior means of information, besides, if the business of the *whole* union is to be managed by one government, there would not be time. Do not we already see, that the inhabitants in a number of the larger states, who are remote from the seat of government, are loudly complaining of the inconveniencies and disadvantages they are subjected to on this account, and that, to enjoy the comforts of local government, they are separating into smaller divisions.

From this investigation into the organization of this government, it appears that it is devoid of all responsibility or accountability to the great body of the people, and that so far from being a regular balanced government, it would be in practice a *permanent* ARISTOCRACY.

But our situation is represented to be so *critically* dreadful, that, however reprehensible and exceptionable the proposed plan of government may be, there is no alternative, between the adoption of it and absolute ruin.——My fellow citizens, things are not at that crisis, it is the argument of tyrants; the present distracted state of Europe secures us from injury on that quarter, and as to domestic dissentions, we have not so much to fear from them, as to precipitate us into this form of government, without it is a safe and a proper one. For remember, of all possible evils, that of *despotism* is the *worst* and the most to be *dreaded*.

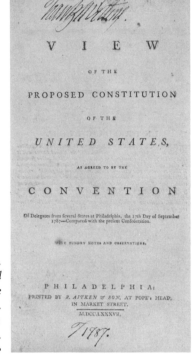

Many critics of the Constitution, like John Nicholson, a Pennsylvania official, compared the new frame of government with the Articles of Confederation, to the former's disadvantage. Others, like young Samuel Bryan, entirely rejected the major principles and assumptions of the document—the separation of powers, a legislature not wholly dependent on the popular will, the authority granted to the central government to maintain an army in time of peace, the power to levy taxes, unequal representation in Senate and House. These iniquitous measures, with the absence of a bill of rights, constituted, in Bryan's view, "the most daring attempt to establish a despotic aristocracy among freemen, that the world has ever witnessed." The United States would "be melted down into one empire," whose government would be "devoid of all responsibility or accountability to the great body of the people, and . . . would be in practice a *permanent* ARISTOCRACY." Bryan urged the states to reject the hateful instrument and to call together a new convention, which should do better.

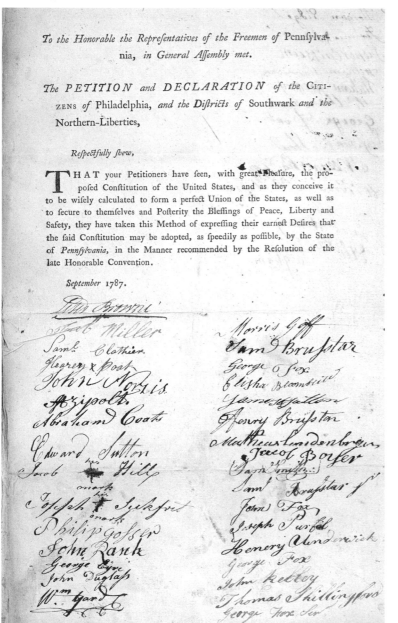

State of *Pennsylvania.*

In GENERAL ASSEMBLY,

Saturday, September 29th, 1787. A.M.

RESOLVED,

THAT three thousand Copies of the Resolutions which the House have this Day adopted for calling a Convention on the Fœderal Constitution, recommended to them by Congress, be struck off, and transmitted by the Clerk to the Members of the City of Philadelphia, and the different counties of this state; two thousand of said copies to be in the English, and one thousand in the German Language.

WHEREAS the Convention of Deputies from the several states composing the union, lately held in this city, have published a constitution for the future government of the United States, to be submitted to conventions of deputies chosen in each state by the people thereof, under the recommendation of its legislature, for their assent and ratification. And whereas, Congress, on Friday, the 28th instant, did unanimously resolve, that the said constitution be transmitted to the several legislatures of the states, to the intent aforesaid. And whereas it is the sense of great numbers of the good people of this state, already signified in petitions and declarations to this House, that the earliest steps should be taken to assemble a convention within the state, for the purpose of deliberating and determining on the said constitution.

Resolved, That it be recommended to such of the inhabitants of the state as are entitled to vote for representatives to the General Assembly, that they chuse suitable persons to serve as deputies in a state convention, for the purpose herein before mentioned; that is, for the city of Philadelphia and the counties respectively, the same number of deputies that each is entitled to of representatives in the General Assembly.

Resolved, That the elections for deputies as aforesaid be held at the several places in the said city and counties, as are fixed by law for holding the elections of representatives to the General Assembly, and that the same be conducted by the officers who conduct the said elections of representatives, and agreeably to the rules and regulations thereof.

Resolved, That the election of deputies as aforesaid shall be held for the city of Philadelphia, and the several counties of this state, on the first Tuesday of November next.

Resolved, That the persons so elected to serve in Convention shall assemble on the third Tuesday of November, at the State-House, in the city of Philadelphia.

Resolved, That the proposition submitted to this House by the Deputies of Pennsylvania in the General Convention of the states, of ceding to the United States a district of country within this state, for the seat of the General Government, and for the exclusive legislation of Congress, be particularly recommended to the consideration of the Convention.

Resolved, That it be recommended to the succeeding House of Assembly, to make the same allowance to the attending members of the Convention as is made to the members of the General Assembly, and also to provide for the extraordinary expences which may be incurred by holding the said elections.

Extract from the Proceedings of the House.

PETER Z. LLOYD, *Clerk of the General Assembly.*

Philadelphia: PRINTED BY HALL AND SELLERS.

Federalist members of the Pennsylvania Assembly, encouraged by petitions from voters, took prompt measures to call a convention to ratify the Constitution. But Anti-federalists, though a minority, were numerous and resourceful. To prevent a quorum and thus a vote on a ratifying convention, some absented themselves from the session of the Assembly. The clerk and sergeant-at-arms were despatched to bring at least two absentees to the State House. All refused to come. Next day two Anti-federalists were seized by a Federalist mob, dragged into the Assembly, and held there to make a quorum until a vote could be taken. This high-handed action put the Federalists on the defensive and intensified political divisions within the state.

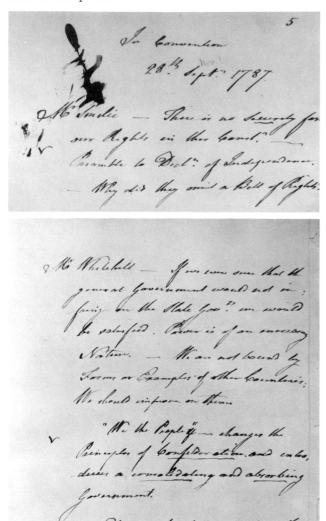

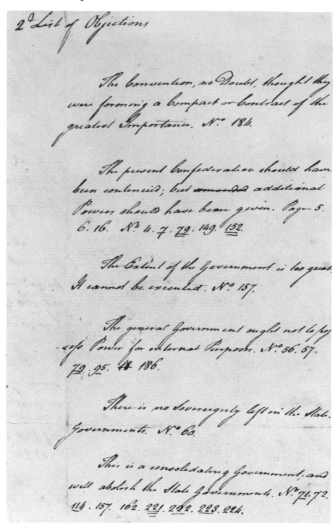

James Wilson. *The Substance of a Speech . . . Explanatory of the general Principles of the proposed Foederal Constitution.* Philadelphia: Thomas Bradford, 1787. LCP

In the Pennsylvania ratifying convention the most effective opponents of the Constitution were John Smiley, Robert Whitehill, and William Findley, all delegates from western counties. They argued that the Federal Convention had exceeded its authority when it created a new government instead of revising the old one; that the Constitution destroyed the sovereignty of the States; and that there was no Bill of Rights. These and other objections were answered by James Wilson, only member of the ratifying convention who had been in the Federal Convention. In a speech at the beginning of the state convention he asserted that the principles of the new government were in fact "purely democratical" and that when one took "an extensive and accurate view of the streams of power that appear through this great and comprehensive plan . . . we shall be able to trace them all to one great and noble source, THE PEOPLE."

Minutes of the Convention of the Commonwealth of Pennsylvania . . . for the purpose of taking into consideration the Constitution framed by the late Foederal Convention. Philadelphia: Hall and Sellers, 1787. HSP

Order of Procession [for Thursday, December 13th 1787]. Philadelphia: Eleazer Oswald, 1786. HSP

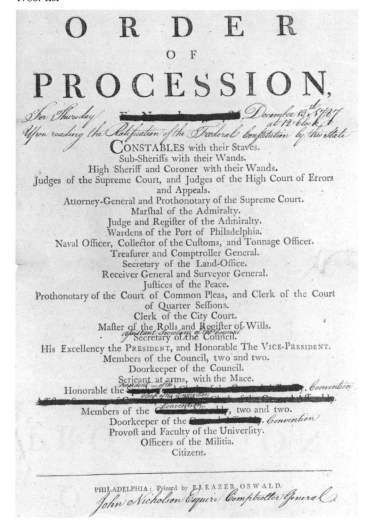

[24]

RATIFICATION.

IN THE NAME OF THE PEOPLE OF PENNSYLVANIA.

BE IT KNOWN UNTO ALL MEN,——THAT WE, THE DELEGATES OF THE PEOPLE OF THE COMMONWEALTH OF PENNSYLVANIA, IN GENERAL CONVENTION ASSEMBLED, HAVE ASSENTED TO AND RATIFIED, AND BY THESE PRESENTS DO, IN THE NAME AND BY THE AUTHORITY OF THE SAME PEOPLE, AND FOR OURSELVES, ASSENT TO AND RATIFY THE FOREGOING CONSTITUTION FOR THE UNITED STATES OF AMERICA.

DONE in Convention, the Twelfth Day of December, in the Year one thousand seven hundred and eighty-seven, and of the Independence of the United States of America the Twelfth. In witness whereof, we have hereunto subscribed our Names.

FREDERICK A. MUHLENBERG, President.

George Latimer,	John Hubley,
Benjamin Rush,	Jasper Yeates,
Hilary Baker,	Henry Slagle,
James Wilson,	Thomas Campbell,
Thomas M'Kean,	Thomas Hartley,
William M'Pherson,	David Grier,
John Hunn,	John Black,
George Gray,	Benjamin Pedan,
Samuel Ashmead,	John Arndt,
Enoch Edwards,	Stephen Balliott,
Henry Wynkoop,	Joseph Horsefield,
John Barclay,	David Deshler,
Thomas Yardley,	William Wilson,
Abraham Stout,	John Boyd,
Thomas Bull,	Thomas Scott,
Anthony Wayne,	John Nevill,
William Gibbons,	John Allison,
Richard Downing,	Jonathan Roberts,
Thomas Cheney,	John Richards,
John Hannum,	James Morris,
Stephen Chambers,	Timothy Pickering,
Robert Coleman,	Benjamin Elliott.
Sebastian Graff,	

Attest. JAMES CAMPBELL, Secretary.

Adjourned until half past nine o'clock to-morrow, A. M.

Friday,

The Federal Procession in New York, 1788. Martha J. Lamb. *History of the City of New York.* New York: A. S. Barnes & Co., 1877. LCP

After three weeks of debate Pennsylvania ratified the Constitution on December 12, the second state to do so, Delaware having ratified unanimously on December 5. Among those voting affirmatively were Dr. Benjamin Rush, James Wilson, who had played a leading role in the convention, Thomas McKean, who had been president of the Continental Congress, and General Anthony Wayne. The next day the act of ratification was proclaimed ceremoniously at the Court House, while Federalists cheered, thirteen cannon were fired, and the city's bells rang out. The "Order of Procession" was only slightly changed from one that inaugurated the General Assembly the year before.

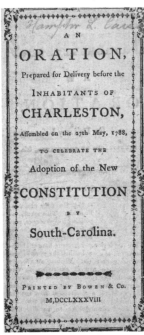

The Governor of New Jersey informs the President of Pennsylvania that his state has unanimously ratified the Constitution (on December 18, 1787), and a Boston lawyer, a member of the Federal Convention and of the Massachusetts ratifying convention, rejoices in the adoption of the Constitution by his state, by a vote of 187 to 168. The minority was large, but "moderate, and say they will with alacrity support the Government"—as indeed the minorities in every state did.

Daniel Carroll. *Letter to Benjamin Franklin,*
Annapolis, December 2, 1787. APS

Benjamin Franklin. *Letter to Charles Vaughan,*
Philadelphia, February 12, 1788. APS

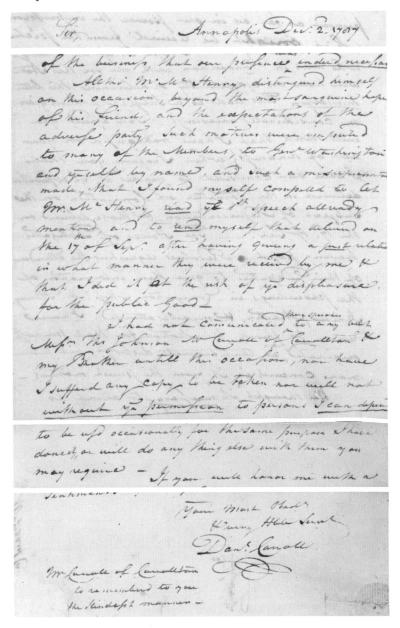

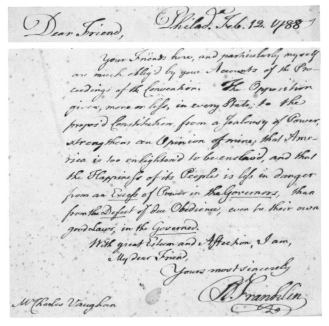

The Federal Ship *Union.*
From: Francis Hopkinson.
"An Account of the Grand
Federal Procession,"
American Museum, IV (1788),
57-78. HSP

A ship was the symbol of the new Federal Union—embarking
on the seas of history. In several of the parades celebrating
ratification of the Constitution, a barge or whaleboat, rigged
like a ship of the line and manned by thirteen sailors, was
drawn through the streets. One little boat, after a voyage
through the streets of Annapolis, was sailed to Mount Vernon,
where it was moored in the Potomac until it sank during a storm.

The oldest and most widely experienced man in the
Federal Convention and, after Washington, the
best known and most respected, Benjamin
Franklin was also a quiet but effective influence in
the debates on ratification. In a characteristically
wise and humorous address on the last day of the
Convention he confessed there were several parts
of the Constitution he did not approve, "but I am
not sure I shall never approve them; for, having
lived long, I have experienced many instances of
being obliged, by better information or fuller
consideration, to change opinions even on important
subjects which I once thought right, but found to
be otherwise;" and he called upon his fellows to
"doubt a little of their own infallibility" and sign
the document to manifest the delegates' unanimity.
Daniel Carroll of Maryland asked for a copy of
Franklin's remarks and, with other observations
made by the old man, quoted it in the Maryland
ratifying convention to win votes for the
Constitution. On Anti-federalist fears generally,
Franklin shrewdly observed that America was in
less danger from too much power in its rulers than
from too little "due Obedience" by the people,
"even to their own good Laws."

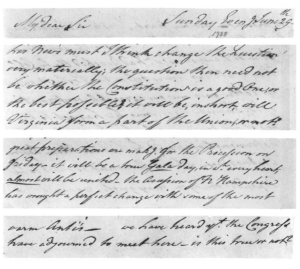

By mid-June 1788 eight states had ratified the Constitution. Only one vote more was required to put the new government in operation—and conventions were then sitting in both New Hampshire and Virginia. The outcome was no longer in doubt; it would be announced in a few days. Rufus King waited impatiently for New Hampshire to "finish the business, and complete the work," confident that that state "would form a solid and powerful Column, on which the Antifederalists of New York could not look with satisfaction." What would become of the remaining states? "The question . . . will then be," observed John Vaughan, "not whether they will adopt the Government, but whether they will join the Union." New Hampshire ratified on June 21 (Virginia on June 25), and the Constitution was accomplished. "The Accession of N Hampshire has wrought a perfect change with some of the most warm Anti's."

William Bingham. Lithograph portrait by Albert Rosenthal. HSP

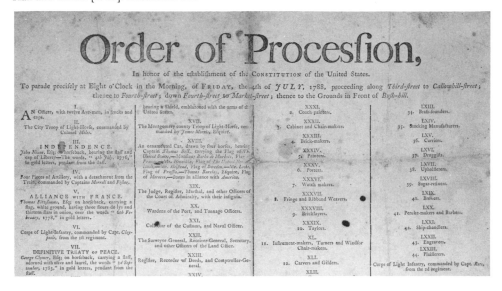

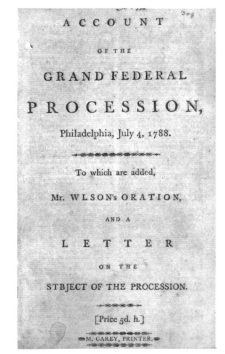

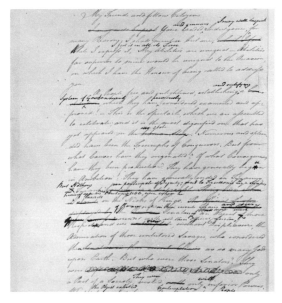

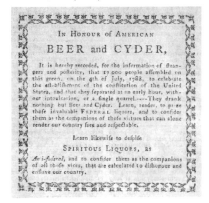

Anticipating the ratification of the Constitution by a ninth state, Francis Hopkinson, Charles Willson Peale, and other Philadelphians planned a great civic celebration for July 4. During the late winter and spring other cities had marked their ratifications with parade and pageantry; but the Grand Federal Procession was by far the grandest of all, for it celebrated the final ratification of the Constitution and, falling on the Fourth of July, linked union and independence indissolubly.

The President of the State, the justices of the Supreme Court, office holders, students, and troops of light horse were in the line of march; so were the farmers, and every trade, guild, and profession, bearing distinguishing insignia, stepping out behind banners of their own

(or Peale's) making. There was a "Grand Foederal Edifice" drawn by ten horses, and other floats of staggering size and ingenious symbolism. Seventeen thousand citizens marched, and an equal number watched them—in respectful silence, it is said—as they moved through the streets, drawing along the Ship *Federal Union*, to the banks of the Schuylkill River. There James Wilson delivered an anniversary and inaugural oration ("Happy Country! May thy Happiness be perpetual!"), and the whole concourse of people dined on barbecued beef and beer. It was because beer, not distilled liquor, was served, Dr. Benjamin Rush believed, that everything went off in orderly fashion.

Simeon Baldwin. *An Oration pronounced before the Citizens of New-Haven, July 4th, 1788; in commemoration of the Declaration of Independence and Establishment of the Constitution of the United States of America.* New Haven: J. Meigs, 1788. LCP

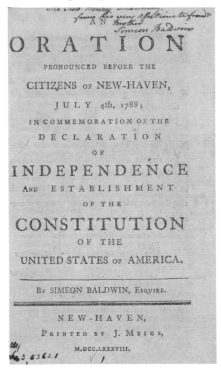

[John Jay]. *An Address to the People of the State of New-York, on the Subject of the Constitution.* New York: Samuel and John Loudon, 1788. LCP

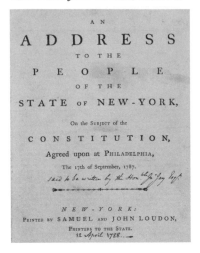

[Melancton Smith]. *An Address to the People of the State of New-York: Shewing the Necessity of Making Amendments to the Constitution.* New York? 1788. LCP

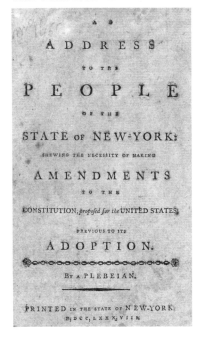

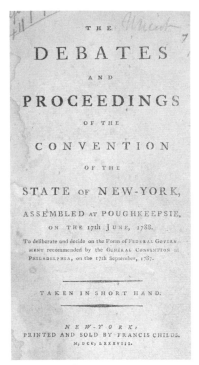

The Debates and Proceedings of the Convention of the State of New-York, assembled at Poughkeepsie, on the 17th June, 1788. New York: Francis Childs, 1788. HSP

Not only in Philadelphia did Federalists link the Constitution of 1787 and the Declaration of 1776. The former, asserted a Connecticut lawyer, was "an event, if possible, more interesting than independence itself. That gave us birth as a nation. This will give duration and happiness to our existence."

New York ratified on July 26, the eleventh state to do so. Alexander Hamilton was the leading advocate for the Constitution, Melancton Smith the able spokesman for the Anti-federalists. The convention finally approved the Constitution, with the understanding that amendments should be promptly drafted and considered by a second Federal Convention.

The two remaining states ratified the Constitution in the next two years—North Carolina on November 21, 1789, and Rhode Island, other-minded now as throughout its colonial history, on May 29, 1790.

Peleg Arnold. *Letter to Welcome Arnold*, New York, July 11, 1788. HSP

New York 11th July 1788

Sir/

We have this Day Thirteen States on the Floor of Congress which has not before been until the present case since the year 1776 —

Ten States having Ratified the New Constitution, Congress are now Deliberating on the Time for the States to annoint Electors to Choose a President

and am your assured Friend

W. Arnold Esqr.   *Peleg Arnold*

By the United States in Congress Assembled, September 13, 1788. [New York, 1788]. Broadside HSP

By the United States in Congress assembled,

SEPTEMBER 13, 1788.

WHEREAS the Convention assembled in Philadelphia, pursuant to the Resolution of Congress of the 21st February, 1787, did, on the 17th of September in the same year, report to the United States in Congress assembled, a Constitution for the People of the United States; whereupon Congress, on the 28th of the same September, did resolve unanimously, "That the said report, with the Resolutions and Letter accompanying the same, be transmitted to the several Legislatures, in order to be submitted to a Convention of Delegates chosen in each State by the people thereof, in conformity to the Resolves of the Convention made and provided in that case:" And whereas the Constitution so reported by the Convention, and by Congress transmitted to the several Legislatures, has been ratified in the manner therein declared to be sufficient for the establishment of the same, and such Ratifications duly authenticated have been received by Congress, and are filed in the Office of the Secretary——therefore,

RESOLVED, That the first Wednesday in January next, be the day for appointing Electors in the several States, which before the said day shall have ratified the said Constitution; that the first Wednesday in February next, be the day for the Electors to assemble in their respective States, and vote for a President; and that the first Wednesday in March next, be the time, and the present Seat of Congress the place for commencing Proceedings under the said Constitution.

A Sonata, Sung . . . as General Washington passed under the Triumphal Arch raised on the Bridge at Trenton, April 21, 1789. [Trenton, 1789]. Broadside. LCP

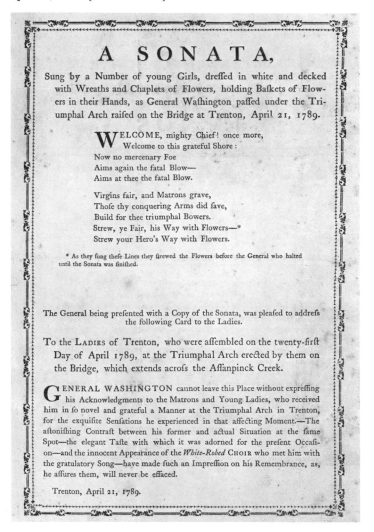

A SONATA,

Sung by a Number of young Girls, dressed in white and decked with Wreaths and Chaplets of Flowers, holding Baskets of Flowers in their Hands, as General Washington passed under the Triumphal Arch raised on the Bridge at Trenton, April 21, 1789.

WELCOME, mighty Chief! once more,
   Welcome to this grateful Shore:
Now no mercenary Foe
Aims again the fatal Blow—
Aims at thee the fatal Blow.

Virgins fair, and Matrons grave,
Those thy conquering Arms did save,
Build for thee triumphal Bowers.
Strew, ye Fair, his Way with Flowers—*
Strew your Hero's Way with Flowers.

* As they sung these Lines they strewed the Flowers before the General who halted until the Sonata was finished.

The General being presented with a Copy of the Sonata, was pleased to address the following Card to the Ladies.

To the LADIES of Trenton, who were assembled on the twenty-first Day of April 1789, at the Triumphal Arch erected by them on the Bridge, which extends across the Assanpink Creek.

GENERAL WASHINGTON cannot leave this Place without expressing his Acknowledgments to the Matrons and Young Ladies, who received him in so novel and grateful a Manner at the Triumphal Arch in Trenton, for the exquisite Sensations he experienced in that affecting Moment.—The astonishing Contrast between his former and actual Situation at the same Spot—the elegant Taste with which it was adorned for the present Occasion—and the innocent Appearance of the *White-Robed* CHOIR who met him with the gratulatory Song—have made such an Impression on his Remembrance, as, he assures them, will never be effaced.

Trenton, April 21, 1789.

With ratifications received from ten states by mid-July, Congress, its attendance better than at any time since 1776, took steps to inaugurate the new government. On September 13 it appointed dates for choosing presidential electors in the several states, for their meeting to cast their votes for President, and "for commencing Proceedings under the said Constitution." Washington was chosen President unanimously and, having been formally notified of the fact, once again set out from Mount Vernon in his country's service. His journey to New York (the temporary capital) was marked by several local tributes. At Trenton, N. J., for example, he had to pass beneath a triumphal arch while a chorus of maidens of the village, clothed in white and wearing wreaths and chaplets, strewed flowers in his path as they sang a "sonata" in his praise. It was quite different, he recalled, from the Christmas night in 1776 when he had crossed the ice-filled Delaware to reach Trenton.

*This book was designed by Sam Maitin with the
assistance of Beth Wickenden in Philadelphia.*

*It was printed by The Meriden Gravure Company
of Meriden, Connecticut.*

*It was printed on Mohawk Superfine Paper,
80 lb. text.*

*It was bound by Robert Burlen and Son of
Hingham, Massachusetts.*

*The type was set by Walter T. Armstrong, Inc.
of Philadelphia. The type is Bembo Monotype.*